Designing
Commercial
Interiors

Designing
Commercial
Interiors

Christine M. Piotrowski, ASID, IIDA
Elizabeth A. Rogers, IIDA, IDEC

JOHN WILEY & SONS, INC.
New York • Chichester • Weinheim • Brisbane • Singapore • Toronto

Published by John Wiley & Sons, Inc.

Published simultaneously in Canada.

No part of this publication may be reproduced, stored in a retrieval system or transmitted in any form or by any means, electronic, mechanical, photocopying, recording, scanning or otherwise, except as permitted under Sections 107 and 108 of the 1976 Unites States Copyright Act, without either the prior written permission of the Publisher, or authorization through payment of the appropriate per-copy fee to the Copyright Clearance Center, 222 Rosewood Drive, Danvers, MA 01923, (978) 750-8400, fax (978) 750-4744. Requests to the Publisher for permission should be addressed to the Permissions Department, John Wiley & Sons, Inc., 605 Third Avenue, New York, NY 10158-0012, (212) 850-6011, fax (212) 850-6008, E-Mail: PERMREQ @ WILEY.COM.

Library of Congress Cataloging-in-Publication Data:

Piotrowski, Christine M., 1947-
   Designing commercial interiors / Christine M. Piotrowski, Elizabeth A. Rogers.
     p.   cm.
     Includes bibliographical references and index.
     ISBN 0-471-17103-4 (cloth : alk. paper)
     1. Commercial buildings—Decoration—Unites States.   I. Rogers,
Elizabeth A., 1939– . II. Title.
NK2195.C65P56   1998
747'.852—dc21   98-29967

Printed in the United States of America.

10 9 8 7 6 5 4 3 2 1

To my parents, Casmier and Martha, for watching
over me while this was written.
Christine M. Piotrowski

To the Max and Maxine Rogers family.
Elizabeth Rogers

Contents

Preface

Interior design, stripped to its essence, is problem-solving. The client has a problem. He or she comes to the interior designer, as well as to other design related professionals, to get help in solving that problem. But no designer can solve the problems the client presents without understanding the problems in as great a depth as possible. Understanding the basic organization of offices, for example, and the job functions within the office is part of the problem-solving mode in the interior design of all office projects. Having some understanding of what is involved in the work areas of the imaging department and work that occurs around a nurse's station help the interior designer make more informed decisions when responsible for the design of a hospital. Far too often, however, students and professionals with limited commercial interior design experience attempt to plan and design commercial spaces with little knowledge of the character and functions of those spaces.

We should know something about the business of the client before we go after the job or begin to plan the project. Unfortunately, students generally do not like to research information about a facility before beginning to design and plan a project. Professionals often feel that they just don't have the time. Although there is research material available for students and professionals, it is presented in numerous specialized books. Thus it is prohibitively expensive for students and even many professionals to obtain all these references.

The purpose of this text is to provide students and professionals with a practical reference for many of the design issues related to planning commercial interior facilities. From a practical standpoint, the text is not all-inclusive. Rather, it focuses on the types of commercial design spaces most commonly assigned as studio projects and those typically encountered by the professional interior designer who has limited experience with commercial interior design. It contains a large amount of information—both as drawings and text—to give the student and professional a concise reference to the generic issues of commercial spaces.

The text is organized to allow the subject units to be used by professors in whatever sequences are required for the focus of their specific class. Because of the outline of the book, professionals seeking information about specific types of facilities can easily direct their attention to the chapters that satisfy their informational needs. Thus the book does not need to be used from beginning to end.

The first eight chapters concentrate on explaining the functions and design concepts of the most common categories of commercial facilities. Each of these chapters begins with a brief explanation of the functional business concerns of the facility being considered. Following this discussion, examples are presented, illustrating the planning and design concepts critical for the success of such facilities. Information concerning key mechanical interface issues and the codes has been included as well, and numerous illustrations are provided to clarify space layouts, specialized equipment, and to help the reader understand aesthetic applications. Chapter 1, on office design, includes a discussion of concepts related to designing computer workstations, while Chapter 8 concludes with a brief discussion on the planning concepts of public rest room facilities. The information in those discussions, of course, applies to many types of commercial facilities.

Chapter 9, the final chapter, provides an overview of concepts dealing with project management. This topic is very important to the overall success of a design project and frequently is not discussed fully in studio classes. An in-depth glossary of terms used throughout the text and appendices with additional resource material conclude the text.

In addition, each chapter contains its own reference list, directing the reader to additional sources of information on that chapter's topic. With these references, students, professionals, and professors can obtain more detailed and specific information that could not be included in this text. This combination will make this text an important reference for all readers.

Commercial interior design is a very exciting and challenging way to make a living. To the inexperienced, it is also filled with what seem to be mysterious terminology and perplexing design decisions. The authors hope that this text will help the reader, whether he or she is a student or a professional, understand the mysteries and enjoy the challenges of planning and designing commercial interior facilities.

Christine M. Piotrowski
Elizabeth A. Rogers

Acknowledgments

A project of this magnitude can never be accomplished without the help of many people. The authors would like to acknowledge those who provided information and played important roles in the completion of this book.

Christine would like to thank Ms. Judy Voss at Haworth, Inc., who provided invaluable information on the history of open office systems, Robert Viol, Corporate Archivist at Herman Miller, Inc., who sent a huge amount of information on the history of the company and open office systems; and Sandy Frantom of Herman Miller, Inc. She would also like to extend a special thanks to Robert Krikac for his comments on several of the chapters and to David Petroff, IIDA, of Office Designs in Phoenix for once again providing his time and expertise on office design and Steelcase, Inc., and Carl Clark, FASID for his contribution "at the last." Thanks also to Gwen Mason of Facilitec in Phoenix and Barbara Kumlin of Goodmans Design Interiors for their assistance in obtaining additional information on Haworth and Herman Miller products. She would also like to thank Tim Eaton at the American Hotel & Motel Association and John Pile for their assistance with important illustrations. And Christine would like to acknowledge the assistance provided by the Northern Arizona University library, and Arizona State University libraries.

A special thank you to former students Barbara Clapp and Alisha Newman for researching a variety of information while students at Northern Arizona University. Christine would also like to give a special thanks to the students who had the patience to put up with her while she was writing this manuscript, and who inspired the book in the first place. She would also like to extend her thanks to family and friends, especially Dr. Nancy Oliver, Al Hunt, Barbara Wallis, and Dr. Alyce Jordan for helping to get her through the final stages of this project.

Elizabeth would like to acknowledge the assistance given by the following libraries: Clarinda Public Library, Iowa Western Community College Lisle Library, Utah State University libraries, Iowa State University design library, and the University of Nebraska libraries. In addition, she would like to thank Dr. Bonita Wyse, Dean of the College of Family Life at Utah State University, and staff, Dr. Joan McFadden, Head of the Department of Human Environments, Utah State University, and staff, and the Nora Eccles Harrison Museum of Art, Utah State University.

She would like to extend many thanks to the students who participated in the computer aided drawings.

For their expertise and suggestions regarding information to be included in the book, Elizabeth would like to thank Dr. Joanne Graham, veterinary oncologist at Iowa State University; Dr. Mark Mosier, DDS; Mr. Michael Thompson, banker, and Dr. Bernard Hayes, educator, Utah State University.

Thanks from Elizabeth to Merrily Tunnicliff for providing office space to conduct research and writing, and to Frank and Millie Iarossi for their inspiration and contributions to the text. To Bettie Anderson and Samantha Carlisle for their encouragement. A special thanks to her mother, Maxine for her intellect and research abilities. And a special thanks to all of Elizabeth's commercial clients, who provided the design experience and background to participate in this project.

Sincere thanks to all the individuals, photographers, publications, design firms, and companies who have allowed us to reprint photos or other graphics for use as illustrations. There are too many to individually acknowledge in this space.

Finally, special thanks goes to Amanda Miller, Senior Editor at John Wiley, for having so much patience, understanding, and encouragement in bringing this book to completion.

Christine M. Piotrowski
Elizabeth A. Rogers

Chapter 1

Office Facilities

For the commercial interior designer, the planning and design of office spaces is a fact of life. Whether one works in an office furnishings dealership or some sort of independent studio, one is never very far removed from at least occasionally designing an office. There are, of course, all kinds of offices: accountants, real estate, banking, lawyers, advertising, architects, interior designers, government agencies, education, consultants, doctors, dentists, and so on. Offices are also part of manufacturing facilities like the offices of General Motors, Apple Computer, and a meat packing plant. Office facilities are provided as part of the makeup of retail stores, hospitals, hotels, airports, churches—you name the facility and at least one space somewhere in the business is labeled "office" (Figures 1-1 and 1-2).

There are literally hundreds of specialized work activities conducted in offices. The layout and design of an office must support the functional needs for the jobs within the specific kind of business activity. These needs will depend upon such things as clientele, type of business or service, size of the company, the geographic location, and the condition of the business, to name just a few factors.

The planning and design of offices introduce the student or designer who is unfamiliar with commercial design to a new list of job names, furniture names, and space requirements. And while we have all been to offices of one kind or another, personal exposure to office spaces does not provide the designer with the understanding of the workings of an office or the equipment requirements of the different jobs. It is important for the student and designer to understand the goals and functional responsibilities in an office in order to best develop working adjacencies into space plans and make design specification decisions.

Today's office is also changing. The era of downsizing of the early 1990s has created new concepts and theories of office design and office work. These new concepts have most dramatically affected the way work is done and the planning of office environments for large businesses that have dozens, even hundreds or thousands of employees. Although these concepts are slowing affecting smaller companies and businesses, such as a retail store that has an office, they are not the only design challenge the student will face in projects and early work experience. The concepts and challenges of the changing office environment are discussed in Chapter 3.

The purpose of this chapter is to explain the functional characteristics of office work as a basis for design decisions. Traditional though they may be, these design concepts and

Figure 1–1 The reception room of this office space is innovative in approach and creativity. (Photograph courtesy of Randy Brown Architect.)

functions still hold true in many office facilities. It would be impossible to detail the functional requirements of the numerous kinds of specialized offices. This chapter uses the basic traditional office environment to explain functional and design needs in planning general offices.

The chapter begins with a brief discussion of facility planning and facility management. These two areas of design are strongly associated with office design. Of course, they are associated with many other kinds of commercial facilities as well. The chapter continues with an overview of office operations based on a traditional office facility followed by a section that describes specific criteria relevant to the planning and design of offices. The chapter concludes by outlining specific planning and design guidelines for an office facility.

Facility Planning and Facility Management

Facility planning and facility management are relatively new terms for activities and professions in commercial interiors. The terms for these activities and professions came into accepted use in the early 1980s, although the jobs actually existed for many years. Almost all major corporations and medium to large business enterprises, regardless of the exact nature of the business, utilize facility planning and facility management activities. *Facility planning* involves the programming and space planning of offices and other areas of commercial businesses. *Facility management* involves the total nonfinancial-asset management of a business. According to the International Facility Management Association (IFMA), "facility management combines proven management practices with the most current technical knowledge to provide humane

(a)

(b)

Figure 1-2 *(a)* A small real estate office circa 1900, depicting use of office space and furnishings popular at the time. (Photograph used by permission, Utah State Historical Society. All rights reserved.) *(b)* A present-day real estate office, depicting changes in the use of office space and furnishings. (Photograph courtesy of Coldwell Banker Gold Key Realty, Inc.)

and effective work environments. It is the business practice of planning, providing, and managing productive work environments."[1]

In the context of this discussion, it is important to point out that all businesses consist of the facility and the people who work there. For example, the facility in a store is the space and the display fixtures used to display the merchandise. In a hotel, the facility is the space and all the guest rooms, restaurants, and other features of the hotel. In an interior design or architecture office, the facility is again the space and the furniture, drafting boards, computers, and other equipment needed to provided design services.

Facility planners, sometimes called space planners, are most involved with the layout of the spaces and generally have little responsibility for the aesthetics of the interiors. For enterprises such as banks, corporate office complexes, and service intensive businesses, facility planners are concerned with space planning and layout of office areas, support operation areas such as training rooms, and space needed for other business functions. Many retail chains use facility planners to determine the best layouts for merchandise display to encourage sales. Hospitality enterprises—especially hotel chains—use facility planning to maximize guest services and convenience. Government agencies also use facility planners to determine office layouts.

Facility managers are concerned with planning and management of offices as well as production spaces and maintenance of the physical plant. "Facility manager" is a position that formerly was often called plant manager, buildings and grounds superintendent, director of physical plant, or even office manager. These professionals are involved in decisions related to the best utilization of assets to help create the most productive environment for the business. Today's facility manager is involved in: long-range facility planning, the management of the furniture, fixtures, and equipment (FF&E), the manufacturing equipment, real estate acquisition, and interior space utilization. In other words, these individuals are in charge of managing the enterprise's capital assets.[2] Facility managers are also responsible for the aesthetic design and space planning of the facility, but many do not do the actual "work" to create the plan or the aesthetic design. They work with employees at all levels. In addition, they must coordinate with outside architects, interior designers, contractors, and others in the planning and construction of the facility.

An Overview of Office Operations

In one way or another, we have always had offices. In earliest of times, it may have been the space two people occupied as they shook hands on a deal for, say, one caveman to make a wheel for another caveman. Offices became more formalized as economies and industry grew throughout the world. Specialized office work developed as a way of recording the transactions of a business and enhancing the effectiveness and profitability of a business.

In offices, owners, managers, supervisors, and staff employees go about activities necessary to plan, manage, and control any and all of the activities required to maintain the business. Each person's job, each department or division of a business is charged with specific responsibilities that enhance the likelihood of the business achieving its goals. From the designer's point of view, each of these different job functions might require variations in the sizes of individual office spaces and the furniture provided to execute job responsibilities.

Let's look at some terminology that is consistent with the operations of offices.

Manager is a term associated with any individual at any level whose responsibilities are to plan, control, organize, provide leadership, and decision-making for his or her employees.

A *line manager* is an individual responsible for the "firm's activities directly related to the production of goods or services which the enterprise offers society. Production/operations

---

[1] International Facility Management Association, Houston, TX, USA date unknown, p. 1.

[2] *Capital assets* is an accounting term that generally means any property, buildings, and equipment that a business requires in order for that business to conduct the mission of the enterprise.

management, marketing, financial management, and general management are generally considered line functions."[3]

A *staff manager* is an individual who provides support, advice, and expertise to line managers. For example, public relations, legal counsel, accountant, and personnel are typical staff functions.

The *Chief Executive Officer* (CEO) is the job title for the highest ranking individual in the business. In smaller companies, he or she might have the title president or principal rather than CEO.

Vice Presidents are the second highest layer of management. They work primarily with the CEO and are responsible for specific departments or divisions of the business. Examples would be Vice President of Marketing and Vice President of Product Development.

Department managers are another level down in the hierarchy. They are responsible for more specific work activities. For example, the managers for the accounting department and the payroll department are responsible for the staff members who perform those specific functions.

Supervisors are an additional level down in the hierarchy in many businesses. They usually make up the greatest number of managers in a business. These individuals are responsible for the work activities of the individuals who actually perform most of the work in a business. An example might be the supervisor of the group of accounting individuals responsible for only the accounts receivable section in the accounting department.

Other terms associated with the design of office spaces will be a part of the chapter text.

The goal of office work is to provide individual specific task accomplishment that assists in the achievement of overall business goals. The office provides the environment for individuals to do the required work of the business, dependent upon the specific purpose of the business. The type of business will affect the design requirements to which the interior designer must conform even though the basic goal and concept of office facilities is the same regardless of the type of business.

In order to understand the specific job functions within offices, it would be a good idea to understand the overall nature of the traditionally organized enterprise. This section looks at the responsibility centers of a large corporation, so that the reader can see where the job functions fall within the operations of a business. Keep in mind that these same areas or divisions exist in many smaller business, though, of course, not as formally as described for the larger corporation.

Traditionally organized businesses have clearly defined organizational structures. The larger the organization, the more defined this structure becomes. Structure helps define roles and responsibilities so that each segment of the business can effectively meet the goals of the enterprise. The designer's primary concern with the organizational structure is to understand what each department does, how departments relate to each other, what individuals do in the department, and the relationship of these individuals to each other. In part, these relationships are explained by the use of the corporation's organizational chart (Figure 1-3). In the downsized organization of the 1990s, these layers will be less defined, as the reader will see in Chapter 3.

Organizational charts explain the formal reporting structure of the business. Yet the formal chart is often merely that—a formal description of organizational structure. Often day-to-day work relationships that keep the enterprise going do not strictly relate to this chart. Designers find out about these informal channels of communication by the use of common programming[4] techniques, such as one-on-one interviews, on-site inspections, or by using questionnaires.

---

[3] Glueck, 1980, p. 39.

[4] *Programming* is, as most readers know, the first phase of any project where information about the project is obtained by the interior designer.

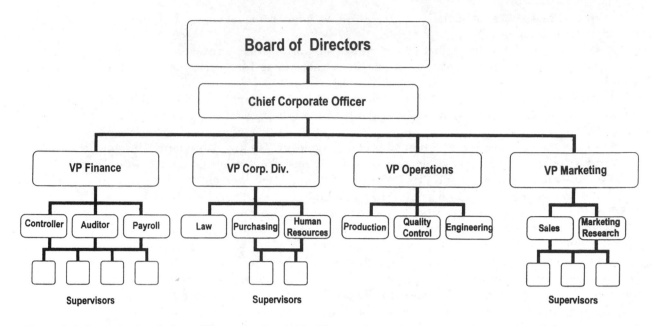

Figure 1–3 Organizational chart. (Illustration by: Alisha Newman).

Large business enterprises are commonly broken down into several divisions or departments. Our sample business is broken down into the following divisions:

1. Executive
2. Corporate/Legal
3. Finance
4. Operations or Manufacturing
5. Marketing
6. Administration

The *Executive Division* commonly includes the chairman of the board, CEO, or president, along with executive staff, and perhaps several vice presidents. This division of the enterprise determines overall policies and implements the policies of the board of directors.[5] The executive division is responsible for financial planning and overall general administration. As for the interior design concerns for this portion of the facility, it is common for these areas to "set the design tone" of the business through the use of the highest grades of furniture and furnishings. Many upper level executives ask designers to provide a setting to impress clients, visitors, and the board of directors.

The *Corporate or Legal Division* would consist of the many departments related to the operations on the corporate level. These might include law, taxes, communications—especially publicity and public relations—corporate planning, real estate and insurance, employee relations, and purchasing. The legal department looks after the business's best interests in terms of any legal services the business may need. The tax department will work closely with finance concerning taxes. The communications group will insure that the proper image is maintained in all public communication and coordinate activities with the marketing division

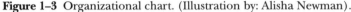

[5] The *board of directors* are individuals elected by shareholders. The board is legally responsible for such things as selecting the president and other chief officers, delegating operational power, and setting policy on matters concerning stocks, financing, and executive pay levels.

in the promotion of the business. Leaders in planning the corporation's future direction will be housed in the corporate planning department. The real estate department will be responsible for obtaining land and buildings for the business. The insurance department will be responsible for the numerous kinds of insurance needs of the business. Purchasing departments are often housed within the corporate division in order to best control the purchasing of all the goods and materials required to operate the business, from those needed to produce the goods of the business to the paper clips and furniture used in the offices. The employee relations area, most often called the human resources department or personnel department, is responsible for the recruiting, interviewing, and hiring of employees. Depending on the organizational structure of the corporation, other activities may also be housed within this corporate division.

The *Finance Division* includes individuals responsible for corporate finance, financial planning, financial analysis, accounting, and the preparation of financial reports. All of the other financial aspects of the company, such as processing of receivables and payables, payroll, and other matters dealing with finances, would also fall under the finance division's responsibilities.

The *Operations Division* is responsible for all aspects of producing the goods or services of the enterprise. The work responsibilities of this division includes such things as: engineering, production, distribution, materials management, purchasing, and quality control. These terms relate to a corporation involved in the production of goods rather than the provision of services, but the concepts are similar. For example, the operations of an architectural firm would involve the production and delivery of construction drawings and specifications, as well as site supervision during construction. The operations of an accounting office would involve bookkeeping, producing managerial reports for business owners, perhaps tax accounting, and possibly conducting required audits.

The *Marketing Division* would include all areas of responsibility related to marketing, advertising, and sales. This group of departments determines how best to convey the information about products or services the business makes or offers to the consumer. The marketing division is also responsible for the company's actual efforts to sell its products or services to its customers. Whatever the corporation is selling, it is up to the marketing division to determine the consumer's needs or wants regarding the company's "goods," to determine how to best make those products known to the consumer, and to go about the actual selling of the product or service.

Within the *Administration Division* would be those departments that are responsible for providing services to the other departments. One of the departments commonly located in this division would be Management Information Services (MIS). Individuals is the MIS department look at the operations of the corporations and analyze how things are done. They also analyze the data they collect, providing department, division, and corporate managers and executives with reports related to efficiency and productivity. A major portion of the work done in this area is done on computers. The main computer center would also commonly be located in or near this department.

Another department located in the administration division is Facility Management. This group is responsible for the maintenance and planning of the office "plant" and any actual manufacturing facilities. These individuals would be the department that would work with outside architects, contractors, interior designers, and vendors whenever facilities are built or remodeled.

Other departments in administration are the central or main reception area, mail room, copy centers, central files, supplies storage, and training areas. In large corporations, the administration division would be responsible for training of new employees. Conference or classroom space, training rooms, audiovisual facilities, and storage areas for equipment and paper supplies would be the primary areas needed in this department. Some corporations with several locations may also have satellite hookups for teleconference or multisite training sessions.

Do not forget that each of the above areas will have slightly different space requirements and furniture needs. For example, attorneys use legal size paper and require larger file cabinets than other departments that use letter size paper. The real estate department may need to view large blueprints, just like an architect, in order to review development drawings and site plans. Individuals working in communication departments may still be reviewing storyboards, which are used to lay out proposed advertising campaigns.

In its own way, each specialized business—regardless of size—has spaces and functional requirements similar to those described above. It is all rather relative, in a way. For a doctor's suite, one could describe the spaces that the doctors use for themselves as the executive division. The officer manager of a doctor's suite performs many jobs of the corporate division. The area where patients check in and pay for services, as well as the spaces occupied by office workers responsible for these activities, can be thought of as the finance division. The patient exam rooms, perhaps small surgery, lab, and other medical specific spaces are the operations divisions of a medical suite. Marketing is not generally an issue with physicians, but that function would be part of the doctor's or office manager's responsibilities. And one could argue that all areas except the medical treatment areas are similar to the administration division.

Types of Office Facilities

Office facilities have existed for many centuries. Business was conducted in the great rooms of the Pharaohs and the palaces of kings; administrative spaces existed within the great cathedrals, and in side rooms or portions of residences of craftsmen and tradesmen. As civilization grew and industry and trade became more sophisticated, the need for office facilities and office furniture expanded.

Offices moved away from the home and into a separate business space perhaps as early as the 16th century.[6] However, the major change in the development of offices occurred during the Industrial Revolution. The change in economies from an agricultural to an industrial base influenced the growth of office functions along with the numbers and kinds of businesses. In addition, an increasing number of offices were conducting more and more specialized tasks.

In the late 1800s, business offices primarily used a closed plan. The closed plan for office design at the time involved a private space for the boss or owner with clerks and secretaries in separate spaces. Recall the private office of Ebenezer Scrooge and his clerk, Bob Cratchit, sitting in an outside room at a tall desk lit by a single candle in Dickens' *A Christmas Carol.* If the business was large enough, the clerks would be in a large open space (Figure 1-4). The offices of the owners and managers were often more opulent and decorative in comparison to the sparse desk, chair, and lamp on the workers' desks.

The 20th century saw the real growth in offices and functional specialties along with the infant emergence of commercial interior design as a specialty. As industries absorbed production workers, the offices for companies increased in size. Closed plans in offices continued into the early part of 20th century until designers such as Frank Lloyd Wright, with the Larkin Administration Building (1904), started to open up office space plans.

After World War II, corporations, which often had offices located in different parts of the country, began to move all their offices into central corporate headquarters. Unlike previous office architecture, where more than one company would be located in a building, these corporate headquarters created a single tenant in a building. This gave the building owner much more control of the architecture, the interior space planning, the interior finishes, and furniture specification.

A major impact on the design of office facilities occurred in the early 1950s in Germany.[7] A design group called the Quickborner Team created a new office planning concept that was called Office Landscape. This planning methodology did away with all private offices and

---

[6]Klein, 1982, p. 10.
[7]Pile, 1978, p. 18.

Figure 1–4 Office space circa 1900 with open area shared by various employees. (Photograph used by permission, Utah State Historical Society.)

placed both managers and staff members in an open plan. Although designers and business owners had used a concept of open plan for decades, this was the first time in modern office design that the whole of the facility utilized an open plan. Open office is discussed in detail in the next chapter.

Open landscape, now called open office planning, and the furniture products introduced in the 1960s by Robert Probst, a designer working for Herman Miller, Inc., had a profound effect on the design of all offices (see Figure 1-5). This change in space planning affected how businesses were managed, because it placed greater emphasis on work groups than on the individual workers. Office design in the 1960s and 1970s actually became more humanistic, with greater concern for the ability of the individual to have some freedom in the design and specification of his or her work area.

In the late 1970s, several designers focused their efforts on the creation of ergonomically designed seating. Today designers utilize concepts of ergonomic design in everything from letter openers to keyboards to any piece of the vast variety of office products used by businesses and the consumer.

The design of the office environment has changed again in the 1990s. Chapter 3 discusses some of those changes. Office planning and design today encompass a combination of the approaches that have evolved over the history of office design. Open plan, closed plan, systems furniture, and traditional case goods or *stick*[8] furniture, all can be applicable to the needs of the client. Enhanced environmental planning has also become important in today's offices, as has the challenge of incorporating technological changes into office equipment setups. Personal computers are on every desk; laptop computers and cell phones allows for mobile offices; telecommuting permits workers and clients to be on different continents and still conduct business "one-on-one."

With all these changes in the way offices were and will be designed, along with the changes in furniture and technological interfaces required in today's offices, one thing has remained relatively unchanged: The boss still gets the biggest office with the most furniture

---

[8] Many designers refer to wood furniture as *stick* furniture.

Figure 1–5 Action Office workstation. (Photograph courtesy of Herman Miller, Inc., Zeeland, MI.)

and furnishings, while the staff and production workers get spaces and furniture adequate to do the job.

Regardless of the type of business and the exact purpose of that business, the types of office facilities within businesses are relatively similar. Naturally, if the business is small, such as a real estate office or an accountant's office, the types of office facilities described in this section may not actually exist or will exist in a different context. But in some way, shape, or form, they will be there. The following discussion focuses on the traditional office hierarchy, not on the downsized corporate hierarchy of the 1990s.

Executive suites and offices house the highest ranking individuals in the enterprise. These offices are generally private offices, assigned to one individual, quite frequently with a private secretary or administrative assistant located just outside. The executive office area is often located on the uppermost floor or most premium location in the facility. In some cases, the highest level executives are provided with a private entrance via private elevators. The executive suite often has a separate reception area and receptionist along with a controlled or separate entry for visitors. A large board room or conference room for meetings is important in this area as well.

The largest offices are reserved for the president or chief executive officer and other upper level managers. Because the CEO is the top person in the organization, he or she is given many more amenities and better quality design treatments than anyone else in the organization (see Figure 1-6 and 1-7). Vice presidents will also have a private office, smaller in size than the president but furnished in a similar manner (see Figure 1-7). This second level of management also is provided with a private secretary located just outside the private office door.

The executive suite often provides space for several other kinds of space usages. A secured storage area for confidential corporate records and an on-site safe or vault are often provided. Large corporations may have an executive dining room, lounge, even an exercise area for the use of upper level executives, either in the executive suite or in some convenient area.

Smaller businesses and professional service offices will have their own versions of the executive suite. The owners or managers of the business will have the most space, generally in the premium locations. They will often request that larger sums be spent planning and designing their office spaces, providing them higher grade desks, seating, fabric selections, and architectural finishes. They may not have a separate reception area, but the owner/manager almost always has a private secretary who works closely with him or her.

Figure 1–6 Executive office of Estee Lauder, furnished with Louis XV and Louis XVI furniture as well as other luxurious appointments. (Photograph © Scott Frances/Esto. All rights reserved.)

Figure 1–7 Traditional executive furniture which could be used in a vice president's office. (Photograph courtesy of Harden Contract, McConnellsville, NY.)

Staff offices are another type of office. For managers and some supervisors, these offices will be private offices, providing them privacy to accomplish their work and conduct some meetings with staff members. In some cases, the staff offices will be areas within the general work area, probably partitioned with movable panels to provide a limited amount of privacy. For managers, their offices are smaller in square footage than those of the vice president, but can be equipped with similar furniture, just on a smaller scale. In many organizations, supervisors do not even have an enclosed or private office, but are located in the same general area as the group of employees for whom they are responsible. For example, a factory foreman's "office" might actually be a desk in a reasonably quiet corner of the production area. As we see in Chapter 3, many of the upper level staff offices have disappeared due to the downsizing of large corporations in the 1990s.

Another type of office facility is sometimes called the *general office*. In general offices, the space is not designed for anyone in particular. People move in and out of these spaces as they leave and enter the company or get promoted to higher ranking positions (see Figure 1-8). The only specialization to the design of a general office is for the particular work being done in the office area. General offices are sometimes thought of as spaces for "production employees." Production employees are individuals such as designers, real estate agents, accountants, sales representatives, computer programmers, and so on. The specific furniture and equipment needs vary a great deal with the company and the department. The designer obtains the information about these specific needs in generally through interview questions or by the use of questionnaires during the programming phase of a project. Unless general office areas are visited by clients of the company, less money is spent on these areas and they are usually specified with lower grades of furniture and finishes.

All office facilities have a *reception or waiting area*. The reception area is the place where visitors are greeted, queried as to whom they wish to see, and wait for the appropriate person to come and receive them. The larger the business, the more elaborate this reception area becomes. Smaller businesses may merely have a few chairs located near the entrance door so that customers have somewhere to sit. In large corporate facilities there may be subreception areas located at the entrance to departmental areas. In most businesses the reception area is an important location from a design standpoint as it is where the visitor receives the first

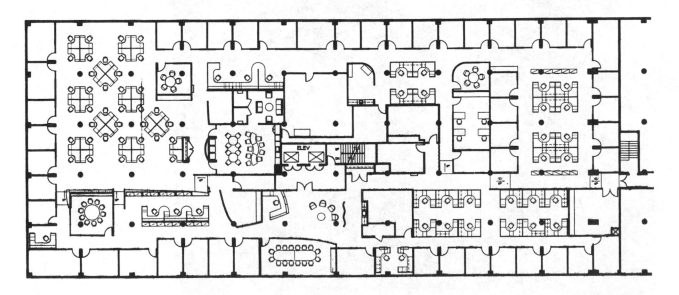

Figure 1–8 This floor plan is an example of a general office with a core of workstations in the midsection and enclosed offices placed around the perimeter of the building. (Plan courtesy of Richard Pollack & Associates, Architecture/Interior Design.)

impression of the business. Companies often spend considerably more money and attention on this area to help create the right impression (Figure 1-9).

There are many kinds of *support spaces* (sometimes referred to as ancillary spaces) in business offices. First, conference rooms or presentation rooms can serve one of two functions: for in-house employee conferences and for client conferences. In-house employee conferences might involve such business as: weekly staff meetings, team meetings concerning a current project, strategy planning sessions for upcoming client presentations, or group discussions of changes in policies and procedures. Conference rooms can also be places for company personnel to meet with clients. Meetings such as the taking of depositions by attorneys, the final design presentation by interior designers and architects, and client meetings with accountants all are examples of client meetings in conference rooms.

Other common support spaces are: mail processing, supply storage, copying, central filing, and perhaps a resource library. In large businesses, these support services will be in separate areas. Many medium to small businesses will combine these support areas into one or two areas, depending on the size of the office complex. In large office facilities, services such as copying, supply storage, and resource material areas may be located throughout the office building as well as in a central location.

An employee break room or lunchroom is another kind of support space. The larger the firm, the more elaborate this support area will be. The break room will be a separate room, possibly with minimal kitchen facilities in larger companies, or perhaps simply a small area to hold a coffee machine and supplies in smaller businesses. A break room might exist on

Figure 1–9 Reception area promotes a welcoming environment for Steelcase WorkLife, New York, NY. (Photograph courtesy of Steelcase, Inc.)

each floor in very large businesses, and a large employee cafeteria, with complete food service capabilities, might be provided.

Planning and Design Concepts

This section presents basic information on planning and design concepts applied to many of the office and support areas of office facilities. Recognize that it is not possible to discuss each specialized type of business or specific job function in this chapter. The information included in this section provides the reader with sufficient background information to understand the basic space and functional equipment needs of the most common job levels in offices.

Image and Status

The design of a firm's office reflects the firm's attitudes toward budget, goals, and plans, as well as its attitudes toward its employees, customers, visitors, and vendors. All of these reflect the image of the company. An important part of the designer's job is to interpret what the company wants as its design image.

Image is not just the finishing touches—a Knoll Barcelona chair rather than a budget wood armchair, for instance. Image is the entire design solution, from early programming decisions to the completion of the project. The company image is an expression of the company itself. The designer must attempt to express that image through his or her selection of the products, colors, textures, and styles that create the final interior design of the facilities. A conservative, traditional image may be appropriate for a law office or bank. A high-tech contemporary image may be appropriate for an advertising agency. No matter how up-to-date it might be, a traditional law office done in glass and chrome furniture does not reflect the traditional, conservative image that is often desired by the conservative client.

Today, very few clients give designers a blank check for the budget. The professional designer must strive for a design solution that:

- Projects a well-organized functional arrangement of space and furnishings

- Uses colors and textures that enhance the function of the space and make a statement about the business

- Exhibits a concern for detail in the design work

- Creates an environment in which the client is happy

Status in an office environment is generally provided by one or more of these three features: size of the office, location of the office in the building, and quality and quantity of furniture. Even in a small organization with only a few employees, it is obvious who is in charge—the person in the largest office. Space allowances are often set by company policy. An individual, based on the job title not the job function, gets X square feet of office space. Many times this allowance is appropriate to the function when the office is planned using conventional full-height wall planning concepts. It is the designer's responsibility to respect these space standards whenever possible as part of the status requirements of the company.

A second way of showing status in an office is by location. The corner office with windows on both sides is a prime location in many companies. It is much more desirable than an office with only one window or one in the central core with no windows. Generally, highly desirable offices are reserved for management, even if they are not in their offices very much. There are not too many enlightened companies that believe in putting the secretarial staff at or near the windows so that they can have a view and natural light in which to work.

The last status criteria relates to quantity and quality of furniture and treatments in an office. We have already seen how an employee at the executive level receives a larger desk and extra pieces of furniture when compared to the "production employee." The higher up the ladder one is in an organization, the better the quality of the furniture. This is not only a part of the status "perks" of an organization, but relates to the image projected to clients. The president's office must impress visitors so that they know they are dealing with a successful company and a successful individual. High quality furniture in the lower levels of the organization is not unheard of but is less common. However, as with anything else— you get what you pay for. If the client buys budget furniture for employees who are hard on equipment, the furniture will not last long, and in the long run will have to be replaced sooner.

The higher up the corporate ladder, the more furniture the individual office worker will have. Often the size of the furniture is the key to status. One employee has a larger desk than another doing a similar job. The larger desk, or even the higher-backed posture chair, is the status symbol signifying rank in the office. In bank branches, for example, where it is often uncommon for the manager and loan officers to have private offices, status is shown by giving the bank manager a large size desk and a high-back posture chair while the loan officers are given smaller desks and lower-backed chairs.

Interior Design Concepts

The office exists so that the work of the business can be done. The design of the office plays an important part in how well the work is done. Countless studies have been conducted to show this connection. The most famous is probably the study done by the Buffalo Organization for Social and Technological Innovation (BOSTI), published in 1984 and 1985. Researchers uncovered statistical data that showed that factors such as layout, design, and appearance affected job satisfaction and job performance.

Designing an office effectively means understanding the business of the client, work relationships and job adjacencies, communication patterns, and furniture needs. All of this information is gathered during the programming phase. Information about client needs, the office site, preferences, and other information needed to complete the project is obtained long before the designer begins any space planning or selection of products. Keen observation, reading books such as this and the ones listed in the chapter references, asking the client thoughtful questions, and listening to his or her answers all help the student and inexperienced designer learn about the business of the client.

Understanding work relationships and job adjacencies helps the designer to locate each type of office space in the facility and each individual in each department. Adjacency matrixes are a key aid to the designer in understanding how to develop the floor plan. Just as the student learns that in planning a residence it is most effective and common to locate the dining room adjacent to the kitchen, he or she will learn the business's chain of command, and understand all the different work relationships and adjacencies in a variety of office environments.

Designing an office to encourage productive employees involves consideration of communication patterns as well. First of all, communication patterns have a lot to do with work relationships. Individuals who need to communicate frequently with each other need to be located near each other. Secondly, the way the office is planned will affect whether communication between workers and work groups is inhibited or supported. Meetings take place in private offices, in staff offices, and in conference rooms—even in the lunchroom. It is also important that privacy exist somehow so that a supervisor can reprimand an employee. Sound control is needed, for example, when a team of designers hash out a tricky solution to a problem with a project. Individuals who work together on projects must find that the facility allows for those group communications if they are to be able to do their jobs. And those whose jobs require more individual concentration must have the privacy or acoustical planning to keep distractions to a minimum.

Furniture needs are also discovered during programming. Some designers use formal questionnaires while others determine these product needs by observation and an inventory of existing items. Almost every non-highly-specialized job in an office will require at least a desk, space for filing, one or more drawers for storage of reference materials and a limited amount of office supplies, seating for the worker, and today, space for a personal computer. What size and style of each piece of furniture, whether an individual gets any additional items, and the price of each item will vary based on the individual's level in the hierarchy and other factors such as: whether the office is a corporate headquarters or a branch office; the type of business and the target market of clients with which the business is trying to work; the location of the office; and the general philosophy of the business about providing a quality work environment for its employees.

This background information is necessary to effectively make planning and design decisions, regardless of the type of business and the specific office facility type under contract. Let us now look at specific issues concerned with the design of generic office facilities.

Space allocation for each office and support space is determined during the programming phase of a project. In many cases, large businesses will have predetermined allowances for many levels of job functions. For example, a major electronics and semiconductor company has a corporate standard of 250 square feet for senior managers, 200 square feet for midlevel managers, 168 square feet for supervisors, and 48–64 square feet for secretarial and clerical staff. The designer is normally required to plan the facility using these corporate standards.

Square foot allowances not formulated or controlled by corporate policy are easily determined by developing typical plan sketches of the different areas. Pieces of furniture and equipment require the space they actually occupy along with the space around one or more sides to use the furniture and equipment. The designer must add space allowances for traffic paths. Finally, some areas will be allotted additional square footage for "status." In certain instances, code requirements will also necessitate additional square footage for the job or function. This is especially true to meet the needs of employees who fall under the Americans with Disabilities Act (ADA) provisions. Bringing all these factors into account, a typical plan sketch can be developed that shows the necessary square footage required for each office and function. Figure 1-10 shows several typical floor plans for office spaces based on hierarchical level or specific job responsibility.

Experienced designers have extensive knowledge about how much space is typically allocated for many jobs or support functions. Students and professionals beginning to design commercial office spaces may depend upon the development of typical plan views as described in the preceding paragraph. Figure 1-11 provides a chart of square foot ranges for support spaces common to office facilities.

When all these space allowances are determined for all workers, the result is the *net area required* to plan the facility. But this net area has not allowed for architectural features and spaces that are considered part of the space the client rents or builds. These additional areas include general circulation space, columns, wall thicknesses, electrical closets, and other similar spaces.

When the client is moving into a building and leasing or renting the required office space, a few other terms need to be understood. The first is demising wall. A *demising wall* is any partition used to separate one tenant space from another. When calculating allowances for needed square footage, each tenant is responsible for one-half the thickness of all demising walls. Partition walls separating the tenant space from the public corridors are not demising walls, and the tenant does not "pay for" that thickness.

The total amount of square footage required for office and support spaces and including allowances for demising walls, and interior architectural features such as columns, mechanical chases or closets, and even a portion of the exterior walls, is called the *rentable area*. When clarifying usable square footage, to determine if the client has rented too much or too little space, the designer needs to calculate and subtract the square footage represented by demising walls, exterior walls, any structural columns, chases, and electrical closets that may exist within the space. In order to determine the actual usable square footage, designers need to know whether or not the demising walls, and so on, are part of the rentable square footage. This information can be obtained from leasing agents and building managers.

Once space allocations for the various office facilities are determined and the functional adjacencies of each job function and department are clarified, the designer is ready to begin

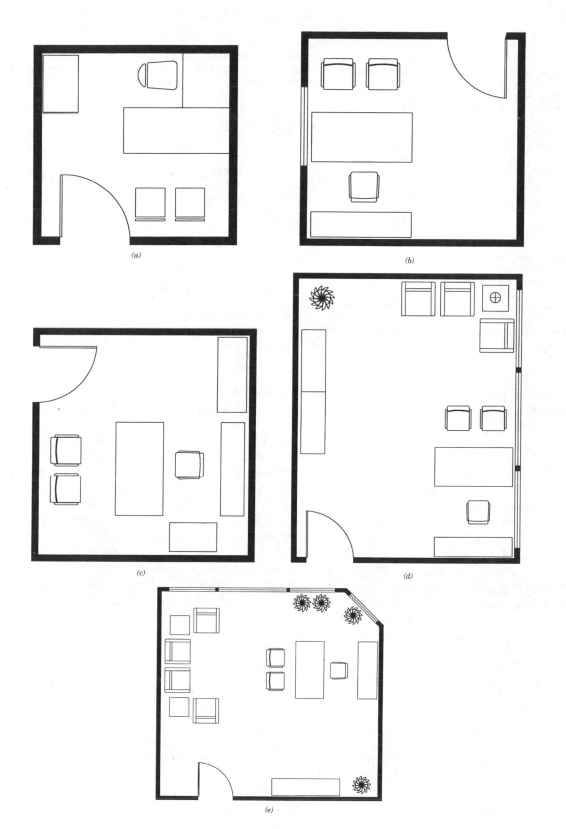

Figure 1–10 Some typical floor plans for office spaces based on hierarchical level or specific job responsiblity. *(a)* Secretarial and clerical staff: 48 to 64 square feet. *(b)* Supervisor: 168 square feet. *(c)* Midlevel manager: 200 square feet. *(d)* Senior manager: 250 square feet. *(e)* Execuitve office: 330 to 360 square feet. (Plans courtesy of HENV: Interior Design.)

Support Space	Sq. Footage Range (30,000 SF office or less)	Sq. Footage Range (30,000–100,000 SF office)	Sq. Footage Range (100,000 SF office or more)
Reception	250 SF / 300 SF	300 SF / 400 SF	1000 SF
Conference Room	250 SF / 300 SF	300 SF / 500 SF	750 SF
Workroom	250 SF	250 SF	300 SF
Training Room		750 SF	1500 SF
Computer Room	400 SF	1000 SF	2500 SF
Equipment Rooms	120 SF	250 SF	250 SF
File Room	120 SF / 200 SF	200 SF / 400 SF	1200 SF
Copy Room	200 SF	300 SF / 400 SF	1000 SF
Mail Room	200 SF	300 SF / 400 SF	1000 SF
Library	200 SF / 300 SF	400 SF / 600 SF	1200 SF
Pantry	200 SF	300 SF	300 SF
Day Care Center			8000 SF
Fitness Center			4000 SF / 6000 SF
Cafeteria			10000 SF / 12000 SF
Conference Center			12000 SF
Auditorium			5000 SF

Figure 1–11 Chart of square footage for support areas. (From Rayfield, *The Office Interior Design Guide*. Copyright © 1994. Reprinted by permission of John Wiley & Sons.)

schematic planning of the floor plan. Schematic plans will be developed to test the information obtained in the programming phase and to begin to show the client potential layouts for the project.

Circulation paths to move people through the office facility must be determined. "The circulation path defines the skeletal framework of the office. Whether an enclosed corridor or a pathway through an open work area, a circulation path is meant to get people easily from place to place."[9] A major circulation path is provided to move people in and out of the general office space. This may be a major fire rated corridor from the elevator around the building core providing access to the one or more office suites on the floor. The major circulation path might only be the path from the front exterior door through corridors and aisle ways in a small office on the ground floor of a building. It is necessary for the designer to insure that these major circulation paths are designed to adhere to all applicable building codes. Circulation paths that are defined by floor to ceiling walls and any partitions of over 69 inches high are required by code to be a minimum of 44 inches wide unless the occupant load is less than 49.[10] Actual width of major circulation paths and exit corridors may need to be larger, based on the number of occupants in the suite and on the floor of the building. Circulation paths may also be required to meet the ADA guidelines or other accessibility guidelines in effect. Special design elements, such as areas of refuge, wheelchair turnaround space, and maneuvering alcoves, to name just a few, may also be required by ADA guidelines.

Secondary circulation paths are required to move people from the major path to more remote places in the facility. Building codes will again guide the designer in the size of these secondary paths. In most situations, as long as the partitions or counters are less than 69 inches high, the pathway width will be 44 inches unless, again, the occupant load is less than 49. In some situations, however, it is possible for the width of aisles used by employees to be narrower than 44 inches. The appropriate code book should be referenced.

Circulation paths require 25 to 40 percent additional floor space. This does not include space for the major traffic paths that are considered exit paths from suites into core exit access.

---

[9] Brandt, 1992, p. 96.

[10] Dimensions related to building, fire safety, and ADA codes used throughout this book were based on 1997 codes. Local regulations may be different than those provided. The reader is responsible for verifying actual current codes.

The exact amount will be influenced by whether the project is primarily private offices versus open office systems, the requirement or desire for generous circulation paths, the number of spaces required in the project, and the footprint of the space. Open office projects generally take up more space than projects with full-height walls. Another thing that will affect the amount of circulation space is whether the circulation paths are designed with twists and turns (some sort of maze) or straight "bowling alley" effects. Straight paths are more efficient, but can be boring in a large layout. Mazes take up a lot of space, as does trying to do floor plans on angles. Although there is no sure-fire way to determine how much space should be allowed, the guideline noted above will help the student estimate how much total space is needed to plan office facilities.

Office *furniture* is selected on the basis of function, price, and aesthetics or style. The item, be it a desk, seating unit, file cabinet, or whatever, must first satisfy performance criteria. A desk that is too small or a file cabinet that will not hold the file folders used by the client is not a successfully specified product, regardless of aesthetic success. There are many price points for office furniture from low budget, very inexpensive pieces to semicustom and custom furniture items with very high prices. Most projects for most designers will be budgeted based on medium to medium-high priced goods. Fortunately, there is a great deal of quality performance and quality aesthetics in this price range. Lastly, furniture is selected on aesthetics. We realize this is an arguable point by many professional designers, but for the vast majority, it is true. The majority of clients are more concerned with product performance and price than with aesthetics. That is always unfortunate from the designer's point of view!

Office furniture is categorized as either *general use furniture* (sometimes called conventional furniture) or *systems furniture*. General use furniture includes desks, credenzas, bookcases, file cabinets, and seating, while systems furniture are items created from less than full-height movable panels with components that become freestanding units or cubicles. This section deals only with general use furniture since systems products are covered in the next chapter.

General use furniture is further categorized into case goods and seating. *Case goods* are items made of "cases," like desks, credenzas, bookcases, file cabinets, and the like. Some designers also think of tables as case goods, but many just refer to them as—tables.

Desks are the common denominator in offices. Few office jobs can be performed without some kind of desk. These furniture items come in a variety of sizes and types (see Figure 1-12). Desks have drawer units on one or both sides called pedestals. A desk with only one pedestal is called a single pedestal desk; if it has two, it's a double pedestal desk. Some jobs require a desk with a return. A return is an additional case unit that creates an L or U shaped desk. Traditionally, secretaries had L shaped desks with a return to hold the typewriter. In many offices, the computer now replaces the typewriter on the return. Standard 18 inch deep returns are not deep enough to properly manage the computer and keyboard. L or U shaped desks can be specified with returns that are slightly lower in height than the desk or at the same height, creating a large continuous desk surface. It is most common that managers and executives receive an L or U shaped desk with a continuous height while secretaries and other clerical or lower level staff be given a lowered height return.

Some executives like a table desk. Table desks are either beautiful tables or specially designed tables with a center drawer. Obviously, they have no drawer pedestals so that the specification of a storage unit, called a credenza, is necessary.

Designers will almost universally provide a *credenza* for managers and upper level staff . A credenza is a storage unit much like a buffet cabinet in a home as is shown in Figure 1-12. It is used for extra storage and filing, accomodates some kinds of office equipment like an adding machine, and is almost always positioned behind the desk. It is specified the same basic width as the desk, though many manufacturers make credenzas about 2 to 4 inches narrower than the matching desks. Credenzas also have pedestals, the number being dictated by the width of the unit. Credenza pedestals are configured similarly to those in desks.

Another storage item found in many office spaces is the file cabinet. The paperless office is not yet a reality. In many businesses, paper files must be kept for several years. There are

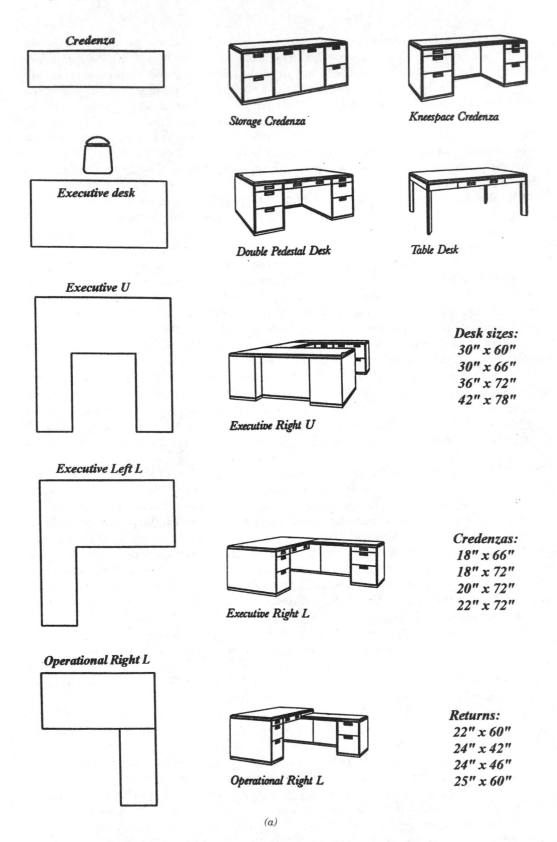

Credenza

Storage Credenza

Kneespace Credenza

Executive desk

Double Pedestal Desk

Table Desk

Executive U

Executive Right U

Desk sizes:
30" x 60"
30" x 66"
36" x 72"
42" x 78"

Executive Left L

Executive Right L

Credenzas:
18" x 66"
18" x 72"
20" x 72"
22" x 72"

Operational Right L

Operational Right L

Returns:
22" x 60"
24" x 42"
24" x 46"
25" x 60"

(a)

Figure 1–12 Desks are manufactured in a variety of shapes and sizes. Credenzas are used for storage as well as for computer use. (Line drawings courtesy of Kimball Office Group.)

two kinds of file cabinets most commonly used in the office: vertical and lateral files (see Figure 1-13). A vertical file is the traditional filing unit. Because it takes up so much floor space, many designers prefer to use lateral files. These are not as deep as vertical files, but wider. Not only are they more efficient when it comes to floor space, but more filing inches are available in a lateral file versus the same number of drawers of a vertical file. When a company has to store large amounts of files, the standard lateral and vertical file cabinet is not cost effective. Open shelf filing units provide storage for large quantities of file folders (Figures 1-14 and 1-15).

When planning central filing areas where numerous file cabinets of any style are to be used, the designer must be careful about the live load[11] added to the structure. For example, a four drawer, 42 inch wide lateral file cabinet filled with paper can weigh 720 pounds[12]. When these units are massed together in one area, it is very easy for the combined weights to exceed the load limits of the floor. It is necessary for the designer to estimate the total load amounts of these massed storage units. Designers obtain the live load limits of the floor from the facilities managers, leasing agents, or the architect to insure that the floor will not sag or even fail. If the estimated load of the massed units exceeds the safe load limits, it will be necessary to either reinforce the floor or relocate the storage units to more than one location.

There are several kinds of seating units used in offices. The seating piece used behind the desk for the office worker is called desk seating, posture chair, desk chair, or any of a number of other names created by manufacturers (Figure 1-16). Side, guest, and conference chairs are items used by office guests and in conference rooms. Other office chairs include: secretarial, operational, management, stools, high-back executive, stacking, sled base, and others. Soft

Figure 1–13 Typical filing units: lateral five drawer file on the left and a vertical five drawer file on the right. (Drawing courtesy of S.O.I. Interior Design, Houston, TX.)

---

[11] *Live load* is such things as the weight of people, furniture, and equipment added to the building. The permanent structural elements part of the building are considered *dead loads*.
[12] De Chiara et al., 1991, p. 287.

Figure 1–14 Mobile open shelf filing units provide storage for extensive amounts of filing. (Photograph courtesy of Jim Franck, Franck & Associates, Inc.)

Figure 1–15 Open unit provides high-density, high-access filing in a modular structure. (Photograph courtesy of TAB, Palo Alto, CA 94304, 1-800-672-3109.)

Contemporary executive chair   **Traditional executive chair**

Traditional client chair   **Conference chair**

Management chair   **Task chair**

Figure 1–16 Seating units used in offices. (Drawing courtesy of Gunlocke.)

seating is another type of seating unit. This group includes lounge chairs, love seats, settees, modular seating, and sofas—seating pieces generally fully upholstered.

An office worker spends eight hours a day behind the desk. He or she should be provided a comfortable chair that supports function and supports the body properly. Since the introduction of ergonomic seating for office workers in the 1970s, desk seating has become more comfortable and healthful. Ergonomic chairs are designed not only for greater comfort but also to be more specifically useful to the jobs of individuals. Manufacturers and chair designers have created a variety of ergonomically designed seating to meet job functions and also provide the "status" requirements of the different ranks.

Chairs also come in different designs and options, some for function, some for status. Casters allow chairs to move more freely. However, the designer must specify the right kind of caster for the floor surface: single wheel casters for hard surface floors, double wheel casters for carpet. Chairs can swivel and tilt. These options are most appreciated for the office worker, regardless of job or rank. Chairs with sled bases rather than legs are generally easier to move. And chairs come with different height seat backs, finishes, and of course, fabric options to help provide status differences.

Color preferences are incredibly varied in office facilities. Some businesses will have color standards for their offices. For example, Red Carpet Realty uses red as the primary design color. In most situations, however, the designer must question the client about color likes and dislikes and develop a workable color scheme for the business, space, and planning concepts. Color selection, in conjunction with proper lighting, can increase productivity and worker comfort in office facilities; thus color schemes should be selected carefully.

Sandra Ragan, a noted commercial interior designer, feels,

The placement of color in commercial environments plays a major role in creating the mood of the space. In fact, color strongly affects the way an environment is perceived by its occupants. . . . Color contributes to the productivity and to the psychological satisfaction of the occupants in a space.[13]

The balance and the mix of colors should be undertaken with care and thought, based on standard color relationships, the type of space, and the lighting designed for the space. Designers should remember light reflectance factors related to color choices. Light values will reflect a high percentage of light while dark values will reflect very little light. Office areas with few or no windows should not be specified with dark colors.

Color in offices is also dictated by trends and fashion. Many offices want to be "up to date" and will ask designers to specify colors based on trends. The bright red-oranges and full intensity hues of the 1970s gave way to the grayed colors of the 1980s. Steel gray, mauves, and the other darker grayed hues have been popular in the early 1990s. However, almost any color combination can work in today's office facility if it is planned carefully and if it meets the wishes of the client.

Lighting design and fixture specification is very important in the office environment. Lighting specification not only relates to providing the proper amount and kind of light for the various jobs in the office, but lighting will also affect color usage and success of the color schemes in office environments.

Until the energy crisis of the late 1970s, most offices were provided with numerous rows of fluorescent fixtures. The high cost of energy and electricity finally forced designers and building owners to look for alternative methods of providing the lighting necessary for workers while keeping costs down. Lighting levels are based on the amount of light needed to perform different tasks. Designers use guidelines such as those from the Illuminating Engineering Society to calculate required lighting for the different tasks and areas of an office facility (see Figure 1-17).

Offices can have two to three different sources of lighting, depending on the size of the space and overall design goals. The most important types are ambient, task, and accent lighting. *Ambient lighting* is lighting designed to provide a uniform level of illumination throughout an area, exclusive of any provision for special task requirements. This has most commonly been accomplished with direct ambient lighting using fluorescent fixtures surface mounted or recess mounted on the ceiling throughout the facility. In the late 1970s, the quality of ambient lighting was improved by the use of indirect ambient lighting fixtures; light is bounced off the ceiling from fixtures that are floor standing, placed on top of shelves, or suspended from the ceiling rather than directed down from the ceiling.

Task lighting is light delivered to the specific area of work from a closely placed source. In this case, lighting fixtures such as a desk lamp and a drafting lamp at the drafting table are selected to provide specific light to a work area. Task lighting is of particular importance where indirect ambient lighting fixtures are used, since indirect ambient fixtures are generally planned to provide a lower general light level than is needed for office work. Task light provides

Accounting, and other business machine operation	150 foot candles
Regular office work—original copy	70 foot candles
Regular office work—fair quality copy	100 foot candles
Corridors, elevators, stariways	20 foot candles
Drafting	200 foot candles
Training/lecture rooms	100 foot candles

Figure 1–17 Chart of recommended minimum foot candles for office applications. (From McGuinness et al., *Mechanical and Electrical Equipment for Buildings*, 6th ed. Copyright © 1980. Reprinted by permission of John Wiley & Sons, Inc.)

---

[13]Ragan, Sandra L. *Interior Color by Design*, 1995. Reprinted with permission from Rockport Publishers, Inc., 33 Commercial St., Gloucester, MA 01930, p. 33.

each office worker with the additional light levels to comfortably work on papers and the computer.

A third source of lighting would be accent lighting. Not all office facilities use wall washers, soffits, spotlights, and other kinds of accent lighting. However, these light sources will provide design interest to the interior. The designer must calculate accent lights into the overall light levels since these fixtures will contribute to the general lighting level.

A most difficult situation for designers concerning lighting designs occurs when the client is leasing office space. Most often, the building owner has dictated the type of lighting fixtures, the sizes of fixtures, and even the colors of the lamps in the fixtures. Some landlords will allow the tenants to replace lighting fixtures or lamps; others will insist on retaining "building standards" to insure a uniform appearance of the interior from the exterior. In these situations, the interior designer will need to do more careful planning and specifications of colors, materials, and textures to design a space that is functional and aesthetic.

Computers are a fact of life in most businesses. The proliferation of the desktop computer over the last 20 years or so has given workers in every business situation a new tool to accomplish a larger variety of tasks than ever before. But this efficiency sometimes carries a price. Many workers are at keyboards all day, with constant repetitive movements resulting in injury to hands, fingers, and arms. Others suffer eyestrain from glare on monitor screens and still others report back, head, and neck problems. In many cases, these injuries are related to the design and specification of the work area.

For the interior designer, the introduction of one or more computers into a work environment by the client goes beyond specifying some aesthetically pleasing piece of furniture to house the equipment. A responsive computer workstation also requires proper lighting design to reduce eye strain and glare. Comfortable seating is needed, especially for those who will be doing a full day's worth of data entry or other repetitive computer tasks. Furniture that is appropriate to the computer workstation is necessary to avoid physical traumas. Appropriate mechanical interface must also be achieved, but this last factor, of course, is primarily the responsibility of the architect.

Unfortunately, there is no ideal or perfect solution to the problem of creating a healthy, responsive computer workstation. People being people, they have varying body dimensions, vision characteristics, and even different ways of working. However, there are some standards that have been discovered that help create a responsive workstation when computers are part of the job. The research on these standards has primarily been performed by modular systems furniture and computer hardware manufacturers. This section discusses important planning considerations for computers in work environments. It is placed in this chapter since the planning and design criteria apply to all computers regardless of the actual business description.

Most readers will be familiar with the terminology of computer hardware—computer, monitor, drives, scanners, modems, and different types of printers. However, a list of terms associated with equipment that some clients still use needs to be presented. A few other terms associated with the challenges of designing computer work stations are also provided.

Carpel tunnel syndrome "is one of a group of musculoskeletal disorders believed to be caused by repeated trauma to the body. This group of disorders . . . is referred to by the umbrella term cumulative trauma disorders or CTDs"[14] It is usually associated with disorders affecting the arms, wrists, and fingers.

CPU (central processing unit) is the hardware "brain" of a computer where the actual computations and data manipulation take place.

CRT (cathode ray tube) is another term for the computer screen or monitor.

Ergonomics is the "study of human beings and their functions in the environment."[15]

---

[14] Herman Miller, Inc., 1991, p. 1.

[15] Kilmer and Kilmer, 1992, p. 190.

VDT (visual display terminal) displays the data generated in the CPU. Note that some people use the acronym VDU or visual display unit rather than VDT.

Work surface is the common name for systems furniture products, "desktops."

Computer work areas should be designed and specified to achieve a workstation that does not contribute to health problems. The best designs are based on flexibility in product specification so that the employee can modify the computer work area to his or her own needs. This is, of course, especially necessary in the many employment situations where more than one employee is using the same workstation. Key issues in the design of a ergonomically healthy computer work area are: the location of the monitor (VDT), position of the keyboard, the seating unit, and proper lighting. Let us first look at the location of the monitor.

Monitors should be located within a maximum 40 degree field of view (see Figure 1-18). This means that the top of the monitor should be level with the worker's eyes and the user's chin should have a slight downward slant. Many who complain of neckaches find they are caused by the monitor's being too low. There is no consensus as to how far the monitor should be from the worker's eyes; the distance must be based on body sizes and personal preference. However, a range of 18 to 22 inches seems common, with some workers located up to 28 inches from the monitor.

Keyboards should be at a height so that the workers forearms are in a nearly horizontal position with a maximum of 10 degree angle of the wrists when the fingers are on the home keys on the keyboard. The wrists should not be sharply bent, resting on the desk top, nor resting on the edge of the keyboard. Wrists should be kept as straight as possible. This can be done by using a lowered keyboard tray or the business owner may provide employees with a padded wrist rest. Ergonomically designed keyboards came onto the market in the 1990s and are very useful in limiting CTD injuries.

These ergonomic factors must influence the designer's specification of furniture. The desktop or work surface depth must be a minimum of the overall depth of the monitor plus approximately 3 inches for cables plus an allowance for the keyboard. Thus the depth of the work surface or desktop will required to be between 28 and 36 inches, depending on the size of the monitor. The minimum width of the work surface should be 36 inches. Additional desktop or work surface space is required on one or both sides of the VDT, depending upon the worker's actual job responsibilities. For many workers the standard desk height of 29 to 30 inches locates the monitor at the wrong height for proper vision and keyboard comfort.

Interior designers should caution business owners against using the standard desk or credenza to house a computer, especially if the employee will be using the computer for most of the day. Modular systems furniture (discussed in Chapter 2) provides flexibility in the layout and specification of furniture products specifically designed for jobs requiring computers. Case goods manufacturers have also designed many products specifically to house the computer. For users in wheelchairs, an adjustable table height is an effective special needs solution.

In designing these workstation areas, the designer needs to make certain that the table does not obstruct the leg movements of the user, that the user has sufficient table surface for the intended tasks, and that bilevel surfaces are supplied where applicable.

Seating is another important part of creating a healthy computer work area. Ergonomically designed seating that allows the worker to sit comfortably at the computer reduces the problems of back, leg, and arm problems. Certain features are needed if the desk chair is to achieve that goal.

Chair seats and backs should be adjustable so that the chair easily "fits" the worker. For example, the backrest should have lumbar support and the backrest position should be adjustable so that the lumbar support area "fits" the user's back comfortably. There should also be an adjustable or movable angle between the seat back and the seat pan. It should be a minimum of 90 degrees.

The seat pan itself should have an angle between 10 degrees above and 30 degrees below horizontal. A *waterfall front*, which is a rounded soft edge at the knee edge of the chair, aid in comfort and helps prevent stress against the back of the legs. The seat pan itself should be 16 inches deep and at least 18 inches wide. If the chair has armrests, the distance between them

Basics of Ergonomic Seating

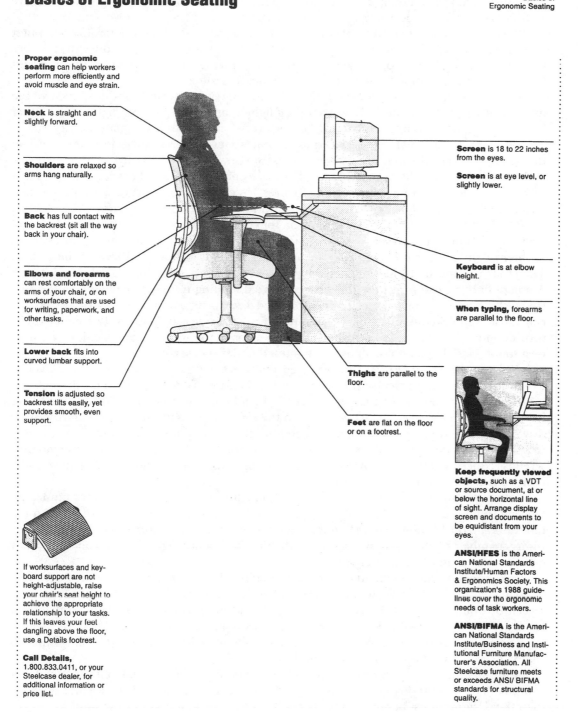

Proper ergonomic seating can help workers perform more efficiently and avoid muscle and eye strain.

Neck is straight and slightly forward.

Shoulders are relaxed so arms hang naturally.

Back has full contact with the backrest (sit all the way back in your chair).

Elbows and forearms can rest comfortably on the arms of your chair, or on worksurfaces that are used for writing, paperwork, and other tasks.

Lower back fits into curved lumbar support.

Tension is adjusted so backrest tilts easily, yet provides smooth, even support.

If worksurfaces and keyboard support are not height-adjustable, raise your chair's seat height to achieve the appropriate relationship to your tasks. If this leaves your feet dangling above the floor, use a Details footrest.

Call Details, 1.800.833.0411, or your Steelcase dealer, for additional information or price list.

Screen is 18 to 22 inches from the eyes.

Screen is at eye level, or slightly lower.

Keyboard is at elbow height.

When typing, forearms are parallel to the floor.

Thighs are parallel to the floor.

Feet are flat on the floor or on a footrest.

Keep frequently viewed objects, such as a VDT or source document, at or below the horizontal line of sight. Arrange display screen and documents to be equidistant from your eyes.

ANSI/HFES is the American National Standards Institute/Human Factors & Ergonomics Society. This organization's 1988 guidelines cover the ergonomic needs of task workers.

ANSI/BIFMA is the American National Standards Institute/Business and Institutional Furniture Manufacturer's Association. All Steelcase furniture meets or exceeds ANSI/ BIFMA standards for structural quality.

Figure 1–18 Illustration of an ideal computer workstation (Illustration by Alisha Newman.)

needs to be a minimum of 18 inches, and they should be recessed from the front edge of the chair so that the chair can be pulled up to the keyboard, providing proper seating distance.

Seat heights need to be adjustable too, and a range from 16 to 23 inches allows for the greatest flexibility for the largest number of workers. When the worker is seated, his or her feet should rest flat on the floor or be supported by a small footrest.

Finally, chairs that can change position by tilt, swivel, or caster mechanisms help the worker who must be at the computer for long hours relieve the strain of stationary positions. Figure 1-18 shows an ergonomically designed chair as part of an ideal computer workstation.

It is also important to maintain proper posture while operating a computer. The computer operator must avoid long hours of repetitive work in the same position to reduce the number of injuries caused by improper use of the computer. Taking frequent mini breaks of at least ten minutes every hour aids the user's eyes and muscle groups.

Lighting design in commercial interiors with computers is an interesting challenge for the interior designer. Computer monitors are self-lighted and normal room lighting—whether from artificial light sources or natural light sources—can easily cause glare and eyestrain. Technically, no additional lighting is required to view data on a computer monitor other than the light emitted by the monitor. However, most workers are also referring to other materials and need additional light sources. In many businesses, and especially offices, general lighting is provided by the use of fluorescent ceiling fixtures. Unless these fixtures are carefully specified and planned, too much light will result, along with glare on monitor screens.

The best solution to the lighting problem for computer work areas is the combination of properly designed ambient or low level general lighting with task lighting at the workstation. Ambient lighting uses different types of light fixtures that are pointed toward the ceiling. The light is bounced off the ceiling, creating a more diffused, glare-free light in the interior. Ambient lighting can provide sufficient generalized lighting to make maneuvering through the work space safe. Properly specified and diffused direct ceiling mounted fluorescent fixtures can also accomplish this task, but it is far more difficult to achieve in that way. Task light fixtures provide more intensive levels of light to specific areas of the workstation. A task light might be a simple desk lamp or a small fixture mounted under shelves.

Glare, uncomfortably bright or reflected light that makes it difficult for an individual to see properly, is a particular problem in office lighting. Glare occurs when the light an individual encounters is brighter than that to which he or she was accustomed. We all have experienced the glare of the headlights from the car behind us in the rearview mirror as we drive. Unfortunately, too many office workers also experience glare on computer screens, due to poor lighting design decisions or to locations of monitors. Filters placed over the monitor screens reduce the glare from overhead and other lighting sources, and some also protect the user from electromagnetic field radiation.

Computer monitors are also susceptible to veiling reflections.[16] Designers must plan lighting to limit the possibilities of veiling reflections by limiting the amount of light on the monitors and the location of both lighting fixtures—especially task fixtures—and the monitors. Indirect ambient lighting supplemented at the desk with a task light will help alleviate many glare problems on computer screens.

It is generally recommended that the combination of general and task lighting be approximately 50 foot-candles. Workers who are looking from source documents to the computer screen or doing other off the computer work should be provided a task light so that light levels are in the range of recommended light levels shown in Figure 1-17. Work areas where employees are not referring to source documents but are working exclusively on computers can be provided with less than 50 foot-candles.

Monitors should be positioned so that glare from windows is minimal. It is suggested that computers be at a 90 degree angle from windows to eliminate glare. If that is not possible, then the designer must be sure to specify blinds, shades, or drapery over the windows.

Another factor in the design of computer workstations is electrical interface. Although the responsibility for designing electrical plans in commercial interiors generally rests with the architect, the interior designer needs to be aware of a few basic principles. Few desktop computers require power sources greater than the standard 110–120 volts. However, 110–120

---

[16] "Veiling reflections are the reflected image of a light source that obscures the reflecting surface of work surfaces (particularly, computer screens)." Rayfield, 1994, p. 185.

volt power is not very "clean," meaning it is susceptible to power surges and power spikes as other equipment on the line is turned on and off. In general electrical service design, many circuits can share the same ground wire. A computer plugged into a receptacle on a circuit with a shared ground wire can be damaged or data lost if surges occur. Independently grounded circuits (also called dedicated circuits) are the best way of protecting sensitive computer equipment from power surges. Circuits with an independent ground only have the one ground wire to the circuit, and this ground wire goes all the way back to the electrical service box. This reduces the problem of power spikes and surges when equipment is turned on and off on the circuit.

Some businesses, such as hospitals, will require backup generators in case regular power service is interrupted. Backup generators prevent the loss of data and access to computer information. Although this is something that will be handled by the architect, the need may come up during the programming interviews conducted by the interior designer.

Computer areas should be designed with architectural finishes in a light color value, with color accents restricted to seating or minor accessories. This will provide better light reflectance and help prevent eyestrain. Acoustical or textured commercial quality wallcoverings will aid in reducing noise to some degree. Desktops or work surfaces should also be kept in light tones to reduce eyestrain problems that result from the contrast of reading a white sheet of paper against a dark surface. Carpeting is recommended to aid the reduction of noise, but only those carpets with low or no static discharge possibilities should be specified.

Although this discussion of the design of computer work areas has concentrated on the office application, the design principles and guidelines apply to computer stations, regardless of the type of business. Other planning issues related to electrical and telecommunications service are covered in Chapter 2.

When a client owns the building housing the offices, any improvements to the structure increase the value of the building. That is to say, if paneling is specified for the walls in the executive area, paneling will add more value to the building than painted walls. When a client rents a portion of a building, improvements to the building made by the tenant belong to the landlord, not the tenant. That is why many clients are reluctant to spend a great deal of money on special architectural finishes. The costs for those materials come primarily out of the pocket of the tenant, but the value goes to the landlord.

Tenants receive a built-out allowance from the landlord to pay for certain improvements to the space. A *built-out allowance* is an amount per square foot to furnish the cost of building partitions, basic plumbing fixtures, lighting fixtures, and architectural finishes. In many cases, there are preselected building standards for architectural finishes and details. This is done to keep some continuity of design in exterior and interior public spaces. Some of these, like window treatments and door styles, must be used. If the interior designer is not able to utilize the building standards or wishes to specify materials that are priced beyond the built-out allowance, then the client may approve of upgrading the materials. The client pays the difference between the allowance and the upgrade. These upgrades are called *lease-hold improvements* or tenant improvements. An upgrade from vinyl tile in the entry to marble is an example of a lease-hold improvement. The landlord is generally in favor of these improvements since they serve to increase the value of the property. Some improvements, however, may be discouraged as they make renting the space to another tenant in the future difficult.

Materials specified for office environments must meet code and the demands of heavy wear. Architectural surfaces in office occupancies that will qualify for classification as businesses must be Class I when used in enclosed stairways, Class II when used in other corridors, and can be Class III in other areas. Commercial grade materials should be used in corridors and exit ways. The designer may have the option of using residential grade materials in private offices and conferences rooms, depending on local codes. Hundreds of patterns and colors of commercial wallcoverings are available to create the right backdrop for the interior spaces. If the student or professional wishes to use textile wallcoverings, he or she must check with local codes since some jurisdictions will only allow textiles on walls if a sprinkler system is in the facility.

Carpeting in offices helps to reduce noise and lend comfort to the office workers. It must be selected carefully due to the heavy foot traffic and wear and tear produced by chairs being moved across carpet. These points lead most designers to specify tightly tufted or woven carpet with a reasonably short level looped surface. Cut pile surfaces will show traffic patterns faster unless they are extremely dense carpets with a short nap. It will also be much harder to move office chairs on a plush surface than a looped surface. On the other hand, executive areas that receive less wear can be specified with cut pile surfaces and more luxurious materials. Code requirements will also vary for carpets depending on the space where the carpet is used. ADA requirements limit the height of the pile with backing to one-half inch.

Designers began using carpet tiles or modular carpet in the late 1970s. Carpet tiles are manufactured and installed in sections 18 to 24 inches square. Depending on the manufacturer's instructions, carpet tiles might be installed without adhesives so that the tiles can easily be replaced if damaged or if they show heavy wear. Interesting custom designs can be created with carpet tiles that might not be possible with broadloom carpet. However, the initial cost of the tiles is greater than that of an equivalent quality of broadloom carpet. The ADA requirements cited above also apply to carpet tiles.

Resilient and hard surface materials are noisier than carpet and are used sparingly in office environments. Utilitarian areas, like mail rooms and storage rooms, are ideal for economical resilient materials like commercial grade sheet vinyl and vinyl tiles. The heaviest traffic areas, like entrance lobbies, public corridors, and rest rooms, are commonly specified using resilient and hard surface flooring. Of course, some areas of the office that require higher-end design specification, such as portions of executive suites, might also see the use of woods, ceramic tiles, or stones for flooring materials.

Upholstery should also be selected with maintenance in mind. Light colors look great and make rooms look larger, but they also will show dirt faster. Commercial upholstery textiles are available in a huge variety of colors, textures, and patterns to suit aesthetic goals. Commercial chair manufacturers have a wide range of materials available from the factory and selections from these items are guaranteed to look right and stand up to the hard use of office seating. Designers can also use customer's own materials (COMs), where the designer selects goods from a source other than the chair manufacturer. However, some seating companies will not guarantee performance of COMs. This type of specification, though creating something very special, will also be more costly.

An architectural component that needs to be discussed in the context of the design of offices is *demountable* walls. A type of partition, demountable walls are full-height partitions that are held in place by tension rather than "stick built" on the site. Thus they can be relocated when the needs of the office require a new space plan without the expense and downtime of demolition and new construction. Demountable walls can be finished with drywall and painted, but are most commonly finished with a vinyl wallcovering that meets Class A fire codes. Demountable walls can also accommodate windows and doors so that fully private offices of almost any size or configuration can be created. Cavities within the walls allow electrical and communication cables to be integrated. Plumbing is generally not accommodated since the the walls are not thick enough to handle waste pipes. Demountable walls are installed over carpet and held in place by a gripper system on the bottom of the wall and attached to the T-bar in suspended ceilings at the top. This type of installation also reduces the cost of installing the carpet since less cutting is required.

Office facilities are subject to several important *code* considerations. The student and designer must first determine which codes apply to the project. Many jurisdictions adopt one of the model building codes:

- National Building Code (NBC), used by many of the states in the Northeast
- Standard Building Code (SBC), adopted by most of the states in the Southeast
- Uniform Building Code (UBC), used primarily in the western United States
- National Building Code of Canada (NBC), the primary code used in Canada

However, any jurisdiction can write its own building and safety code rather than adopting a model code. In addition, jurisdictions that are neighbors, such as any large city and its suburbs, can have different code requirements. It is the designer's responsibility to know what codes are applicable to the project location, not the codes applicable to the designer's office location. A number of code requirements specific to space planning an office facility were discussed in a previous section. In Canada, each province may have specific code variations that affect elements of the design and specification of structures.

Along with the building codes, the design of office facilities will also be affected by the ADA and by fire safety regulations. Depending on the designer's legal and project responsibility, he or she may also have to investigate the appropriate plumbing code, the National Electrical Code, and the possibility of other codes or regulations that are applicable to the project.

All the building codes classify office facilities as business occupancies. This classification, as the reader probably already knows, will direct many decisions concerning space planning and architectural finish specification. The actual number of occupants allowed in the space will also affect planning decisions. For example, a small office having only 20 occupants can generally be designed with only one exit door. However, an office with 50 or more occupants will require two exits. And as the number of occupants increases, additional exits may be necessary. Naturally, these general statements may not be true in all cases and in all jurisdictions. The designer must check applicable codes. The building codes will affect design choices in areas such as: sizes, numbers, and locations of egress doors; sizes of corridors and aisles; specification of architectural finishes; and permissible lengths of corridors. Of course, there are many other code issues that will influence the design of individual projects.

Business offices that are considered public buildings, that is offices open to the general public, must meet the ADA's accessibility design guidelines in every respect. Guidelines will affect such things as: the size of corridors and aisles; locating areas of refuge; design and location of signage; heights of reception counters and drinking fountains; flooring specifications, and, of course, the design of public toilet facilities. The reader is directed to refer to the accessibility design guidelines for specific accessibility requirements.

Several cities and states have adopted specific fire safety codes concerning upholstery or seating units. Smolder resistance tests such as the Cigarette Ignition Test determine the smolder resistance of a textile or a seating mock up. The California Technical Bulletin #133, referred to as CAL 133 or TB 133, is a very strict smolder test that requires that the entire seating item—fabric, stuffing, and frame—pass the test. Manufacturers must test the seating item and certify that it passes the test or the whole unit cannot be used in many types of occupancies. If any one item in the unit fails the test, the unit cannot be used. This test has been applicable to occupancies that contain ten or more seating units, especially in places of assembly and institutional occupancies. However, some jurisdictions may require that seating items pass this test in large office environments as well. This fire safety code has been adopted by many states in addition to California. The reader should verify whether some version of TB 133 is applicable to his or her jurisdiction.

Design Applications

Whether one is designing a large corporate office or a small neighborhood office of some kind, design guidelines exist to direct the creation of a functional and aesthetically pleasing environment. It would indeed be impossible in this context to discuss every type of office function in every type of business. This section will concentrate on the large business office, providing detailed guidelines on the interior design of office facilities. However, as often as is practical, comments will be provided on how these design guidelines affect the design of a small office facility. Figures 1-19 through 1-24 are floor plans of different sizes and kinds of office facilities to help the reader get an overall understanding of office space plans.

The *main reception area and waiting area* are the public's introduction to the business. Creating the right public image means that the business will also ask the designer to plan and

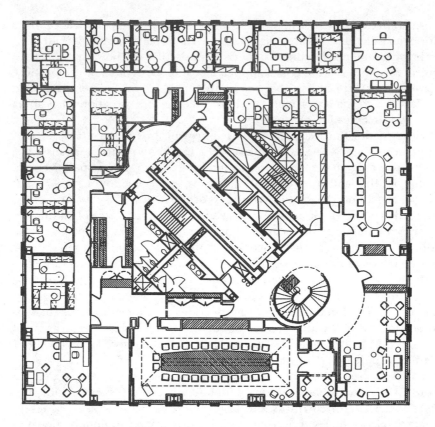

Figure 1–19 Floor plan of a corporate office in a multistory office building. (Plan courtesy of Fox & Fowle Architects.)

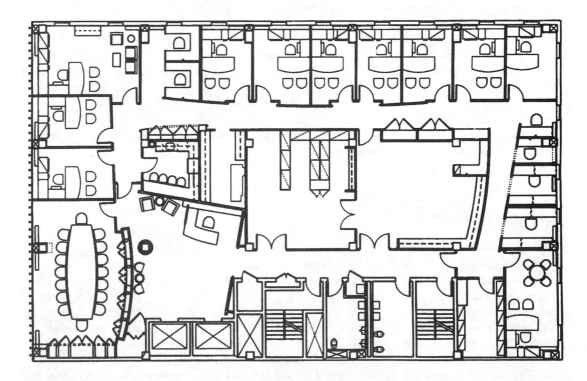

Figure 1–20 Floor plan of a corporate office. (Plan courtesy of RTKL Associates, Inc.)

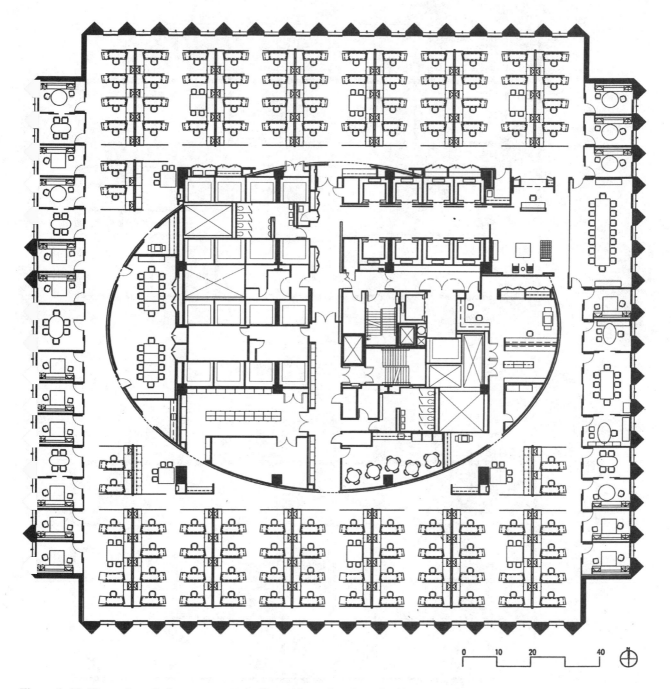

Figure 1–21 Floor plan of a large corporate office with workstations flanking two sides. (Plan courtesy of Gary Lee & Partners.)

specify this space using higher quality furniture and materials than those used in the general office areas (refer to Figure 1-9). Reception and waiting areas are usually specified with a desk or counter area for the receptionist, seating units for visitors, and end tables. These areas may also be designed with magazine racks, display cabinets, even tables and chairs for holding a brief conference. Because people generally do not like to sit next to individuals they do not know, it is common that the seating units in a reception area be individual chairs rather than sofas, love seats, or settees. There are, of course, businesses that request sofa units and situations when sofas of sufficient size would be effective and appropriate.

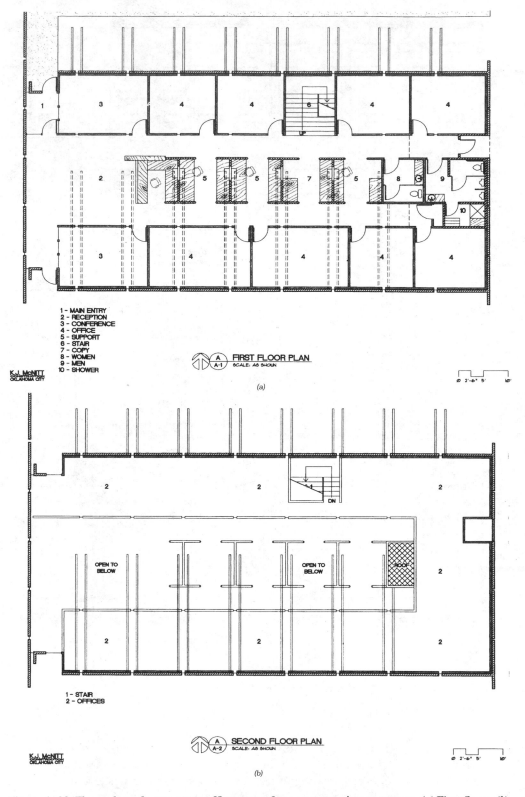

1 - MAIN ENTRY
2 - RECEPTION
3 - CONFERENCE
4 - OFFICE
5 - SUPPORT
6 - STAIR
7 - COPY
8 - WOMEN
9 - MEN
10 - SHOWER

FIRST FLOOR PLAN
SCALE: AS SHOWN

(a)

1 - STAIR
2 - OFFICES

SECOND FLOOR PLAN
SCALE: AS SHOWN

(b)

Figure 1–22 Floor plan of a two story office space for a construction company. *(a)* First floor. *(b)* Second floor. (Plan courtesy of Rand Elliot, FAIA, Elliot + Associates Architects.)

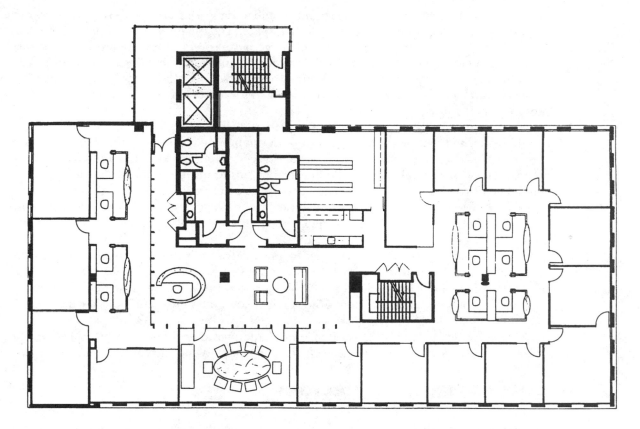

Figure 1–23 Floor plan of a corporate office depicting reception area, conference room, workstations, and individual office locations. (Plan courtesy of AREA.)

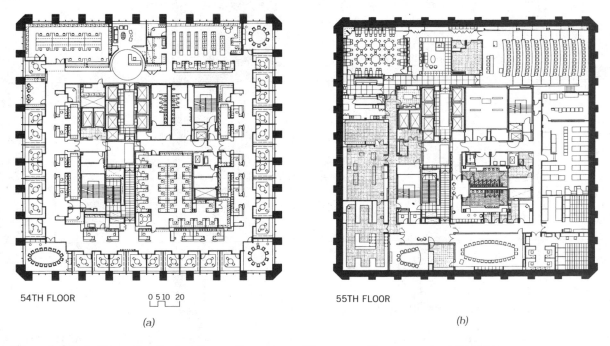

54TH FLOOR   0 5 10 20

(a)

55TH FLOOR

(b)

Figure 1–24a, b Floor plan for two floors of corporate office space. (Plan courtesy of DMJM Rottet Interior Architecture, Lauren Rohen, FAIA.)

In all but the smallest offices, the reception and waiting areas are rooms requiring visitors to pass through doors into the general office space. This planning arrangement provides the security that many businesses, especially large businesses, require. Major corridors and circulation paths move visitors from the reception room to the different departments and areas of the office facility. Spaces such as training rooms, personnel offices, and some conference areas are often located adjacent to the reception area so that visitors are restricted in how far they may enter the total facility.

Reception room layouts have some standard guidelines. The reception desk or counter should be located to insure that the receptionist can monitor incoming and outgoing traffic (Figure 1-25). The receptionist not only serves to greet visitors, but also is charged with various administrative or clerical duties including typing, answering the phone, and doing paper work. The desk or counter must be large enough to accommodate these work activities and equipment needs. Since these work activities can be somewhat messy at times, it is also common that the face of the desk or counter be high enough to hide the work surface from the view of incoming visitors.

Executive office areas are those utilized by the upper level of management or ownership of the company. Executive offices are almost always private offices, usually placed on the perimeter of the floor and located in a prime location in the building or floor. In smaller facilities, business owners locate their office to the rear of the suite, even if this means they do not enjoy any windows.

Office space for executives is often quite large providing not only work space, but a conference area and almost always a soft seating group. While the furniture needs of this

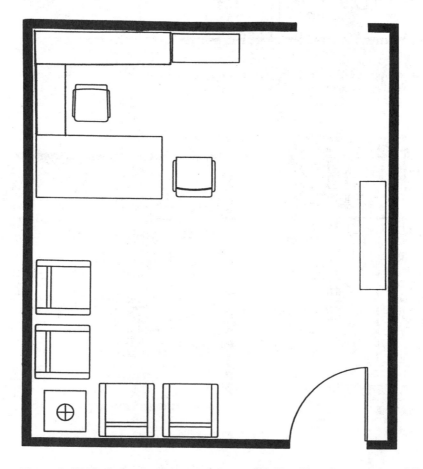

Figure 1–25 Typical reception area for a small office (Drawing courtesy of Cody D. Beal and Kotie L. Mitchell.)

type of space are more attuned to the specific desires of the individual executive, it is common to specify a large size desk and matching credenza unit; a large posture chair for the executive; two or more guest chairs at the desk; a soft seating group consisting of club chairs, love seats, settees, or sofa and club chair arrangements; and perhaps additional storage units such as bookcases or display cabinets (Figure 1-26). Many executive offices have file cabinets or extra file drawers in credenzas. If an executive wants file cabinets in his or her office, these are usually of a higher design quality than a standard metal file cabinet. And, of course, depending on the executive and the industry he or she is in, other kinds of furniture or equipment would be necessary.

Right outside the office of the president or in a separate room adjoining the president's office would be his or her secretarial support. Today, this person's job title is likely to be administrative assistant or executive secretary. The administrative assistant usually has a larger size desk than other secretaries and also a better quality of furniture and finishes as is fitting for the executive suite. The administrative assistant must have a secretarial return, typing return, or an appropriate cabinet to accommodate the typewriter or computer terminal. He or she would also have more file cabinets to hold records for his or her boss. If the entrance to the president's office is through a separate area, a few seating units for those waiting to see the president are often provided.

The offices of vice presidents are smaller in size than the president's but are furnished in a similar manner. Each office generally is furnished with a large desk and credenza, posture chair, guest chairs and probably a soft seating group or unit (refer to Figure 1-7). Vice presidents often have more files in their offices than the president. These individuals also spend a lot of time with clients, but are more involved in paperwork than the president.

Support staff for the vice presidents are also located right outside or adjacent to the vice presidents' offices. These other upper level secretaries are rarely in private offices, though this might be found in very large corporations or specialized industries. The furniture and

Figure 1–26 Executive office featuring desk, conference area, and soft seating. (Photograph by Peter Paige.)

equipment is similar to all the rest of the clerical staff, but a secretary to a vice president would generally have a slightly larger size desk and higher quality of goods than other lower level secretarial staff.

The executive suite commonly has a large conference room called a boardroom. Boardrooms of large businesses project image and status of the company to the visitors invited to this space (see Figure 1-27). From a space allocation point of view, the boardroom is commonly located with its own reception area in the largest of businesses or very near the main entrance for other companies. This provides convenience to visitors in finding this space. This spacious, well-appointed conference room is designed as much to impress as it is to functionally hold meetings. It is not uncommon that the conference table be custom designed in beautiful woods, and large comfortable chairs are specified. Designers also provide projection screens, marker boards, and cabinets that can house a beverage service, and other accouterments for high-level business meetings. In some cases, a projection room behind the boardroom is provided to house the necessary audiovisual equipment and setups for projection into the conference space.

Materials and furniture used in the executive suite or executive offices are of the highest quality the business can afford. Executives and owners know well that the place to impress the client is the executive area. Thus high-end products are specified. Exactly what this means would be impossible to state here. Even when comparing two like business offices, the amount of money and quality of products specified can be quite different. The designer's observation and experience, along with careful discussions during programming, help him or her determine exactly what level of merchandise is appropriate for each client.

Management staff areas are much smaller than those of higher ranking executives and located farther away from the prime areas in the facility. Unless the business is using office systems furniture extensively, the manager may have a private office. The designer would specify the management staff offices with a desk and credenza of a smaller size with appropriate guest seating. A soft seating unit or conference table is possible, but is less likely at this level. These individuals, however, seem to have more need for files and storage equipment, like bookshelves or display cabinets. The furniture requirements of the supervisor are usually a desk, possibly a credenza or other storage unit, and maybe one guest chair used when it is necessary to talk to one of the employees in the group. The quality of the furniture and materials in these offices is also downgraded from that used for upper level executives.

Production employee areas require specialized equipment determined during programming (see Figure 1-10). However, everyone needs a desk surface to handle general paperwork. Even if the individual uses a computer a great deal, all workers still must have space to review and work on paper copies of documents. For most "production" level employees, that space will probably be a 30 by 60 inch desktop. Production category employees may also have a file cabinet and perhaps a bookcase for storage of additional reference materials. A good posture chair behind the desk and perhaps one or two guest chairs, depending on the exact nature of the job, would also be included.

Specific job needs may necessitate additional furniture for "production" employees. Architects and designers, for example, need drafting surfaces or tables to spread out large sheets of drawings, while attorneys need more filing and storage equipment. Accountants may need to refer to large ledger books and sheets, and thus may require larger desks to accommodate these bigger books. Advertising and public relations workers need display space and perhaps drawing boards for the production of drawings and storyboards needed to explain promotional ideas. Computer programmers and designers require more return space for additional computers. And so on.

It is typical that the furniture and materials specification for production employees will be very similar to that of the management staff. This is because there are only so many levels of quality that can be used to differentiate staff hierarchy before the quality of the goods cannot meet the functional requirements of employee usage.

Design guidelines exist for *support personnel areas.* Ideally, secretaries are positioned right outside or very near the executive or manager for whom they work. When a secretary is

(a)

(b)

Figure 1–27 *(a)* Traditional conference table in a conference room with a media wall housing a rear projection screen. (Photograph courtesy Architectural Design West Architects. Scott Theobald, project architect. © USU Photography Services.) *(b)* "Butterfly" conference table, which allows good sight lines for viewing the media screen when the boat shaped table is pivoted open on slides. It closes for normal use. (Photograph courtesy of Meyer, Scherer & Rockcastle, Ltd., Architects, for Koop Investment Advisors. Conference table custom design: MSR. Manufactured by: Harbinger Industries. Photographer: Philip Prowse.)

utilized by two or more executives or managers, the secretary would be located for easy access to the different managers. In general, secretaries have a medium sized or larger desk (depending on level) for doing standard paperwork, and an attached typing return to hold the typewriter, word processor, or computer terminal (refer to Figure 1-10). Secretaries have small armless chairs so that the chair can be easily pulled up close to the desk or return. Secretaries also have file cabinets (as they usually maintain most of the files needed by the executives, management, and other employees). In addition, secretarial support personnel often have storage cabinets for office supplies unless there are storage rooms in their departments. As a group, secretarial support personnel rarely have a guest chair or other seating near their desk.

Large businesses have secretarial or clerical "pools," that is, a large group of clerical staff located in one area (Figure 1-28). Generally one or more supervisors are also located in this "pool" area. The equipment needs of secretarial staff located in a "pool" will be similar to those of a regular secretary, though individual file cabinets at the desk are unusual.

Clerical staff are often thought of as lower level or entry level secretarial staff. They occupy less square footage for their "offices" and will have smaller desks. The main function of clerical staff is typing, so they generally have fewer file cabinets and storage units for extra furniture items than do secretaries. The clerical staff's filing work is most commonly done in file cabinets located in a central file area rather than in individual files in their offices or stations.

Support or ancillary spaces provide needed workrooms or backup spaces to the main office functions. We discuss some of the specification needs of the most common support spaces—conference rooms, resource areas, and copying areas.

Conference rooms provide space for employee meetings, presentations to clients, training room space, and even mini lunchrooms. This spaces should be designed as a backdrop for presentations and meetings. Depending on the size of the company, their furnishings will be less high-end than those of a boardroom. The designer must plan the size of the space to meet

Figure 1–28 Secretarial or clerical work area for a large business. (Photograph courtesy of Teknion, Inc.)

the required numbers of expected participants without those individuals feeling crammed into the space. Remember to provide circulation space around the table and chairs as well as proper visual planning for the type of presentations to be made. If presentations are made with a leader standing at a podium, allow that extra space at the front of the room. Even if a podium is not used, be sure that sufficient circulation space has been provided so that someone can write on a chalkboard or point at a screen.

The furniture in a conference room is fairly standard, regardless of the exact nature of the company's business. Conference rooms are most commonly furnished with a table and chairs (Figure 1-29). Round tables are very good for small groups, though rectangular tables are also used. The number of seats available at any specific size table will be dictated by the chair specified. The larger the chair, the fewer seats available around any table. A boat shaped table is common in larger conference rooms. The shape of this table, which looks like the plan view of a boat with its ends flattened, makes it easier for every one at the table to see everyone else. Chairs are often specified with casters or sometimes a sled base for ease of movement. In the more important conference rooms, the chairs may also be specified as swivel/tilt chairs. These features help to make sitting in the meeting more bearable. Of course, small staff meeting rooms may have smaller chairs with fewer features than chairs specified in conference rooms where presentations to clients will take place.

Conference rooms are often furnished with many types of support equipment. Chalkboards, liquid writing surfaces, tackboards, screens for showing films or slides, and televisions and VCR equipment are examples of the most common types of support equipment. As with a boardroom, some conference rooms may have a projection or audiovisual room at the rear. Many companies serve simple beverages such as coffee and tea, so it is also quite common to find a small counter area and even a small sink and refrigerator unit. Conference rooms used by clients are often designed with higher grades of furniture and furnishings than those used only by the employees.

When the designer is planning a conference room with audiovisual equipment, he or she should carefully consider lighting options in that space. Multiple lighting systems, such as fluorescent fixtures for normal lighting and spotlights on dimmers for the times audiovisual equipment is used, are common lighting solutions. Fixtures should be on multiple switches and dimmers when appropriate to help control and modify the lighting in this multipurpose room. Plan the furniture locations and lighting fixtures so that sufficient light is provided on

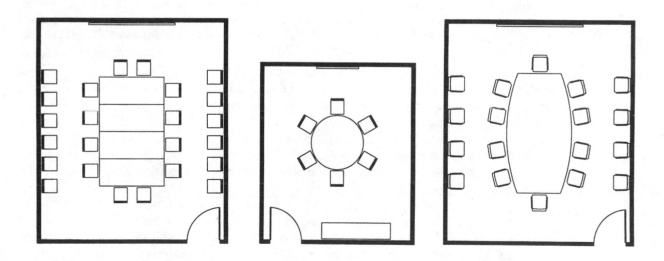

Figure 1–29 Three standard conference rooms. The one on the left has four tables banked together, which allows for versatility in placement. The one in the middle shows a small conference table. The one on the right shows a typical boat shaped conference table, which provides good sight lines for communication. (Drawing courtesy of Cody D. Beal.)

the table surface, not behind guests. Conference rooms are a good location for the use of egg crate or parabolic reflectors so that the light is concentrated on the table and "washes" the circulation space around the table. Appropriate spotlights might then be needed for the podium or front of the room.

Some conference rooms are actually training rooms. By nature, these would be larger than the average conference room, capable of seating 20 or more individuals. Training rooms may be planned with tables and chairs similar to a conference room, but more frequently they are designed using narrow table and chairs arranged classroom style. Since the training room may be utilized for a variety of training programs, folding tables and stack chairs are common. This allows the room to be converted to other uses. In addition, in today's office, much training revolves around technology changes in the office. Extensive use of audiovisual equipment and connections for computers or other office machines should be planned to allow for each of these mechanical interfaces. In some cases, this may require custom cabinets to house the computer equipment rather than the use of tables.

Resource materials areas have a few special considerations in their planning. The first of these is that the design student should remember that there are many different kinds of furniture units that can be utilized to handle resource materials. Resource materials for businesses might include the law library for an attorney, samples and catalogs for architects and designers, computer tape and disk storage for many kinds of businesses, and advertising brochures for the marketing departments of many kinds of businesses, to name a few examples. This variety of readily accessible reference items requires different kinds of shelving to house the goods. A shelf unit designed to hold law books is inadequate for storing samples needed by an interior designer. So the designer must be clear on exactly what is being stored and any special environmental or security requirements concerning the goods when deciding on the exact specifications.

Copy areas are commonly located throughout large office facilities. These satellite copy centers save time and increase employee productivity. Space must be provided for the machine and storage of supplies for the copier. Large corporations also have primary copy and/or print shops so that major duplicating and printing jobs can be done in-house. These main copy centers might be located in the central core or even on the basement level. Designers need to understand what size copy machine is being planned by the business to insure electrical service of the proper kind is provided to the locations. A small desktop copy machine can be plugged into a standard outlet but may use sufficient amps to require a separate circuit. However, a large collating copy machine would require a 220 line. This must be noted on drawings and in specifications.

There is no absolute rule of thumb for the space allowances for any of these areas. What must be considered are three items: first, the actual size of the equipment utilized in these areas remembering that counters, tables, or desks that the equipment sits upon are also equipment. Second, the space needed to access the equipment. For example, a copy machine must have space not only on the side where the operator stands to make a copy, but also space to feed paper and remove the copies. Mechanized pieces of equipment like copy machines also need to be serviced. Depending on the size of the machine and its configuration, sufficient space must be allowed for a service representative to move the equipment or have access to all sides of the machine. A file cabinet takes up floor space when the drawers are closed, of course, but additional space is required in front of the cabinet to open the drawers and for someone to stand to get into the file drawers. The third item of consideration would be how many people might be in the area with the equipment at one time. The more people in the area, the more room will be required for general circulation around the equipment.

Businesses often provide additional support areas for their employees. Unfortunately, it is not possible to discuss in any detail all these additional spaces that might be planned into large or even some smaller office facilities. Figure 1-11 mentions examples of these other spaces.

Summary

It is quite probable that long into the 21st century, offices will be an important specialty in the work of interior designers. Downsizing and the use of technology is changing the way offices function and the manner in which they are designed, but we will always have offices. As a student in a commercial interior design class, whether you are interested in entering commercial design practice or not, you should be constantly observing and learning about offices every time you have an opportunity to enter one. Observe how the spaces have been planned, what kinds and styles of furniture are used as well as the size of each item. Examine the treatments to floors, walls, windows, and fabrics. And, if you have the opportunity, use a journal to sketch ideas that are interesting to you. These sketches might provide valuable ideas for solutions in the future. It is also important to read the trade magazines that feature office projects. These are full of great design ideas for a variety of offices and all commercial spaces. *Contract, Interiors,* and *Interior Design* magazines all feature commercial facilities in each issue.

This chapter has focused on an explanation of the functional characteristics of the office environment. It has briefly discussed the work responsibilities of the divisions of a corporation as well as provided planning and design considerations relevant to the different levels and job functions of an office facility by use of the corporate structure as a model. The chapter also looked at the design and planning considerations of the many kinds of support spaces that are part of most offices. The reader may wish to research the references listed for this chapter for further information and ideas on how to design the interiors of office facilities.

References

Becker, Franklin. 1981. *Workspace. Creating Environments in Organizations.* New York: Praeger.

———. 1982. *The Successful Office.* Reading, MA: Addison-Wesley.

Brandt, Peter B. 1992. *Office Design.* New York: Watson-Guptill.

Brill, Michael and the Buffalo Organization for Social and Technological Innovation (BOSTI). 1984, 1985. *Using Office Design to Increase Productivity,* 2 vols. Buffalo: Workplace Design and Productivity.

"California Technical Bulletin 133 Questions and Answers." 1992. California State Department of Consumer Affairs Bureau of Home Furnishings and Thermal Insulation. January.

Cotts, David G. and Michael Lee. 1992. *The Facility Management Handbook.* New York: American Management Association.

Dana, Amy. 1992. "Glare and VDT." *Interiors.* March. P. 81.

De Chiara, Joseph, Julius Panero and Martin Zelnik. 1991. *Time Saver Standards for Interior Design and Space Planning.* New York: McGraw-Hill.

Farren, Carol E. 1988. *Planning and Managing Interiors Projects.* Kingston, MA: R. S. Means.

Friday, Stormy and David G. Cotts. 1995. *Quality Facility Management.* New York: Wiley.

Glueck, William F. 1980. *Management.* Hinsdale, IL: Dryden.

Gould, Bryant Putnam. 1983. *Planning the New Corporate Headquarters.* New York: Wiley.

Harrigan, J. E. 1987. *Human Factors Research.* New York: Elsevier Dutton.

Harris, David A. (Editor), Byron W. Engen, and William E. Fitch. 1991. *Planning and Designing the Office Environment,* 2nd ed. New York: Van Nostrand Reinhold.

Haworth, Inc. 1993. *Ergonomics and Office Design.* Holland, MI: Haworth, Inc.

Herman Miller, Inc. 1991. *Cumulative Trauma Disorders*. Zeeland, MI: Herman Miller, Inc. May.

———. 1994. *Input and Pointing Devices*. Zeeland, MI: Herman Miller, Inc. August.

———. 1996. *Issues Essentials: Talking to Customers About Change*. Zeeland, MI: Herman Miller, Inc.

International Facility Management Association. Date unknown. *"Official Statement on Facility Management"* (Brochure).

Kaiser, Harvey H. 1989. *The Facilities Manager's Reference*. Kingston, MA: R. S. Means.

Kearney, Deborah. 1993. *The New ADA: Compliance and Costs*. Kingston, MA: R. S. Means.

Kilmer, Rosemary and W. Otie Kilmer. 1992. *Designing Interiors*. Fort Worth, TX: Harcourt Brace Jovanovich.

Klein, Judy Graf. 1982. *The Office Book*. New York: Facts on File.

Knobel, Lance. 1987. *Office Furniture. Twentieth-Century Design*. New York: E. P. Dutton.

Lueder, Rani (Editor). 1986. *The Ergonomics Payoff: Designing the Electronic Office*. New York: Nichols.

Marberry, Sara O. 1994. *Color in the Office*. New York: Van Nostrand Reinhold.

Pelegrin-Genel, Elisabeth. 1996. *The Office*. Paris, France and New York: Flammario.

Pile, John. 1976. *Interiors Third Book of Offices*. New York: Watson-Guptill.

———. 1978. *Open Office Planning*. New York: Watson-Guptill.

Ragan, Sandra. 1995. *Interior Color by Design: Commercial Edition*. Rockport, MA: Rockport.

Random House Unabridged Dictionary, 2nd ed. 1993. New York: Random House.

Rappoport, James E., Robert F. Cushman, and Daren Daroff. 1992. *Office Planning and Design Desk Reference*. New York: Wiley.

Rayfield, Julie K. 1994. *The Office Interior Design Guide*. New York: Wiley.

Raymond, Santa and Roger Cunliffe. 1997. *Tomorrow's Office*. London: E & FN SPON.

Saphier, Michael. 1968. *Office Planning and Design*. New York: McGraw-Hill.

Shoshkes, Lila. 1976. *Space Planning: Designing the Office Environment*. New York: Architectural Record.

Shumake, M. Glynn. 1992. *Increasing Productivity and Profit in the Workplace*. New York: Wiley.

Steelcase, Inc. 1991a. *The Healthy Office: Lighting in the Healthy Office*. Grand Rapids, MI: Steelcase, Inc.

———. 1991b. *The Healthy Office: Ergonomics in the Healthy Office*. Grand Rapids, MI: Steelcase, Inc.

Tate, Allen and C. Ray Smith. 1986. *Interior Design in the 20th Century*. New York: Harper and Row.

Tillman, Peggy and Barry Tillman. 1991. *Human Factors Essentials; An Ergonomics Guide for Designers, Engineers, Scientists, and Managers*. New York: McGraw-Hill.

Yee, Roger and Karen Gustafson. 1983. *Corporate Design*. New York: Van Nostrand Reinhold.

Additional references related to material in this chapter are listed in Appendix A.

Chapter 2

The Open Office

Open office is a specific way of doing space planning without using full-height permanent partitions and traditional casework desks. It utilizes specialized furniture products to achieve the space plan and furniture specification. Some refer to open office as modular or systems planning. This is because the panels and components are manufactured on a module—or system. Other designers use the term open landscape. These are all terms that mean the same thing as open office. For the sake of simplicity, we use the terms open office or open office planning in our discussion in this chapter.

Open office as used in this context is a relatively young methodology, dating from the 1950s, when the term office landscape was first used. Even though it is relatively new concept, it has had a profound impact on office design throughout the world, as well as on the furniture industry, and on commercial interior design in general. More recently, the changes in office management philosophy and advances in office technology have further contributed to the use of open office. Downsizing and advances in office technology are constantly changing the planning concepts and products available to designers and end users to achieve productive work environments, thus changing how open office is utilized.

The purpose of this chapter is to introduce the student and professional to the concept and methodology of open office planning so that the reader will be able to understand how this nonconventional furniture product goes together to create office spaces. The chapter begins with an overview of open office planning followed by a brief history. The major portion of the chapter discusses how a generic component system is constructed, and the chapter concludes with an introduction to the mechanical interface, acoustic, and code issues associated with a successful open office project. Although we focus on a specific type of open office product, the reader can apply the basic planning concepts to any of the products manufactured where vertical panels are used to separate office stations.

An Overview of Open Office Design

Open office planning uses freestanding, less than full-height movable divider panels and individual component pieces to create functional work environments called stations. The freestanding panels are not fixed to the floor or ceiling (Figure 2-1). The configuration of the panels and components is stable because of the layout of panels. Traditional or conventional office planning as described in Chapter 1 was the method of designing office facilities for decades if not centuries before the introduction of open landscape. Of course, conventional office planning is still used by many companies today.

In order to understand open office planning, there are a few terms that are used throughout this chapter.

Office landscape is a design methodology developed in the 1950s using conventional furniture and plants, but few if any wall partitions.

Conventional furniture means the use of desks, credenzas, file cabinets, and bookcases.

Station is the common term for the individual work area. A station is created by the use of vertical divider panels and components.

Systems furniture, or *modular systems furniture,* consists of divider panels and components used to provide station functionality.

Divider panels, or simply *panels,* are the vertical support units that form the stations and from which components are hung.

Work surface is the term for the product that serves as the desktop.

Components are the individual items, such as shelves, work surfaces, drawer units, and so on, that are hung from the divider panels and provide the actual functional items for the stations. Other component terms are discussed later in the chapter.

Connector usually refers to the "hardware" used to connect one panel to another. Connector styles vary by manufacturer. Some manufacturers use plastic hinges; others use steel poles or steel hinged connectors.

Open office planning concepts are used in virtually any kind of business organization and commercial facility to outfit almost every kind of office job and function. Used in large corporations to save space, provide flexibility, and improve worker productivity, these concepts can also provide smaller companies with these same advantages. In the last 15 or so years, open office has found its way into the home office as well.

One of the main goals of using open office planning is to enhance worker communications and interaction. With the full-height walls of conventional planning eliminated, workers have

Figure 2–1 Freestanding panels in open office plan. (Photograph courtesy of Kimball Office Group.)

more opportunity to productively communicate with each other to accomplish their jobs. Stations are located to enhance this communication interaction and work flow. Locating supervisors and managers in stations nearer their staff provides supervisors heightened interaction with employees. This also allows managers to be part of the team, not just the leader. Many companies embrace the idea of teaming and shared work responsibilities, which makes it important for groups of workers to easily communicate with each other. Open office planning tears down the physical barriers that separate workers and work groups so as to encourage this needed interaction.

A second important goal of open office planning is the opportunity for the business to use less space to house its employees. With the vertical use of space afforded by the components hanging on panels, stations can be functionally designed to meet the individual job requirements while saving many square feet of floor space. This by-product was an important selling tool of open office planning in its early days and remains a benefit appreciated by many businesses that have downsized. For example, a small manager's office using conventional offices will require a minimum of 120 to 140 square feet. This same manager's station could be accommodated in 80 to 100 square feet (Figure 2-2) with an open office design. Assuming that the stations are planned based on true functional needs rather than on status or old company standards, the total space savings could reduce the amount of square footage the company needs to rent or build, thus reducing rental or construction expenses significantly.

The well-thought-out design of stations consistently leads to more productive workers. Distractions can be held to a minimum if the project is planned carefully. Time and motion studies over the years have shown that the vertical arrangement of components in the stations cuts down on the extraneous movement the worker requires to have access to files, references, and materials needed to do his or her job.

Open office planning has some definite advantages and disadvantages beyond the goals mentioned above. The most commonly cited advantages to the end user include:

- *Cheaper construction costs.* With fewer full-height partitions to construct along with the reduction in some mechanical construction materials, it will be cheaper—and faster—to initially build the facility.

- *Potential energy savings.* When using a minimum number of full-height partitions, open plan will result in a significant decrease in the amount of money spent on creating the

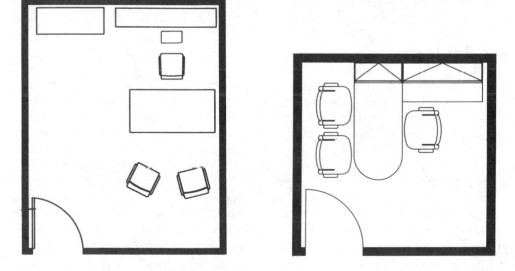

Figure 2–2 Plans of two manager's offices showing savings in square footage with the use of systems furniture, on the right, as opposed to the conventional office, on the left. (System plan courtesy of Herman Miller, Inc., Zeeland, MI.)

heating, ventilation, and air conditioning (HVAC) system. Less duct work, wiring, and other kinds of hard equipment at the time of initial installation would be required.

- *Potential tax savings.* Panels are considered furniture and as such are subject to depreciation calculations based on approximately a 7 year usable life. This larger and faster tax reduction helps the bottom line of corporations and businesses.

- *Changes in the facility are easier and generally cheaper.* The downtime and construction costs of removing and rebuilding full-height walls is far higher than the downtime and reconfiguration costs of using open office products. Employees get back to work quickly without having more than minimal construction confusion in the work areas.

Some of the most commonly cited disadvantages to using open office planning are:

- *Lack of privacy.* A common problem expressed by many people is not having a private office. Proper information gathering and planning of the project should provide adequate privacy for those in sensitive jobs and provide convenient conference rooms for holding private meetings.

- *Noise.* Designs sensitive to acoustical considerations can eliminate most concerns about the open office project creating a noisy environment. Attention to surface materials on the ceiling, floors, window treatments, and surfaces of panels help to reduce noise. Development of sufficient ambient noise to mask conversations yet not distract other workers also reduces or eliminates this problem.

- *Lack of status.* This problem was often expressed back in the 1970s when open plan was first being introduced. The styles of furniture and finishes available today make it easy for the designer to provide status considerations as might be required.

With all the advantages and disadvantages, it should also be remembered that not all clients need open plan. Likewise, the designer must remember that not all areas in a client's facility require open plan. Today's planning philosophy sees the compromise of using open plan for many areas in a facility and using conventional partitioned offices for others. To stay within the framework of open plan, there are several options of full-height *demountable*[1] walls that provide all the advantages of open plan and yet provide the privacy and status of fully enclosed office spaces. The decision of whether to use conventional partitions or open office partitions should be made jointly by the designer and client.

Types of Products

The products used for open office planning have gone through many changes since their early introduction in the 1960s. There are almost 300 manufacturers of products for use in open office projects. Each manufacturer has its own version or versions of products and how the products actually are put together. There are also numerous finish options that help to make each project different than the project across the street. But when all the differences are noted by the manufacturers' representatives, there are really five types of systems products that have been developed over the years.

First, there are the projects that use some type of vertical divider panel and conventional office furniture either without components or only capable of holding overhead shelves. These panels might be a specialty furniture product made by any of a number of manufacturers or they might be the panels that go with a component system. Some clients use only panels for

---

[1] *Demountable walls*, also called movable walls, are a type of floor-to-ceiling partition that is held in place by tension and can generally be easily relocated with little demolition and new construction.

budgetary purposes. They may feel they cannot afford to replace the desks and other furniture items with the components, but want to have the separation that panels allow. The designer's job in this situation will be to determine which heights of panels are needed, which product is most appropriate for the client's needs and budget, and then design a layout of panels and specifications that provides the desired separation for each work area.

A second type of product is what is sometimes called a "case goods product" (Figure 2-3). This product provides open plan methodology while retaining the look of conventional furniture. In most cases, the components are attached to and supported from the side panels rather than from the back panels. This limits the lengths of the components, and thus the sizes of the stations. Case goods products have always been popular with financial institutions, law offices, and many businesses that like to present a more conservative aesthetic to their customers.

Figure 2–3 Use of open plan systems furniture with a case goods appearance. (Photograph courtesy of Kimball Office Group.)

Probably the most commonly used type of product is what is commonly called modular systems or full component products. This third type of product consists of vertical panels that are able to support a wide variety components anywhere along their height (Figure 2-4 and 2-5). Components are hung cantilevered from the back panels, not the side, and are adjustable, generally in one inch increments, so that components can be hung from the top to very near the bottom of the panel (depending on the actual product). Since components are cantilevered, it is very important that the back panels be properly supported by panel configurations or special support hardware. This is the type of product that is discussed in detail later in the chapter.

The fourth type of product is the frame and tile based product (Figure 2-6). In this case, a steel frame is used to make the stations. A series of components are either cantilevered or hung from side panels (depending on the product) and horizontal tiles are used to finish the interior and exterior surface of the frames. This product is an exciting way to treat the interior and exterior of the stations from a design and functional standpoint. In addition, because of the thickness of the frames, this type of product gives a more architectural look to the systems furniture.

The last and newest type of systems furniture product, or a furniture system as one manufacturer says in its advertising, is called freestanding or raceway systems. In this case, vertical panels are not used or are not essential to creating the configurations of component parts (Figure 2-7). However, some of the products have been designed so that the freestanding units can be integrated with existing panel systems a business may already own. The freestanding units have an integrated "raceway" below the work surface or work table to carry the necessary electrical, computer, and telephone cabling. In most cases, this freestanding product is more movable as well, allowing employees to rearrange the pieces themselves for changes in the group needs. This is especially important in the face of the changing work environment where teams are developed that last for a few months or even days, and are then broken up for a new project.

Figure 2–4 Vertical panels, at varying heights, can support a wide variety of components. (Photograph courtesy of Kimball Office Group.)

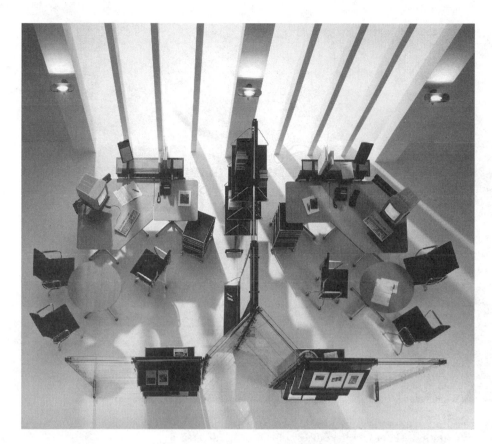

Figure 2–5 Aerial view of workstations showing a variety of components supported by vertical panels. (Photograph courtesy of U. Schaerer Sons Inc. / Haller Systems.)

Figure 2–6 Receptionist's workstation done in mahogany and translucent glass tiles of varying heights. (Photograph courtesy of Herman Miller, Inc., Zeeland, MI. Photographer: James Terkeurst.)

Figure 2–7 Freestanding systems furniture where vertical panels are not used or are not essential to the components' configuration. (Photograph courtesy of Haworth, Inc.)

Arguably the most complex type of product for planning and specification is the cantilevered full component product, since there are so many options possible and so much care must be used in the planning. It is generally recognized by designers who work primarily with open office that if a designer can understand how to put this type of product together, he or she will also be able to design with all the others quite easily. That is why the major discussion of this chapter focuses on the full component type of product.

Historical Perspective

The office environment began significant changes in the early part of the 20th century, but especially around the time of World War II. The numbers of workers in corporations grew enormously during and after World War II. At this time, social scientists started researching organizational structures and employee productivity. Other researchers theorized on the changes to come in the office environment as technology impacted how work was done in the office. In addition, the better educated professional in the office environment was increasingly dissatisfied with the way in which offices were planned—the bosses on the perimeter with other workers in open "bull pens."

Open office planning has its roots in the open planning of Frank Lloyd Wright, who started designing large corporate office facilities in the early 20th century. However, the historical beginning of open landscape was 1958 in Germany.[2] A management consulting group called the *Quickborner Team für Planung und Organisation*, headed by Eberhard and Wolfgang Schnelle,

---

[2]Pile, 1978, p. 18.

was looking at ways to improve office layouts to improve performance and productivity. With the help of a planning expert, they developed the concept of open landscape by laying out the "offices" to increase communication between workers (Figure 2-8). The office workers who worked together or in close relationships were grouped together to improve productivity.

The original planning concept consisted of laying out office space in an open manner, without the use of any kind of partitions. The Quickborner Team coined the term *Bürolandschaft,* which translates into "office landscape,"[3] to define their planning idea. The rather irregular arrangement of the furniture was not based on any geometric plan and seemed to be done more by accident than by planned thought—at least that is what designers and office managers who did not understand the new ideas believed. However, the planning was actually based on work relationships between individuals and work groups and based on very sound principles.

The designers who created this planning concept did not have any specialized furniture to specify for the projects. They used standard desks, file cabinets, bookcases, and other standard office furniture. The divisions between workers were created by the furniture items themselves, along with a few simple panels and the extensive use of plants in the interior. The use of plants probably provided the "open landscape" term.

The open landscape concept slowly made its way to the United States in the 1960s, where it was met with shock and laughter. The planning concept violated every precept of conventional office planning that was well accepted in the United States at the time. "Architects, interior designers, and office planners who felt that their existing work was being called into question tended to oppose office landscape with considerable hostility."[4] One of the biggest objections was the randomness of the layouts. Yet, as previously mentioned, the

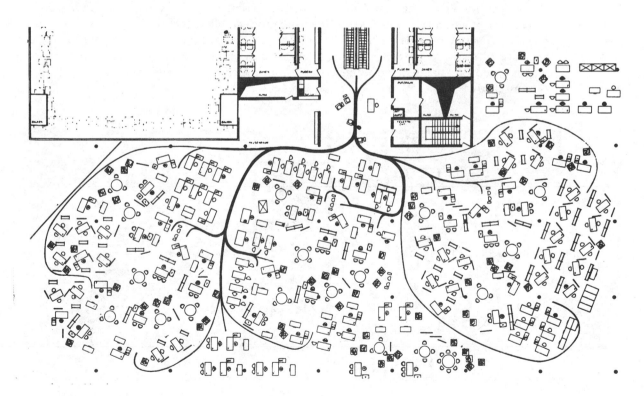

Figure 2–8 Quickborner office landscape.

---

[3] Pile, 1978, p. 9.
[4] Pile, 1976, p. 38.

randomness was not random at all, but the result of the careful analysis of work relationships and work patterns.

Another strong objection was the absence of private offices. Private offices were strong status symbols at the time with the size, location, and increased amount of furnishings all a part of creating that status. But private offices, according to the Quickborner group, also represented the lack of flexibility of the company and the "class differentiation" of employees. Getting the manager out of the private office and into the floor area with the people he or she supervises creates the team of workers and supervision needed to get jobs done.

In 1967, the first project utilizing open landscape in the United States was a department within the DuPont Corporation in Delaware (Figure 2-9). It was part of an experiment in planning and productivity that included another floor, planned in a conventional manner, as a "control." With the "experimentally designed" floor and the "conventionally designed" floor, it was possible to compare costs, acceptance, and other considerations. The experiment was not very successful since it did not really meet all the criteria of Quickborner. Over the years it received reasonably good comments. No other department at DuPont opted for the concept at that time. However, more and more companies tried the planning concept. With each of these attempts, more acceptance of open plan occurred.

In 1960 Herman Miller, Inc. hired a researcher and inventor named Robert Propst to "design things." By this time, Herman Miller, Inc. was fully committed to manufacturing and selling office furniture. The company needed and wanted innovative ideas in office furniture to lead the commercial furniture industry. Robert Propst's pioneering study on the way people worked resulted in the 1968 publication *The Office: A Facility Based on Change*, which discusses his work and the philosophy behind what would become a new product for the office environment.

Propst worked on the design of office furniture that would be functional and original. In 1964 the company introduced his first furniture product called "Action Office."[5] This furniture product consisted of a series of work surfaces, rather than desks and storage units, that utilized the vertical space in an office rather than spreading out in a horizontal fashion. Storage pieces could be attached to the edge of the work surface or hung on freestanding panels (Figure 2-10).

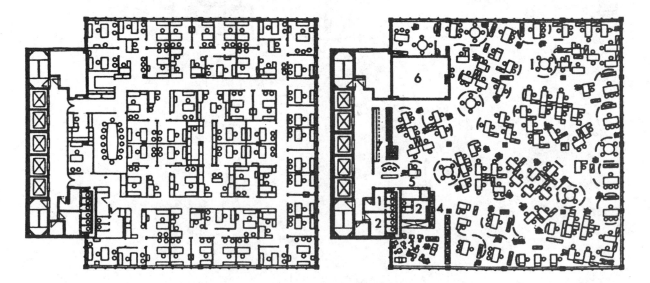

Figure 2–9 First office landscape in the United States, for the DuPont Corporqation. The plan on the left is for the "conventionally designed" floor, while the one on the right is for the "experimentally designed" floor.

---

[5] Herman Miller, Inc., 1996.

(a)

(b)

Figure 2–10a,b Action Office systems furniture, introduced in 1964. (Photographs courtesy of Herman Miller, Inc., Zeeland, MI.)

Action Office was originally designed to fit into the conventional private office. But since its introduction coincided with the acceptance of open landscape, Action Office began to be used in open landscape projects. It was redesigned in 1968, incorporating vertical divider panels and the hanging components with which we are familiar today. Although Action Office in a sense violated the rules of the Quickborner group, it seemed to be a clearly acceptable solution to furnishing the open landscape project. The panels and vertical stacking components helped create "privacy" while still maintaining the essence of the openness. Because of the flexibility in the selection of items that could be hung on the panels, users liked the idea of being able to create a personal office. As open office planning caught on, other furniture manufacturers created products that could be used for this planning concept.

Over the years, open office products have gone through many changes. Special components, panels, and finishes have been produced to provide better aesthetics and custom appearances. Several manufacturers have introduced product with thicker panels to give an "architectural" look to the interior. Panels that simplified interface with electrical and communications needs were developed in the 1970s. Specialized components have been designed to better accommodate personal computers. New lighting solutions were developed to accommodate the rapidly growing use of movable panels. And in the 1990s, numerous new product designs give office areas a more open look with freestanding table units and other components that give open office projects an entirely different look today.

The "big three" manufacturers, Steelcase, Herman Miller, and Haworth, along with numerous others have continually modified, redesigned, upgraded, and created new products in order to keep up with changing demands of the client and design industry. We hope that the reader will understand that in the context of this book it is impossible to list each manufacturer and describe each product used in open office planning. It is suggested that the reader attend one of the trade shows, such as NEOCON in Chicago each June, West Week in Los Angles in March, InterPlan in New York in late October, or any of the other regional shows to view the many different products available. There the reader will be able to obtain information and brochures on many different kinds of product and learn how each may be applicable for a particular client and project requirement.

Planning and Design Concepts

The discussion of open office products in this section is generic in nature and is based on full component systems products. It is based on the general nature of the three most widely used open office products in today's market—Action Office from Herman Miller, Inc., Series 9000 from Steelcase, Inc., and Places from Haworth, Inc.

Open office space planning projects are similar to conventional office planning in that the information required regarding numbers of individuals and their job relationships, support spaces, equipment utilization, and mechanical interface, are all necessary to properly plan the office. Designers of open office projects must pay strict attention to job functions, work relationships, and specific equipment needs as translated into the variety of components. These are of critical importance to a successful floor plan using open office products.

Proper and dedicated use of programming techniques is very important to a successful open office project. In programming, of course, the designer is responsible for finding out everything he or she needs to know about the client's requirements and the physical facility. With an open office project, particular attention must be paid to equipment needs of all the employees. The information can be obtained using formal preprinted questionnaires, one-on-one interview techniques, or by the designer making personal observations of the existing work environment. This information gathering is undertaken to establish which open office components are required for each job function.

Space allocation begins with the decisions concerning equipment needs for each job. Components, even though they are hanging on panels, naturally take up floor space. The organization and configuration of the components on panels, in part, determines the square footage needed for the station of each employee. Other factors also influence the amount of square footage allocated to different job functions. As mentioned in Chapter 1, many companies have standards relating to workstation square footage allowances. Status may also be a factor in some companies. In addition, work methodologies, such as use of teaming versus individual work assignments, also affect square footage requirements. All these must be

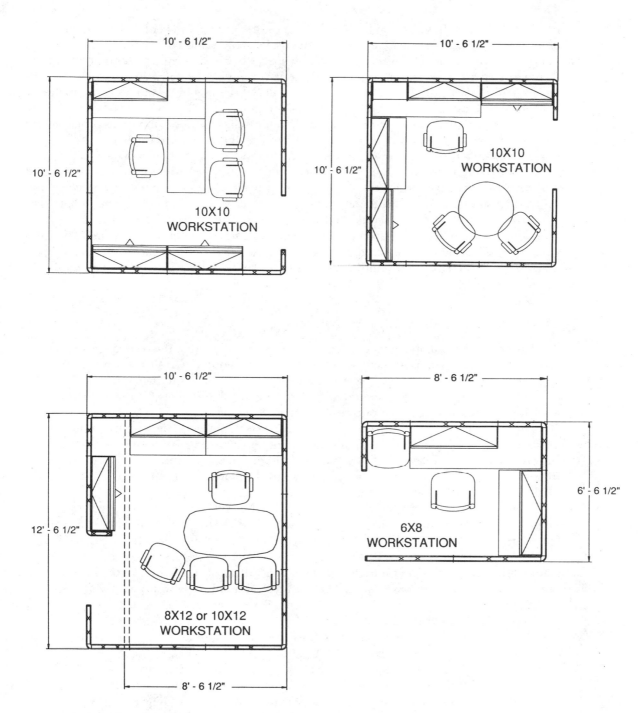

Figure 2–11 Four floor plans showing a variety of open office space planning units. (Courtesy of Milcare, Inc.)

honored in determining the layouts. Figures 2-11 represent some of the typical configurations of open office stations for a variety of job functions.

Circulation space will be determined as in traditional office planning. However, a few notable exceptions must be kept in mind when dealing with open office planning. The designer must differentiate traffic aisles from traffic corridors. The building code defines a *corridor* as any circulation space having partitions, rails, or dividers of over 69 inches in height. When a corridor is defined in a plan, the size of the corridor is required to be a minimum of 44 inches if it is in a space with an occupant load of over 50. This affects open office planning projects whenever the designer uses systems panels of over 69 inches to create stations or support areas. *Aisles* are circulation spaces between furniture items and between furniture items and partitions as long as those partitions or divider panels are less than 69 inches high. An aisle can be less than 44 inches unless it serves a high volume of occupants or must meet Americans with Disabilities Act (ADA) regulations.

An allowance of 25 to 40 percent for circulation space is common in systems projects. The more generous allowance will be common in projects that are more open and provide for flexible working areas, which have become common today. The tighter end of the allowance will be more common when a plan is based on a "cubicle" approach with a majority of individual workstations. Of course, wider circulation spaces provide for a more open, spacious feeling. Circulation spaces that are too generous, however, waste space. Main traffic spaces that carry the largest amount of traffic should be five to six feet wide (or wider if the codes require), with other traffic spaces sized according to occupant load and code requirements. The ADA guidelines will also affect the size and configuration of traffic corridors and aisles in the open office plan. Sufficient turnaround spaces must be planned along all corridors and aisles to insure accessibility.

Panels and Panel Support Systems

The skeleton of an open office systems project is represented by the vertical divider panels (Figure 2-12). The panels divide one workstation from another, permit the use of numerous kinds of components, create passageways and aisles, and provide varying amounts of privacy. Panels also provide a certain amount of acoustical control and allow for the distribution of electrical, telephone, and data transmission throughout the space.

The panels can be laid out in numerous different configurations, depending on the client's needs and the available product. Layouts of panels and stations can create basically enclosed cubicles or, where privacy is less of a concern, rather open configurations. Since panels are freestanding, care must be taken in the design of the station and the way components are used, especially when stations are more open.

Panels come in several different *sizes* to meet the various needs of facility work and support functions. Width and height dimensions of panels are given in nominal dimensions. For example, a 24 inch wide panel is not necessarily 24 inches wide, but might be slightly smaller, depending on the manufacturer. Widths and heights of panels vary a little between manufacturers. The designer must become familiar with the specific sizes of the product line with which he or she chooses to work. The most typical nominal generic panel widths are: 12, 18, 24, 30, 36, 45, and 48 inches. A few companies have 60 inch wide panels as well. The most typical panel heights are: 30, 36, 39, 45, 47, 53, 63, 72, and 85 inches (Figure 2-13).

Certain panel heights are usually used for certain functional needs. The lowest height panels (30 to 39 inches) are commonly used to create "desk height" configurations. This means they are trying to imitate a standard desk appearance. They are also used in cases where some separation is required, where open communication and team work is important, and where supervisors wish to have more visual control of employees. The next group of panel heights (39 to 47 inches) is commonly thought of as "counter height" panels. These are used to create transaction counters where an individual, such as a client, would approach a workstation of a receptionist. This group of panels provides a height suitable for use with a counter cap (transaction surface) at the top of the panel so that a visitor may write or leave papers on the counter. Counter height panels hide some of the work and equipment of the receptionist from view by clients (Figure 2-14). Panels from 53 to 85 inches high provide what is called "sit-down privacy." This means that the individual within the station, when seated, generally cannot be seen by individuals passing by the panel layouts, assuming a more enclosed cubicle station. These panels are often used for job functions where a moderate amount of storage is required and for supervisors and higher level employees. In addition, the 72 to 85 inch high panels provide what is commonly called "stand-up privacy." This means that the individual in

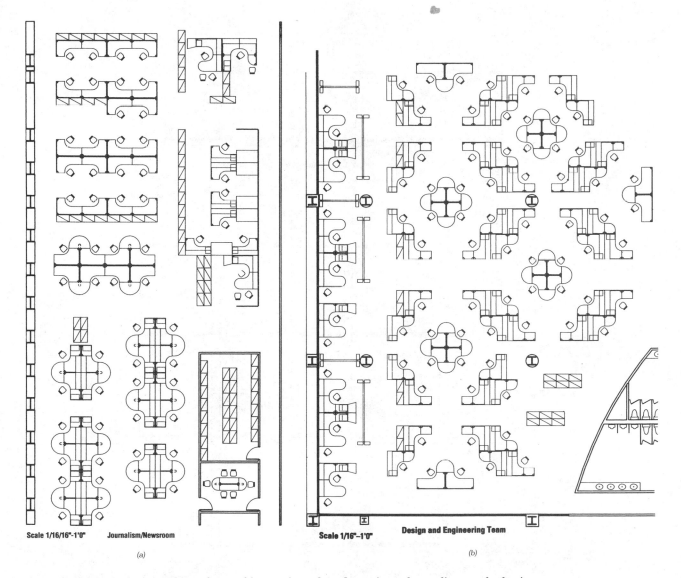

Figure 2–12a,b Vertical panels can be used in a variety of configurations, depending on the business profile. Two examples are shown. (Copyright Steelcase, Inc., used with permission.)

the station, even when standing, generally cannot be seen by someone passing by. This height panel is often used for upper level personnel and for conference spaces. The highest height panels also allow for the greatest storage capability and are often used to create libraries, mail rooms, and other support spaces.

Connecting hardware, provided by the manufacturer, is used to secure panels together. Panels are almost always connected so that one corner of a panel is connected to a corner of the next panel. When panels are connected together forming a straight line, a "straight line connector" or simple hinge is used. When this is done, components can be butted up against each other. A straight line connection is also used when a curved panel is connected to any straight panel. When the layout requires that panel connections form an angle—to create an L configuration workstation, or to create two to four different stations from one connecting point—hinge connectors are used. The most common angle connection for a work station would be a right angle turn (90 degrees). However, most manufacturers' products allow for connections of many degrees of angle. The exact kind of hinge connector depends on which manufacturer's product is being used.

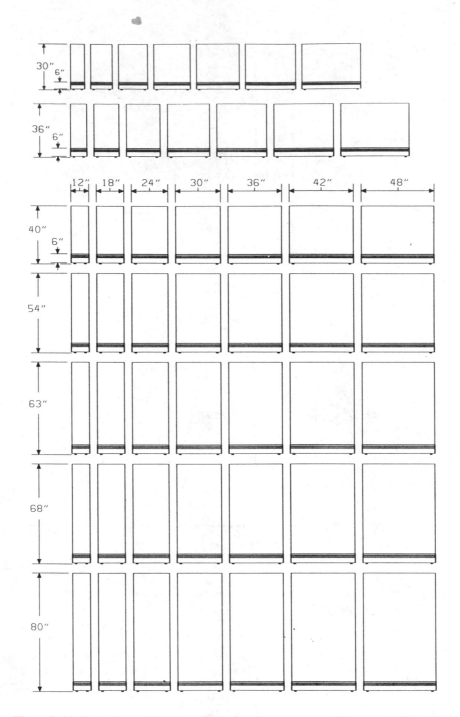

Figure 2–13 Typical panel heights. (Line drawings courtesy of Herman Miller, Inc., Zeeland, MI.)

Hardware connections and products that allow for specialized connections of panels to other panels or to the building structure are also available. The most common type of specialized connection hardware is called a T-connector, which allows a panel to be connected to a wall or to the face of another panel. This is done for support needs when the designer or client chooses not to use an end panel for support. Figure 2-15 shows these various methods of connecting panels.

As panels are not fixed to the floor or the ceiling, they must be configured to be self-supporting. A single panel or a straight run of panels always requires support on both ends.

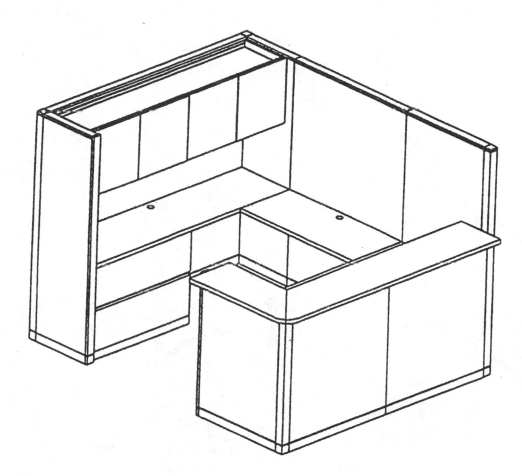

Figure 2–14 Receptionist's area using systems furniture.

One cannot design a layout with a panel or a series of panels in a straight line without any support. The panel configuration must make a turn for it to remain standing. Support panels on the ends of a run of panels are generally required for a configuration of 8 to 12 feet of length, depending on the type of panel, and on whether the configuration is load bearing or non-load bearing. A load bearing panel is one from which components are hung on one or both sides. When a panel is supported by another panel—the most common method of support—the panel heights do not have to be the same unless the main panel is 65 inches or higher. Manufacturer's guidelines should be reviewed to insure that the manner in which panels are configured and supported meets the recommendations for the product being specified. Figure 2-16 provides illustrations of the most common requirements based on the Steelcase 9000 product.

A panel support foot is a component that is attached to the base of the panel. It sticks out 12 to 18 inches from the panel and can be used as an intermediary support. Most manufacturers do not recommend its use with fully loaded panel configurations. Short panels (30 to 48 inches high) are also used as support end panels, especially when stations are set up next to windows.

Panels also have thickness. Most commonly, a panel is a nominal 2 inches thick. Some panels are thicker, so again the designer must be sure to check the specifications of the product he or she is using. This thickness is important because it affects layouts every time panels are added at right angles or in any direction other than in a straight line (Figure 2-17). Designers who forget to plan systems projects with the proper panel thicknesses and allowances for panel connection hardware find their floor plans often do not fit the space. This miscalculation of the panel size and configuration is referred to by many designers as *systems creep*. Every time the plan makes a turn with a panel, the designer must allow the thickness of the panel and

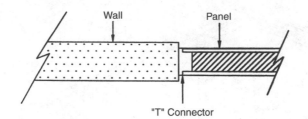

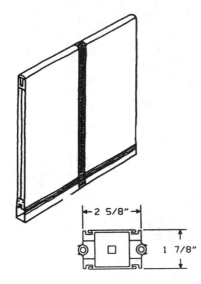

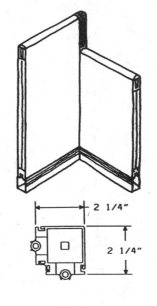

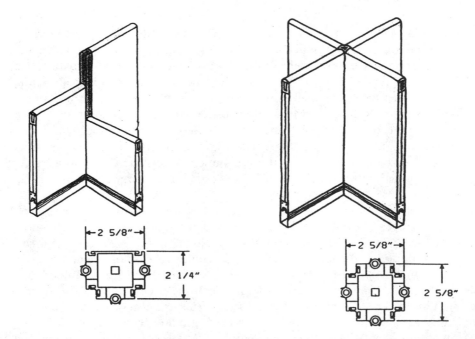

Figure 2–15 Top visual indicates method of connecting panel to wall. Lower four visuals depict use of connectors for various configurations. (Top drawing courtesy of Cody D. Beal, bottom four drawings courtesy of Herman Miller, Inc., Zeeland, MI.)

Two-Panel Runs

8' maximum

Three-Panel Runs

 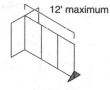 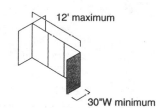 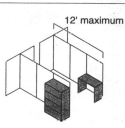

12' maximum

12' maximum

12' maximum

30"W minimum

Unstable. Requires additional support at end of panel run.

Stabilizer feet provide stability at end of panel run.

Perpendicular panel provides stability at end of panel run.

Furniture provides stability at end of panel run.
Tip: Not recommended on 75"H panels in a 12' run.

Four-Panel Runs

 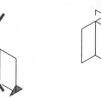 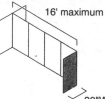 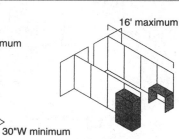

16' maximum

16' maximum

30"W minimum

Unstable. Requires additional support at end of panel run.

Unstable. Requires a perpendicular panel or furniture as support at end of panel run.

Perpendicular panel provides stability at end of panel run.

Furniture provides stability at end of panel run.
Tip: Not recommended on 75"H panels in a 16' run.

Five-Panel Runs

Unstable. Requires additional support.

Figure 2–16 Illustrations indicating proper panel runs in regards to stability. (Copyright Steelcase, Inc., used with permission.)

any connection hardware to the scale of the station. A minimum of 3 inches for the panel and connecting hardware should be added to the over-all length of the layouts for most full component products as described in this section.

Panels also come in a variety of *finishes and types*. The most commonly used panels are hard surface panels and acoustical or fabric covered panels. Hard surface panels are steel faced panels painted in neutral tones or covered in a melamine finish to imitate wood. These

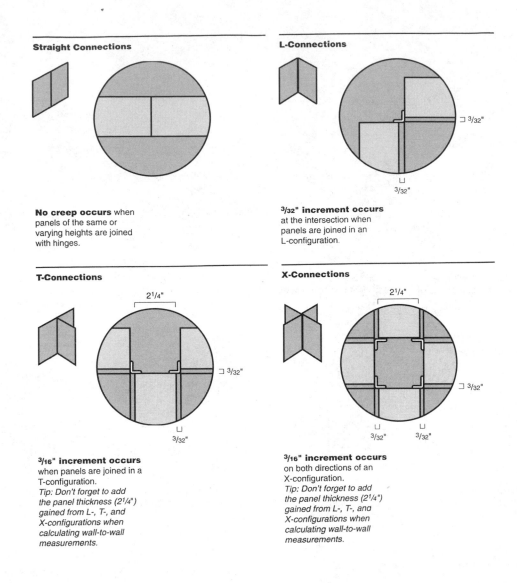

Figure 2–17 Considerations regarding panel creep when additional increments occur. (Copyright Steelcase, Inc., used with permission.)

panels have no acoustical values. Fabric covered panels can be acoustical or nonacoustical. Acoustical panels are designed to absorb sound. They are used in high noise areas to help baffle the ambient noise levels in an office environment. Nonacoustical fabric covered panels are used to provide color, but these have minimal acoustical value. Some manufacturers provide veneer for panels to give a more executive look. And there are also "glass" panels, which are panel frames with a tempered, safety glass, or Plexiglas material in the frame. Of course, specific manufacturers may have a variety of specialized panel finishes or types available for specialized needs. Panels generally have the same finish on both sides, making it easier to reconfigure the floor plan in the future. However, fabric panels can be ordered to have a different fabric on each side.

Panels also come with or without built-in electrical components. The power bases of panels are connected together to carry electrical service from the building to the freestanding workstations. Space in the power base is provided to carry telephone and computer cables as well. A more complete discussion of the power base is provided in the section on electrical interface.

Finally, at the edges of the panels on both faces are a series of slots. These slots, most commonly on one inch increments, allow for the cantilevered hanging of component pieces that complete the workstation. Coordinating the panel widths with the components to be hung from them is sometimes the most difficult part of planning with open office systems products.

Components

Components are the many different parts and pieces that provide horizontal surfaces in place of desktops and table tops, open or closed shelving, file units, drawer configurations, and numerous miscellaneous pieces to provide the total work environment of the stations. For the fully modular component panel systems, components can be hung on both faces of the panels. Generally, components can be hung anywhere from the top of the panel to nearly the bottom. These components can be hung on one inch increments in height, making the panel system a totally customizable furniture product.

Open office furniture products have some unique product terminology. Exact terms and definitions may vary depending on the manufacturer, but most are similar to these:

Work surface refers to the component that takes the place of the desktop, credenza surface top, and table tops. Work surfaces are usually 24, 30, or 36 inches deep (front to back) and can be 24, 30, 36, 45, 48, 60, and 72 inches wide. Some manufacturers have wider work surfaces. Curved work surfaces are also available. These fit inside the curve of curved shaped panels. Other specialized work surfaces, especially for the integration of computer equipment, are available as well.

Convergent or peninsula work surfaces are work surface components that attach at one end to another work surface (or maybe the wall) and jut out into the work station to create a desk-like appearance. They are 30 to 36 inches deep (front to back) and 48 to 72 inches wide. Many are curved and supported by a leg at the "free" end. They are often used when conferences or team work is required in stations.

Corner work surfaces are the often oddly shaped corner work surfaces commonly used in L-shaped stations to hold a computer in the corner of the station. They usually have a corner "cut-off" so that the keyboard is more easily accessible.

Freestanding work surfaces are various sizes of tables, which may be round or rectangular. Most common rectangular sizes are 24 by 48, 30 by 60, and 36 by 72 inches. Freestanding work surfaces are used as table desks or for holding heavy and/or delicate equipment.

Shelves come in a variety of sizes. Shelves come in various heights and widths. Most common are 24, 30, 36, 42, and 48 inches wide by 12 inches deep.

A *flipper door* is usually a part of a component that creates an enclosed storage unit rather than an open shelf. Some manufacturers sell the flipper door as a separate item for their storage shelf and others include the shelf as a unit.

A *storage bin* is a closed shelf unit with a door as a total unit item.

Open storage shelves are used for various storage needs such as books, files, supplies, and so on.

Display shelves are angled shelves used to display work or magazines.

Electronic data processing (EDP) shelves are large shelves intended to store oversized computer printout paper and binders.

Specialized shelves are available from various manufacturers, providing specialized storage unique to their systems.

File units are single drawer lateral file units that are suspended from the panels. They usually accommodate either letter or legal size filing by the use of hanging file folders.

Task lights (or shelf lights) are the luminaries that are sold to fit under shelf units. Task lights are usually specified under any shelf that is over a work surface.

Tack surfaces (visual display surfaces) are items such as tack boards that can be added to the panel surface to provide for visual display needs.

Marker boards are another visual display surface. Marker boards use specially coated steel surfaces used in conjunction with water based liquid markers.

Pencil drawers are small drawers used for personal storage of small supplies under a work surface. They are generally, only about 2 to 3 inches high.

Box drawers are about 6 inches high, and can be used to store bulkier items. Some manufacturers provide or make available dividers so this drawer can be used to store stationary.

File pedestals are drawers that can usually accommodate either letter or legal size filing using hanging file folders. They are suspended below work surfaces.

Drawer pedestals are available from manufacturers in a variety of styles that are sold as one unit.

Counter caps (*also called transaction surfaces*) are primarily used on low panels (34 to 48 inches high) in reception areas to create a more private across-the-counter transaction area. They can also be used on higher panels to locate ambient light fixtures or plants.

Accessories are available to complete the work station. Accessories include paper handling equipment to organize paper flow, shelf dividers, paper trays, keyboard trays, and many other items.

For the major systems, components are cantilevered from the face of the panel. Since components can be hung vertically at one inch increments on the panels, the designer has an almost unlimited number of configurations of component arrangements on the panels. The only limitations will be the height of the panels selected and any weight limit recommendations by the manufacturer. For example, using a 65 inch high panel that is 48 inches wide, it is possible to specify one work surface with one shelf/cabinet, or one work surface with two low open shelves, or five or six low open shelves or three shelf/cabinets, or even two work surfaces—plus potentially other configurations of components depending on the product offerings of the manufacturer. And that is only on one side of the panel!

When a component (or multiple components) is hung on a panel, the panel requires support to keep it from tipping over. Exactly how many components may be put on one or, the other, or both sides of the panels and what kind of support is required is dictated by the manufacturer. In general, it depends both on how high a panel is being used, and on how many and what kinds of components are on each side of the panel. As a general rule, however, always provide support to the side of the panel on which components are hung.

Component widths basically match panel widths, except there are generally no components smaller than 18 inches wide or wider than 60 inches. An exception to the 60 inch width is for work surfaces. Manufacturers make work surfaces 72, 84, and 96 inches wide.

As stated earlier in this section, components can be hung on both sides of any one panel. Thus the configuration of components can be different on either side as well. Since components must be supported at the vertical strips on the edges of the panels, the configuration of components and panels is very important. It is more economical to use both sides of a panel as much as possible, rather than only one side, to hang components.

While a component may overlap a straight connection of panels, components *cannot* overlap a spot where panels have turned a corner. For example, if the designer wanted to hang a 6 foot wide work surface and a 4 foot wide shelf on panels, a 4 foot panel and a 2 foot panel in a straight line connection would be needed. Because it is most economical to utilize both sides of the panels wherever possible, the designer must consider having the same kind of station on either side of the panel whenever feasible. At the very least, stations should be designed so that components of compatible sizes are specified on each side of the panels. Again, it is only possible to hang components over straight line connections of panels, not where panels turn.

Mechanical Interface

Open office systems projects require careful consideration of the mechanical interface of the product to the structure. Because systems products are not fixed to the walls or the floor and often do not even touch the walls, the planning of electrical, telephone, and data communications service to the stations is critical to the overall design. Lighting and acoustical planning are additional challenges to the designer. Overhead shelves reduce the amount of light on work surfaces. Poor lighting can cause glare and veiling reflections on computer monitors, leading to eye fatigue. The use of less than full-height partitions creates an opportunity for a acoustical problems in an open office project.

Today's open office products come with the option of integrated *electrical service*. Manufacturers provide panels with or without electrical service and with a variety of options. Planning electrical service involves consideration of three basic issues: first, how power and cable channels are provided in the product; second, how will panels be connected to the building electrical service; and third, how many circuits are provided in the panel system.

The most common way of integrating electrical and communications cabling in panels is by a base feed system. In this situation, a 3 to 4 inch channel has been added along the base of the panel into which is placed electrical wiring in a rigid conduit. Special connectors allow for the flow of electricity from one unit to another. A second channel is provided for telephone and data communications cabling. By code these cables must be separated from electrical wiring.

Other options may be available from some manufacturers on some of their products. One option is a *belt-line electrical* channel. A belt-line feed has the outlets and channels at approximately 30 inches above the base of the panel. That height allows for plug-in above the work surface. A vertical channel along one side of the panel brings the service from floor entries or base feeds up to the belt-line feed unit. This type of system allows for much easier access to outlets and helps to clean up the tangle of wires that normally must be fed behind the edge of the work surface and down to the outlets in the base. A second option is an in-line feed down a vertical channel on one edge of the panel. This would be connected to the building system either with a power pole that extends to the ceiling or through a base feed. Figure 2-18 shows the primary methods of providing electrical service to the panels.

Commercial buildings generally have single phase or three phase electrical service. *Single phase service* is called 240/120 V service. It is the former standard for electrical service in most buildings. Now it is found in older commercial buildings. It is designed to support two sets of 120 volt circuits. *Three phase electrical service* is the present standard in newer commercial buildings. It is called 208 Y /120 V service. It is designed to support three sets of 120 volt circuits. This will take care of standard needs in the office space. However, 480 Y / 277 V systems are needed for major equipment like the air conditioning system. It is important to note that you cannot fully utilize all the circuits of a multiple circuit panel system if the building has single phase service. In that situation, you will be required to recommend rewiring the building, or providing additional electrical drops (or starts) to power up the panels.

It is most common for systems products to have three or four electrical circuits. Some products have two circuits and others have up to six circuits. The differing number of circuits is in response to today's heavy demand for electrical service in stations. Multiple circuit systems are important so that the electrical load of the office layout is distributed without overloading the service. Since the majority of manufacturers provide a three circuit system for panel products, this discussion focuses on that type of product.

In a three circuit system, it is common that one circuit is used for auxiliary service items such as shelf lights, calculators, typewriters, and other small office equipment. The second circuit is provided to accommodate the use of ambient lighting fixtures. If ambient lighting is not used, the second circuit is used for additional standard office equipment. The third circuit is dedicated to computers. This "clean" circuit with its own ground helps prevent loss of data due to in-house power surges.

There are a few electrical terms that are associated with open office systems products.

Amperage is the amount of electrical current required to operate any kind of electrical device.

A *dedicated circuit* is a separate circuit with its own hot, neutral, and ground wires, having none of these wires shared with any other circuit. It is most often used to provide power to a specific piece equipment such as a computer.

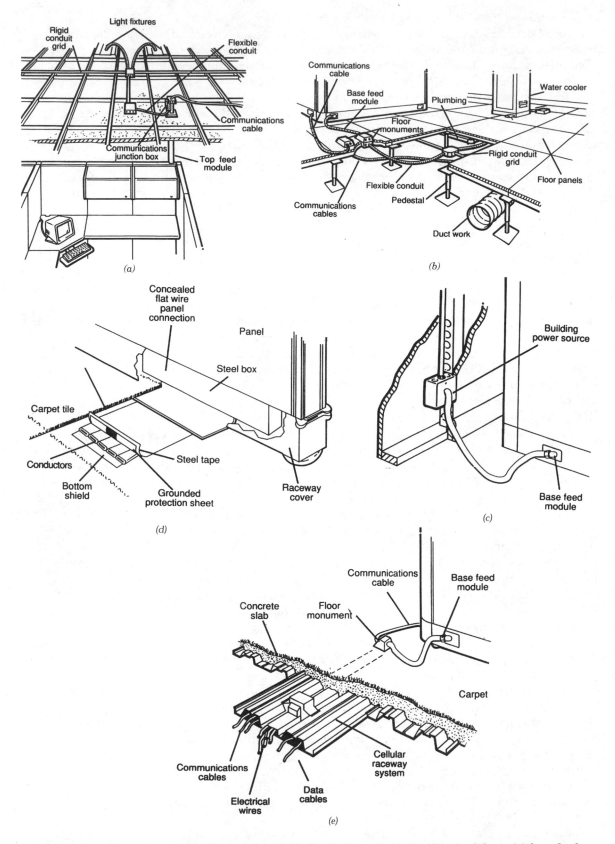

Figure 2–18a-e Electrical service to the panels. (*a*) Topfeed with power pole, (*b*) raised floor, (*c*) base feed from wall, (*d*) from flat-wire cable, (*e*) floor raceway. (Drawings courtesy of Haworth, Inc.)

Power entry is a generic term for the point where the building electrical service is wired to a special vertical panel that starts power to a series of panels.

A *plenum* is an air space between the ceiling tiles and the structural ceiling in commercial buildings in which HVAC ducts, lighting fixtures, electrical cabling, and other cables can be located.

The National Electrical Code (NEC) provides the standards necessary for all planning of the electrical systems. Although the code standards for the building will be the responsibility of the architect, there are some standards that are the responsibility of the interior designer. For example, the NEC allows a maximum of 13 receptacles on each 20 amp circuit and each standard receptacle must be rated at 1.5 amps/120 volts. The reader is urged to check the NEC and local code interpretations to properly plan powered panels.

In order to properly plan the electrical system for panels and determine the type of electrical service needed, the designer must know the amperage of common office equipment that will be placed in the stations. Since the electrical code limits the number of receptacles on each circuit, the designer must know the amperages to be sure that he or she provides sufficient power entries to handle all the electrical needs of the project layout. Figure 2-19 lists the amperages for many common pieces of office equipment.

The most common building interface for electrical service is through walls. This method was shown in Figure 2-18(*c*). If the existing outlets are in the right place, this is an inexpensive way to connect panels to the electrical system. If the client is willing to rewire the building space, you can make connections almost anywhere you want. This is not always possible because of problems with the existing structure that will make adding extra receptacles cost-prohibitive. If a column does not already have electrical service provided, you will need to show how you will frame the column so that electrical service can be run down the column.

A second very common way of providing electrical service is through drops from the ceiling plenum. In commercial buildings with plenums, it is possible to provide power drops exactly where they are required. This method necessitates the use of power poles, which are attached to the ceiling tile grid and the ends of divider panels. It is an effective way of providing electrical interface since connections are unlimited. However, designers and some clients do not like the aesthetic appearance of the power poles. This method was shown in Figure 2-18(A).

Another method of providing electrical service is by a poke through system. Wiring is brought up from the plenum below by drilling holes in the slab where the floor monument

Answering maching	.08
Adding machine	.05
Large electronic calculator	.2
Pencil sharpener	.25
Electric eraser	.25
Radio	.05
Clock	.03
Fan	1.0
Typewriter	1.5
Computer equipment	
Personal computers (VDTs and PCs)	0.08–4.80
Stand-alone printers	3.0–11.0
Processor/disk drive unit	0.08–12.0
Modems	.15
Copiers	
Stand-alone	15.0
Desk-top	7.0–10.0
Coffee brewer	10.0
Microwave	8.0–12.0

Figure 2–19 List of amperages of common office equipment. (Copyright Steelcase, Inc., used with permission.)

connections will be needed (Figure 2-18(E)). Surface mounted or recessed boxes are installed and the power entry panel is wired to the building service. Drilling holes in the floor, called core drilling, can only be done if the amount and locations of the holes does not destroy the structural integrity of the floor system.

In many older buildings, electrical service may be provided with a floor grid. Troughs recessed in the floor contain the conduits for electrical, data processing, and telephone service. This is an expensive initial installation, and has some problems for the designer. Not all installations are on a grid that will work with the panel system and stations sizes. Most commonly, the grid is not lined up with the panels since the grid was done prior to the furniture arrangement being designed.

A very flexible interface system that was developed in the late 1970s is flat wiring. Flat wiring uses electrical, telephone, and data processing wiring that has been flattened. This is attached to the floor using special installation techniques (Figure 2-18(D)). It is wired to a starter box along the wall or a column, and runs out to where the connection needs to be made with the panel system. Additional boxes can be added along the run as long as the number of receptacles does not exceed code. It is expensive, but the advantage of infinite placement options is attractive to the designer and clients. The electrical code does not allow the use of broadloom carpet with flat wire installations. It is necessary to use carpet tiles. It is also possible that, in certain jurisdictions, local codes may prohibit or restrict the use of flat wire electrical and cabling service

The last kind of electrical interface is the raised floor (Figure 2-18(B)). In this situation, a second floor is created over the slab. The space between the slab and the raised floor allows for the introduction of electrical, telephone, and data processing interfaces. It is an expensive installation, but provides unlimited arrangement of the open office systems since power can be brought up anywhere from the floor. This situation will most commonly be encountered in remodeling projects in older buildings.

Telephone and data communications interface is handled in a very similar way to the electrical service. Technology has created intense demands on the communication interface in offices today. The designer needs to clearly understand what types of computers and printers are being used and how they are networked. Many other technological choices and equipment items that will find their way into the office environment must also be understood. Manufacturers have provided space within panels to accommodate telephone and data cables of many kinds. The designer must determine through programming activities the nature of the communications service required for the project so that he or she is again specifying the correct type of systems products to handle the cabling. Recall that the code requires that electrical wiring and communications cables cannot be in the same exact space. Notice how the two items are separated in Figure 2-20.

Because the cables for communications are fed through the building in the same manner as electrical service, the main points of information here are to clarify the terminology associated with communications.

Data and voice communication starts most simply with a *twisted pair cable*—two copper wires twisted together, shielded by an insulator. It is the common cabling in homes and the basic cabling to individual phones and modems in offices.

Four pair cable has four sets of two copper wires twisted together covered by an insulating material. It is the most common voice and data cabling used today since it is inexpensive.

Twenty-five pair cable is like four pair except it has 25 pairs of copper strands. An older method of providing voice and data communications, it is rarely installed in new buildings but exists in many older structures.

Fiber optic cable is a data cable utilizing a thin glass filament wire for the transmission of signals.

Coaxial cable is a data cable with a central core conductor surrounded by insulation material that is then covered by a metal sheath that acts as a second insulator. This cable is finished with an outer coating.

A *local area network* (*LAN*) is a telecommunications network that has been designed to eliminate the possibility of signals that would interrupt the network.

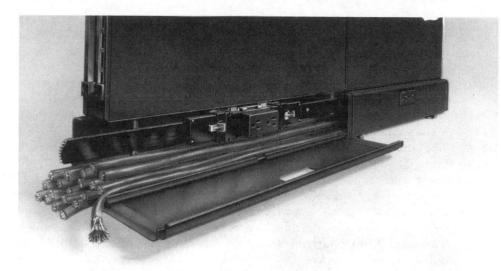

Figure 2–20 Action Office energy distribution system. (Photograph courtesy of Herman Miller, Inc. Photographer: David Jackson.)

Traditionally, *lighting design* for offices emphasized a uniform quantity of light throughout the space. This uniform quantity of light did not consider the visual comfort or quality of the lighting nor the aesthetics of the light in the interior. Since the 1970s, an increased emphasis on lighting layouts has occurred. This is due in some part to designers wishing to have more input in the design of lighting in the interiors for which they are responsible. Of equal if not greater importance has been the effect of the high cost of energy and the need for energy conservation.

As with all aspects of the interior and space planning, lighting decisions and lighting design should be initiated as early in the planning process as possible. It is too late to suggest task or indirect ambient lighting, for example, when the electrical contractor is installing a grid of 2 by 4 foot fluorescent fixtures.

This discussion of lighting design concentrates on the concepts of task/ambient lighting. This has been done since the key lighting design solutions must commonly occur using these concepts. In open office planning, task lighting is relatively easy to provide. It generally makes use of small fixtures placed under shelves or on the desktop. In most cases, task light fixtures are fluorescent fixtures, commonly using a 40 watt tube. Task lights should be specified with reflectors or lens that help reduce glare, eyestrain, and veiling reflections. Task lights may also be smaller fluorescent or halide lamp fixtures, generally about 10 by 7 inches wide and fitting under the shelf just like the other luminaries. Due to their small size and reduced wattage, it is often necessary to use two of these under a 4 foot or longer shelf.

Ambient lighting can either be a direct system in which fixtures are located on the ceiling, such as the standard grid of 2 by 4 foot fluorescent fixtures, or an indirect system where the light source is commonly hidden and light is bounced off another surface. A type of light fixture that is commonly used in the indirect method is the high intensity discharge (HID) fixture. HID fixtures have grown in popularity due to their energy efficiency and high quality of light. The three kinds of HID light sources often used as ambient fixtures are:

- *Mercury vapor.* This type of lamp uses mercury vapor and argon gas as its light source. It often has a bluish to greenish color of light.

- *Metal halide.* This type of lamp uses mercury vapor and metallic vapors as its light source. The color of light from the lamp varies depending on the kind of metals used in the arc tube. The light generally has a bluish or greenish tint (most often seen when the light shines on the ceiling).

- *High-pressure sodium.* This type of fixture produces light when electricity passes through sodium vapor. It is the most efficient of the HID lamps but it has color problems. It often has an orangish colored light—like street lamps.

High intensity discharge luminaries can be used for indirect ambient lighting as floor standing kiosks or units within shelves. They can be panel hung fixtures that are placed on hanging devices of various kinds or can fit into a cavity of an overhead shelf as part of a system. They also can be pendants mounted from the ceiling or fixed to the walls.

Lighting an office area where computer monitors are used presents another challenge to the designer. Eyestrain, fatigue, and blurred vision are some of the problems that are caused by poor lighting design in computer areas. Users of computer monitors can see the screen even in a dark room—the tube provides its own light source. But few users of monitors are looking only at a screen. They must also read from printed or handwritten documents and sketches (for CAD users). These source documents require illumination to be read carefully. Individuals who are inputting from some kind of source document must continually shift from the source document to the computer screen. The source documents are usually dark letters on a white background and the monitor screen is light letters on a dark background. Added to this is the fact that the individual is also shifting from two different light source quantities.

One other factor has to be taken into consideration. The ability to read and work with clarity and without fatigue is also affected by glare. There are two kinds of glare; *direct glare* is glare coming from a light source and *reflected glare* is glare coming from surrounding equipment. Glare occurs when the light levels in the field of view vary greatly from the light levels to which the eyes are adapted. If you are reading a book and someone changes the angle of the light so that it is very intense, the glare makes it difficult for you to read the book anymore. The light from a window reflecting on a computer screen makes it nearly impossible to see the screen. It is also suggested that computer monitor be at a 90 degree angle to adjacent windows rather than facing windows or having the windows behind the screen. Do not locate the computer monitor directly under a shelf light or task light as glare may also be created.

To the authors' knowledge, it is not possible to run *plumbing* through any standard office systems panels. Plumbing design for a coffee area sink, for example, should be planned along perimeter walls or adjacent to a wet column rather than as part of the open area. Providing plumbing areas in the larger open area also makes reconfiguration at a later date much more difficult.

Acoustical design is another important interface challenge for the designer. One of the biggest complaints about open office has always been that they are too noisy. Elimination of private offices and putting everyone "into the open" brings complaints concerning the lack of privacy and general noise. An open office space can be designed so as to control the sound level of the environment, but it will never be noise-free—just as any conventional office plan cannot be noise free.

Trying to make the office environment as quiet as possible is the wrong approach. When a room is very quiet (no ambient sounds), any little sound can be distracting. The idea is to create an environment that is free of distraction, not free of noise.

Theoretically, any sound is audible to the human ear. What must be determined is not if sounds are audible in the office environment, but if they are intelligible. Intelligibility refers to the ability of our hearing mechanism to gather information from the available sounds. As few as 15% of the words in a sentence may make the meaning of the entire sentence clear to the listener. If this drops to fewer than 10%, intelligibility almost vanishes. Sounds may be "audible"—stimulate the ear—without carrying any intelligibility or without being annoying. In open plan, the designer must limit the intelligibility to specified zones while limiting other sounds to tolerable levels.

The most common method of controlling sound in an open office project is by the use of acoustical panels. Commonly these panels have an internal baffle to help keep sound from passing through the panel. This is covered by acoustical material on both sides and finished using standard panel fabric. Acoustical panels are classified by a noise reduction coefficient

(NRC) rating or sound transmission class (STC) rating. The *noise reduction coefficient* is a number value between 0 and 1.0 representing the fraction or percent of energy (striking the material) that is absorbed. A rating of 0 means no sound is absorbed. A 1.0 means all the sound is absorbed. For acoustical panels the NRC can vary quite a lot based on the way the tests were conducted. However, better quality acoustical panels will have an NRC of .80 or higher.

Sound transmission class is a one-number rating that describes the ability of a panel surface to block the transmission of sound. An STC of 0 means there is no drop in level through the panel. An STC of 50 means very little sound goes through. In general, good quality acoustical panels should have an STC of not less than 23.

Decibel or *dB* is the scale of measurement of sound. All sounds have different decibel levels. Figure 2-21 provides some common decibel levels. Normal speech between two persons takes place at a distance of about 3 to 3½ feet and produces a level of about 65 dB at the listener's ear. This is such a common level that people tend to adjust their voice level or physical separation to establish this level. Levels below 30 dB are considered very quiet; levels about 85 dB are very loud, and speech is almost impossible.[6]

Normal speech was said to be at a 65 dB rate at a distance of 3 feet, but this is too high a level of background noise to be tolerated by most people. Most office workers who need to concentrate as they work will not tolerate background levels of much more than 45 to 47 dB.[7] If this range is achieved so that those who do not wish to hear (or should not hear) conversations, don't, then acceptable privacy will be achieved.

Acoustical control can be achieved by controlling the source, the path, and the listener. A few simple methods for dealing with the source of sound include: (1) when people do not need to be in direct communication with each other, face them away from each other; (2) try to locate phones so as to encourage talking into acoustical panels; (3) noisy office machines like copiers should be located away from areas needing privacy; (4) if noisy computer printers must be in the office area, house them under special covers; and (5) those who don't or won't adjust their voice levels to the new environment must be identified so that special provisions can be made in their location and the treatment of their spaces.

Sound spreads out in all directions, not just forward from the source. Other surfaces besides panels contribute to noise or acoustical control. One of the most important transmission paths in the office is the ceiling system. Lighting fixtures, for example, that replace the absorptive ceiling tile seriously add to acoustical problems. Try to locate such items to avoid reflecting sound between work stations. With light fixtures, replace flat lens with parabolic or egg crate diffusers. Cover fixed walls with an absorptive material or panels attached to the walls. Work stations near walls should have panels tight against the walls. If possible, cover the wall surface at least from the floor to 6 feet above floor with acoustical materials. Windows are commonly a serious contributor to noise unless they are covered in fabric drapes and the drapes kept closed—an unlikely occurrence. Try to use window walls as traffic aisle walls

Deafening	Thunder	dBA of 140
Very loud	Loud street noise	dBA of 100
Loud	Noisy office	dBA of 60
Moderate	Average office	dBA of 50
Faint	Quiet conversation	dBA of 20
Very faint	Normal breathing	dBA of 10

Figure 2–21 Table of decibel ratings. (From Harris et al. Planning and Designing the Office Environment, 2nd ed. Copyright © 1991. Reprinted by permission of John Wiley & Sons, Inc.)

[6] Harris et al., 1991, p. 49.

[7] Harris et al., 1991, p. 50.

rather than as part of the workstations. And floors should be carpeted to absorb sound. Specify carpets that provide an NRC of about .40.

The control of the listener is achieved by providing background noise through masking out undesirable signals. Masking does not eliminate or reduce noise, it increases the sound level in the space. It should be used when the existing background level is too quiet so to mask annoying sounds or to cover up speech sounds that should not be overheard. The quality of the sound is somewhat like a whispering hiss—like wind in trees.

Masking can be done by using: (1) a fixed volume ventilation system, (2) a music system that plays nondistracting music, or (3) an electronic noise generating system.[8] Masking systems should be planned with the aid of an acoustician.

Good acoustical design cannot be achieved if only one factor or one surface is treated. Sound source, path, and receiver must all be considered.

Even though open office products are furniture, the plans for projects using these products may have to meet various building, life safety, and ADA code requirements. First, the products themselves should meet minimum code standards. Although this may not be covered under a building or fire code, most products meet standards on a voluntary basis. This is insured by the manufacturers through their research and design of the panel systems and component pieces. All vertical surfaces, regardless of finish, meet Class A fire safety standards when specified with the standard vertical surface fabrics or materials. Fabric covered component pieces should also be Class A. Other components, generally manufactured of metal, will by their nature meet fire safety standards. Care must be taken by designers when they specify customer's own material (COM) fabrics for any panel or component item. COM fabrics must be selected that are considered class A or the fabric must be treated to conform to this standard. To neglect to do this will leave the interior designer liable for bringing the noncompliant materials up to code.

Building codes affect the design of open office projects primarily due to the height restrictions that define corridors. Recall that any circulation path defined by full-height walls or by partitions over 69 inches high are considered to be corridors. This will necessitate the corridor to be a minimum of 44 inches wide in these locations. For the most part, circulation paths within systems projects can vary from 24 inches to wider than 44 inches, depending on the use of the circulation path. It is important for the designer to know the local code requirements that will dictate the widths of all circulation paths and corridors. Additional code factors concerning circulation space were discussed in the section on space allocation earlier in this chapter.

Building codes will also determine how many exits are required from the office space and their locations. As in all cases, this is determined by the number of occupants and the type of facility within which the office area is located. For example, there may be different requirements for a medical records area in a hospital than for a real estate office in a strip shopping center. In conjunction with the number of exits would be the location of any required fire walls. Systems projects are often installed on a whole floor of an office building utilizing many thousands of square feet of floor space. In some jurisdictions it may be necessary for the designer to include full-height partitions as fire walls to subdivide very large systems projects in order to compartmentalize the space in case of fire.

Projects that fall under the ADA as a public building or that must meet the ADA due to employee considerations are becoming the norm, not the exception. Designers must be careful to provide circulation paths that are a minimum of 44 inches wide, to provide turnaround areas at intersections of paths, and to design entrances into stations that are a minimum of 36 inches wide. Sensitivity to other issues, such as employee workstations designed to accommodate the individual's disability, specification of carpet height, and reception counters that accommodate visitors in wheelchairs are also important.

The examples discussed above are the key code issues for designing projects using systems furniture products. Other challenges concerning proper design of electrical and communication service to the stations have been discussed earlier in the chapter. Local jurisdictions

---

[8]Sometimes called "white noise."

may also have specific standards for dealing with projects designed using open office products rather than conventional partitions and conventional furniture. As always, it is the designer's responsibility to know and apply those standards to his or her project for the jurisdiction in which the project resides.

Summary

Open office products have given the interior designer and architect incredible flexibility in the design of functional office spaces for those clients who find the product suitable to their needs. Whether the project is to design a few stations for a real estate or insurance office, provide an office with a small footprint in a retail store or restaurant, or set up thousands of workstations for a major employer, systems projects challenge the designer to design differently from a conventional office project.

Systems planning goes beyond determining whether the desk faces the door or the window. Rather, the designer must determine if the station should be enclosed, providing a measure of privacy, or open to allow greater team interaction. The designer must also determine what assortment of component parts are needed to furnish each station to meet the functional needs of the various jobs within the project. Options in sizes, heights, and numbers of specific items challenge the designer to learn job requirements beyond the simple "desk and credenza" specification. These projects also challenge the designer in the specification and interface of electrical and communication equipment. The proper kind and location of panels and accessory equipment to accommodate appliances is needed in all systems projects.

This chapter has presented the reader with an overview of the open office concept and generic planning challenges. Information has been provided to inform the student and professional about the development of the planning concept and products used in this type of project as well as some key points that are used to determine if systems projects are appropriate for the client. Chapter material has focused on the fully component system products and how to plan with that product as well as how to integrate the building mechanical system into the product. The reader, however, is encouraged to obtain planning and specification guideline information from a specific product manufacturer before becoming involved in any systems project. Up-to-date lists of the manufacturers of systems products are printed in the buyers guide issues of each of the trade magazines.

References

The authors have been provided dozens of articles, brochures, and catalog materials by Haworth, Inc., Herman Miller, Inc., and Steelcase Inc., which have been invaluable to the preparation of this chapter. It is impractical to list all of those materials. Only items that were quoted or might be of specific interest to the reader have been listed in this reference section.

The ADA and the Workplace. Date unknown. Grand Rapids, MI: Haworth Inc.

ASID. Date unknown. *Sound Solutions: Increasing Office Productivity Through Integrated Acoustic Planing and Noise Reduction Strategies.* Washington, DC: American Society of Interior Designers.

Becker, Franklin D. 1981. *Workspace: Creating Environments in Organizations.* New York: Praeger Scientific.

Brandt, Peter B. 1992. *Office Design.* New York: Watson-Guptill.

Brill, Michael and the Buffalo Organization for Social and Technological Innovation (BOSTI). 1984, 1985. *Using Office Design to Increase Productivity,* 2 vols. Buffalo: Workplace Design and Productivity.

Complying with Electrical Standards. Date unknown. Grand Rapids, MI: Haworth, Inc.

Designing with Haworth. 1986. Grand Rapids, MI: Haworth, Inc.

Edwards, Sandra and the editors of *Industrial Design Magazine.* 1986. *Office Systems.* Locust Valley, NY: PBC International.

Gissen, Jay. 1982. "Furnishing the Office of the Future." *Forbes.* November 8. P. 78.

Harris, David A., Byron Engen and William Fitch. 1991. *Planning and Designing the Office Environment,* 2nd. ed. New York: Van Nostrand Reinhold.

Herman Miller, Inc. 1996. News Release. "Herman Miller Is Built on its People, Values, Research, and Designs." December 15.

Keeping Your Options Open. Date unknown. Grand Rapids, MI: Herman Miller, Inc.

Klein, Judy Graf. 1982. *The Office Book.* New York: Facts on File.

Maassen, Lois. 1989. "The State of the Office: 1990." *Herman Miller Magazine.* Grand Rapids, MI: Herman Miller, Inc.

Marberry, Sara O. 1994. *Color in the Office.* New York: Van Nostrand Reinhold.

Pile, John. 1976. *Interiors Third Book of Offices.* New York: Watson-Guptill.

———. 1977. "The Open Office: Does it Work?" *Progressive Architecture,* June.

———. 1978. *Open Office Planning.* New York: Watson-Guptill.

———. 1984. *Open Office Space.* New York: Facts on File.

Propst, Robert. 1968. *The Office: A Facility Based on Change.* Grand Rapids, MI: Herman Miller, Inc.

Pulgram, William L. and Richard E. Stonis. 1984. *Designing the Automated Office.* New York: Watson-Guptill.

Ramsey and Sleeper. 1988. *Architectural Graphic Standards,* 8th ed. New York: Wiley.

Rappoport, James E., Robert F. Cushman, and Karen Daroff. 1992. *Office Planning and Design Desk Reference.* New York: Wiley.

Rayfield, Julie K. 1994. *The Office Interior Design Guide.* New York: Wiley.

Raymond, Santa and Roger Cunliffe. 1997. *Tomorrow's Office.* London: E & FN SPON.

Steelcase. The First 75 Years. 1987. Grand Rapids, MI: Steelcase, Inc.

Steiner, Sheldon. 1991. "Power to the People." *Contract.* June. Pp. 83–84.

Shoshkes, Lila. 1976. *Space Planning: Designing the Office Environment.* New York: Architectural Record.

Thiele, Jennifer. 1993. "Go Team Go!" *Contract Design.* March. P. 29 ff.

Voss, Judy. 1996. "White Paper on the Recent History of The Open Office." February 26. Holland, MI: Haworth, Inc.

Wiring and Cabling: Understanding the Office Environment. 1986. Grand Rapids, MI: Steelcase, Inc.

Wolf, Michael. 1992. "Furniture: A New Breed of 'Knowledge Worker' Requires Office Environments of the Future." *I.D. Magazine.* October. P. 40 ff.

Additional references related to material in this chapter are listed in Appendix A.

Chapter 3

The New Office Environment

Downsizing. Delayering. Right-sizing. Reengineering. These terms and others have shaken the organizational boots of large and small businesses alike during the late 1980s and into the 1990s. For many companies today, the effects of what these terms mean has resulted in a change in how businesses are organized and how office work is accomplished. The changes in business organization and changes in the work process and organization have also lead to new definitions of the office environment. Of course, the organizational structure and design concepts discussed in Chapter 1 still exist, but are disappearing—especially in the largest businesses.

Reorganization, downsizing, and the like are not the only factors that have influenced the office environment. Technological advances have transformed how and where work is executed. Just as few business owners, a mere 25 years ago, foresaw the rapid progression of desktop computers into virtually every job function and business type, so too few foresaw telecommuting, which allows employees to work virtually anywhere.

The interior designer of the new office environment must be familiar with the changes in how work is being done and what will be expected from employees. Clients demand interior designers have an understanding of the new work methods and organizational structures. Those who do not have little chance of working successfully with many businesses in the future. At the same time, the new office environment requires planning and specification with product solutions and planning ideas that respond to these new initiatives. Flexible furniture products, innovative space planning, designs that accommodate a diverse work force, and responsive mechanical interface, are all part of the changing work environment.

This chapter provides a brief overview of the forces bringing change to the world of office work. It also discusses the most prevalent design and planning solutions developed by designers and suppliers to meet the challenges of the new office environment. The chapter concludes with an in-depth discussion of the home office environment, one of the fastest growing office environments and design challenges.

The Changing World of Work

Many businesses, from the largest corporations to the smallest firms, have redefined how work is accomplished and how the environment provided to accommodate that work is organized.

Downsizing, reengineering, globalization of the market place, and advances in technology are a few terms associated with these changes. For the student and design professional faced with the challenge to creatively solve the design problems of the new office environment, it is vital to understand this new work structure. Indeed, students will find themselves working in design firms that embrace many of these concepts. This section briefly discusses how the structure of work has and is expected to continue to change into the next millennium.

IBM, Ernst & Young, General Electric, AT&T, and Anderson Consulting have been just some of the leaders in changing the way office work is accomplished. Thousands of other companies are also changing the world of work and the work environment for their employees. Most corporate officers will say that they have reorganized their company to respond to changing market needs and customer demands, and, of course, that is true. However, corporations also reorganized in order to survive the economic problems of the 1980s and early 1990s. One of the best known words associated with the changing structure of work is *downsizing*. Downsizing means reducing the number of a business's employees with the goal of being both more responsive to customer demands and more cost-effective. Downsizing has resulted in massive reorganization in many firms, leading to the elimination of jobs for thousands of employees—especially those in middle management positions.

Another term associated with the changing structure of work is *reengineering*. According to Hammer and Champy, reengineering is "the fundamental rethinking and radical redesign of business processes to achieve dramatic improvement in critical, contemporary measures of performance, such as cost, quality, service, and speed."[1] All processes and procedures change in the business due to reengineering, not the least of these is the way work is done.

Both these changes have affected the basic reporting structure of many businesses. Instead of the pyramidal structure represented by the traditional organizational chart, companies today have a flatter structure with more interdisciplinary work groups functioning as teams to achieve business goals. Sometimes called *delayering*, this change in structure means there are fewer management and supervisory layers, resulting in the enlargement of the responsibilities of the worker. This added responsibility, or empowerment,[2] makes many employees feel they are more a part of the business. "Joining a Workplace 2000 company will be more than contracting for a 'fair day's work.' Rather, it will be more like joining a 'family' or 'team' with all of the consequent benefits, responsibilities, and obligations."[3]

Advances in technology have made it easier for many kinds of work to be done faster and more accurately, and, as the reader well knows, to be done from almost anywhere. The computer allows workers to communicate with each other and have access to information that hitherto had been the privilege of upper level mangers. This access allows empowerment to occur at the "local level," giving the employees access to information to make decisions. How to use the information technology makes available is one of the greatest challenges in the new workplace. In addition, telecommuting allows an individual to work away from the main office, at home, on the road, or at a satellite office. This takes appropriate workers to the customer, solving problems, taking orders, and generally satisfying the customer quickly.

Technology also changes how companies work in the global arena. Companies that never worked with foreign markets now have the opportunity to provide goods and services to any other country. Entrepreneurs working for themselves are also able to secure customers in foreign markets. Globalization brings diversity as American workers must learn to deal with the cultural subtleties of foreign countries, whether or not they physically travel abroad.

The restructuring of businesses also changes how work is done. In a traditional company, an end product is broken down into parts; each part is the responsibility of an individual or a

---

[1] Hammer and Champy, 1993, p. 32.

[2] *Empowerment* means that the employee is allowed to make certain decisions him- or herself, rather than going through many layers of managers and perhaps waiting days for decisions to be made.

[3] From *WORKPLACE 2000* by Joseph H. Boyett and Henry P. Conn. Copyright ©1991 by Joseph H. Boyett and Henry P. Conn. Used by permission of Dutton Signet, a division of Penguin Books USA Inc., p. 42.

small group who, after accomplishing some goal will pass the part down to the next individual or group, and so on, like an assembly line. In the new world of work, an individual or team is responsible for all the parts of the project from beginning to end.

Teaming has become a key to the future of work. Teams today are flexible creatures, consisting of two or three people one day and maybe dozens the next, depending on the scope and problem facing the team. Teams may work together in the morning and break into individual assignments in the afternoon, only to come together again the next day. Some individuals are members of more than one team at a time. The team will not function effectively if free-flowing interaction between the team members does not exist.

One of the reasons for the switch to teaming is the need for businesses to develop new products faster and hit the market with the new product ahead of its competition. Problems need to be solved more quickly. A client is no longer willing to wait three weeks, three months, or years for an answer. Even in interior design and architecture, clients need responses now, and the firm that can deliver that response in a hurry usually gets the project.

A paper published by Herman Miller, Inc. describes three kinds of teams. *Linear teams*—those performing repetitive tasks—are teams where each person performs a part of the task needed to complete the total job. The work is passed from one person to another in the team until the task is complete. A second kind of work team is called a *parallel team*. These team members "are assembled for a project that requires specialized skills from each member. Team members often come from different departments, and the project usually isn't their only job."[4] A team assembled to do a design project would be an example of this kind of team. This team could stay together after the project is done, but since they are also working on other projects, they could move their main responsibility to some other project when any one project is completed. A third kind of team is a brainstorming or *circular team*. In this case, a team is organized to do very creative and innovative work. Members could come and go through the course of the project and the team disbands when the project is completed.[5]

In one way or another, it is predicted that all workers will have to be innovators and entrepreneurs, even if they work for someone else. The day of the steady job with gradual, promotions and salary increases, the day when an employee would stay with a company for 40 years, then retire, is gone, say many futurists and business management philosophers. According to Boyett and Conn, "the average American will most likely work in ten or more different types of jobs and at least five different companies before he or she retires."[6] Flexibility and creativity will be the key issues for the success of employees. Rewards will come for those characteristics joined with employee performance and contributions. Thus the employee with a breadth of knowledge will be of more value to many businesses than the narrow specialist.

Where work is done is also a major change. Some jobs in the new office require space and planning for team association and work to occur. Flexible work spaces must be able to accommodate a team set up to handle a project that could last from a few days to over a year. Then the space must be able to be reconfigured for a new team and a new project. Other jobs are handled by individuals via telecommuting. The telecommuter is on the road visiting clients rather than being in the office. Perhaps he or she has been provided a computer at home to complete job responsibilities without leaving home. Telecommuting has become popular with many businesses and employees as expanding technology by use of wireless communication provides the medium for this dramatic change in how many individuals do their jobs.

The virtual office takes telecommuting one step farther. The concept of a *virtual office* is that the worker has everything he or she needs to work in a briefcase or car—cell phone, modem, portable laptop computer, fax, and printer. Thus the virtual office can be anywhere:

---

[4] Herman Miller, Inc. (616-654-5680), 1996a, p. 2.

[5] Herman Miller, Inc., 1996a, p. 2.

[6] From *WORKPLACE 2000* by Joseph H. Boyett and Henry P. Conn. Copyright ©1991 by Joseph H. Boyett and Henry P. Conn. Used by permission of Dutton Signet, a division of Penguin Books USA Inc., p. 3.

a car, airport terminal, restaurant, the customer's location, home—wherever the worker sits down to work.

Changes in how work is accomplished and in the work environment have not only affected the lower level employees. With the delayering of corporations, the amenities that were associated with upper level management jobs have disappeared. The coveted corner office with high-end furniture and accessories has been replaced in many businesses with smaller offices or workstations. The executive dining room and big offices have become old-fashioned in the new workplace. Of course, for these new methods and theories to work in reality, the management of the business must be committed to making the necessary changes. They must be committed to giving the authority to the employees to follow through, make the system within the company support these work groups, and never forget to include the employees in the design of the system and the environment.

In addition to changing the office environment back at the main office, there is a growing demand for the home office. The dramatic explosion in technology has made working at home possible at inexpensive costs. Through careful planning and analysis, a company will determine that certain kinds of jobs can be accomplished from home. Employees given this option are often furnished with the appropriate office equipment while the employee provides the space in the home. Of course, many thousands of entrepreneurs start businesses from their home, setting up an office space in a spare bedroom or possibly in a remodeled garage.

And so what does all this mean? "Work anywhere, anytime is the new paradigm. Your car, your home, your office, even your client's office. Work alone, coupled, teamed. Work in real space or in cyberspace."[7] All these changes in work philosophy and structure have created the need for alternative work environments. Many of these are discussed in the remainder of this chapter.

Alternative Office Environments

As a solution to accommodating the new work strategies, private offices—except for the very highest levels of a corporation—are disappearing as flexible open workstations increasingly become the norm. Managers, and even vice presidents, are being located closer to their employee groups rather than in executive areas as described in Chapter 1. The new workplace has either eliminated or drastically reduced the number of individuals in the traditional private office.

Alternative officing has come to be "a collective term used to describe different strategies which have changed the design of the workplace and how people work."[8] According to a Haworth, Inc. and International Facility Management Association study in 1995, by the year 2000, 94% of office workers are expected to participate in some version of alternative officing.[9]

With the changed office environment becoming more fluid than its traditional predecessor, it is important for the designer to carefully discover during programming the variety of space requirements the business will need. The designer must place more emphasis on understanding the corporate organization and culture as well as furniture needs. Changes in work philosophy and organization also mean that the space and equipment standards for many of today's jobs are too generous by these new requirements. The efficiently designed workstations that have become common today do not have a large amount of filing or storage, and provide virtually no space for visitors. These auxiliary office functions are provided for in common areas. The availability of electronic storage reduces the amount of filing, and electronic reference storage further reduces space needs in any work area. Flexibility in the layout and in the products selected to create the actual work area is very important.

---

[7] *Business Week*, 1996, p. 109.

[8] Haworth, Inc. and IFMA, 1995a, p. 3.

[9] Haworth, Inc. and IFMA, 1995a, p. 7.

Team areas must be designed to accommodate the many different types of work styles that may occur. Some designers refer to one style of team areas as *caves and commons*. In this layout, the "caves" are individual work areas surrounding the "commons," where team members can come together to work on the problem or discuss issues. It is most often associated with group or shared work spaces (Figure 3-1). A team area will often require individual workstations along with meeting spaces. In some cases, these personal work areas need to be very private, yet remain flexible for future change (Figure 3-2). In others, semiprivate or even open workstations, similar to standardized open office systems designs, function perfectly.

Meeting or conference spaces, whether the traditional conference rooms discussed in Chapter 1 or informal gathering places, are also needed (Figure 3-3). Some teams need to retain a conference or work area for the duration of the project. Teams may need to spread out materials and documents without having to put them away each day, secure in the knowledge that the materials will not be disturbed overnight. Depending on the needs of the group, the conference space could be permanently assigned to the project, or organized like free-address individual stations that can be reserved for a period of time. Conference areas also need to have arrangements for teleconferencing or video conferencing. Since a member of the group may be out of town, or even working for a different branch of the firm, teleconferencing and video conferencing facilities need to be designed and planned into many companies' facilities today.

A popular method of changing the office environment for individuals is the use of unassigned offices. An *unassigned office* is an open systems station of some kind or an enclosed office that is not designated for one individual worker. It can be used by any number of people on any given day. These unassigned offices are reserved through a *reservation desk*. In this situation, a salesperson who primarily works out of the office can reserve a station when he or she must return to the main office for a few hours or a few days. In other companies, the salesperson might simply show up at the main office and check with a receptionist or seek out an unassigned work area. Other terms for these nonterritorial unassigned office spaces are: hoteling, hot desking, free-address offices, and just-in-time offices; many other terms have been developed by manufacturers and designers.

Hoteling is a system of unassigned work spaces that are available to workers by reservation—like a hotel. It was first used by Ernst & Young in Chicago. A support person, sometimes called

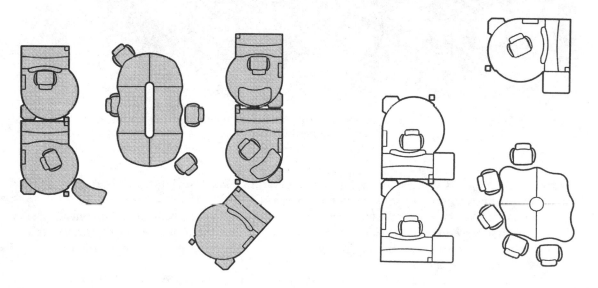

Five-member team space   Three-member team space

Figure 3–1 Three and five member team spaces with individual workstations flanking the commons. (Copyright Steelcase, Inc., used with permission.)

Figure 3–2 Personal work space that provides privacy while still remaining flexible for future adaptations. (Copyright Steelcase, Inc., used with permission.)

a *concierge,* is assigned the task of taking the reservations and insuring that the spaces are equipped properly when the employee "guest" arrives.

Free-address is another system of unassigned work spaces that are available to anyone on a first-come, first served basis. No reservations are needed and the individual using the space could be from another department. For example, an accounting person could use a free-address station in the sales area.

A *hot desk* is the same as the free-address station. It gets its name from the reality that the desk may be "hot" from the previous user.

Landing sites are unassigned workstations that cannot be reserved. Like a hot desk, the employee "lands" in an unoccupied work area when he or she arrives at the main or satellite office building.

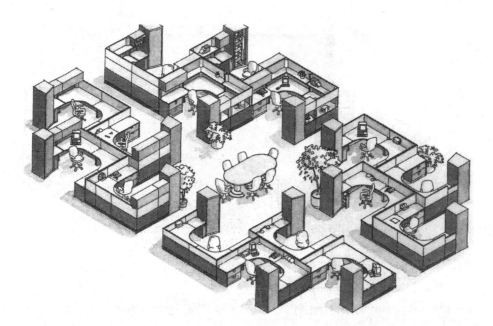

Figure 3–3 Small conference area for use by the surrounding work areas. (Copyright Steelcase, Inc., used with permission.)

Just-in-time stations are another type of unassigned work space. These are often very open and flexible work areas that individuals and even groups can congregate in by bringing their mobile files and laptop computers to the station to work for a period of time. Movable screens and easily assembled components are available to make the just-in-time work area functional for the individual or group members. Mobile files are commonly used to store and transport personal items and personal files from a central storage area to any of the unassigned work areas.

Shared assigned work areas are those stations that are shared by one or more individuals. It might be a secretarial station where two or more workers working part-time use the same work space. The workers develop their own work schedule with the consent of the manager.

Guesting is an assigned or unassigned work area provided to a visiting worker from another company. Many office furnishings dealers, for example, provide a guest office space that can be used by manufacturer's representatives while they are in the dealership.

Satellite offices are work centers established away from the main office but convenient to the territory of the outside workers. These are generally not branch offices with complete full-time staff and assigned workstations. There are some assigned workers, but much of the facility is provided for those transient workers, like salespeople, who may be located too far from the main office for convenient travel. Some entrepreneurs have even set up satellite offices where home-based entrepreneurs can rent a conference room for presentations to clients.

Furniture for these new office environments must be flexible and easily accommodate office technology. Whether specifying casework in an executive area or systems in most other areas, the designer needs to choose furniture items that can accommodate both computer usage and manual paperwork. In executive areas, U-shaped configurations rather than the standard desk and credenza provide plenty of surface space for equipment and regular paperwork as well as a conference surface (Figure 3-4). A minimum of an L-shaped work area for computers with a table desk is a common specification in today's corporate executive offices. U-shaped and L-shaped work areas are also the norm in many staff areas, whether the work station is assigned or unassigned (Figure 3-5). Office seating must be fully adjustable to accommodate the different work responsibilities and styles of individuals and teams. The types of chairs shown in Figure 1–16 work well in the alternative office as well.

Furniture manufacturers have responded to these new officing ideas with new products. Steelcase's "Harbors," Haworth's "Crossings," and Herman Miller's "Arrio" panel systems are

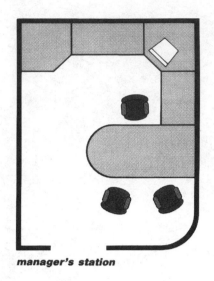

manager's station

Figure 3–4 A U-shaped configuration provides extended surfaces for equipment and paperwork, as well as a conference area. (Plan courtesy of Panel Concepts, Inc.)

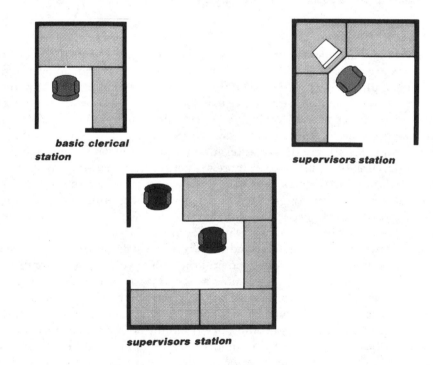

basic clerical
station

supervisors station

supervisors station

Figure 3–5 L-shaped and U-shaped workstations for assigned and/or unassigned areas. (Plan courtesy of Panel Concepts, Inc.)

just a few of the new products available to designers and end users to accommodate furniture needs in the changing work environment.

Designers point out that the employees who will be affected by unassigned office spaces should be involved in the planning process. Too often it seems that the reduced work area and the elimination of a specific "home" for many of these workers leads to a deterioration in the success of their work. The most annoying problem for these workers is the lack of sufficient space when too many of these outside employees return to the home office at any one time. Workers also complain about the lack of the privacy they feel they need to conduct business with their customers. Each of these stations or offices should be identical, even down to where the office supplies are stored, in order to gain employee acceptance.

Although it is up to a business's managers to decide whether to use one of the nontraditional office concepts discussed in this chapter, involving the employees in the programming and design phases encourages acceptance. For a client that has not used one of these methods before, pilot programs, where only a portion of the office facility is converted to the new officing concepts, may make the conversion more acceptable to employees.

Today's office workers are doing their jobs in ways that rarely exist in the traditional office environment. The reengineering of corporations and work strategies has created new ways for employees to work, requiring changes in the office environment. Technology and mobility have also moved many office workers out of the main office's four walls and into the outside world or into their homes. The remainder of this chapter discusses many of the issues involved in designing an office in the home environment.

Home Offices

One of the ways of meeting the challenges of changing office environments is through the movement of individuals from the central office setting to the home office. It is estimated that over 40 million people work from home, whether for themselves as entrepreneurs, for their employers, or on their own part-time after hours. Twenty-five years ago, only seven million people worked from home.[10] LINK Resources Corporation, a New York research firm, predicted in 1996 that by 1998 nearly 60 million Americans would be working from their homes.[11] Although retailers have understood and met the needs of the home office market for many years, interior designers have largely ignored this market until recently.

Because of the tremendous growth in the home office market, the authors felt it was necessary to explore the fundamental design issues inherent in locating office work in the home environment. The focus of this section is on the true home business office, not a space used to pay bills. This section will not differentiate space or equipment needs for home offices of an entrepreneur versus those of employees working at home.

Planning the home office should be done with the same programming skills and methods as any other office. The designer must work with the client to understand the nature of the home business, the type of equipment that will be used, reference materials or supplies that will be needed, amount of filing, and so on. In the design of an home office, the interior designer must also clearly understand the client's "family connection." By this is meant the extent of the client's interaction with family issues during the work day and in the vicinity of the home office. This is necessary in order for the designer to recommend if a space in the family room with the children nearby will be appropriate, if a spare bedroom will be utilized, or even if an addition to the house is necessary for separating work time from family time.

Many entrepreneurs operate their businesses from home to keep costs down by eliminating the expense of a remote office space. The selection of inexpensive, poor quality furniture solutions is also common by home office clients for the same reason. Although a door laid over two small file cabinets is an inexpensive solution to the need for a desk, it creates a safety hazard not commonly considered by the budding entrepreneur. In this case, the "desktop" is not fixed to the file cabinets and the top can be easily knocked off. Proper desks, adjustable chairs, properly designed filing and storage solutions, lighting to meet office work, and electrical/cabling needs are all important parts of office design for the home environment. Selection of appropriate office furniture will also eliminate ergonomic problems caused by utilizing unsuitable furniture.

---

[10] Hastings and Waller, 1996, p. 92.

[11] *Seabrook Journal*, 1996, p. 8.

The *location* of the office within the home is an important issue. Depending on the client's needs for the home office, it can be located in a part of the master bedroom, a separate bedroom, part of the guest room or family room, even the dining room or kitchen. In many cases, the owners are able to convert a garage, basement, or sunroom/porch into the office or in some cases, build an addition to the house. In some developments, builders are making an office room with a separate entrance door a option on some of their models.

Whenever possible, it is best to locate the office in a separate room not used for other purposes. This will provide needed privacy and the ability to separate "work" from "home and family" responsibilities. When the office has to be located as part of another space like the family room, the designer should make the office space seem different from the family space (Figure 3-6). Visual cues, like the bookshelves of reference materials the client will need, or certificates that relate to the business, help to differentiate the space. It is also necessary to locate and design this space to provide as much privacy as possible—especially for those easily distracted. An entrepreneur locating an office space in the family room near the television or play area will have little privacy to accomplish his or her business tasks. Freestanding divider panels or tall bookcases that create a "room" within a room can help in this case.

If it is necessary to locate the home office in a guest room, the client should realize that the access to the office part of the guest room will be limited when the family has guests—naturally. If guests are frequent, then the home office worker may not have needed access to the desk area.

The designer and client should be sure that the layout of the desk and other furniture items is planned as would be appropriate in a corporate office. Obviously, where the office is located in the home has a great deal to do with the actual layout of the space, regardless of the type of work performed. Programming discussions will determine what size desk is needed, what equipment needs to be accommodated, whether conference space is needed, and if any other tabletop surfaces are called for (Figure 3-7). Easy access to reference materials and files is also very important in the home office. Sufficient space must be allowed so that the desk chair does not hit other pieces of furniture or make it difficult to get around the desk (Figure 3-8). These comments are, of course, just common office planning sense, but many clients do not think about such issues.

To insure safety and comfortable working conditions, appropriate *furniture* should be selected for the home office. The designer and client need to analyze what kind of work is being done at the home office and what types of office equipment are being used. Since many home-based businesses start on a shoestring, the owner has a hard time seeing the necessity of purchasing quality furniture items when he or she can go to a superstore and buy budget priced

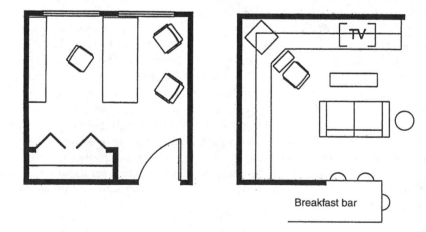

Figure 3–6 On the left, a conventional office space in a designated room in a residence, and on the right, a small family room that incorporates both family entertainment and office space. (Plans courtesy of Cody D. Beal.)

Figure 3–7 Photo of work space in a designer's office located in his residence. (Photograph courtesy of Craig A. Roeder, Designer.)

items. However, designers need to clarify to the client the advantages of buying quality for the long run, rather than looking at short-term budget pricing. As was pointed out above, using inexpensive or inappropriate furniture for the home office can lead to safety and ergonomic problems for the user.

Standard commercial office furniture can be used, but it is often difficult for the worker to move a heavy 36 by 72 inch desk down the narrower halls and through door openings found in most homes. Many of the commercial office and systems furniture manufacturers have begun to offer products designed for the home office. Steelcase, for example, created a subsidiary company called Turnstone to address the home office furniture market. Davis Furniture, Geiger, Brickel, Haworth, Herman Miller, and many others all have modified and designed products specifically for the home office. In furniture for the home office, the axiom "you get what you pay for" is certainly true.

Furniture should be selected to encourage good working posture for the job. Desk heights that comfortably accommodate both computer keyboards and standard paperwork are important.

Figure 1–18 shows the proper configuration of a computer workstation. When using a computer, the desktop should be such that the location of the keyboard keeps the arms parallel to the floor with the wrists straight. Standard desk heights of 29 to 30 inches are generally too high if the keyboard of a computer is placed on the desktop. In order to have the arms parallel to the floor, the keyboard should be 25 to 27 inches above the floor.

Adjustable chairs that provide proper seated posture for the long hours are just as important in the home office as they are in the standard office. One of the many ergonomically designed chairs shown in Chapter 1 will be the best option, rather than the use of an extra dining room chair or a stool. At the very least, the desk chair should be fully adjustable.

Filing and storage is another place where many home-based office owners try to skimp on cost. It could be argued that the home office worker will actually use files and storage units

Figure 3–8 Design elements create an interesting and functional space in this home office. (Photograph courtesy of Craig A. Roeder, Designer.)

to a greater degree than someone working in an office in a corporate setting. The designer should be specifying at least mid-price level filing and bookcases to give the worker a piece of furniture that will last until he or she is ready to move to a freestanding office site.

Color and finishes can help make the room or space within a room seem different. The opportunity of have the office "your way" instead of being stuck with the muted colors of corporate offices is very appealing to many home office workers. Residential designers know that clients choose color schemes and surface materials for their home that are less frequently, if ever, used in office design. The home office does not have to be as dull as some corporate offices, but care should be taken in the use of bold colors and patterns in these smaller spaces. The designer needs to help the home office owner choose colors and materials that will enhance the office space, but not create uncomfortable surroundings. This is especially true if the office is in a back bedroom, traditionally a small space. Bright splashes of color should be provided in art work rather than in strong wall colors, which can cause eye fatigue.

Lighting is very important in the home office. Most homes today do not have built-in lighting fixtures provided in bedrooms or even family rooms. The building codes require either a ceiling fixture or one outlet for a table or floor fixture that can be turned on and off with a switch by the door. This is commonly located so as to be convenient when the room is used as a bedroom, but that site may not be convenient for an office. The designer should provide a low, even amount of ambient light with task lights at the desk or work surface. This will also help reduce eye fatigue from glare on the screen for those home office workers utilizing computers.

Glare from windows can also be significant problem when most of the office work is done on computers. Placing the side of the monitor toward the window will eliminate this form of glare in most situations. Do not plan the office with the computer facing toward the window either. Clients may like the chance to look outside, but the strong outside light will produce eye fatigue. Following the guidelines in Chapter 1 will also aid the designer in creating an effective home office for clients.

Mechanical interface beyond lighting is another issue that should be considered. Except for recently built homes that have been specifically design to accommodate computers and extra telephone lines, bedrooms or family room electrical service is likely to be linked to receptacles in other rooms. Power surges can occur that can damage sensitive computer equipment, fax machines, and other office electronic equipment. Although a surge protector is a must, whenever possible, a dedicated circuit for the computer provides even greater safety. Copy machines and printers use enough amps to create small surges or fluctuations in home offices, especially if used at the same time as the computer. Even turning on a task light could overload the circuit and damage the computer. Suggest to the home owner that an electrician check the circuit to the space or room to be used and have the electrician add one or more dedicated circuits to that space. Refer to Figure 2–19 for electrical usage of electronic appliances to help with planning.

A second or even third phone line to accommodate business calls and dedicated fax lines is also commonly needed for the home office. This can be easily accomplished by the local phone company and is beginning to be commonly planned in newer homes as a standard construction item.

Should the home owner and designer determine that remodeling the garage or adding an attached or freestanding home office is in order, the designer will need to carefully design the spaces with building *codes* in mind. Some cities and homeowner's associations will not allow for the conversation of a garage to livable space. And some clients may not have sufficient space on the property to allow for the building of a new addition. A designer engaged to do this kind of project must investigate the zoning restrictions for these situations first, then proceed with the actual design work. Building codes for conversions and additions used as office spaces generally do not vary from those applied to residential construction, but that may not be true in all cases and all jurisdictions.

Working from home is not for everyone. It is lonely with no coworkers around. It is easy to get distracted by children, nonbusiness-related interruptions, and household chores. Clients may want to come to the "office" and one's home may not be designed to provide the image the businessperson is trying to project. Creating an appropriate home office is not the key issue in whether the entrepreneur or other office worker will be successful. However, the appropriate atmosphere will help.

Summary

Where once it was enough for a commercial designer to understand how to plan and design office spaces, the interior designer must now add an in-depth understanding of the new concepts in business operations. Downsizing, reengineering of work, technology, and many other forces have changed the structure of businesses, the way work is accomplished, and the environment of the office. It is expected that these forces and perhaps others will continue to influence the work environment, and thus the work of the commercial interior designer specializing in office design.

Technology will likely have one of the strongest influences on the world of office work. As technology continues to advance, the impact of these changes in the office of the future is in some ways unknown. Will more people now working in offices be working at home or in virtual offices? Probably. Will technology take over even more job functions? Probably. The design industry must remain on top of the technological changes and designers must learn more about their customer's business and the methods of business in order to react positively to their needs.

This chapter has briefly discussed the way office work is changing in terms of methodology and structure. It has discussed several current ways to create useful work spaces to accommodate these new work methods. The chapter concluded with a discussion of the home office environment, one of the fastest growing segments of the office design market.

References

There are numerous articles, books, and manufacturer's publications continually being published on the topics within this chapter. It is impossible for the authors to provide all those references. Students and professionals should seek additional information from suppliers or through literature and Internet searches at their local library.

Addi, Gretchen. 1996. "The Impact of Technology on the Workplace," a paper presented at the ASID National Conference.

Allie, Paul. 1993. "Creating a Quality Work Environment in the Home Office." *Interiors and Sources.* September/October. Pp. 128 ff.

ASID Report. 1993. "The Home Office: A Design Revolution." November/December.

Becker, Franklin and Fritz Steele. 1995. *Workplace by Design.* San Francisco, CA: Jossey-Bass.

Blake, Peter. 1991, "Something Amiss in Offices." *Interior Design.* May. Pp. 208–209.

Boyett, Joseph H. and Henry P. Conn. 1991. *Workplace 2000: The Revolution Reshaping American Business.* New York: Plume Books (Penguin Group).

Business Week. 1996. "The New Workplace." April 29. Pp. 107–113 ff.

Cornell, Paul and Mark Baloga. 1994. "Work Evolution and the New 'Office'." Grand Rapids, MI: Steelcase, Inc.

Cutler, Lorri. 1993. "Changing the Paradigm: Is it Workplace or Work Environment of the Future?" Zeeland, MI: Herman Miller, Inc.

DeVito, Michael D. 1996. "Blueprint for Office 2000: The Adventure Continues." *Managing Office Technology,* December. Pp. 16 ff.

Gunn, Ronald A. and Marilyn S. Burroughs. 1996. "Work Spaces that Work: Designing High Performance Offices." *The Futurist.* March-April. Pp. 19–24.

Hammer, Michael and James Champy. 1993. *Reengineering the Corporation.* New York: Harper Collins Business.

Hastings, Judith and Tony Waller. 1996. "Stay at Home and Go to Work," *Interiors and Sources.* January/February. P. 92.

Haworth, Inc. and International Facilities Management Association. 1995a. *Alternative Officing Research and Workplace Strategies.* Holland, MI: Haworth, Inc.

———. 1995b. *Work Trends and Alternative Work Environments.* Holland, MI: Haworth, Inc.

Herman Miller, Inc. 1993. "Effectively Managing the Office of the 90s." Zeeland, MI: Herman Miller, Inc.

———. 1994. "Office Environments: The North American Perspective." A research summary. Zeeland, MI: Herman Miller, Inc.

———. 1996a. *Evolutionary Workplaces.* "Office Alternatives: Working On-Site." Zeeland, MI: Herman Miller, Inc.

———. 1996b. "Issues Essentials: Talking to Customers about Change." Zeeland, MI: Herman Miller, Inc.

Kruk, Leonard B. 1996. "Facilities Planning Supports Changing Office Technologies." *Managing Office Technology.* December. Pp. 26–27.

Lundy, James L. 1994. *Teams: Together Each Achieves More Success.* Chicago, IL: Dartnell.

Parikh, Anoop. 1995. *The Book of Home Design.* New York: Harper-Collins.

The Seabrook Journal. 1996. "Designing Around Technology: The Home Office." Fall.

Steelcase, Inc. 1993. "Understanding Work Process: To Help People Work More Effectively." Grand Rapids, MI: Steelcase, Inc.

————. 1994. "Teleworking: Supporting Work Process." Grand Rapids, MI: Steelcase, Inc.

Stewart, Thomas A. 1993. "Welcome to the Revolution." *Fortune.* December 13. Pp. 66 ff.

Sunset Books (Editors). 1995. *Ideas for Great Home Offices.* Menlo Park, CA: Sunset.

Tetlow, Karin. 1996. *The New Office.* New York: PBC International.

Thiele, Jennifer. 1993. "Go Team Go!" *Contract Design.* March. Pp. 29–31.

Vischer, Jacqueline C. 1996. *Workspace Strategies: Environment as a Tool for Work.* New York: Chapman & Hall.

Zimmerman, Neal. 1996. *Home Office Design.* New York: Wiley.

Additional references related to material in this chapter are listed in Appendix A.

Chapter 4

Lodging Facilities

Lodging facilities are businesses that provide temporary housing to people away from their primary residences—the hotels and motels located in nearly every city, town, or area around the world. Lodging facilities are a part of the one of the fastest growing industries today—the hospitality industry. "The word hospitality has ancient roots, dating from the earliest days of Roman civilization. It is derived from the Latin word *hospitare*, meaning 'to receive as a guest.' "[1] The hospitality industry is broken down into three distinct areas: lodging, food, and beverage. Of course, many lodging facilities combine these three areas. This chapter focuses on lodging facilities. Chapter 5 discusses specific issues of food and beverage facilities.

Guests check into lodging facilities for all kinds of reasons. Perhaps it's for a one night stop during a car trip from one part of the country to another, or possibly it's for a few days while one attends a series of business meetings or a conference. It may be a week of well-earned vacation. A guest's reason for checking into a lodging facility will have a great deal of influence on the type of facility chosen. It is important, therefore, that the interior design of the lodging facility be in harmony with the type of facility and with guest expectations. A motel that targets the auto traveler cannot be designed as elaborately as a luxury hotel in a large city. Thus the interior designer must have an appreciation for the business goals of the lodging facility owner or management company.

This chapter begins with a brief discussion of the business of lodging through an overview of responsibility areas and management structure of a generic hotel. The purpose of this discussion is to assist the design student and professional understand the functional concerns of lodging as the designer approaches a project. It is followed by a discussion of the different types of lodging facilities, accompanied by a brief history of the hospitality industry. The chapter continues with discussion of specific criteria that affect the planning and design of lodging facilities. The last section focuses on application of design criteria to the lobby, function areas, and guest rooms.

An Overview of Lodging Facilities

It is important for the designer to have an understanding of the lodging business to better appreciate the operational goals that will affect the interior design of the spaces of the facility.

---

[1]Dittmer and Griffin, 1993, p. 4.

Let us begin with some terminology that affects the operation and design of this type of commercial property.

A *lodging facility*, sometimes called a lodging property or a transient living facility, is a facility that provides sleeping accommodations for individuals away from their permanent home. Larger lodging facilities also provide food and beverage services.

Front of the house refers to those areas where employees have the most contact with guests, such as registration desk, guest rooms, and food and beverage areas.

Back of the house refers to those areas where employees have minimal contact with guests, such as facility offices other than registration desk, laundry, mechanical systems areas, and kitchens.

Guest services are the services provided to enhance the guest's stay at the facility, such as room service, valet, bell service, health clubs, and dining rooms, to name just a few.

Amenities are the little guest room "extras" that are provided to make the guest's stay a bit more convenient or pleasant, such as in-room hair dryers, bath robes, extra telephones, and in-room beverage service, to name a few.

Hotel management company would be a group of individuals or a company that has made an agreement with the hotel owners to operate the hotel facility.

Bay is the amount of space required to house a single standard guest room.

The overall goal of lodging facilities is to provide a comfortable and safe temporary home for travelers. While all guests would suggest that safety at this temporary home is an absolute necessity, the level of comfort expected varies greatly. This leads us to the overall goal of the design of lodging facilities: to provide an atmosphere in congruence with the type of facility and guest target market. The design treatment and detail of the interior specification will vary greatly based on the type of facility and target market. For example, a budget facility utilizes simple design treatments while a luxury hotel may be filled with antiques. The interior designer will be faced with providing an atmosphere and design specification that will appeal to guests and make them feel that this hotel is the kind of place where they wish to spend one or more nights.

An important part of the designer's programming efforts will therefore be to understand what the lodging facility is really selling to the public. Is it simply selling a clean room, a place to hold a convention, or a family vacation place with numerous conveniently located recreational activities? The designer must remember that while the facility is selling a temporary living space to guests, they are also selling its ambience and services. A guest makes a selection as to which lodging facilities he or she will stay at based not so much on the fact of getting a room for the night or nights required—that is a given. The selection is based on price and on an expectation of what that interior environment may look like, as well as on the services and amenities provided.

Responsibility Areas

Lodging facilities, regardless of size, can be divided into a minimum of three distinct responsibility areas: front office, housekeeping, and security. Front office activities are those related to guest check-in and checkout, guest information, and reservations. Check-in and checkout are commonly handled at a registration desk or counter in the lobby. Information activities are handled at the registration desk and, in larger hotels and motels, through a concierge. The concierge provides guest assistance for many guest needs like theater tickets, car rentals, and sightseeing recommendations. Reservations services may be performed by registration desk clerks or by reservation clerks, commonly located away from the registration desk.

The housekeeping department is responsible for the daily care of guest rooms and all other areas of the facility. The daily cleaning and preparing of guest rooms, corridors, lobby and other public spaces of the facility, as well as offices and other service areas, are part of the housekeeping department's responsibility. Guests do not so much see these activities as experience them. Poor housekeeping services cause many guests to try another lodging facility on their next visit. The housekeeping department will also work with interior designers in all issues related to the planning and design of the facility.

The security area is charged with making the lodging facility and its property safe for guests and employees. Security staff attend to guest complaints about noise or suspicious activity, monitor safety equipment such as sprinkler systems and smoke detectors/alarms, and inspect the parking lot or garage to insure safety of guests' automobiles. These and many other activities are provided so that guests, employees, and the property is protected from hazards.

In addition to other services provided by the main responsibility areas, most lodging facilities today provide additional services for guests. Additional front services include taxi services, luggage handling, mail and message service, and opening doors. Additional security services might include in-room safes or safety deposit boxes at the front desk for guest's valuables. Housekeeping might provide the loan of hair dryers, irons and ironing boards, and valet service for laundry and dry cleaning.

Guest services will vary based on the type of facility. For example, hotels that cater to business travelers will have special sections of the hotel that provide fax service, copy machines, even computer areas where guests can use hardware provided by the hotel. Urban hotels and resort facilities provide access to health clubs along with the ubiquitous swimming pool and spa found in even the smallest facilities. In-house game rooms for children, tennis courts, affiliation with a regulation golf course, and access to alpine or cross country ski areas, are just a few of the entertainment options that might be available. Personal services such as laundry and dry cleaning, hair salons, newsstands, and gift shops are other optional guest services. And of course, food and beverage service is found in many lodging facilities. Food service may be as simple as a vending machine or coffee urn in the office or as elaborate as a five star gourmet restaurant. Even those facilities that do not have in-house food and beverage facilities often recommend nearby restaurants for guests through in-room brochures or menus.

The reason for providing any or all of these additional services is to make a guest's stay as pleasant, stress-free, and enjoyable as possible. Whether these services are provided or not will impact the scope of the project for the interior designer as well as have some effect upon the design and specification of the different areas affected by the accommodation of these extra services.

Management

Lodging facilities may be managed by only a few people, in the case of small motels and inns, or may involve several levels of management for larger facilities. Generally speaking, there are three levels of management in the hospitality industry: Top management, middle management, and supervisory management. Top management is made up of the individual owner (in the case of the smallest types of lodging facilities) or the chairman of the board, president and vice presidents, and the board of directors (in the case of the larger types of facilities).

Middle managers will be the level of management most associated with the work of the interior designer. They may be employees of the owner or a management company that operates the facility. Note that some organizations may use other titles than those listed below. The general manager and assistant general manager have responsibility for the overall operations of the lodging facility. The director of housekeeping is responsible for upkeep of guest rooms and the whole of the facility. He or she would interface with the designer on design and remodeling assignments. The food and beverage manager is responsible for the operation of restaurants and other food services such as catering for banquets and room service. The plant engineer is responsible for the supervision of all areas related to the building itself— mechanical systems such as heating, ventilation, and air conditioning, plumbing systems and, of course, general repairs needed in guest rooms or other areas of the facility. Marketing and sales managers work toward attracting guests and guest groups to the facility. The job of the security manager is obvious from the title. Other middle managers may also be assigned, depending on the size of the facility and ownership organization.

Supervisors are responsible for smaller groups of employees and may have more direct contact with guests. For example, the front office manager is responsible for the supervision of staff that interface with guests at the registration desk and other front office functions, while the restaurant manager and executive chef are specific supervisory individuals in food and beverage areas of the lodging facility.

Types of Lodging Facilities

As the reader knows from his or her own experience, there are many different types of lodging facilities (see Figure 4-1). These differing types of facilities cater to the diverse needs of the public and have grown in reaction to the demands of the market. The industry itself dates back many centuries, beginning with simple inns and taverns. As civilization grew and became refined, lodging services also became more refined. Although inns were still available for the lower classes, hoteliers saw the need for grander lodging facilities with more amenities that would appeal to the wealthy travelers.

Hotels began taking on their grand size and opulence in the 19th century. Resort hotels like the Grand Hotel on Mackinac Island, MI, and the Hotel del Coronado in San Diego, CA, both opened in the 1880s. They are two magnificent examples of early resort hotels (see Figure 4-2). The 19th century also saw the development of grand hotels in the large cities and even luxurious tourist facilities in national parks. The El Tovar Hotel at the Grand Canyon provided early park travelers a chance to experience the "wild west" with accommodations that were only mildly "wild."

In the early part of the 20th century, hotels were often the most elaborately designed buildings in cities and towns. The Conrad Hilton in Chicago (1920s) was the largest hotel in the world for many years with its 3000 rooms. The Beverly Hills Hotel in California (early 1900s), the Arizona Biltmore in Phoenix (built in 1929), and the Houstonian Hotel, Club, and Spa in Texas are other early examples of these grand hotels (Figure 4-3).

Today's hotel facilities provide a large range of services and exciting entertainment venues. The industry caters to a wide variety of guests from business travelers and conventioneers to families on vacation. A guest might be looking for a grand hotel such as those mentioned above, or a resort hotel that combines all aspects of hospitality in one location such as Opryland in Nashville, and DisneyWorld hotels in Orlando. Perhaps the guest seeks a purely recreational location such as a ski lodge in Colorado or a dude ranch where guests become cowboys and cowgirls for a few days. Perhaps the guest needs a convention hotel or a place to hold a meeting (Figure 4-4). Then again, the guest may choose a bed-and-breakfast inn to spend a few days luxuriating away from home. All these types of lodging facilities are available to serve the

Hotels	Motels
Downtown or City Center	Downtown or City Center
Suburban	Suburban
Airport	Airport
Freeway	Freeway
Convention	Motor Inn
Conference	Bed and Breakfast
Casino	Lodges
Super Luxury	Inns
Commercial	Hostels
Residential	Tourist Home
Resort	Health Spa
All-suite	Boarding House
Mega hotel	

Figure 4–1 List of different types of hotels/lodging.

(a)

(b)

Figure 4–2 (*a*) The Grand Hotel on Mackinac Island, MI. (Photograph courtesy of the Grand Hotel, Mackinac Island, MI.) (*b*) Hotel del Coronado in San Diego, CA. (Photograph courtesy of Hotel del Coronado.)

diverse market of guests in this country and throughout the world. Let us now define some of these specialized lodging types.

Hotels are generally large facilities offering a variety of rooms, from standard guest rooms to luxurious suites, along with a variety of restaurant and beverage service and other services and amenities. There are a great variety of hotels in today's hospitality marketplace, serving

Figure 4–3 Reception/waiting room adjacent to the main lobby. The Houstonian Hotel, Club, and Spa in Houston, TX. (Photograph courtesy of the Houstonian Hotel, Club, and Spa.)

various locations and target markets. There are convention hotels that cater to large business, professional, social, or other organizational groups, where the emphasis during the stay is on meetings and exhibits or related activities. Conference centers are hotels specially designed and organized for smaller meetings and conferences than those held at the conventions hotel. They offer many of the same facilities as the convention hotel, but for meetings on a smaller scale. Casino hotels are those located in states and cities where legalized gambling is allowed (Figure 4-5). Commercial hotels are those that cater to business travelers and are commonly located in urban centers or near central business districts. *Resort hotels* are lodging facilities that have as part of their services extensive recreational facilities or activities. Residential hotels are those in which the largest portion of guests are accommodated for long-term stays, perhaps months or even years at a time. All-suite hotels are lodging facilities where all the guest rooms are suites consisting of a separated bedroom and living area. Many all-suites hotels also offer kitchen facilities in-room.

The automobile made for a very mobile population in the United States in the early part of the 20th century. Travelers required lodging and food service along the roadways, as well as increasing the demand for resort and tourist facilities. This demand was met by the development of motels. *Motels* are those lodging facilities that cater to the traveler using an automobile. Arthur Hineman is credited with opening the first motel in California in 1925.[2] Early motels and smaller hotels along the highway system were often small structures on one floor. Many "motor inns" were small cabins providing privacy from neighbors, but little space. Motels are usually much smaller than hotels and have fewer services and amenities. Kemmons Wilson, a building contractor from Tennessee, improved the design of early motels when he conceived the Holiday Inn Motel in 1952. That first Holiday Inn led to the corporation that

---

[2] Walker, 1996, p. 56.

Figure 4–4 Exterior of the Hyatt Regency in Dallas, TX. (Photograph courtesy of Hyatt Regency Dallas.)

today represents the largest lodging business in the world.[3] Motel parking is commonly right at or near the guest rooms, making it convenient for guests to unload luggage from their cars. Some motels have food and beverage services and many provide swimming pools, but there

[3]Dittmer and Griffin, 1993, p. 105.

Figure 4–5 Exterior view of The Mirage in Las Vegas, NV. (Photograph courtesy of The Mirage.)

are usually few other services. This is due to the fact that most motel guests do not stay at the facility for more than one or two days.

Bed-and-breakfast lodging facilities have become popular. In some situations, individuals have converted part or all of their private residences into bed-and-breakfasts, welcoming travelers to stay in a more homey environment than most hotels and motels provide. Most bed-and-breakfast establishments offer guest amenities for the guest's comfort, but not entertainment. For example, few offer swimming pools, but many offer room options with in-room Jacuzzis. Bed-and-breakfasts offer the full breakfast or a substantial continental breakfast as part of the room rate, but few have full food and beverage facilities for other meals.

A lodging establishment called a *lodge* is a facility commonly associated with some kind of recreational activity such as skiing or fishing. These are usually smaller facilities in basically rural areas or areas close to the recreational activity. Since they are commonly found in more remote locations, food and beverage service is provided to guests.

Another lodging establishment, an *inn,* is a small to medium sized facility that wishes to convey a feeling of a small comfortable home to guests. It may be in a rural area or a big city, one story or multistoried, offering a full-range of guest services including food and beverage services. Many people think of inns as "motel or hotel" facilities in the country, especially in the eastern states.

Hostels are economy lodging facilities that often cater to students and budget-minded travelers who are looking for a clean room and few other services. Hostels have very simple rooms, often do not have in-room bathrooms, and some even require guests to bring their own linens.

The modern traveler is faced with multiple decisions when planning a stay at a lodging facility. What type of lodging facility, what kind of amenities are expected, what kind of guest services are a necessity along with price for the stay are decisions the guest must contemplate. Although these decisions affect every guest, they also affect the design program and concept with which the interior designer, architect, and owner must contend in the development of the lodging facility.

Planning and Design Concepts

From the previous discussion of the types of lodging facilities, it should be easy for the reader to imagine that the planning and design concepts of these various facilities will vary—sometimes greatly. The design of a small bed-and-breakfast will be very different from the design of a chain motel/hotel like a franchise member of Best Western, Inc., and both will differ from the design of a large resort, convention, or conference hotel.

However, there are also similarities in the design of lodging facilities. For example, guest rooms take on standard sizes and furniture configurations regardless of the type of facility. All lodging facilities need a lobby with a place for guests to register and pay their bills. And the basic operational functions discussed above must be considered as well. In this section, we discuss the planning and design concepts of a nonspecific type of hotel, since hotels will encompass the greatest challenge to the design team. Remember that the exact size and type of lodging facility will affect how design concepts are applied.

A hotel has three basic products to sell to potential guests. The definition and specifics of these products create the differences between the types of hotels. The first product is "guest accommodations" or guest rooms. The guest accommodations are often thought of as the key product in lodging facilities. Guest rooms can be small and simple, as is found in many roadside motels, or elaborate luxurious suites, found in super luxury hotels. The interior design can range from the simple "cookie cutter" hotel and motel furnishings found in thousands of facilities to exquisite antiques found in super luxury hotels. The second product is "services." The services product of the mix are all the additional services that are available to guests. This might be as simple as an alarm clock in the room, to gift shops and newsstands, recreational activities of some sort, and varying levels of food and beverage service. The third product used to set the theme and design of the hotel is "ambience." As the reader knows, ambience gives the facility its look and personality. Interior architectural finishes, lighting design and fixtures, style of furniture, accessories, fabrics, and many other elements create the desired ambience. However, ambience is not only the effect of the interior. The exterior design and landscaping should be working together with the interior to create an overall theme. A guest's impression of a lodging facility will start with the exterior design. As the guest moves into the lobby and other public areas around the lobby, this overall theme is continuous, even into the hallways and corridors and continuing into the guest rooms.

Feasibility Studies

The decision to develop a lodging facility, regardless of its size, is not taken lightly by owners, developers, and property managers. Due to the complexity of the modern hotel, design planning begins with a feasibility study. This is done to clarify the space needs and options that the owner seeks to include in the facility and will help the owner, architect, and interior designer determine if achieving the original goals is possible. It is true that all major commercial design projects involve feasibility studies. They are discussed here due to their importance in the design of a hotel property.

The feasibility study is a thorough analysis of the goals and objectives of the project to determine if it is possible and will succeed. For a hotel project, the feasibility study is generally prepared by a consultant who specializes in this type of work. It may take the consultant months to prepare the study and will cost the project owner many thousands, perhaps hundreds of thousands, of dollars. The time and money spent "at the front end," however, could save the owner and developer the study's cost many times over.

Feasibility studies for a hotel project will look at the demand for guest accommodations and hotel services projected for the type of hotel concept in the expected location. In order to determine this, the consultant will study competition, lodging demands, future growth of the location, and the surrounding business or recreational impact. The consultant will also study any impact from the geographic location and points of interests to tourists. This is done as part of good business planning to prevent building another hotel that is minimally different from the exiting facilities in a saturated market.

The feasibility study carefully analyzes financial factors. Costs for generating the design documents, site development, actual construction, and finishing costs are only one part of what will be required to build a hotel. Estimated operational costs for such things as staffing the hotel front and back of the house, running the mechanical systems, operating full-service kitchens, providing laundry and housekeeping services, maintaining security systems, providing parking services, even watering interior and exterior plants are all considered in the feasibility study. All these costs of doing business cannot exceed reasonably attainable revenues, or the project will not be profitable.

Revenue projections are based on industry standards with adjustments for the local competitive market and are based on the desired types of guest rooms and other services that will bring in revenues to the hotel. The feasibility study is an objective report on the possible success (or lack of success) of the hotel concept. It is reviewed carefully by the owner, developer, and property management team to determine where, if any, changes to the concept need to be made before actually beginning architectural programming and design.

Exterior Design Concepts

Guests form an impression about the hotel from its exterior design, and that design is defined by: number of guest rooms and guest services, overall theme, geographic location, and target guest. A key element in exterior design is the main entrance. Depending on the size and type of hotel, there may be several "main entrances." In convention and conference hotels, many visitors to the hotel do not need to go to the main lobby, but need to easily find their way to the entrance to exhibit space, conference rooms, or the ballroom. For a casino hotel, the entrance to the casino space is always prominent and exciting, but it may not be the entrance to the registration desk.

The *main entrance* serves to draw the guest to the lobby. An architectural element called a *porte cochere* is often used to help draw the guest to the main entrance. A porte cochere is a canopy located over the driveway by the main entrance and is used to protect guests from the weather as well as to call attention to the main entrance. The area surrounding the porte cochere needs to be large enough to accommodate peak loads of pedestrian, auto, taxi, and tour bus traffic.

In many climatic areas, architects design vestibules as part of the main entrance. The vestibule limits cold air, rain, or snow from blowing into the lobby as the doors are opened. Depending on the actual total size of the hotel and number of occupants, the building codes may require multiple doors at the front entrance. Many architects use revolving doors at the main entrances. The revolving door cannot be the only exit door since building codes require that leafed doors must be used as the required exit doors from the hotel lobby to the outside. Sizes of doors, type of doors, floor finishes, the kind of glass required in doors and in windows surrounding doors, all these are also regulated by building codes. Should the interior designer have any responsibility for these details, he or she must carefully review local codes and conditions to insure proper specification.

The design of exterior *signage* is focused on two main goals: identity and way-finding. Exterior signage commonly incorporates the hotel logo (also called a "mark") with the name of the hotel and may incorporate the logo of a management group such as Best Western, Inc. Sight lines must be determined by the architect to insure that signs can be seen from roadways as well as parking areas. Exterior identity signage might be as extravagant as that used by casino hotels or subdued—even almost nonexistent, in most luxury and super luxury hotels.

The second goal of exterior signage is for way-finding. Way-finding is a term that came into use in the 1960s.[4] *Way-finding* is a methodology of signs, graphics, and directional arrows used

---

[4]Arthur and Passini, 1992, p. v.

to help individuals find their way around complex properties and building interiors. On large properties, directional signs are used to help guests get to the main entrance from parking areas, locate restaurants that have access from the exterior of the hotel, find entrances to conference centers or convention displays, as well as to recreational facilities on the property.

Interior Design Concepts

Planning and design decisions for the interior of a hotel vary greatly based on the type of lodging facility. Although many elements in the design of the interior of hotels are similar, it is vital to the success of the property that design directions and goals be clarified before the actual planning and specification activities are begun. Along with the information in the feasibility study, the design team will next work with the owners to develop a concept for the hotel. The *concept* is an overall idea that unifies all parts of the facility and provides a specific direction for all aspects of the design. It focuses the planning and design of functional spaces as well as the design of uniforms, graphics, types of service offerings and recreation spaces available, even the colors of linens for guest rooms, and every other detail of the hotel's operation.

In the development of the concept, it will be necessary to examine the exact type of hotel, the guest target market, service offerings, the mix of accommodation offerings, and, of course, the ambience. Elements that are appropriate in a resort hotel might not work effectively in a downtown hotel catering to the business traveler. If the hotel is targeting upscale guests who enjoy luxury accommodations, different specification decisions will need to be made than for those for a budget hotel beside a freeway. The kind of services offered impacts design in terms of space allocation and budgetary factors. While a small hotel will have only a few options for guest accommodations, larger hotels and many of the specialized types of hotels will have several. Designers need to understand the projected mix of guest accommodations in order to plan appropriately for the interior treatment of each different type of guest room. For the interior designer, the ambience is especially important. Ambience involves many elements from wallcoverings and the style of furniture to the colors of guest linens, decorative elements in guest rooms and public spaces, and the many other items that make the interior, general concept, and operations all come together in an unified whole.

As with any commercial facility, the elements of a hotel that are important to the successful interior design and specification include space allocation, traffic patterns, furniture and finishes, lighting and mechanical interface, and code considerations. This section discusses these items in a brief overview as they apply to a generic hotel property, focusing on the interior designer's responsibility for these areas.

An important part of the programming phase of the project is the *space allocation* section. In this portion of the study the owner and designer determine how much of the total space will be devoted to guest rooms and how much to other service areas. As can be seen in Figure 4-6, the amount of guest space can vary from around 90 percent for motels to around 55 percent for mega hotels. Larger portions of the total structure in some types of hotels will be devoted to such things as food and beverage facilities, banquet or meeting rooms, and recreational spaces.

Allocations are categorized into the amounts of space needed for front of the house and back of the house activities. It is important for the architect, owner, and interior designer to work together to determine estimated space needs for all the functions of the hotel property. The interior designer assists in this process through his or her knowledge of space standards needed for layouts of furniture for different functions. Figure 4-7 provides guidelines on total space allocation for the various areas of a lodging facility.

Traffic patterns for a hotel encompass two distinct models. First is the organization of all the functional spaces, especially the footprint for the arrangement of guest accommodations, which influences the traffic patterns for the whole of the facility. These traffic patterns are the responsibility of the architect. Second is the traffic patterns within the specific functional spaces. The designer must provide sufficient traffic aisles for the expected number of occupants and activities based on the exact use of the space. Occupancy classification and the

Lodging Type	No. rooms	Service Level	% of total hotel space devoted to guestrooms*
Motel	100	Economy to mid-price	85–95
Motor Inn	100–200	Mid-price	75–85
Commercial Hotel	200–400	Mid-price to luxury	75–85
All-Suite Hotel	150–300	Mid-price to first class	75–85
Suburban Hotel	150–300	Mid-price to·first class	75–85
Convention Hotel	200–2000	First class	65–75
Resort	varies	Mid-price to luxury	65–75
Mega-resort	> 1000	First class	55–65
Conference Center	100–300	Mid-price to first class	55–65

* Includes guestroom corridors, stairs, elevators, and linen storage.

Figure 4–6 Guest space for different types of lodging properties. (From Stipanuk and Roffmann, *Hospitality Facilities Management and Design.* 1992. P. 365. East Lansing, MI: Educational Institute of the American Hotel & Motel Association.)

	Motor Inns	Commercial	Convention	All-Suite
Number of Guest Rooms	150	300	600	250
Number of bays[1]	150	315	630	250
Net guestroom area (sf.[2])	310	330	350	450
Gross guest room area (sf.)[3]	420	480	500	675
Total guest room area (sf.)	63,000	151,200	315,000	168,750
Total public area	9,000	27,000	67,500	22,250
Total back-of-the-house area	6,750	23,400	67,500	20,000
Total hotel area (sf.)	78,750	201,600	450,000	211,000
Total hotel area/room (sf.)[4]	525	672	750	844

[1] A bay is the space equivalent to a standard guest room; many suites are two (or more) bays, or the equivalent of two (or more) typical guest rooms.

[2] sf. = square feet

[3] Gross guest room area includes an allowance for corridors, stairs, elevators, walls, etc.

[4] Total hotel area per room includes a portion of all public and back-of-the-house space.

Figure 4–7 Chart indicating total space allocation. (From Stipanuk and Roffmann, *Hospitality Facilities Management and Design.* 1992. P. 365. East Lansing, MI: Educational Institute of the American Hotel & Motel Association.)

number of occupants will be important criteria for the interior designer in the layout of furnishings and needed traffic aisles and corridors within the different types of functional spaces in a hotel. As hotels are so varied in overall design, it is impossible to provide typical floor plans of the overall hotel footprint. However, Figure 4-8 provides sample layouts of typical guest room floor configurations. Typical traffic flow systems for specialized areas are provided later in this chapter.

Furniture specifications, colors, and materials used in the specialized areas of a hotel are as varied as the types of facilities. The specification of these items will differ depending on the type and location of the hotel. The most important generalization that can be made about these items is that all the products need to be aesthetically appropriate for the concept as well as selected for easy maintenance while standing up to the abuse of heavy use. Just as the fabrics selected for a guest room will require more constant cleaning than those in the lobby, the fabric selected for lobby seating for a rough and tumble dude ranch resort will need to be quite different from that for a big city resort such as one in Phoenix, Arizona.

The interior designer must delicately balance creating the mood and carrying through the concept of the hotel with appropriate specifications of the number of items and the quality

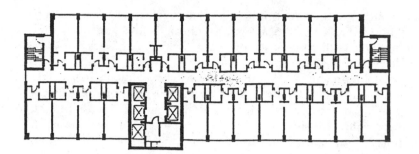

Double-Loaded Slab

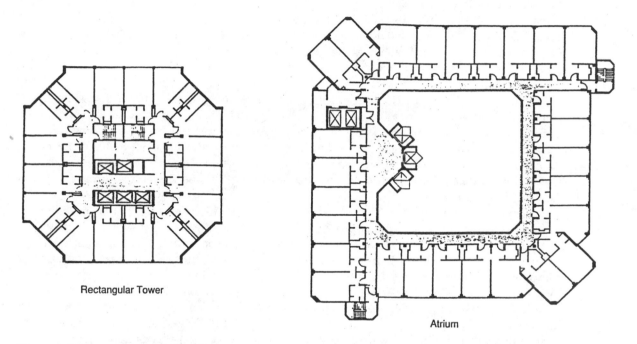

Rectangular Tower

Atrium

Figure 4–8 Layouts of guest room configurations. From Stipanuk and Roffmann, *Hospitality Facilities Management and Design*. 1992. East Lansing, MI: Educational Institute of the American Hotel & Motel Association.)

needed to provide long life and reasonable maintenance. Generally, the highest quality of furnishings and materials will be reserved for the lobby and the guest rooms. These spaces are the primary places that influence the guest and therefore must be given the most careful consideration. The lobby sets the mood for the whole of the facility and the guest spends so much time in the guest room. Unfortunately, even though the lobby sets the mood, depending on the type of facility, the guest does not spend much time in the lobby. Spending an inordinate portion of the budget on the furnishings for the lobby could be a waste of resources. On the other hand, putting significant dollars into guest rooms also can "break the budget." The designer must remember that deciding to add even one more accessory item to a guest room might involve thousands of dollars, not just the few dollars of the item's cost, because that accessory item might need to be repeated dozens, even hundreds, of times in all guest rooms.

The success of lobbies, meeting rooms, food and beverage areas, and all other public areas also depends on effective *lighting* design. The three kinds of lighting that can be used in these areas are general lighting, accent lighting, and sparkle. General lighting will be needed for overall visibility to allow for general movement through the space. Accent lighting could be used for calling attention to certain areas or elements in a space. For example, accent lighting can call attention to a small piano bar that might be part of a large hotel lobby. In some areas a type of lighting called sparkle lighting can be used. *Sparkle lighting* is produced from a variety of light sources that create special effects and give atmosphere to a room. Commonly used in food and beverage facilities, sparkle lighting is also effectively used in hotel lobbies. An example of sparkle lighting in a lobby would be the use of very low wattage strip lighting along the underside of the nose of stair treads.

Lighting in the other public areas needs to be adaptable to accommodate varied activities that can be going on in these spaces. Meeting rooms or the ballroom will require overall lighting for users to find their way through the space, various lighting levels for meals, as well as subdued lighting if slides or movies are presented as part of a conference. A coffee shop will require bright lighting for breakfast and lunch service, and might provide more subdued lighting in the evening to encourage the use of the coffee shop for dinner service.

Lighting in guest rooms also needs to accommodate a variety of activities. Bedside lighting is needed for guests to read, general lighting is needed when a guest enters the room, and quality task lighting is a necessity for shaving and applying makeup. Additional lighting for reading or doing work would be necessary at a desk or table area, especially in hotels catering to the business traveler. Inadequate lighting in any aspect of the guest room would adversely affect the guest's satisfaction and might encourage him or her to stay somewhere else on the next trip.

Back of the house areas will need high quality task and general lighting that will support functions and aid employees in performing their jobs. Lighting fixtures that provide energy efficiency and cost-effectiveness are of primary concern in the back of house work areas. Though color rendition is less important in most of these areas than in front of the house areas, careful selection of lighting in the kitchens is important. Proper lighting levels and color renditions will be necessary to insure the freshness of foods and the preparation of foods to the chef's satisfaction.

There are *other mechanical systems* regarding which the interior designer may have limited input or need to interface with appropriate engineers and the architect. Designers may have responsibility to design business areas for guests on guest room floors or in specialized areas. Here, the designer will work with telephone, data, and computer consultants for equipment hookups. The design of the registration desk must be done in coordination with consultants who will be supplying the computer equipment that is used today for registration, payment, and voice messaging. Designers who plan interior fountains and elaborate interior live plant landscaping need to consult with water systems engineers and plumbing contractors as well as with the project architect. A wide variety of consultant work on specialized mechanical needs will be required in the design of food and beverage facilities and their commercial kitchens. Should recreational facilities be included in the program, the designer may coordinate and consult with the architect and others on specialized needs related these activities.

The interior designer has many *code responsibilities* in the design of hotels and the numerous areas part of the occupancy. Hotels are considered to be residential occupancies in the building codes. However, all but the smallest lodging facilities are actually mixed occupancies. A hotel property not only has the guest rooms that create the residential occupancy but can have food and beverage areas and meeting rooms that will be assembly occupancies; retail stores and service spaces like a hair salon that are business or mercantile occupancies (depending on the model code being used); offices that are also business occupancies; and many might have some spaces classified as hazardous areas such as in-house dry cleaning plants or paint shops. The interior designer must be clear on how these different classifications will affect the furniture and space planning along with product and material specification of the facility.

The Americans with Disabilities Act (ADA) significantly affects lodging facility design in many ways. First, all public and common use areas must be designed to comply with the basic design guidelines of the Act. This would include such things as the paths of travel, lobby, restaurants, public toilet facilities, meeting rooms, and recreational facilities. Second, all lodging facilities are required to have a portion of the guest rooms designed to meet accessibility standards. It is important to note that rooms in each of the different configurations (queen or king, double-double, or suites) must be accessible, not just one type of room. In addition, hotels with 50 or more sleeping rooms are required to have a percentage of those rooms designed with roll-in showers. Figure 4-9 shows a typical double-double room that is accessible. Visual and auditory emergency signals are required as well. Third, counters such as the registration desk and the cash desk in retail stores within the hotel property need to be designed to have either a section of the counter no higher than 36 inches above the floor, an auxiliary counter nearby, or a folding shelf to facilitate registration and business transactions.

As the size of the hotel property and the number of services provided increase, the interior designer's responsibility for meeting ADA requirements will also increase. The greatest responsibility will be in the design of new buildings. However, remodeling of older structures will place a burden on the owners to make numerous "readily achievable" modifications to the public spaces and guest rooms. As always, it is the interior designer's responsibility to know how the law affects the project.

The designer must also be careful to select products and materials that will meet local codes. For example, carpet specified for traffic corridors needs to be Class I while the carpet in guest rooms and hotel offices can generally be Class III. This is also the case for other architectural finishes. Although most jurisdictions only regulate the architectural finishes in hotels, some jurisdictions have specific restrictions on furniture items and fabrics used in this type of facility. California Technical Bulletins CAL 117 and CAL 133, discussed in Chapter 1, apply to upholstered furniture used in spaces where more than ten seating units are located. The designer must clarify if this code requirement or other local code requirements affect the specification of furniture items—especially seating—or design furnishings elements for the project.

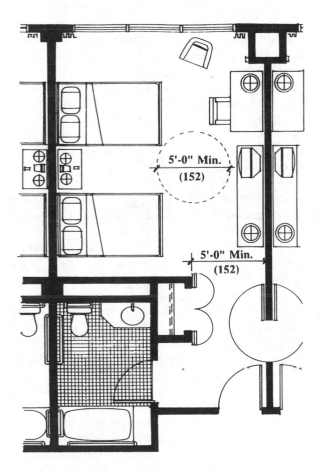

Figure 4–9 Double-double room that is accessible as noted by the 5 foot minimum dimensions. (From DeChiara et al., *Time Saver Standards for Interior Design and Space Planning.* © 1991. Reproduced with permission of the McGraw-Hill Companies.)

Design Applications

In the context of this book, it would be impossible to describe in detail all the design issues of even a generic hotel, let alone all the different types of lodging facilities. However, the reader seeking to venture into the design of lodging facilities must have some reference to guide him or her in his or her efforts. This section discusses specific design and planning principles for areas of a generic hotel most likely to be the responsibility of an interior designer. Included in this discussion are: the lobby, function spaces, and guest accommodations. This section concludes with a brief discussion of the planning of food and beverage facilities as part of a lodging property. Chapter 5 deals with food and beverage facilities in depth.

The Lobby

The design of the lobby sets the critical first impression and design theme for the hotel (Figure 4-10). Hotels did not have lobbies until the 19th century, and until the 1960s most hotels—other than the grand luxury hotels—had lobbies that were small. The atrium hotels, first introduced at the Hyatt Regency Atlanta by John Portman, showed designers and property owners that a lobby could be a prominent feature of any hotel property. Even as large and multistory lobbies became popular, however, the smaller intimate lobby remained the norm for many types of hotels and suite hotels that sought to create the intimacy of the older grand hotels.

The lobby can be a busy place. It is, of course, where the guest registers. It is also the main circulation space helping guests to public spaces in the hotel such as restaurants, recreation venues, and conference spaces. In addition the lobby serves as a place for guests to meet other guests and visitors, and to relax away from guest rooms, thus becoming a gathering place.

Clear circulation space is very important to the successful design of the lobby. The traffic patterns must not only meet codes, but adequately handle expected peak volumes of traffic. Primary traffic paths need to move the guest from the front entry to the front desk, elevators, escalators, retail outlets like gift shops, public rest rooms, and restaurants. Secondary traffic paths must accommodate guests to and through seating provided in the lobby.

A key element of the lobby for guests will be the front desk or registration desk (see Figure 4-10). It is common that guest registration, checkout, and guest information is provided at the front desk. Sufficient space must be provided to handle the numbers of guests registering at any one time, along with queuing space for those waiting. For example, a convention or conference hotel may have busloads of guests arriving at any one time. Small hotels or hotels that do not attract large convention groups will need a smaller space for the front desk and waiting guests.

The front desk is not just the actual desk area. Other front office functions are commonly part of the front desk (see Figure 4-11). Depending on the organization of the hotel, space and design consideration must be made for these other functions. Figure 4-12 provides a list of these other functions.

The number of stations for registration, cashier, and information are based on the occupancy of the hotel. It is suggested that a desk space of 6 feet be allowed for each of these functions and that two stations be allowed for the first 150 rooms and one additional station be planned for each 100 additional rooms.[5] Calculations must be made as to how many guests would be arriving at peak times to determine the amount of circulation space needed for queuing.

The front desk must be positioned so that the desk can be easily located by arriving guests and so that desk clerks can have visual control over the entrance and main lobby area. Obviously, in larger hotels of many types, the entrance visibility factor by the desk clerks is mitigated by the addition of security staff and other employees who can monitor entrances. It

---

[5]Rutes and Penner, 1985, p. 181.

(a)

(b)

Figure 4–10 (*a*) Lobby of the Inter-Continental Hotel in New York, NY. (Design by Kenneth E. Hurd and Associates.) (*b*) Lobby of the Castle in Tarrytown, NY. (Design by and photograph courtesy of Peter Gisolfi Assoc., Architects.)

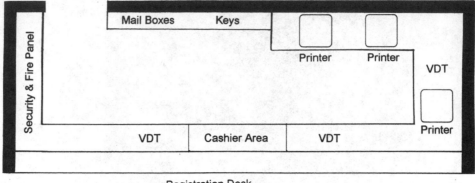

Figure 4–11 Small registration desk indicating space for various functions in front desk/lobby area. (Drawing courtesy of S.O.I. Interior Design, Houston, TX.)

Guest registration stations
Guest check-out and cashier stations
Guest mail and messages
Key boxes
Guest information (concierge)
Space for assistant manager
Reservations
House and pay phones
Events directory
Bellman station (nearby)
Bellman carts storage (nearby)
Luggage storage (nearby)

Figure 4–12 Typical front desk functions.

is also common to locate some seating near the front desk. This seating is provided for those accompanying the person registering or checking out (see Figure 4-13).

Many hotels provide concierge services in the lobby. The concierge provides information, assistance in ticket sales for theaters or sporting events, and other aid to the guest to make his or her stay more enjoyable and trouble-free. The concierge desk is usually located close to the front desk to make it easy for guests to seek the assistance they need.

Convenient to the front entry and the front desk would be space for luggage storage and the bellperson area. In larger hotels, room will also be provided for a bell captain podium or counter where a supervising bellperson will assign individuals to assist guests. It is also important to have a locked storage room to hold luggage when guests check out early but have a later departure time. The designer must also remember to plan space for the large luggage carts used by bellpersons.

The total ambience of the lobby and hotel in general will determine the architectural and millwork finishes, styles of furniture, fabric choices, and accessory items. The actual size, number, and kind of seating provided in the lobby will again be determined by the kind of hotel facility. A small suburban hotel located to serve highway travelers usually has a small lobby with a few sofas or other soft seating units. A large convention hotel's lobby will be quite large and have numerous sofas and soft seating units arranged in conversation groups of four to ten. Some hotels also provide a few desks or tables where the guests can write letters or postcards in the lobby. Resort hotels require more lobby space than most suburban and downtown hotels since guests have more time to lounge and socialize at a resort. Luxury and super luxury hotel lobbies are commonly small, private, and very elegant.

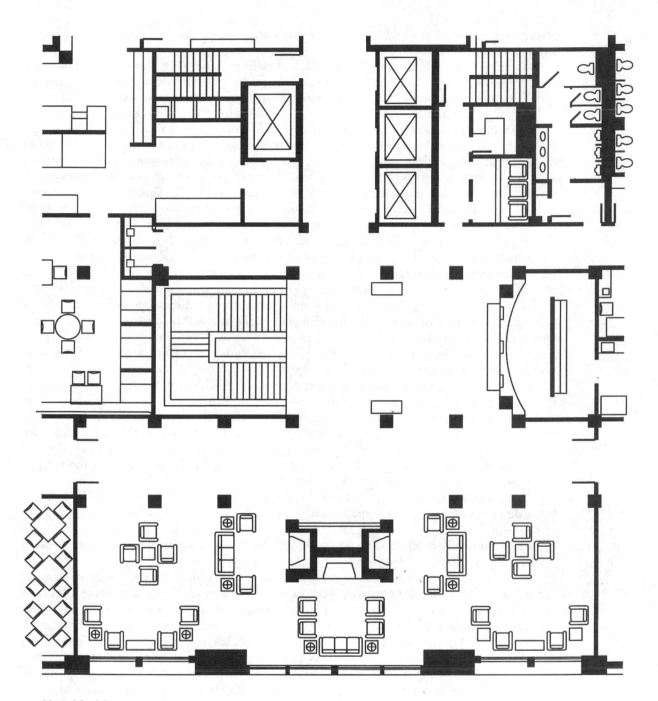

Hotel Lobby

Figure 4–13 Registration area and lobby in a small hotel. (Design by and plan courtesy of Cody D. Beal.)

Signage is an important element in the total detailing of the lobby. Of course, the registration desk will be identified with prominent signage. Guests will also require signage to direct them to the elevators, restaurants and cocktail lounges, stores, and recreational venues. Almost all but the smallest hotels provide function spaces for meetings, receptions, and seminars. It is necessary for the designer and architect to locate and specify appropriate directories or letter boards so that guests will know what events are scheduled each day and where they can be found. In large hotels, floor standing or wall mounted directories are supplemented by television screens.

Materials in the lobby need to be durable and easily maintainable. Hard surface flooring is commonly used for primary traffic paths. Carpeting can be used in seating areas, and if careful specification is done, used in traffic paths as well. It is quite common to use patterned carpet in large areas to help hide traffic paths and spills. Walls can be treated with many materials that will meet appropriate codes. However, the designer should consider the potential economic effect of replacing wallcoverings should a wall be damaged. Upholstery fabrics must also be durable and easily maintainable. Upholstery specification should be made with concern for spills, feet on the furniture, dust and dirt on clothing (especially in vacation and some resort hotels), and traffic volume in the space. Colors and patterns of fabrics should either be selected to help hide spills and dirt, or the fabric should be treated with a high quality stain repellent.

There are several mechanical interface challenges in lobby areas. The first is lighting. High quality general and task lighting will be required by the front desk. It is recommended that 40 foot-candles be specified here. This must be planned with the consideration that most hotels use computer systems for registration, checkout, and messaging. The lighting at the desk must not contribute to glare on the computer screens. General lighting will also be required in the seating areas of the lobby. General lighting in the lobby is recommended to be 10 foot-candles. Depending on the concept and furniture arrangements, task lighting for reading and writing letters might be needed. Accent lighting to call attention to art work, signage, and display features is often required in the lobby. Finally, lighted signage helps guests find the front desk, retail stores, restaurants, and public restrooms.

Electrical and communication cabling is another mechanical interface of concern to the interior designer in lobby areas. Extensive cabling will be required for the front desk and auxiliary functions that require computers and other telecommunications equipment. Furniture layouts in the lobby must be done to insure wall and floor outlets are provided for table fixtures and other task lighting. Cabling will also be necessary for security systems, public address systems, and fire alarms. These items might not be the responsibility of the interior designer, but may affect detail specification that is the responsibility of the designer.

Computer work stations are part of many functional areas in a lodging facility. As for lobby design considerations, computers will be needed for registration and checkout of guests, reservation checks, even messaging. Most of these stations are stand-up stations using terminals similar to any business office. Depending on ADA requirements in specific locations, sit-down stations may also be provided.

Other areas that will need design consideration for computers are the administrative offices and food and beverage areas. Computers are heavily utilized in administrative areas of the hotel for a variety of office functions. These uses are, of course, similar to any office function. Specialized terminals will be found in the food and beverage areas to accommodate on-line ordering of meals and beverages. These terminals will also aid the hotel in inventory control and product ordering. Other functional areas may need computers. The designer needs to understand what kind of computer equipment will be utilized in the various areas of the hotel to accommodate appropriate furniture, lighting design, and seating to house the worker.

Function Spaces

Function spaces are those areas used for conferences, meetings, trade shows, banquets, seminars, various receptions, and other activities requiring space for large numbers of guests. Hotels began adding function spaces to their space mix in the late 19th century in order to accommodate civic meetings. Lodging facilities recognize the availability of extra revenues from these spaces as they generate food service, guest rooms for exhibitors, and extra money spent at the hotel by participants in gatherings of many kinds.

Function spaces can be individual rooms or large rooms such as a ballroom that can be partitioned with full-height movable walls. Hotels commonly have a mixture of function room spaces to attend to the specific expected needs (Figure 4-14). For example, a conference hotel may require quite a few small meeting rooms or rooms that can be subdivided into smaller meeting rooms to hold seminars, small workshops, and business meetings. A convention hotel will have need for larger spaces for business meetings and exhibitions.

Function spaces should be located close to the lobby. Many larger hotels provide exterior access to the section of the hotel dedicated to function spaces. This is done because many of the individuals using the function spaces are not hotel guests. It is also common for larger hotels to have secondary lobbies off these exterior entrances. These secondary lobbies provide a gathering space and room to set up registration desks or even required food service. It is important to have rest rooms, public phones, and coat rooms nearby as well. Easy access from the hotel kitchen should be provided.

A key to the success of a function space is its flexibility. It might be a room set up with individual chairs for a business meeting or presentation one morning, used for a luncheon in the afternoon, and set up for a trade show display in the evening. The space allotted to function areas will depend upon the type of hotel and the guest target market. Conference centers and convention hotels will allow 60 to 100 square feet per guest room for function areas while a small hotel might only allow 10 to 20 square feet per guest room.[6] The actual

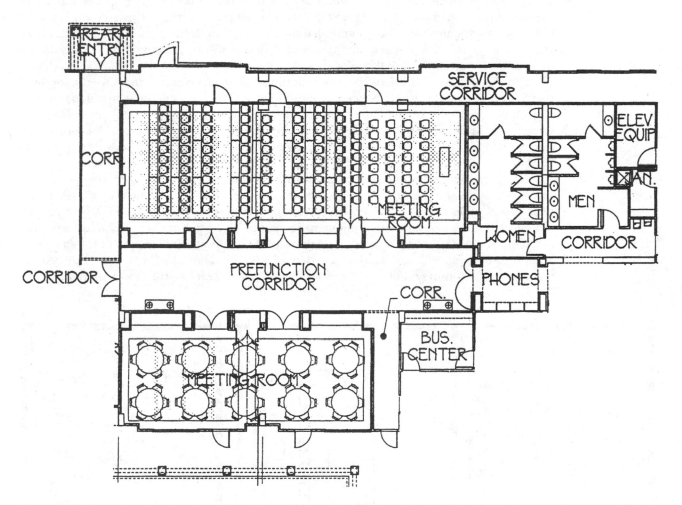

Figure 4-14 Floor plan showing the prefunction corridor and service corridor flanking the various meeting rooms. The lobby is in close proximity. (Plan courtesy of Holiday Inns.)

---

[6]Stipanuk and Roffmann, 1992, p. 378 (hardcover edition).

size of the rooms needs to be planned to accommodate three basic kinds of furniture setups: individual chairs set as theater seating, conference or "classroom" seating with small tables and chairs that can be arranged in numerous configurations, and food service seating with round tables that will handle six to eight diners (Figure 4-15).

Storage facilities will be required near the function spaces. A room may need individual chairs for one meeting, seating or tables for a reception, seminar tables and chairs for another event, and round tables for yet another. These tables and chairs must be foldable and stackable so that hotel staff can move them easily from one function space to storage space to another function space.

Interior materials, treatments, and furniture of function spaces will vary with the type of hotel. Although the types of items needed in these spaces are the same from hotel to hotel, the actual items must be appropriate for the target market of the hotel in terms of their style and quality. Products in function spaces must be specified in order to sustain the heavy traffic, spills, and movement of furniture. Patterned carpets are often specified to help disguise spills and traffic patterns. Wall finishes need to be very durable. In many cases, chair rails are used to decrease the possibility of chairs scuffing the walls. It is also suggested that fabric wall panels be used to help with acoustics. Should one or more walls in a function room include windows, the designer must specify full blackout drapes or blinds. In most function spaces, chairs are small and easily stackable. Upholstery fabrics on chairs are commonly vinyl, although strong nylon fabrics are also used. Budget-minded hotels might use folding chairs with no fabric or vinyl fabric on the seat. Patterns and colors of materials will be selected in keeping with the overall themes or concept of the hotel.

Function areas will need additional way-finding signage. It is very common for the rooms to have names in common with the theme or location of the hotel. For example, function rooms in many hotels in the Phoenix, AZ, area have rooms with names such as: Grand Canyon, Flagstaff, Camelback, and Sedona, themes in keeping with the Arizona landscape and localities. Wall hung or floor standing signs need to be provided to identify the function within the room as well.

Although most of the mechanical interface challenges in function rooms are the purview of the architect, the designer must coordinate a variety of issues. Speakers may wish to use film, easels, slide projectors, overhead projectors, or computers to augment their presentations. Although not all these equipment items will be stored in each function room, the mechanical interface must be present to allow this equipment to be utilized in the spaces. In addition, rooms must accommodate a variety of audiovisual setups for the different seating arrangements. Sound systems and acoustic design must make it easy for those within the rooms

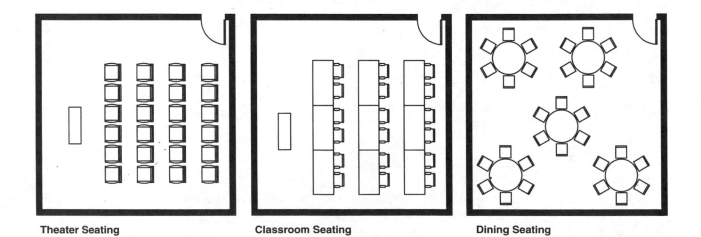

Theater Seating   **Classroom Seating**   **Dining Seating**

Figure 4-15 Three floor plans of mulipurpose room layouts in a hotel. (Drawings courtesy of Cody D. Beal.)

to hear speakers and the presentations from any point in the room, but these same sounds should not be heard outside of the function space.

Several lighting options are also needed in function spaces. Low lighting will be needed to allow viewing of movies or slides or to focus on a speaker, adjustable lighting levels will be desired for dining, and high levels of lighting will be required for exhibits and displays. A variety of fixtures from accent to functional to spotlighting, even chandeliers, might be required in any one functional space. The design of the ceiling and the incorporation of the lighting fixtures into that ceiling often makes the most dramatic design statement in function spaces—especially large ones like the ballroom. Because of the large numbers of people in most of these rooms, ceilings are high so that guests and visitors do not feel closed in. Ceilings are visible regardless of the function taking place in the room so much thought is put into the design of the surfaces, selection of fixtures, and lighting design possibilities in these spaces. Do not forget that ceiling design will also involve selection and spacing of smoke detectors, sprinkler heads, emergency lighting, speakers, and mechanical grills for heating/air conditioning. The ceiling is a complex design element that cannot be ignored.

Guest Rooms

Recall that 55 to 85 percent of all the space in a hotel is devoted to guest rooms. In the design and specification of hotel guest rooms, the designer must remember that adding one item to a room may not seem like much, but that item will be multiplied by dozens or even hundreds as it will likely be repeated in each room. The actual cost of furniture, fixtures, and equipment (FF&E) in guest rooms can become quite high if this consideration is ignored by the designer.

The actual size and configuration of the guest floors and rooms will vary greatly based on the type of hotel. The small hotel will have compact guest rooms with a minimal amount of furniture and accessories. The luxury hotel will have larger rooms with additional pieces of furniture and many more accessory items. The design team's planning goals in this area will be to provide as many of the different size rooms considered essential based on the type of hotel being developed without providing too much extra space. Guest rooms that might be only one foot wider than actually required for the type of hotel could lose the hotel several additional revenue-producing spaces.

There are two aspects to planning guest room areas: guest room floor planning and the design and specification of the guest rooms themselves. Guest room floor planning involves determining the greatest number of rooms and suites on each floor as well as providing space for guest and service elevators, stairs, and service areas such as linen rooms, vending areas, and circulation space. Depending on the type of hotel, other areas may be planned for each floor. For example, in a hotel that will cater primarily to business people, the hotel may provide a business communication area where a fax machine, copy machine, and other office equipment may be available for guests to utilize.

A number of slab floor plans are possible (see Figure 4-8). The most efficient type of floor slab is the double loaded slab. It allows for the greatest number of rooms in the smallest gross square footage. Tower plans have guest rooms along the outside of the tower with the service areas in the central core, just like many office buildings. In atrium plans, the guest rooms are arranged on the perimeter with room entrances along the corridors that overlook the lobby atrium. Guest elevators in atrium plans take advantage of the view from the elevator by use of glass elevators that allow guests to see the atrium space from ground level to some upper floor level. Service functions for atrium hotels are placed away from the atrium itself.

In determining the plan slab and actual floor plan of the hotel, the design team must carefully consider the *room mix,* which is the configuration of different types of rooms required based primarily on the size and number of beds in the room. Each floor for a hotel will rarely have all the exact same size and configuration of rooms. Hotels will have some rooms with a king or queen size bed, others with two double beds (called a double-double), others that will be small and/or large suites with separate sleeping and sitting areas, and so on. The room mix will also be affected by the number of connecting rooms required, the number and types of suite rooms, and the shape of each room. Three terms are related to the actual number of guest rooms available in the design: *key*, which refers to a rentable unit; *room* which is a separate unit whether rentable or not;[7] and *bay*, which is the space equivalent to a guest room.[8] For the hotel management, the term *key* is most important, since it represents the number of rentable guest rooms available. Figures 4-16 and 4-17 illustrate common guest room layouts.

The interior plan and design of the guest rooms themselves are influenced by the architectural decisions mentioned above along with decisions concerning the location of the bathroom, the location of the doors, and windows. The interior designer's primary responsibility is to provide the appropriate amount of furniture and accessories to make the rooms pleasant for the type of clientele and type of hotel property (Figure 4-18).

Design of the guest rooms itself can be done by zoning the "functional" areas of the typical guest room. Those zones include sleeping, lounging, working, dressing, and the bathroom. The sleeping area requires a bed or beds, bedside tables with lighting fixtures, and room around the bed for access by guests and housekeeping. The lounging area requires soft seating for easy viewing of the television and lighting to read. If the room is large enough to provide a sofa, this is usually a sofa bed to allow for extra sleeping accommodations. The work area is a table or desk with one or more chairs. Chairs are usually dining room style chairs and the work area is accessorized with a table or floor fixture. Depending on the type of hotel and services, an extra telephone may be located at the work area, perhaps with an extra wall outlet as well for the accommodation of computer modems for the business traveler. In many hotels, the working zone doubles as an eating area when room service is requested by the guest.

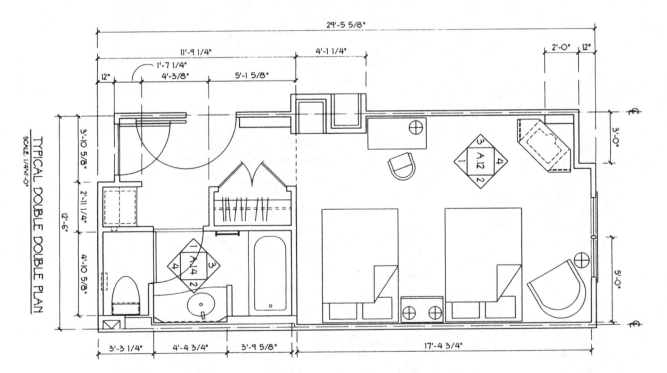

Figure 4-16 A typical double-double floor plan in a hotel. (Plan courtesy of the Holiday Inns.)

---

[7] Rutes and Penner, 1985, p. 167.

[8] Stipanuk and Roffmann, 1992, p. 371 (hardcover edition).

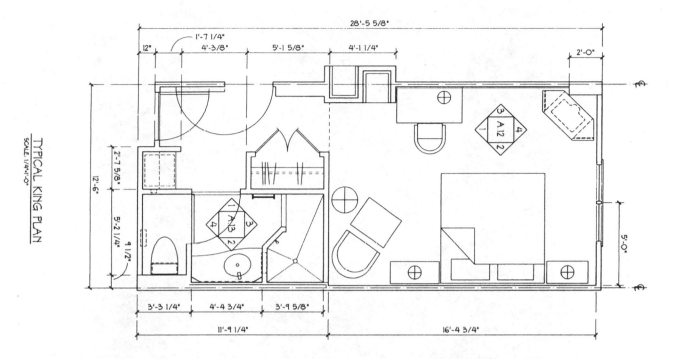

Figure 4–17 A possible guest room layout with option of an adjoining room. (Plan courtesy of Holiday Inn.)

Recently, many types of hotels have added another small "eating zone" by providing small refrigerators with chargeable bar and snack service, and coffee makers. In some types of hotels, the eating zone could become a full-service kitchen where the guest could prepare his or her own meals. In many smaller hotels, the lounge area is the work area, and no soft seating is provided.

Dressing areas require a dresser, closet, mirror, and space to accommodate luggage. How much room is allowed for these areas will vary with the type of hotel. Facilities where guests will be spending only one or two nights will have a dresser with a small number of drawers, small open closet, and folding rack for the luggage. Hotels where guest will be staying for several days or possibly even a few weeks will have more dresser space, larger closets, and storage space for luggage.

The basic design of the bathroom is a lavatory, water closet, and a bathtub or shower stall. Some hotels will provide lavatories separate from the water closet/tub area. Many designers also include drawers in the dressing and/or bath area. Bathrooms are of simple design in smaller hotels and motels. But competition has forced more upscale hotels to recognize that a luxurious bathroom is an important part of marketing the hotel property. Larger spaces, elegantly designed fixtures, handsome materials, and extra amenities have been added for the discerning guest to feel at home. Remember that ADA regulations and the building codes will also affect the design of bathroom facilities in lodging facilities. Recall that this was discussed earlier in this chapter.

The FF & E specification of the interior will typically involve selections for wallcoverings, flooring, window treatments, furniture styles and fabrics, bedspreads, accessories, and lighting fixtures. Let us first look at the preferred types of materials for walls, floors, and windows. Commercial grade vinyl wall covering and commercial grade carpets are a must in guest rooms. In most situations for the standard size room, small patterns are used for the carpet and wall coverings with larger patterns being reserved for bedspreads and draperies. Of course, larger rooms might find the opposite specification. Ceramic tile for the bathroom walls and floors is preferred. Highly glazed ceramic tile should not be used for flooring for obvious reasons.

(a)

(b)

Figure 4–18 (*a*) Luxurious guest room at the Monte Carlo Resort and Casino. (Design by and photograph courtesy of Anita Brooks/Charles Gruwell Interior Design International, Las Vegas, NV.) (*b*) Interior design of a guest room reflecting the tropical ambience at the Westin Rio Mar. (Design by and photograph courtesy of Hirsch Bedner Associates.)

The architectural finishes used must meet Class C and Class III materials within the rooms. Window treatments should include both an over drape of some decorative fabric or pattern and an under blackout drape to provide privacy and light control.

Furniture selected for guest rooms must be commercial grade products rather than residential grade. The difference, of course, will be in the construction quality of the bed frames, dressers, and seating pieces. Plastic laminate finishes on furniture items are most commonly selected, though veneers will be used in upscale and luxury hotels. Fabrics for bedspreads and soft seating should be selected with care even though the building and fire codes generally do not regulate those materials.

Accessories are selected to carry out the overall concept and theme of the hotel. Reproduction paintings, prints, and photographs for the walls are most common with small bookshelves and books supplied in many resort and vacation hotels. The designer must make selections of accessories with some consideration for theft in mind. It is common that wall accessories be physically attached by screws rather than being hung as in a home. In many hotels even lighting fixtures are fixed to the walls or tables to make it difficult for items to be stolen.

A standard accessory in hotels and almost all lodging facilities today is the television. A television, and even a VCR, has become an expected accessory in guest rooms. The placement of the TV must be planned for viewing from the bed as well as the lounge area. Placing the TV on a "lazy Susan" on the top of the dresser or in a special TV cabinet and dresser combination allows for this kind of flexibility.

Appropriate lighting for each zone in the guest room is important. General lighting by means of ceiling or movable fixtures with switches at the entry door provides security and safety. High quality lighting is needed in the bathroom for applying makeup and for dressing. Light fixtures are needed at the bedside and are commonly a wall fixture with sections that will accommodate both sides of a bed or table fixtures with multiple light levels. Fixtures are also required for soft seating and work areas. Designer specification of lighting fixtures should also take into consideration energy economy. Incandescent lamps left on by guests will require constant replacement. Longer burning fluorescent lamps will provide better energy economy for the hotel.

The ADA requires certain accommodations to a percentage of rooms in hotels for accessibility. These were discussed in the general section on interior design code requirements earlier in this chapter. The reader is referred to Figure 4-9 for a typical ADA guest room layout.

Guest room suites accommodate an alternative to the standard guest room and present hotels the option to attract different classes of guests. All-suites hotels have become quite popular with business travelers and many families. Suite rooms provide all the function areas discussed above in a more residential setting. The suite room will have separated eating and sleeping areas. Larger suites have multiple bedrooms, conference rooms or dining rooms, and separate lounge areas (Figure 4-19). In many hotels, suite rooms are commonly on the upper floors of the hotel providing better views, quiet, and privacy. Suites on upper floors also may have private balconies whenever the hotel has feature views of the city or area. The designer also will upgrade the quality of materials, furniture, and accessories in the suites, making these rooms worth their upgraded prices. If suites are planned into a new hotel, a portion of these accommodations will also have to be designed to meet the ADA.

Food and Beverage Facilities

Food and beverage facilities are common in the service mix of hotels. A *food service facility* is any retail space that is devoted to providing cooked or prepared foods to consumers. *Beverage facilities* are defined as those providing alcoholic beverage service. They have been part of the mix of service in hotels for decades. Multiple factors conspired to reduce the role of food and beverage services in hotels during the early part of the 20th century. Prohibition encouraged people to seek out less public places to have a drink. Competition from freestanding restaurants reduced guest visits to hotel restaurants. Fast-food restaurants changed the eating habits of many. However, this trend has been diminishing since about the 1960s.

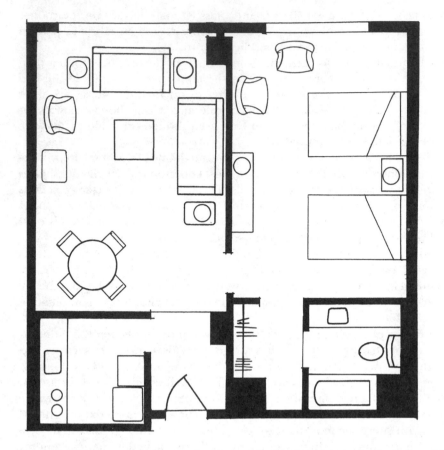

Figure 4–19 Suite rooms in a hotel with double-double layout in the bedroom. (Courtesy of Double Tree Guest Suites.)

The high cost of planning and outfitting a food service space must produce revenue at a profitable level even faced with local outside competition. Therefore, the use of a distinctive theme, type of service, and the menu are all parts of the decision package for food and beverage facilities located in hotels. The type of hotel and its guest target market also play an important part in planning and interior design decisions. For example, for a suburban hotel, breakfast is the main meal serving numerous guests while lunch has a minimal customer demand. Customer use of in-house food service picks up again at dinner time. For resorts and hotels remote from other food and beverage options, all meals will be at a high demand.

Generally, food and beverage facilities are located off the lobby for the convenience of guests. In many situations such as downtown and conference hotels, at least one hotel food service facility is planned with an exterior entrance in order to attract local customers. A hotel might have a coffee shop, a mid-priced restaurant, an upscale restaurant to serve gourmet meals, and some have smaller outlets selling specialized items, outlets like coffee bars, ice cream shops, delis, and snack bars. In recent years, larger hotels have also allowed brand name facilities like McDonalds to offer food service within the hotel complex.

The designer and hotel food and beverage manager must work out the mix of table sizes. In many types of hotels, the common number of diners in a party will be one or two with some fours and fewer large groups. In hotels that cater to families, table seating for four or more is required most often. The number of seats can be approximated by using a factor of

.75 times the number of rooms for restaurant seats and .5 times for lounge seats.[9] This does not mean that each outlet will have that number of seats. Food and beverage managers must communicate to the designer and architect the expected amount of seating depending on the type of hotel, the number of service options, and the possibility of local customers also coming into the hotel. All of these operational factors are important criteria to be determined before any space planning and design specification can occur.

Lobby bars are a specialized beverage service provided in many downtown and larger hotels. They originated as a means to give guests and visitors something interesting to do in the atrium lobbies. They are a good revenue generator for the hotel as guests and visitors have a place to casually meet or hold meetings away from conference rooms. Lobby bars are usually open, meaning they are not in a "walled room" like the bar part of a restaurant. Designers often give them a perimeter by use of plants and low walls that separate the space from circulation space and create a barrier to restrict underage individuals from using the space. A lobby bar must have good visibility, comfortable seating with sofas and soft seating around small tables, a service bar, and access to food service for appetizers and snacks. Some include space for entertainment like a piano and television.

The beverage area commonly called a cocktail lounge usually has a different atmosphere from the lobby lounge. It often provides evening entertainment including a dance floor rather than just a piano player, and is thus generally noisier than the lobby bar. Cocktail lounges are in enclosed areas to reduce noise filtering into the lobby or nearby restaurants. Lower light levels are provided since it is a place for relaxing. Cocktail lounges in hotels also provide seating for guests at small tables and sofas in small to medium groupings; they also need space for the bar itself, along with access to food service space for appetizers, and entertainment areas.

The seating units selected in a cocktail lounge are generally more movable than those in a lobby bar, though the requirement to move seating around is found in both situations. This is true since guests will rearrange furniture to bring larger groups together than are normally accommodated in the furniture plan. Because of the entertainment factor in the hotel cocktail lounge, lighting specification and design is very important and must be flexible to accommodate a variety of entertainment modes. Consideration is also needed for the sound system so that individuals on the dance floor clearly hear the music, while other areas, for guests who are less interested in the music, remain quieter.

Designers who will seek food and beverage projects within hotels should become familiar with all aspects of food and beverages operations and have some knowledge of hotel operations as well. If the reader is involved in a food and beverage space in a hotel, he or she is urged to begin by reading the next chapter.

Summary

Designing lodging facilities, regardless of size or type, is a challenging and exciting facet of commercial interior design. It is also an area of design in which the ability to work with a team is of utmost importance. The interior designer's work supports concepts and goals of the owner and must coordinate with the architect. Attention to detail, thoughtful budget deliberations, and careful working habits are necessary for the designer engaged in lodging interior design as a specialty.

This chapter has explained the purpose, goals, and operational objectives of lodging facilities. It has also provided basic explanations of the different types of facilities. The student and design professional first encountering the design of a lodging facility will find information concerning the planning and design of the interior with special emphasis on the lobby,

---

[9] Rutes and Penner, 1985, p. 183.

function spaces, and guest rooms. The reader may wish to investigate material in the reference list below for more details on the operations and design of lodging facilities.

References

Architectural Record Book. 1960. *Motels, Hotels, Restaurants and Bars,* 2nd ed. New York: McGraw-Hill.

Arthur, Paul and Romedi Passini. 1992. *Wayfinding.* New York: McGraw-Hill.

Bardi, James A. 1990. *Hotel Front Office Management.* New York: Van Nostrand Reinhold.

Davies, Thomas D., Jr. and Kim A. Beasley. 1994. *Accessible Design for Hospitality,* 2nd ed. New York: McGraw-Hill.

Dittmer, Paul R. and Gerald G. Griffin. 1993. *The Dimensions of the Hospitality Industry.* New York: Van Nostrand Reinhold.

Donzel, Catherine, Alexis Gregory, and Marc Walter. 1989. *Grand American Hotels.* New York: Vendome.

Fellows, Jane and Richard Fellows. 1990. *Buildings for Hospitality.* London, England: Pitman.

Hardy, Hugh. 1997. "What Is Hospitality Design?" *Hospitality Design.* Jan.–Feb. Pp. 66–68.

Janjigian, Robert. 1993. "Bathing Beauties." *Hospitality Design.* Sept. Pp. 57–65.

Knapp, Frederic. 1995. *Hotel Renovation Planning and Design.* New York: McGraw-Hill.

Lawson, Fred. 1995. *Hotels and Resorts: Planning, Design and Refurbishment.* Jordan Hill, Oxford, England: Butterworth-Architecture, Linacre House.

Radulski, John P. 1991. "Specifying for the Bath." *Restaurant/Hotel Design International.* Jan. Pp. 22 ff.

Rutes, Walter A. and Richard H. Penner. 1985. *Hotel Planning and Design.* New York: Watson-Guptill.

Rutherford, Denney G. (Editor). 1995. *Hotel Management and Operations,* 2nd ed. New York: Van Nostrand Reinhold.

Sawinski, Diane M. (Editor). 1995. *US. Industries Profiles.* "Hotels and Motels." New York: Gale Research Inc.

Standard and Poors. 1996. *Standard and Poor's Industry Surveys A–L,* Vol. 1. New York: McGraw-Hill.

Stipanuk, David M. and Harold Roffmann. 1992. *Hospitality Facilities Management and Design.* East Lansing, MI: Educational Institute of the American Hotel and Motel Association.

Walker, John R. 1996. *Introduction to Hospitality.* Englewood Cliffs, NJ: Prentice Hall.

Additional references related to material in this chapter are listed in Appendix A.

Chapter 5

Food and Beverage Facilities

The second and third parts of the hospitality industry involve food and beverage facilities. Food service facilities provide prepared foods for immediate consumption, whether that consumption takes place on or off the premises. The beverage portion of the industry provides alcoholic beverages for on-site consumption. There are, of course, many examples of food service facilities or restaurants that serve food and do not serve alcoholic beverages and beverage facilities going by names such as bars, taverns, pubs, and lounges that do not serve much in the way of food. This chapter focuses on the establishment that offers both food and beverage service.

Customers go to food and beverage establishments not just to eat or drink. They go for socializing, celebrating, conducting business, romance, even to give the primary food maker a break. The design of the establishment helps create the psychological atmosphere desired to complete this need:

> Restaurant design has become as compelling an element as menu, food, wine and staffing in determining a restaurant's success. . . . To be effective, restaurant design must strike a nearly impossible balance between three competing agendas: that of the guest, who must feel welcome, aroused and transported; that of the staff, which must be able to complete its tasks in a smooth, stress-free flow that allows for maximum hospitality; and that of the restaurant's owner, for in providing all this comfort for guests and staff, there must still remain the proper ratio of selling area to manufacturing space to allow for maximum profit.[1]

In this chapter we first discuss the business of the food and beverage industry. The chapter continues with a brief history and a discussion of the different types of facilities. Planning and design concepts related to the interior design of food and beverage facilities are also included, focusing on a generic food and beverage facility.

---

[1] Danny Meyer, guest forward. Reprinted by permission of PBC International from *The New Restaurant: Dining Design 2* by Charles Morris Mount, p. 9, © 1995.

An Overview of Food and Beverage Facilities

According to Dittmer and Griffin, "one out of every four retail outlets in the nation is an eating or drinking establishment."[2] The reader need only look around his or her hometown to realize that the food and beverage industry is highly competitive. Yet, according to the National Restaurant Association, three out of four restaurants fail within one year.

The overriding goal of a food and beverage facility is relatively simple to state: to provide food, service, and an atmosphere that satisfies the guests and encourages them to come back. But there are, of course, all levels of food, service, and atmosphere. Each individual owner must first determine what levels of food, service, and atmosphere are the goals for his or her restaurant, and then seek through good planning, design, and operations to achieve those levels. The interior designer must understand these goals in order to assist the owner in achieving an atmosphere that is consistent with the intended food type, quality, and service.

Let us first look at some terminology used in discussing the operation of a restaurant.

Beverage areas are those sections of a restaurant or freestanding facility that primarily serve alcoholic beverages.

Concept represents the ideas brought together by the owner that are used for the basis of all planning and design decisions for the facility.

Independent restaurants are those owned and managed by an individual or partnership and created from the individual's or partners' own imagination and creativity.

Franchise restaurant is one for which the owners have purchased a license to operate the restaurant under the guidance and requirements of the company that holds the rights to the original concepts.

Deuces are tables for two, also called "two tops."

Seat turnover rate is the estimated number of times a table will be used in any one day. This will vary greatly based on the type of restaurant and the type of service offered.

One factor in achieving a successful design for a food and beverage facility rests with understanding the operations of such a facility. The hierarchy in a restaurant is relatively simple. The manager is responsible for overall organizational and operational decisions. He or she will set policy, be responsible for insuring employees are trained and motivated, work with the chef and kitchen staff to insure that the proper amount of and kind of food is available each day, and determine personnel needs for wait staff and kitchen staff.

The staff members who will be in direct contact with the customers are the host, wait staff, and cashier. The host or hostess greets the guests and directs their seating. In some restaurants the host or hostess is called a maître d', which actually is defined as head waiter. This individual is also responsible for the appearance of the dining room, for taking reservations, and for overall customer relations. The wait staff, often called servers, are those individuals who take customer orders, serve the food, and may clean the tables. There are commonly two levels to wait staff, those who work directly with the customer, commonly called waiters and waitresses, and those who clean tables and reset for the next service, commonly called busing staff. Other levels of wait staff may exist, depending on the concept for the restaurant. In a beverage facility, there will also be the bartender and cocktail servers, who will have direct contact with the customer.

The back of the house employees will be the kitchen staff and manager. Kitchen staff include the main chef, specialty chefs, and cooks who, of course, prepare all the food. Then there will be support employees such as ware washers, who scrape and wash dishes, and pantry workers, who assist in pulling foods from storage areas. Other than the main chef, it is uncommon that the kitchen staff have much contact with the guests.

Concept and Menu Development

Critical to the development of a successful restaurant are the concept and the menu. It is important for the owner to establish a *concept* whether the venture to be created is a simple pizza

---

[2] Dittmer and Griffin, 1993, p. 120.

place or an elaborate gourmet restaurant. The concept must present a total impression for the market the owner wishes to attract and includes consideration for location, architectural design, menu, style of service, pricing, mood (formal or informal), interior design, colors, uniforms, and many other factors. The concept might spring from any number of sources. It might come from the region, such as a country inn in New England. Maybe it is based on a particular kind of cooking, like nouvelle cuisine or ethnic food. It might be a gourmet restaurant to cater to the "power lunch" contingent, or simply a hot dog vendor on a city street. Whatever the concept, it must be developed carefully and be based on a clear idea of what the owner wishes to achieve and the kind of guests the restaurant will most likely attract.

A very important part of concept development is the market analysis. A thorough market analysis will look at the demographic and descriptive makeup of targeted customers. It is critical to know if there are enough of the age group, income level, and type of clientele (breakfast, lunch, dinner, business, etc.) in the vicinity to support the venture. Competition analysis will also tell the owner if there are too many existing restaurants of a similar kind in the vicinity to support one more.

The location is an important part of concept development. One must decide if the restaurant is going to be located in an urban or suburban area, small town, along a freeway, near a popular recreational site, or other possible locations. In addition, it must be determined if the facility will be in the business district, near shopping, adjacent to entertainment areas, near other restaurants, in a high-rise, at a freestanding location, or in a strip shopping center.

The location will further define the types of available food and service offerings. Restaurants in the business district, for example, will find that much of their business will be generated during the lunch period. Depending on the actual location, the area may or may not also have a reasonable dinner business. Restaurants near shopping in urban areas provide primarily lunch service. Suburban shopping malls have many levels of restaurants for lunch and dinner service and are commonly surrounded by additional restaurants that may also serve lunch or dinner. In entertainment areas, the meal type will be quite varied. Some forms of entertainment and recreation are all-day activities, like ice skating and bowling; thus breakfast, lunch, and dinner service will be provided. Restaurants adjacent to major sports stadiums are possibly lunch locations, but certainly dinner and evening locations. Food and beverage establishments near theater and movie houses must be prepared to serve dinner before shows as well as provide light food or full service after the show.

The design and concept of the establishment must concentrate on those things that will bring people in the first place and also bring them back—quality food and service and a pleasant atmosphere that relates to the menu / concept. However, those are never enough. The well-thought-out and superbly designed restaurant of today may not be in existence for long if the owner does not keep up with the changing tastes and demands of customers. According to Lundberg, "Restaurant decor is said to have a half-life of somewhere around five years."[3] Concepts become stale as new ones emerge. In this highly competitive industry, today's hot concept could be a vacant space in the future if owners do not constantly look at refining the concept and offerings to stay current and to keep customers coming back. The interior designer, architect, and other consultants will assist in the complete development of the concept and the design elements necessary to make it all come together.

The menu is not a responsibility of the interior designer. It does, however, provide the direction of the overall concept and interior design. For example, a menu of ethnic food such as Asian will often suggest oriental themes in the interior specifications. A seafood restaurant could utilize many different themes from sailing, fishing, and the ocean. "The menu tends to reflect the character and mood of the establishment, not only by which items are being presented but also how those items are represented, the typeface used, the layout of the menu itself, and the colors employed."[4]

---

[3]Lundberg, 1985, p. 12.
[4]Lundberg, 1985, p. 55.

Types of Food and Beverage Facilities

Food and beverage facilities as we know them today are a relatively recent phenomenon. Before the late 18th century, citizens who sought food and beverage service went to inns, taverns, and roadhouses. More often that not, the food quality at these establishments was poor. In Paris in the 1760s, a man named Boulanger opened a shop specifically to sell prepared food. One of the key food items he sold was bouillon. In those days, bouillon was one of the foods considered to be a restorative or *restaurant*.[5] This French word gradually became associated with establishments that provided food service.

As for the United States, restaurants grew in numbers and types as the demand for food service increased in the cities during the industrial revolution. The quality of food improved since the upper classes demanded high quality food and decor. In the cities, a market developed for quick meals, mostly for city workers. The first attempt to deal with this market were lunch wagons which were horse drawn carts or push carts. Late in the 1880s, these carts became large enough to provide indoor sit-down service of sandwiches, soups, and beverages. These larger carts become known as diners (Figure 5-1).

For the rail traveler, obtaining a decent meal on the road was a real adventure until Fred Harvey opened a series of Harvey House restaurants along the Atchison Topeka and Santa Fe Railroad. The Harvey Girls, waitresses at the restaurants, provided good service and decent food in the minimum time the railroad allowed for meal stops.

Many specialized types of restaurants developed in the 20th century, all trying to entice customers through their doors (Figure 5-2). Roadside restaurants became popular in the 1940s, especially after World War II. Competition for the travelers' dollars brought about roadside restaurants with every kind of food and many styles of architectural design (Figure 5-3). Today, every conceivable type of food, quality of service style, and design atmosphere exists to satisfy the preferences of the public.

It is hard to classify today's different types of restaurants since it is a constantly evolving area of commercial design. Frankly, there is a lot of argument by many in the hospitality business as to how to classify the different types of food and beverage facilities. Some food and beverage facilities even fall into more than one classification, making it even harder to identify them definitively by type. However, there are several classifications of food and beverage facilities that stand out.

First, a food and beverage facility can be classified either as independent, as part of a chain, or as a franchise. An *independent facility* is one that is owned and managed by an individual or partnership who create the facility from his, her, or their own imagination and creativity. It often has only one location, where the owner plays a very integral part in the operations and activities of the facility. When this individual location becomes successful, the owner may open an identical or very similar facility in another location—perhaps on the other side of town or in a nearby city. Each additional location increases the size of the "chain." A *chain*-type restaurant would then be multiple locations of one restaurant concept.

A *franchise* is a concept whereby the owners purchase a license to operate the facility under the guidance and requirements of the company that holds the rights to the original concept. Franchises—which are also chains—grew starting in the 1950s. Howard Johnson's was one the first chain restaurants. Chains and franchises grew as local residents increasingly enjoyed eating meals away from home. Patrons became familiar with the food and service provided by this type of restaurant and knew that no matter where they were, across town or across the country, their expectations would be met. The person who buys the franchise—the franchisee—benefits by owning a restaurant that has an established reputation, which brings in customers who are preconditioned as to what to expect from the facility.

The other way of classifying food and beverage facilities is by the type of service they provide. For the purposes of limiting the discussion for this book, we classify restaurants

---

[5]Dorf, 1992, p. 12.

(a)

(b)

Figure 5–1 (*a*) Exterior view of an early restaurant in the Oklahoma frontier. (*b*) Interior view of a cafe/bar circa 1900. (Photographs used by permission, Utah State Historical Society. All rights reserved.)

into fast food, specialty, and full service. Any of these might be fit into any of the ownership categories.

Fast food (called quick service by some) is one type of restaurant. Today, we are all familiar with the fast-food restaurant that serves food that is cooked quickly and served with little or no waiting. Fast-food restaurants began as food carts on street corners. Later sit-down

Figure 5–2 Soda fountains were popular food service facilities. (Photograph used by permission, Utah State Historical Society. All rights reserved.)

luncheonettes and the automat brought fast food to city dwellers (Figure 5-4). The automat requires a bit of discussion.

Joseph Horn and Frank Hardart of Philadelphia came up with the idea of displaying precooked food behind small glass windows. Patrons would walk up to the service line where the food was displayed, insert the proper change into slots by one of the windows, and instantly receive their food choice.[6] In the early 20th century, Horn and Hardart opened an automat in Times Square in Manhattan. It was ornately designed and offered fast service to busy New York businesspeople, shoppers, and tourists for decades. About the only place one can see an automat today is in the Smithsonian Museum of American History in Washington, DC. Unfortunately, it is not operational.

Most readers, however, associate fast food with restaurants like McDonalds, Taco Bell, Kentucky Fried Chicken (KFC), Pizza Hut, and scores of others. According to Dittmer and Griffin, the first fast-food chain was not McDonalds (which started in the 1950s), but White Castle Hamburgers, opening in Kansas in 1921.[7] The atmosphere of a fast-food restaurant is designed to induce the customer to eat quickly and leave after a short time. It must be well organized and, with the chains, the concept rarely changes from one location to another.

Full-service restaurants have a large selection of menu items, sometimes cooked at table side; a wait staff take customer orders and serve. Full-service restaurants can have many types of service style and decor, and are usually independently owned. Menu prices can be from the mid-range to very high. Full-service restaurants got their start in the 19th century when restaurants began offering meals served by waiters. Prior to that, guests would be served "family style" from platters on counters or sideboards. At the fancier restaurants the evening dinner meals were formal affairs with gloved waiters serving multiple courses. Although fine dining was available in the larger cities of the United States, this was rarely true in the smaller towns anywhere in the country.

---

[6] As a side note, the movie "That Touch of Mink," with Doris Day and Cary Grant, features scenes in a New York automat.
[7] Dittmer and Griffin, 1993, p. 99.

(a)

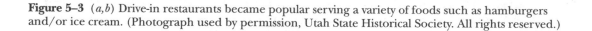

(b)

Figure 5–3 (*a,b*) Drive-in restaurants became popular serving a variety of foods such as hamburgers and/or ice cream. (Photograph used by permission, Utah State Historical Society. All rights reserved.)

High-end full-service restaurants most likely have a high level of service with a host or maître d' to greet guests, captains, and food servers to take customer orders and serve meals, bus people to clean tables, perhaps even a sommelier (a wine waiter). High quality food, sometimes called gourmet or haute cuisine (meaning "high food"), and top of the line interior design are also expected in this type of facility. Restaurants such as the Four Seasons in New

Figure 5–4 Luncheonettes remain popular for their quick service. (Photograph of JoAnn's "B" Street Cafe courtesy of Hayashida Architects, Sady S. Hayashida, Principal. Photographer: Dennis Anderson, Dennis Anderson Photography.)

York, Spago in Los Angeles, Morton's in Chicago, and Christopher's in Phoenix are examples of this type of restaurant at the high end in pricing.

Specialty restaurants are those in which the menu focuses on a certain type of food, a theme, or style of service. A specialty restaurant falls between the limited menu of a fast-food restaurant and the high-end pricing and service style of a full-service restaurant. Many of the specialty restaurants provide service and menu selections similar to full-service restaurants. But it is the price differential that primarily separates specialty restaurants from the high-end full-service ones described above. A specialty restaurant will have a menu larger than a fast-food restaurant, it will likely have a host or hostess to greet customers and seat customers, waiters and waitresses to serve at the table, and even bus persons to clear tables. Coco's, Marie Callender's, Red Lobster, Stuart Anderson's Black Angus, Chili's, Hard Rock Cafe, the

Olive Garden, and numerous other chains and independently owned restaurants fall into this category. It will be beneficial to briefly look at a few of the categories within this broad type of food and beverage facility.

Specialty restaurants can be categorized by type of food such as: pizza, chicken, steak, and seafood, to name a few. There are other classifications of specialty restaurants starting with ethnic restaurants, which focus on traditional ethnic foods; theme restaurants, which rely on a total dining experience rather than a special food group; and family or casual dining restaurants, which are commonly informal places frequented by families.

Ethnic restaurants will usually use the featured foods and ethnic motifs for both the menu and the interior design. For example, it is quite common for Italian restaurants to use the red, green, and white of the Italian flag for their interior color schemes. Ethnic focused restaurants got their start in the 19th century by catering to immigrant groups. Many ethnic restaurants are independently owned, though there are also many chains, like the Olive Garden. Alcoholic beverages are often available, but not all ethnic restaurants will have a separate bar area. Because so many of these restaurants are family owned, the owners often put their own family recipes and twists on the menu preparation and selections, making them fun places to try new foods and recipes.

Theme restaurants develop some specialized theme that is not necessarily related to a type of food or ethnic inspiration. The menu, interior and exterior design, and total concept will focus on the theme. Planet Hollywood uses the movies as its theme. Hard Rock Cafe uses rock and roll music as its theme. Ed Debevick's and Johnny Rockets use a theme of the 1950s. Theme restaurants offer a total experience with the food, interior, and atmosphere taking the guest back to a special idea or place. It might be loud rock and roll music at a Hard Rock Cafe, or movie clips at Planet Hollywood. But the idea is to fully involve the guest in the atmosphere and theme of the facility.

Family dining restaurants are those that had their beginnings with the early coffee shops and highway restaurants. They are generally casual in style, with low-key, simple interiors, friendly waitresses and waiters, and good, wholesome, "home-cooked" food. Many are independently owned, but some chain restaurants like Dennys', Coco's, and Village Inn Pancake House fall into this category as well. Family restaurants often serve all three meals based on a simple, fairly straightforward menu. Limited alcoholic beverage service is available in many of these restaurants, though a bar is not a part of the space plan.

Today, all sizes and types of restaurants cater to all economic levels from coffee shops, cafeterias, and street vendors, to new chains like Hard Rock Cafe, and numerous high-end gourmet establishments. All these different restaurants are vying for the public's patronage, providing varying degrees of service, types of food, and even quality of presentation and the interior.

Planning and Design Concepts

The successful design of a food and beverage facility must consider all parts of the operation. The front of the house areas—entry, waiting, dining room, and bar area—must mesh with the design of the back of the house areas—kitchen, food storage, office, and other service areas. Generally, interior designers are not contracted to design the back of the house. This is done by commercial kitchen design consultants. According to the experts, therein lies the problem. The two consultants do not always communicate thoroughly enough for the two parts to work well together. "If the front of the house is not designed to support the back of the house and/or the back of the house is not designed to carry out the concept manifested in the front of the house, then the operation suffers."[8]

---

[8]Baraban and Durocher, 1989, p. 1.

The remaining sections of this chapter discuss all parts of the design of a food and beverage establishment from exterior design through back of the house. In this way, the student and professional unfamiliar with restaurant design will gain an overview of total design responsibilities.

Exterior Design Concepts

The success of a restaurant is based on how well the parts of its concept mesh. One of those parts is the exterior design. Throughout history, vernacular architecture and symbols have been used to call attention to restaurants. Early inns and taverns would have symbols such as food items incorporated into their signs to indicate that food was available at that establishment. Over the decades, giant root beer barrels, tea pots, igloos, and castles helped owners create an identity for their restaurant and helped the customer find a particular place amongst the competition. In more recent decades, neon lighting and signage beckon the guest to the restaurant.

Although not a responsibility of the interior designer, the exterior design has a direct relationship to customer perception and to ultimate success from the customers' point of view. A facility with a lot of neon lights, gaudy signage, and thematic architecture will indicate such things as fast-food, noisy, the type of food to be served, and so on. A simple exterior design with an elegant sign can be an indicator of high-end, full-service, gourmet food. Any reader who has been at a Planet Hollywood remembers the fun customers have determining if their hands fit into the handprints of celebrities immortalized in the exterior facade. That facade and the other design elements of the exterior provide important clues to the customer as to what they will likely experience on the interior.

Exterior design must attract customers and catch their attention away from competing food and beverage facilities in the same vicinity. Establishments located near highways count on a highly visible exterior design or signage to catch the eye of motorists. They have only a few seconds to attract the motorist as he or she is cruising along the freeway or arterial surface streets.

The *entrance facade* can bring instant recognition. Facades like Planet Hollywood, described earlier in this section, and even the golden arches of McDonalds bring instant recognition of the restaurant and an expectation of what is to come for the guest. "The facade of the building itself can help to differentiate it from the competition and create memorable images in the minds of the customers."[9]

Location is also important to the success of the establishment and relates to many issues of the exterior design. In urban centers, the corner position is considered the best location. Being on the corner allows for immediate visibility by pedestrians and motorists from two directions. A location in the middle of the block reduces visibility, creates more difficulties in entrance location and design, and may dramatically limit total design concept on the interior. Another street-side urban location for a facility is one in which the space is wrapped around an adjacent corner business. The advantage here is that the restaurant can have two entrances from the different approaches. A fourth location is to be wholly inside a building, such as a high-rise office building, with no exterior facade. Visibility by passing pedestrians and motorists is the logical disadvantage to this location. In this case, the establishment is depending on customer traffic from within the structure and the development of the restaurant's reputation, which would bring in additional customers. Restaurants along freeways and highways need eye-catching exterior design with signage that gives an idea of the food and service offered.

Signage helps the guest identify the establishment as well as locate entrances (Figure 5-5). Restaurants along freeways and highways will need larger signs than those located along streets where more pedestrian traffic exists. Signs should identify the restaurant and bring some idea of the kind of food that is offered, the type of meals served (breakfast, lunch, dinner), maybe

---

[9]Baraban and Durocher, 1989, p. 54.

(a)

(b)

Figure 5–5 (*a*) This restaurant on a suburban street displays simple but clear signage. (*b*) This outlet of the same chain located along a highway uses additional signage to attract the motorist's eye. (Photographs courtesy of VICORP Restaurants, Inc., Denver, CO.)

even hours of operation. Even the price of the food can be conveyed with the signage—it seems that the more expensive the restaurant, the smaller the sign!

Exterior lighting goes hand in hand with the facade and signage. Lighting the exterior is done to help set the mood and ambience that will be found inside. Loud, bright neon lighting or colored spotlights usually indicate a casual atmosphere. Subdued exterior lighting often indicates a more formal dining experience. Accent lighting, used in such techniques as small white lights in trees, effectively used at Tavern on the Green in New York City, add interest and sparkle to the exterior.

Finally, the *entrance door* can be a key design element in the exterior. In many cases, canopies call attention to the entrance, helping to provide the needed focal point as well as providing a place where patrons are protected from the weather. When the location for the restaurant is along a busy city street, the entrance area and door design must help identify the restaurant, distinguishing it from all the others. Door specification should also be done in keeping with the Americans with Disabilities Act (ADA) and the building codes. The doors need to swing out into the exterior and be of a weight that does not exceed any applicable limits in the jurisdiction. In colder climates where a double set of entry doors are provided, the designer must insure that the spacing is designed to be at least 48 inches plus the swinging width of the door. Because of the building codes, revolving doors should not be used unless an additional leafed door or doors are provided.

Interior Design Concepts

The interior of the restaurant plays an obvious key role in the success of the restaurant, although to the patron, a great interior with terrible service and disappointing food will not be a place to which they return. For the guest, the congruence of design elements from the exterior through the entry, at the waiting area, and into the dining room itself all, to some degree or another, must fit any preconceived ideas about the establishment for the customer to return. Just consider the confusion of signage that proclaims home cooking, a facade and exterior that resembles a Georgian building, and the interior design lavishly done in a Polynesian motif. Home cooking from where?

If the designer is fortunate enough to be involved in the design of the establishment from the early conceptual stages, then he or she should visit those restaurants in the area that will be competing with the proposed facility. That will give the interior designer some idea of what restaurant themes and planning concepts in the area are already working to attract customers.

In this section of the chapter, we introduce the reader to the interior design and planning concepts of a restaurant with a full-service beverage area. The type of restaurant could be defined as a full-service or specialty restaurant, though no one type of restaurant is emphasized. Although the discussion focuses on a full-service facility, points are made concerning other types of restaurants. This section takes the designer from the entrance through the spaces of the establishment as if walking in the front door and being allowed back into the kitchen. Interior design elements of space allocation and traffic patterns, furniture specifications, colors and materials, mechanical interface, and codes are all discussed.

Space Allocation

Space allocation decisions will be controlled by the estimated number of seats required, the type of restaurant, the style of service, and the menu. The revenue producing areas of the restaurant are, of course, the dining room and the beverage facility. Naturally, the more tables that are provided, the greater potential revenue. However, overestimating the number of tables could jeopardize the concept. Upscale gourmet restaurants and many types of full-service restaurants require a certain amount of spaciousness between tables as part of the conceptual ambience. If the owner and designer plan table arrangements in these types of restaurants as is more common in mid- and low-priced or fast-food restaurants, the concept fails, as might the restaurant.

In our example restaurant, the designer will need to provide for the entry and waiting area, beverage area, dining room, public rest rooms, and perhaps the kitchen and service areas. Although there are "rules of thumb" that help estimate the amount of space required for different types of restaurants, they are just that—estimates. The concept once again drives the actual square footage needed.

Codes will also affect the amount of square footage required. Most restaurants will be classified as A-3 assembly spaces having an occupancy less than 300. Most codes allow an occupant load factor of 15 square feet per person for seating areas. This provides space for aisles and small bus stations, but not for rest rooms, beverage areas, the entry, and waiting area. Of course, this may be satisfactory for a small restaurant with casual service, but the seating allowance may be very low for a more high-ticket gourmet facility. Commercial kitchens are restricted to a minimum of 200 square feet per kitchen staff member. Remember that these allowances are used to calculate occupancy load factors for the number of occupants, not the actual square footage required for the dining room or kitchen.

The owner and designer must carefully consider the combination of tables and chairs, use of *banquettes*[10] and booths, even the size of the chairs to insure sufficient seating for revenue concerns and sufficient spacing to accommodate traffic flow. According to Martin Dorf:

> You can often assume that in terms of square feet per seat, you will need 16 to 18 for a cafeteria, 18 to 20 for counter service, 15 to 18 for table service at a hotel club restaurant, 11 to 14 for fast-food table service, 10 to 11 for banquets, and 17 to 22 for specialty formal dining. Waiting areas, coatrooms and storage areas are not included in these figures.[11]

Seating capacity will also depend on the style of seating. Banquette seating with tables is very efficient, while table and chair seating takes up more room. But banquette seating is not appropriate when the concept calls for privacy—it is more appropriate for conversation and people watching—or for being seen. Booth seating is popular with customers, but booths, usually designed to seat four, are economically inefficient when only one or two people use a booth. The same can be said of a setup when only four-tops (tables to seat four people) are used. Tables to seat two guests, called two-tops or deuces, should also be planned. The easy movement of tables and chairs should be considered when it is necessary to set up for larger groups. Square tables at a diagonal offer more efficient arrangements than tables placed at right angles. It is important to note that codes also restrict minimum square footage allowances on fixed seating units in food and beverage facilities. Applicable code books must be checked to see how these restrictions will affect the overall number of seats and subsequent space planning of the dining areas. Examples of common spacing and table layouts are provided later in the chapter.

Space allocations will also need to be made for service stations. *Service stations* are work areas located in the dining room (and possibly the beverage area) that provide space for storing clean and dirty dishes, glasses, and coffee service. On average, one small service station of approximately 2 by 2 feet is recommended for every 20 seats and one large station of approximately 8 feet by 30 inches for every 50 seats.

Space allocation for beverage areas is our next consideration. "In many areas where there is a bar and seating for the consumption of beverages, from 15% to 25% of the space is devoted to the bar, bar seating, and space around the bar."[12] Put another way, beverage areas usually require 8 to 10 square feet per person plus the space for the bar and back bar. Since the bar itself can be designed in many configurations, it is difficult to give any kind of "rule of thumb" allowance for the early planning. The standard allowance for seating at the bar is 28 inches of

---

[10] Banquettes are upholstered benches along the wall.

[11] Dorf, 1992, p. 41. Published by Whitney Library of Design, an imprint of Watson-Guptill Publications. Telephone: (212) 536-5116.

[12] Kotschevar and Tanke, 1991, p. 61.

bar per stool. The designer must work with the owner and bar manager to determine the kind and size of equipment, amount of bar seating, and amount of storage at the bar to determine the estimated space allowance for this part of the beverage facility.

Space allocation for the kitchen and other back of the house areas will be governed by the menu and the number of seats. According to Dorf, kitchen areas are generally 25 to 40 percent of the total estimated area for the restaurant.[13] When the menu items are primarily fresh food—meaning the restaurant is receiving each day's food in the morning—more space will be needed for the kitchen. Restaurants using more processed foods may be planned with smaller kitchens. Figure 5-6 provides estimates of space for the kitchen functional areas.

The building codes will determine the number of fixtures in toilet facilities for the public and employees. For example, a facility with an occupant load of 100 will require three toilets and three lavatories for the public women's facility and two toilets, three lavatories, and one urinal for the men's.[14] Additional toilet facilities for employees may also be required. The building code and ADA guidelines will determine how many stalls and lavatories will have to meet accessibility standards. Chapter 8 provides standard sizes of toilet facilities in public occupancies.

Functional Areas	*Space Allowed %*
Receiving	5
Food storage	20
Preparation	14
Cooking	8
Baking	10
Warewashing	5
Traffic aisles	16
Trash storage	5
Employee facilities	15
Miscellaneous	2

Figure 5–6 Estimates of space for the kitchen functional areas. (Reprinted with permission. Edward A. Kazarian. 1989. P. 734. *Foodservice Facilities Planning.* 3rd ed. John Wiley & Sons.

Entry and Waiting areas

Entries come in all sizes and shapes, depending once again on total concept and, in no small part, on the type of restaurant and style of service. Entries must be inviting and designed with climatic conditions in mind. As many patrons of restaurants in Phoenix, Arizona, can attest, a glass enclosed waiting area that faces west can feel like a sauna in the summer. One way to deal with climatic conditions is to use a double set of entry doors to create a transition from hot, cold, snowy, or rainy weather.

The type and service style of the facility will create different needs in the entry. For example, in a fast-food restaurant, the main purpose of the entry is to establish the queuing lines for customers to place orders and pick up food. However, in a full-service style restaurant, the entry serves as a transition space for customers from outside into the dining area.

The entry for a full-service facility must be large enough to handle entering and exiting flows, make it easy to find the host or maître d' station, and provide an appropriate amount of seating for guests waiting for tables. When coatrooms are part of the concept, they too will be located off the entry area. Approximately eight to twelve coats can be hung per linear foot of space, depending on climate. The coatroom should be easy to find, and if no attendant is

---

[13]Dorf, 1992, p. 41.

[14]Uniform Building Code, 1994, Table A-29-A.

provided, placed so that the host can watch for potential theft. Public telephones and toilet facilities for guests can be located off the entry or in some other area of the facility. In some restaurants, the cash register is also located in the entry area.

Regardless of the type of restaurant, the entry and waiting areas serve to draw the customer into the restaurant. In table service restaurants, the host podium is placed somewhat back from the door as a way to draw customers into the ambience of the restaurant and maybe even savor some of the food odors to come. Another common design device is to create an entry that allows the patron to make a comfortable transition from the outside world into the smaller world of the restaurant experience to come. For example, in many restaurants, the ceiling in the entry is lower than what will be experienced in the dining areas.

Many restaurants have turned waiting areas into incremental sales areas. Facilities that cater to tourists can use display space in the waiting area to sell T-shirts, mugs, and other items with the restaurant logo. Upscale restaurants may make a wine display part of the waiting area design. Some restaurants provide a display of food in the waiting area. The Fish Market Restaurant in San Diego displays fresh seafood in cases near the maître d' podium. In this way, customers might be encouraged to purchase some fresh fish to take home or view the quality of the day's fresh catch.

It has become common for waiting areas to be provided with bench or banquette seating rather than individual chairs. A greater number of people can be accommodated in this way. Materials and colors selected for the entry set the stage for what the patron will experience in the dining room and beverage area. Architectural surfaces are selected with maintenance in mind as well as the aesthetic statement for which the designer and owner strive. Floor surfaces in the entry need to be specified with a consideration to prevent patrons slipping and falling when the weather is inclement. Materials and finishes used in the entry will be required to meet the same code requirements as those in the dining room and beverage area. Those are discussed later in this section.

Lighting is another consideration in the design of the waiting area. A major problem for patrons concerning lighting in the entry is the transition from the outside to the interior and vice versa. Walking from the bright light of daylight to the dim lighting found in many full-service restaurants is a common problem. Of course, the opposite problem can occur at night. The actual specification of general and accent lighting fixtures and light levels will be done to enhance the concept for the total interior design. A fast-food or cafeteria type of restaurant will have higher lighting levels in the entry and throughout the establishment. Upscale table-service restaurants will have more subdued lighting, often created with indirect ambient lighting and accent lighting. Restaurant designers commonly state that restaurant lighting is similar to theater lighting. The lighting specification and design in the entry "set the stage" for what is to come.

Dining Areas

The interior design of full-service restaurants is as varied as one's imagination and the concepts developed by owners and designers. Interior design can be based on a theme, such as that developed for the Hard Rock Cafe and Planet Hollywood. It can take on interior treatments reminiscent of ethnic motifs, such as the use of sombreros, serapes, and dark woods common in Mexican style restaurants. There are the full-service restaurants of the chains such as Red Lobster, with interior motifs based on fishing, and Applegates, with interiors reminiscent of pubs. And, of course, there are many restaurants of this type with no theme— just great interior design creating a formal or "classy" interior such as Windows on the World at the World Trade Center in New York City (Figure 5-7).

The number of seats having been determined in the programming and concept development stage of the project, the next order of business for the interior designer is the space plan of the dining room itself. Traffic must flow easily from the entry and waiting area and throughout the dining room. Traffic flow must also be considered from the kitchen into the dining room. Designers must remember that wait persons will frequently carry heavy trays of

Figure 5–7 Windows on the World Restaurant, located at the World Trade Center, New York, NY. (Photograph courtesy of Windows on the World.)

food. Maneuvering these trays up or down stairs or through a maze of passageways from the kitchen to the farthest dining areas can be cumbersome as well as a safety issue.

Depending on the actual type, service style, and concept of the restaurant, the main circulation space should be from 3 to 5 feet wide (Figure 5-8). Circulation space between tables will vary depending on the arrangement of the tables (Figure 5-9). In addition to circulation space, the designer must plan for activity space—that is, space that allows the wait person to be standing at a table and not be in the circulation space. The allowance for this space is between 18 and 30 inches. Mid-priced table service and upscale restaurants particularly place tables and other seating arrangements with more generous spacing between tables to give the feeling of privacy.

Since full-service restaurants are usually relatively large in size, the dining areas are commonly divided into smaller sections, creating dining rooms within dining rooms. In some cases, raised or sunken areas are used to subdivide the space. These planning devices are used to create privacy and help with acoustics. The ADA requires that all portions of dining areas be accessible. Should the designer plan raised or sunken areas, even second floor areas, seating areas must be made accessible. This is primarily true of new construction and in some jurisdictions, it may affect remodeled restaurant facilities. When there are smoking and nonsmoking areas in the restaurant, the ADA also requires that accessible seating be provided in each section.

All restaurants have certain tables in locations that are considered "prime"—the best table or tables in the house. Good customers and VIPs expect to get the prime tables. However, one challenge to the designer is to try to make all tables seem like the prime table. Of course, that is not possible in reality. Not all tables can have a window with an unobstructed view of the ocean or be the central tables so that everyone can see the VIPs who choose to be seen by all who dine there.

Sight lines must be carefully considered so that tables do not have views of the kitchen or service areas. Few patrons of few restaurants choose the table closest to where the trash bins and dirty dishes will be located, regardless of the price of the food.

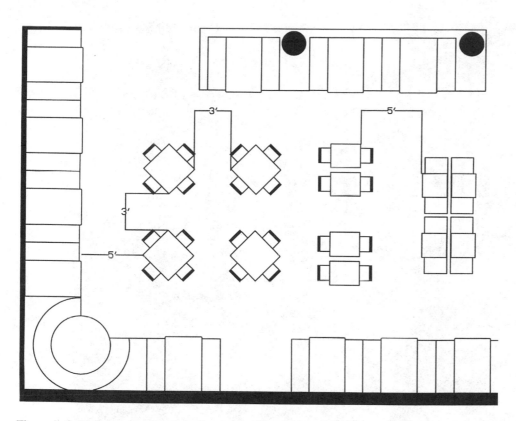

Figure 5–8 Dining room layout indicating traffic and spacing between tables. (Drawing coutesy of Leann Wilson.)

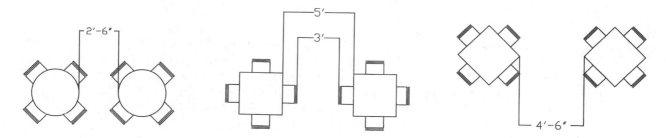

Figure 5–9 Circulation space between tables will vary, depending on the size, shape, and placement of the tables. (Drawing courtesy of Leann Wilson.)

The furniture used in the dining space is an very important part of the concept. The type of seating specified for the dining area conveys a lot to the customer about the kind of dining experience to be had in the facility. Fully upholstered chairs indicate to the customer that the dining experience will be more formal, with a leisurely pace through the meal (Figure 5-10). Arm chairs or armless chairs with upholstered seat and back or just an upholstered seat, gives the impression of a family dining experience and a less formal somewhat more hurried experience. Small chairs like a plastic stack chair signal fast-food, fast eating, informal dining. Many restaurants find it convenient for customers to have chairs on casters. This helps customers move the chairs more easily, especially on carpeted floors. This simple specification device also works well in restaurants that will cater to the business lunch, creating an atmosphere similar to a conference room or office. Dining chairs must be matched to the height of the tables, with seat heights at 18 inches above the floor when the table height is 27 to 30 above the floor.

Figure 5–10 Oak Room Restaurant, Castle at Tarrytown, NY. (Design by and photograph courtesy of Peter Gisolfi Assoc., Architects.)

The designer must be careful in specifying seating heights and table heights when booths and banquettes are used (Figure 5-11). Since booths or banquettes are commonly custom designed, care must be taken so that the seat is not too soft, which would make the table height too high as well as make it difficult for guests to get in and out of the booth. Although older guests often prefer booths, this common design flaw makes it very difficult for older patrons to satisfactorily use the booth or banquette seating.

Fabrics for seating units also vary with style and type of restaurant. Fast-food and many midpriced table service restaurants use vinyl and plastics for seating. Upscale table service restaurants use natural fabrics or other quality textiles to add to the ambience. Patterns should be specified carefully so that the pattern is in scale to the chair or seating piece. Whatever textile is used on seating, the designer must keep in mind soiling, food spillage, ease of maintenance, abrasion resistance, snagging, and pilling. Seating takes a lot of use and abuse (so the owner hopes) and the type of materials used on the seating unit must not only work aesthetically, but be able to handle the expected upkeep.

Architectural finishes must be selected for cleanability, resistance to potential grease—yes, some will escape the kitchen—and abrasion resistance. Painted surfaces should be high gloss and enamels. Wallpapers and other wall treatments should be commercial grade materials that will resist abrasions of chairs banging and rubbing against the surface. The designer will need to decide if the wall treatments are to be a focal point of the interior design or a backdrop. Considering the large spaces, it is most common that the wall treatments and window treatments serve as backdrops and "accents" to the overall design concept. For example, paneling with traditional molding, cornices, and chair rails establish the traditional interior that would accept Queen Anne or Chippendale style chairs in a formal dining experience.

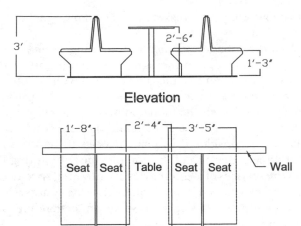

Elevation

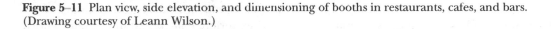

Seat | Seat | Table | Seat | Seat | Wall

Figure 5-11 Plan view, side elevation, and dimensioning of booths in restaurants, cafes, and bars. (Drawing courtesy of Leann Wilson.)

Textile wallcoverings should be selected with care as they will require a higher standard for fire safety. In many jurisdictions the inclusion of fire sprinklers is required if textiles are used as wallcoverings.

All types of flooring materials can be selected. Hard surface and resilient materials will be noisier than carpets and will have little restriction for codes and regulations. However, these materials are more of a safety issue as spills can lead to customers or staff falling. Carpets are commonly specified with medium to large size patterns as a device to add interest but also to hide traffic paths. Carpets need to be tightly woven with a short pile to allow the easier movement of chairs and possibly carts. Nylon and nylon-wool blends are especially good for restaurant carpets, since they will take more frequent cleaning.

Upholstery fabrics and interior treatments and finishes will also have to meet specific local codes for fire safety. In assembly occupancies, vertical exit ways require Class I materials and horizontal exit ways require Class II finishes. Other areas in the space, such as the dining room and cocktail lounge, require Class II or III materials. Materials on seating units are generally not regulated; however, local codes may require specific fire resistive materials to be used on seating units in dining and beverage areas. As discussed in Chapter 1, some states will require the whole seating unit to meet California Technical Bulletin 133 (CAL 133) or a similar fire safety regulation.

Care should be taken in the specification of *accessories*. As with lodging facility guest rooms, it is a good idea to have accessories out of reach or well anchored to prevent pilferage. They also need to be selected with consideration of the size of the item in relation to the size of the space. Small spaces need small accessories, while larger spaces can usually handle large accessories and paintings, but not all large accessories will fit into the space of larger interiors.

Color schemes should reflect the overall concept and type of restaurant and take into consideration current color trends. The bright colors of a fast-food restaurant would not be appropriate in a formal dining area. Many designers feel it is sometimes nice to select color schemes that are unexpected—such as mauves, golds, and walnuts in a Chinese restaurant. The unexpected interior creates a more formal feeling, which may bring a different client to the restaurant. On the other hand, it might turn off the guest who is used to and expects a traditional interior for the theme.

Color psychology can be used in the selection of colors for a restaurant dining area, not only in the area of creating an agreeable interior but also to enhance appetite. Colors that have strong appetite appeal are most colors in the warm section of the color wheel as well as true greens. Colors in the purples and yellow-greens and mustard tones, as well as gray, have little appeal. Blues, seldom used in foods, are good colors for backgrounds. "To be more specific, a peak of appetite and agreeable sensations exists in the red-orange, and orange regions.

Pleasure decreases at yellow-orange, increases again at yellow, reaches a low at yellow-green, and is restored at clear green."[15]

Color decisions should be made together with lighting choices. Since colors are seen because of the lighting introduced, and the lighting selections affect the true or apparent actual colors, the successful restaurant cannot be designed without these two in unison. The designer must remember all the intricacies of color theory and color psychology when selecting the colors for material and services in the food and beverage facility.

Interior *lighting* is a very important part of achieving a successful interior in a food and beverage facility. In fact, it is considered by many experts to be the single most important element of a successful design. Because of the complexities of lighting design, it is common for the owners to retain the services of a lighting designer trained specifically in the application of lighting of interiors and exteriors. However, all interior designers who may be retained to design a food and beverage space should have some understanding of the importance of lighting design in this application.

So much of our psychological response to places, things, and events occurs because of our visual impressions. The lighting ambience plays a significant part in the comfort of the guest and in allowing the guest to have a successful experience at the establishment. Poorly designed lighting can hinder if not destroy that moment.

Lighting design must consider not only guests' visual comfort when they enter and leave the facility at different times of day, but also the safety of guests and staff as they maneuver around the dining room. Sufficient lighting is a must. Successful lighting design must also provide appropriate lighting for guests to be able to read the menu, for the appropriate mood to be set, and for the appearance of the food, and even the people within the environment, to be enhanced.

Dining areas can be planned with indirect ambient, accent, and sparkle lighting. Indirect ambient lighting provides the overall lighting levels for the space to allow comfortable movement and functioning in the space. Accent lighting might be wall sconces or spotlights. Sparkle lighting is produced from a variety of light sources that create special effects both as true lighting and as general mood setting. Pinpoint lights, light reflected off mirrors and glass, and low watt strip lights can produce sparkle.

Many restaurant designers consider lighting as a means to help set the scene. In the dining room and bar areas, lighting levels must be carefully calculated so that the proper selection of fixtures will provide the appropriate levels of light required for the design goals. The dining room, entry, and bar should be on a dimming system to allow any necessary changes in lighting levels throughout the day. This is especially true of those restaurants that might be open for all three meals or at least for lunch and dinner.

Actual lighting levels will vary based on function. In the dining area of a full-service restaurant, 10 foot-candles would be the minimum recommended level, with the dining area of a fast-food restaurant requiring 50 to 100 foot-candles.[16] Figure 5-12 indicates lighting levels in other areas of the restaurant.

Specification of lighting fixtures must consider such things as the type of lamps used, the watts per square foot created, and the heat generated by the lamps. While incandescent lamps are very flattering to people and food, they produce a high heat output for the number of watts produced. This extra heat adds to the heating, ventilation, and air conditioning (HVAC) costs. Energy saving lamps like PAR lamps do provide more light at lower energy costs, but should be "limited to spaces with high ceiling and more theatrical, dramatic environments, because they tend to create harsh, bright spots of light when used too close to objects."[17]

---

[15] Mahnke and Mahnke, 1993, p. 102.

[16] Stipanuk and Roffmann, 1992, p. 132 (hardcover edition).

[17] Dorf, 1992, p. 51. Published by Whitney Library of Design, an imprint of Watson-Guptill Publications. Telephone: (212) 536-5116.

Space	Recommend Minimum Footcandles
Cashier	50
Dining areas	
Intimate	3–10
Leisure	30
Kitchen	30–70

Figure 5–12 Lighting levels in other areas of the restaurant. (From McGuinness et al., *Mechanical and Electrical Equipment for Buildings,* 6th ed. Copyright © 1980. Reprinted by permission of John Wiley & Sons, Inc.)

Lighting must also be carefully planned to avoid "hot spots" and "dark spots." No one wants to sit at a table where the down light is so intense in one spot that the guest seated there feels he or she is "on stage," or where the area is overlit so as to cause glare and visual discomfort—a hot spot. Nor would diners wish to sit at a table where the lighting is so dim they cannot read the menu or comfortably see their dining companions.

Proper *acoustic control* in the dining room plays another important part in the overall success or failure of a food and beverage facility. Almost everything that goes on in a restaurant adds to the noise level of the facility. Guests entering and leaving, guests talking in the dining room, wait staff taking orders and working with guests, activity at service islands, kitchen noise of cooking and preparation, and even the background music or entertainment provided, all add to the acoustical potpourri of the environment.

There are several design options to help with acoustics. Fabric wallcoverings that meet code requirements should be considered rather than painted walls and other hard surface materials like mirrors, metals, paneling, and large expanses of glass. Acoustical panels and baffles made of sound-absorbing acoustical materials covered with fabrics can help reduce the noise levels from the large expanses of wall surfaces. High quality acoustical ceiling treatments and low volume sound systems are also useful in masking the unpleasant noises that will occur in a restaurant. And, of course, carpeting is a major aid in reducing acoustical problems.

There are several other methods to help reduce noise in the dining room. One method is to plan the dining areas into smaller rooms or areas, thus breaking up the noise. For this to be most effective the dividers must go to the ceiling. Booths with high partitions between each unit are another design device that can reduce noise. Choosing upholstery rather than hard surfaces for seating units and using tablecloths to reduce sound of dish ware and utensils are other techniques that will help reduce overall noise levels. Careful design considerations of where the service islands are located, where dirty dishes are stacked, locations and baffling of kitchen doors, even the use of electronic ordering systems rather than waitress and waiters shouting orders, all will help with acoustical problems.

Of course, the noise level of the restaurant also is factored into the total concept. A trendy place like the Hard Rock Cafe is very open with lots of hard surfaces. Such restaurants are noisy by design, but guests expect that and accept the noise level as part of the total experience. The noise levels of a Hard Rock Cafe would not be acceptable for a family table service restaurant or for a full-service gourmet restaurant with a formal service style. The designer should work carefully with the owner and the architect to insure that acoustic considerations have been thought through and appropriately handled.

Computers are now commonly used in larger restaurants for food order entry. Wait staff punch in the entire customer order from a remote specialized terminal or hand-held wireless terminal. This computer application allows for exacting inventory control as well as for reports on the types of food most commonly ordered by customers. Wait staff return to these remote terminals to finalize customer bills and get printouts for cash or credit purchases. Space must be planned at one or more locations in the dining room for the terminal(s), usually at or very near the serving stations on the sales floor. Usually a touch screen rather than a keyboard is part of the special design of these computer terminals. Glare and veiling reflections on the monitor and cleanliness are the key design issues for computer sites in a food and beverage area.

Beverage Areas

Beverage areas are those where alcoholic beverages are served. The earliest beverage establishments date back many centuries. Abbeys and monasteries operated breweries for their own use. When they started to provide a place for travelers to stay, they also offered their beverages to the travelers. Taverns were established along trade routes in many parts of the Western world. These taverns provided beverage service with some food also being available. Taverns were also popular in the American colonies and increased in numbers as the new United States grew in population and geographic size. During Prohibition in the 1920s, consumption of alcohol was forbidden by federal law, but secret clubs, called speakeasies, were established so customers could still purchase their now illegal alcoholic beverages. After Prohibition ended in the 1930s, the beverage portion of the hospitality industry grew. The serving of alcoholic beverages was and continues to be a major reason for the growth of the food service component as a steadily increasing economy gave families and individuals more options in eating out and socializing.

There are two broad types of beverage operations—bars and lounges. *Bars*, usually smaller than lounges, provide less seating and sometimes less ambience than lounges. They might be called bars, pubs, taverns, or saloons and can serve drinks with little or no food service. Bars are also associated with restaurants, as we are discussing in this chapter. Some bars that only serve drinks may have a special focus, such as a sports bar. Other theme uses of bars include airport bars, hotel bars, and piano bars. *Lounges* are beverage areas with seating that is usually more comfortable than what would be found in a bar. A lounge might be an upscale bar with little or no food service, or part of a restaurant. It might also be associated with entertainment, like nightclubs and show lounges in hotels and casinos, or simply have a dance floor with a jukebox or small band.

Note that this book does not discuss nightclubs and show lounges. It focuses on the bar or lounge associated with a restaurant. We use the term "beverage area" in our discussion, reserving the term "bar" to mean the counter area where alcoholic beverages are actually prepared.

Not all restaurants have separate beverage areas, yet many restaurants provide some kind of alcoholic beverage service. A beverage area is commonly separated from the dining room so patrons may use just the beverage service area. Many people do not like to have to go through a beverage area to get to the dining room. In some states building codes do not allow a space plan in which patrons must go through a beverage area to reach the rest rooms. This should be kept in mind during initial space planning. In many smaller restaurants, a small beverage area might be accommodated into the overall space planning of the dining room without making it a separate "room." And then, in the smallest restaurants, the beverage area might be beer on tap or beverages served from out of a cooler in the kitchen.

The beverage area of a restaurant must be designed along the same concept lines as the whole of the facility. Furniture items, finishes, colors, and lighting ambience all need to be planned for beverage service, but in keeping with the interior design concepts developed in the other front of the house areas.

Beverage areas commonly consist of the front bar with stools for patrons and a back bar for display and storage, as well as seating at tables and chairs or booths and tables (Figure 5–13). Elaborate front and back bar cabinets are found in many restaurants, along with creative display methods for bottles and glasses. Figure 5-14 provides dimensional guidelines for these items.

Let us first look at some design concepts concerning the bar area. The bar itself is the guest's view of the bar cabinet. Seating at the bar is primarily stools with a seat height of 30 inches above the floor, assuming the top of the bar is between the standard 42 to 45 inches above the floor. Many beverage establishments use stools that are fixed to the floor, which

Figure 5–13 Photo of a bar with tables, bar stools, bar, and back bar. (Reprinted with permission from *Design Solutions Magazine,* published by the Architectural Woodwork Institute, Reston, VA.)

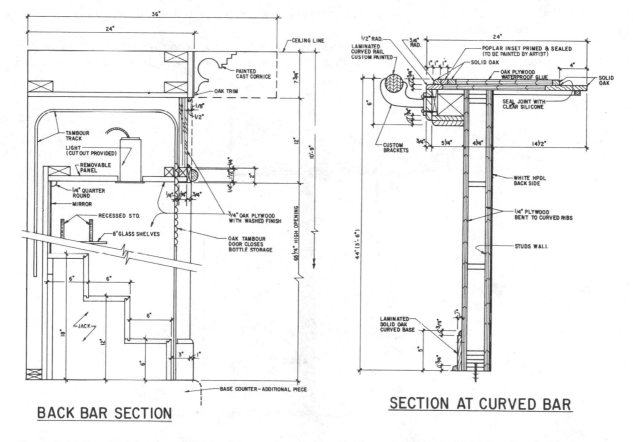

BACK BAR SECTION   ## SECTION AT CURVED BAR

Figure 5–14 Detailed drawing of the back bar and curved bar as pictured in Figure 5-13. (Reprinted with permission from *Design Solutions Magazine,* published by the Architectural Woodwork Institute, Reston, VA.)

would help prevent them from falling over. Some themes also call for the use of a footrest or footrail at 7 to 9 inches above the floor (see Figure 5-15).

Behind the bar are the under bar and the back bar. The *under bar* is the main working area for the bartender as he or she faces the guest. The *back bar* functions as the display area for the different liquors offered and for glasses, with storage space below for beer bottles, extra liquor bottles, and other accessories items needed at the bar. The under bar generally has a four compartment sink for cleaning and sanitizing glassware, draining space for glassware, ice bins and under counter storage, soda guns for dispensing soda, and beer taps. It will need to be between 22 and 26 inches deep, while the bar countertop should be between 18 and 24 inches deep. A speed rail is also placed at strategic spots along the top of the bar cabinet. The *speed rail* holds bottles of the house or "well" beverages so that bartenders can get to these quickly. The back bar will have display space for bottles and glassware as well as under counter refrigerators for cold beer and wine storage and counter space for the cash register or computer. The back bar will be between 24 and 30 inches deep. Bars need a variety of glassware depending on the line of beverages served. Ten or more different kinds of glasses might be needed for a bar serving a full range of beverages.

The space between the back bar and the bar is called the activity zone. It is between 30 and 36 inches wide. This provides a comfortable space for the bartenders to work between the bar and back bar without extra steps. Thirty-six inches allows sufficient space for a bartender to be working at one or the other of the cabinets while a second bartender can walk behind him or her.

The beverage area will need storage space for additional cases of liquor bottles, wines, and beers, as well as space to store extra possible seasonings and mixes for cocktails. These beverages should be kept in a space that is away from sunlight and fluctuating temperatures. Beverage storage is often kept close to the bar, but some establishments keep this extra storage near the kitchen. Considering the high cost of the inventory in this storage room, it must be a secure space.

The designer must also plan a space for a service bar. The *service bar* is where the wait staff orders and picks up beverages that they will take to the dining room. It is commonly planned

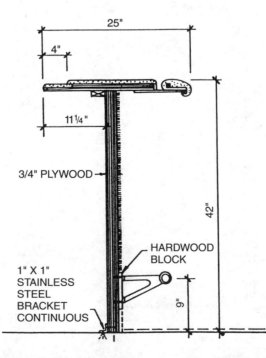

Figure 5–15 Detailed drawing of a footrail and countertop of bar. (Reprinted with permission from *Design Solutions Magazine,* published by the Architectural Woodwork Institute, Reston, VA.)

out of sight of the dining room guests. It is usually very compact and may only be a small window with a shelf. In larger facilities it may be larger, requiring a compact under and back bar and a separate bartender.

Furniture, finishes, and lighting are similar to that in the dining area and should coordinate with the concept in the rest of the establishment. There are a few differences, however. Furniture in a beverage area generally consists of small tables and chairs, bar stools and booths, or banquettes and tables. Tables in beverage areas often are only 25 to 27 inches above the floor. This helps patrons lounge more easily. Chair seat heights in this case will average 16 inches above the floor for this lower table. Since smoking is commonly allowed in beverage areas, the specification of fabrics and seating units that will resist smoldering should be considered, though it might not be a code issue. Lighting is usually more subdued than in the dining areas. Lower light levels by use of the indirect ambient and accent lighting fixtures is supplemented by candles on tables and some accent lights. Should a dance floor or entertainment space be planned, theater style spotlights will be needed.

The main code issue in a beverage facility will be the ADA regulations. The plan must provide clear passage from the entry to seating areas for a patron who is physically disabled. The plan must also allow for access to all parts of the beverage area should there be sunken or raised portions of the plan.

Beverage areas also commonly use computers today, depending on the size of the facility. These units are usually similar to those found in the dining room, but programmed and with keyboards designed for beverage service rather than food service. Cleanliness and protection from dampness are very important considerations in the location of these computer units.

Public Rest Rooms

All food and beverage establishments will be required by code to have rest rooms for use by customers. In all but the smallest facilities, seperate rest rooms will be required for men and women. In smaller restaurants, the guest and employees would use the same facilities. In new construction, rest rooms must be designed to meet the ADA guidelines. Dimensioning of the rest room is covered in Chapter 8. In this section we briefly discuss the interior design of these facilities.

The design treatments of rest rooms are often ignored in all but the more expensive food and beverage facilities. However, the designer and the facility owner should recognize that the rest room facilities, along with all other public areas, help create an impression for the customer of the overall quality of the facility. A tacky looking rest room will provide a negative impression.

Moisture, repeated cleaning, and durability of materials used for rest rooms are all important considerations in materials specifications. Ceramic tile, plastic laminate, moisture resistant vinyl wallcoverings, and moisture resistant high-gloss paints can generally all be used for wall treatments. High quality sheet vinyl or ceramic tiles are most commonly specified for the flooring. Local codes may require specific types of materials behind the lavatories and on the walls by the water closets or urinals. It is also common to have a floor drain in the rest rooms to ease maintenance.

In the women's rest room, it is common to provide extra space and counters for applying makeup, retouching one's hair, and conversation. It is common in upscale restaurant that a separate "ladies lounge" be provided, connected to the actual toilet facilities area, to accommodate these activities. The extra "lounge" area is commonly carpeted, provided with low seating, small chairs, even small sofas.

The Kitchen and Back of the House

Commercial kitchen planning is an interesting design specialty that is primarily done by certified kitchen planners, who may or may not also be experienced interior designers. It is discussed in this section to provide overview functional information and provide an appreciation for the complexities and design decisions necessary to prepare an overall facility plan.

There are a few additional back of the house areas that are a part of or adjacent to the kitchen: receiving, storage, office, and employee areas. These areas are discussed in this section as well. We talk about the planning issues of the kitchen from receiving through the food preparation areas, then the auxiliary areas such as the office. Figure 5-6 provides estimates of space for the many production areas.

The receiving area should be located near a loading dock (for the largest food service facilities or those in hotels and high-rise mixed use buildings) or near the receiving door (for stand-alone facilities). Ideally, the receiving doors will be located so that delivery trucks will not be visible to customers. If the restaurant will be ordering goods by the pallet, then double doors should be designed.

Space is needed for check-in of foodstuffs along with anything else ordered by the facility, such as linen and uniform service. The receiving area should be large enough to hold a delivery until it can be relocated to the proper storage area. Receiving is ideally located adjacent to the storage areas so the foodstuffs can be quickly transferred to proper storage conditions after inspection. Good lighting is needed here to aid in the inspection of food items.

Some jurisdictions will not allow trash and garbage to be removed through the receiving area. This is to insure that fresh foods are not contaminated by garbage. A second door would then be required from the kitchen, generally near the ware washing area, to the exterior where dumpsters and grease dumpsters will be located. The designer should verify local codes to insure proper traffic flow of fresh foods into the facility and garbage out to dumpsters.

Storage areas are commonly located near the receiving area and as convenient as possible to the kitchen. The square footage requirements for each of these areas will depend on the menu offered, the number of seats in the dining area, and the turnover at the facility. As each one of these factors increases, the square footage of the storage rooms will also have to increase.

Food and beverage facilities will need storage space for three classifications of goods: dry, refrigerated, and frozen. A dry storage area will house bottles, cans, and boxes of food and beverage items that can be stored at room temperature. In addition to these items, paper supplies, such as napkins, toilet paper, paper towels, and take-out containers, will be stored here. Cloth items like tablecloths, napkins, uniforms, towels, and other linens will also be stored in the dry goods storage room. One other consideration of the dry storage area is to separate chemical items like cleaning agents, from foodstuffs. This is a common health department regulation to prevent the contamination of food items. Cases of liquor are commonly kept in a separate locked portion of the dry storage area if a separate storage area by the bar is not provided. Of course, wine and beer storage areas require temperature controlled spaces.

Refrigerated spaces—large commercial sized reach-in or walk-in refrigerators—are used to store fresh meats, fish, produce, fruits, and dairy products. Depending on the size of the facility, one or more commercial sized reach-in refrigerators is required. There are many options in the sizes and configurations of refrigerator units. The kitchen planner or designer will discuss these options with the owner to insure that the right equipment is specified for current and anticipated needs.

The third type of storage area is storage space for frozen foods. Reach-in and walk-in freezer units will be available. The kitchen planner or designer must remember to specify an insulated floor if a walk-in freezer is used. A ramp will be needed unless the floor insulation is an integral part of the freezer unit. Walk-in refrigerators and freezers usually have galvanized steel, stainless steel, or ceramic tile surfaces for walls and ceilings.

Finishes in storage areas should be easy to clean and maintain. One should not plan windows into any dry storage areas. This allows opportunity for theft. In fact, it is also recommended that walls in storage areas be from slab to architectural ceiling (not dropped ceiling), also to prevent the opportunity for theft.

Anyone who has spent time observing a commercial kitchen in action during the height of the dinner hour can quickly appreciate the importance of the planning required in a space that seems like chaos. But it must be controlled chaos, as each station and each staff member in the kitchen have roles to play in the food preparation and service preparation of the meals put before the restaurant guest. The complex work tasks of commercial food preparation need to be clearly understood by the planner to insure that the kitchen is planned for efficiencies, safety, and logical work flow.

Kitchens are generally space planned into four basic areas—prepreparation, cold-food preparation, hot-food preparation, and the sanitary or ware washing area (Figure 5-16). Restaurants that offer "home made deserts" will also have a bakery area to prepare them. Some mid- and large sized restaurants also have separate salad preparation areas. The exact breakdown of the preparation areas in the kitchen will vary based on the range of menu items offered and size of the total facility. Display kitchens, which are cooking areas in the dining room, are discussed later in this section.

The prepreparation area is commonly where produce items are cleaned and processed prior to being incorporated into recipes. Prepreparation might include cleaning salad items,

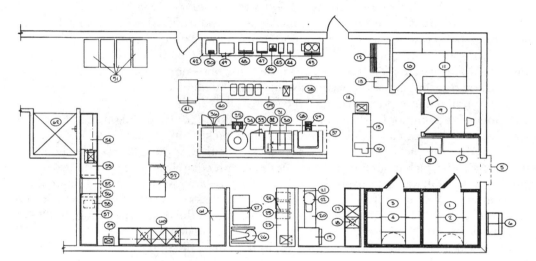

EQUIPMENT LIST

ITEM	DESCRIPTION		
1	WALK IN FREEZER	32	SPACER W/POT FILLER
2	WALK IN FREEZER SHELVING	33	STEAMER
3	WALK IN COOLER	34	40-GAL. KETTLE
4	WALK IN COOLER SHELVING	35	FLOOR GRATE
5	AIR CURTAIN FAN	36	CONVECTION OVEN
6	WALK IN COOLER/FREEZER	37	EXHAUST HOOD W/FIRE SYSTEM
	COMPRESSORS	38	PASS THRU REFRIGERATOR
7	RECEIVING TABLE	39	HOT FOOD COUNTER W/SINK
8	SCALE	40	OVERSHELF
9	OFFICE	41	FREEZER
10	STORAGE ROOM	42	BEVERAGE COUNTER
11	STORAGE ROOM SHELVING	43	COFFEE URN
12	ICE MACHINE	44	HOT CHOCOLATE DISPENSER
13	ICE CART	45	ICED TEA DISPENSER
14	HAND SINK—TABLE MOUNTED	46	WATER DISPENSER
15	WORKTABLE	47	JUICE DISPENSER
16	SLICER	48	MILK DISPENSER
17	VEGETABLE PREP SINK	49	MICROWAVE OVEN
18	DISPOSER	50	TOASTER
19	REFRIGERATOR	51	TRANSPORT CARTS
20	WORKTABLE	52	DISH CARTS
21	OVERSHELF	53	SOILED DISHTABLE
22	FOOD CUTTER	54	RACKSHELF
23	BAKE TABLE W/SINK	55	DISHWASHER
24	INGREDIENT BINS	56	EXHAUST HOOD
25	OVERSHELF	57	CLEAN DISHTABLE
26	MIXER	58	BOOSTER HEATER
27	PROOF CABINETS	59	HAND SINK
28	BRAISING PAN	60	POT & PAN SINK W/DISPOSER
29	FLOOR GRATE		SINK HEATER & OVERSHELF
30	HOT TOP RANGE W/OVEN	61	CLEAN POT STORAGE SHELVING
31	SALAMANDER BROILER	62	CART WASH

Figure 5–16 Commercial kitchen. (From *Manual of Equipment and Design for the Food Service Industry* by Carl R. Scriven and James W. Scriven, 1998, Van Nostrand Reinhold. Reprinted with permission.)

slicing carrots, peeling potatoes, making salad dressings, chopping, dicing, or slicing other produce items needed in hot and cold menu items. Sinks, worktables, and food processors are some of the common pieces of equipment in this area of the kitchen. In larger restaurants, ranges and ovens may also be included in this portion of the kitchen.

The cold-food preparation area is where items such as salads, some appetizers, and cold sandwiches would be prepared. In smaller restaurants, this is also where deserts would be placed on table ware. Proximity to refrigerators and adequate worktables are the major equipment requirements in this part of the kitchen. For restaurants that have a large service of cold items, it is suggested that a separate pickup area at the cold-food preparation position be planned into the total kitchen layout.

The hot-food preparation area requires the largest amount of space and variety of equipment. It is here that the range, oven, broilers, grills, griddles, and deep fryers are organized. Health departments will require ventilation hoods over cooking equipment.

Architectural and surface finishes specifications are very important in the kitchen. All surfaces must be grease resistant and nonporous to allow for easy and frequent cleaning. Light colors for walls and ceiling surfaces will aid in the overall lighting needs in the kitchen. Stainless steel and ceramic tile are used since they are both nonporous and easy to clean. Floors must be nonslippery and grease resistant. Many kitchens use sealed concrete for the floors, but nonglazed, nonporous ceramic tile is also a possibility.

Hot foods are commonly passed to the pickup station. Hot foods might be kept under heat lamps, or on steam tables to keep them hot until picked up by servers. Cold foods will also be passed to the pickup area if a separate pickup station at the cold prep area has not been planned. The pickup area needs to be located immediately adjacent to the exits into the dining room. Roll warmers, soup warmers, and a microwave oven are often located in the pickup station. Here wait staff will add the finishing touches that are not incorporated into the dish by the chefs. This might be adding a bit of parsley to the dish or preparation of toast for a breakfast order. Of course, in many upscale and large restaurants, very little of the dish preparation will be done by dining room staff, as the chef will complete the dish ready for service before it is placed on the pickup station worktable.

The final area in the kitchen will be the sanitation area where dirty dishes are brought from the dining area and then scraped and washed. The sanitation area should be located relatively close to where the servers will bring dirty dishes back to the kitchen. A worktable is needed to store dishes and flatware until they are ready to be put in the dish washers. Garbage bins are needed for scrapings and leftovers. And workspace will be needed at the end of the dishwasher unit for stacking clean dishes and flatware. In addition to the automatic dishwashers, deep sinks in a series of three units are also needed to wash pots and pans and other cooking utensils that will not appropriately fit into dishwashers. The pot washing area can be adjacent to the dish washing area or near the hot-food preparation area, depending on chef's and owner's preference and local code restrictions.

In the kitchen and service areas, sufficient lighting must be provided so chefs and kitchen staff can properly prepare foods and work in a safe environment. Good color rendition is needed in the food preparation area so that chefs and kitchen staff can insure that only fresh food is being prepared. Color-correcting fluorescent lamps or incandescent lamps are recommended. Using incandescent lamps in the kitchen means that the food will be prepared under the same light as what is used in the dining room. White light fluorescent fixtures do not give the color renditions needed in the preparation areas.

With so much stainless steel equipment in a kitchen, it is important for the designer to carefully plan lighting to reduce the chances of reflected glare. "Any luminary that is placed within 30 degrees above the line of sight of the worker should be screened."[18] This will help reduce the chances of glare that would lead to eye fatigue for kitchen staff. Thirty to 40 foot-candles are needed for most working areas and 15 to 20 foot-candles for nonwork general lighting.

---

[18]Kazarian, 1989, p. 149.

Display kitchens are frequent design elements in many types of food and beverage facilities. A *display kitchen* is a cooking area in the dining room positioned so that the guest can watch the chef prepare food. Display kitchens probably got their inspiration from early small diners where the cooks flipped hamburgers and eggs in full view of the customer. Today, many customers feel that the best seat in the restaurant is one where they can get a good view of the chef at work in an elaborate display kitchen. Sight lines and planning must be carefully calculated so that everything about the display kitchen is well ordered and enhances the "show." Placement of display kitchens must put emphasis on seeing the faces of the chefs as they cook, rather than their backs.

The planning and design of the display kitchen will be based on what kinds of food will be cooked in this area. In some situations, some equipment can be eliminated in the main kitchen, when there is a display kitchen. Cleanliness and customer safety is as necessary an ingredient in the design of the space as what will be prepared. Open flame grills need to be on a back wall away from the guest or protected with heat resistant glass. Wall finishes can be more decorative, but must still be selected or treated for easy cleaning of grease. Accent lights will help with the theatrical elements of the display kitchen, but also need to be planned to insure safety and functional needs of the chefs.

An *office* is necessary for the manager. This office is not commonly designed to be large or fancy (Figure 5-17), but it must provide the space and equipment needed to do the work and provide a professional atmosphere for the occupant. The office for the manager should be accessible for staff and guests. It is common to provide a standard arrangement of office furniture with a minimum of 60 square feet being provided. An extra item that might be found in the manager's office is a safe. In larger restaurants, an office is commonly provided to the chef as well. The chef's office should be accessible to and have visual control of the kitchen.

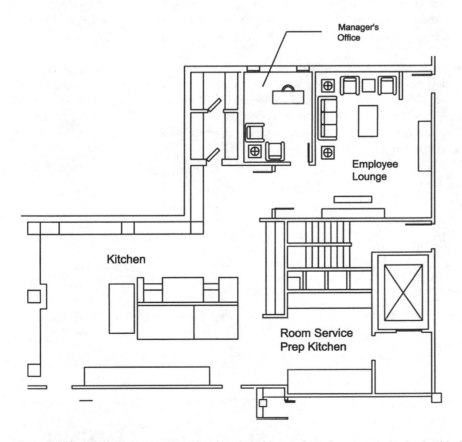

Figure 5–17 Kitchen manager's office in a hotel located in close proximity to the kitchen and auxiliary services. (Design by and drawing courtesy of Cody D. Beal.)

Computers are often provided for the manager and even the head chef. These computers are similar to those in any office area rather than the specialized versions found in the dining room or the beverage area. They are used for inventory control, ordering of foodstuffs and other supplies, bookkeeping and accounting, data control of recipes, and other rather normal office functions.

Many mid to large sized restaurants provide a separate employee area. Employee support areas would provide lockers to store employee valuables and a change of clothes. They should be well lighted and easy to maintain as a way to keep up the morale of staff. Larger restaurants will have separate employee rest rooms as part of the support spaces. This is particularly true of upscale restaurants where the employees would not be allowed to "mingle" with guests in the public rest rooms. If separate employee rest rooms are provided, most codes will require separate men's and women's toilet facilities.

Summary

Designing food and beverage facilities can be an exciting and creative way to use one's skills as an interior designer. The opportunity to design food and beverage facilities will remain high as new establishments are created and older ones are remodeled to stay viable in the face of changing market demands. The cost of developing a property today is very high, and the owner will expect the design consultant to help him or her achieve an interior facility that enhances the opportunities for success.

There are very specific functional needs and goals for the owner of a restaurant or beverage establishment. Bringing the owner's ideas into reality challenges the designer to solve problems of linking the menu to the interior design, acoustics, lighting ambience, and space design, as well as to interior specification. It also requires the interior designer to solve functional issues of traffic flow, workplace design in the kitchen, safety for staff and guests, and code requirements.

This chapter has introduced the student and the professional to the goals and operational issues of food and beverage facilities. We have defined the different types of commercial facilities that fall into this group and detailed the design and planning criteria that apply to a generic full-service food and beverage establishment. The references below are suggested to aid the student and designer in further research of the operations and design applications to this exciting area of commercial interior design.

References

Atkin, William Wilson and Joan Alder. 1960. *Interiors Book of Restaurants.* New York: Watson-Guptill.

Baraban, Regina and Joseph F. Durocher. 1989. *Successful Restaurant Design.* New York: Van Nostrand Reinhold.

Birchfield, John C. 1988. *Design and Layout of Foodservice Facilities.* New York: Van Nostrand Reinhold.

Cohen, Edie Lee and Sherman R. Emery. 1984. *Dining by Design.* New York: Cahners.

Colgan, Susan. 1987. *Restaurant Design. Ninety-Five Spaces that Work.* New York: Watson-Guptill.

Davies, Thomas D. and Kim A. Beasley. 1994. *Accessible Design for Hospitality,* 2nd ed. New York: McGraw-Hill.

Dittmer, Paul R. and Gerald G. Griffin. 1993. *Dimensions of the Hospitality Industry.* New York: Van Nostrand Reinhold.

Dorf, Martin. 1992. *Restaurants that Work*. New York: Watson-Guptill.

Katz, Jeff B. 1997. *Restaurant Planning, Design and Construction*. New York: Wiley.

Kazarian, Edward A. 1989. *Food Service Facilities Planning*, 3rd ed. New York: Van Nostrand Reinhold.

Kotschevar, Lendal H. and Mary L. Tanke. 1991. *Managing Bar and Beverage Operations*. East Lansing, MI: American Hotel and Motel Association Educational Institute.

Lundberg, Donald E. 1985. *The Restaurant: From Concept to Operation*. New York: Wiley.

Mahnke, Frank H. and Rudolf H. Mahnke. 1993. *Color and Light in Man-Made Environments*. New York: Van Nostrand Reinhold.

Melaniphy, John C. 1992. *Restaurant and Fast Food Site Selection*. New York: Wiley.

Mount, Charles Morris. 1995. *The New Restaurant: Dining Design 2*. New York: Architecture and Interior Design Library (PBC International, Inc.).

Ninemeier, Jack D. 1987. *Planning and Control for Food and Beverage Operations*, 2nd ed. East Lansing, MI: The Educational Institute of the American Hotel and Motel Association.

Ragan, Sandra L. 1995. *Interior Color by Design: Commercial*. Rockport, MA: Rockport.

Rey, Anthony M. and Ferdinand Wieland. 1985. *Managing Service in Food and Beverage Operations*. East Lansing, MI: American Hotel and Motel Association Educational Institute.

Scoviak, Mary. 1996. "Hotels: The Next Generation." *Interior Design*. June. Pp. 150–151.

Stein, Benjamin, John S. Reynolds, and William J. McGuinness. 1986. *Mechanical and Electrical Equipment for Buildings*, 7th ed. New York: Wiley.

Stipanuk, David M. and Harold Roffmann. 1992. *Hospitality Facilities Management and Design*. East Lansing, MI: The Educational Institute of the American Hotel and Motel Association.

Uniform Building Code, Vol. 1. 1994. Whittier, CA: International Conference of Building Officials.

Walker, John R. 1996. *Introduction to Hospitality*. Englewood Cliffs, New Jersey: Prentice Hall.

Wallace L. Rande. 1996. *Introduction to Professional Food Service*. New York: Wiley.

Witzel, Michael Karl. 1994. *The American Drive-In*. Osceola, WI: Motorbooks International.

Additional references related to material in this chapter are listed in Appendix A.

Chapter 6

Retail Facilities

Retailing consists of all activities involved in the sale of goods and services to the ultimate consumer. Retail stores are established by independent owners, as franchises of retail chains, and as store ownership groups or corporations. The interior design of a store plays a significant role in the success of that business. The layout and design of a store must provide the backdrop to best present the merchandise mix, and at the same time, encourage customers to purchase the products or services offered.

We have all been in numerous types of retail stores. However, personal exposure does not provide the student or design professional with sufficient information and experience to totally understand how to approach executing an effective and functional interior design solution. It is important to understand the reasoning behind planning and design decisions. Likewise, it is important to understand something about the client's business, and about retail business in general, in order to make appropriate design decisions.

The purpose of this chapter is to provide the design student and the design professional with a basic understanding of functional considerations and design methodologies involved in retail design. The chapter begins with an overview of the business of retail, followed by a brief discussion of the different types of retail establishments. This chapter also describes the specific criteria concerning the planning and design of retail spaces and provides a number of typical layouts for a few of the distinct areas of retail design. The interior design discussions focus on two kinds of retail stores: the clothing store and the furniture store. These two types of facilities were chosen because they represent the kind of stores in which students and professionals have a great deal of experience related to personal and professional needs.

An Overview of Retail

The design of retail facilities is an involved process that depends heavily on the designer understanding the retail business and the specific business of the client. It would not be prudent of any designer to make specific decisions and recommendations about the design of a retail store without this background information, any more than it would be prudent of a designer to take on the design of a medical office or hotel without some understanding of those businesses.

Let us begin with the basic terminology of retail.

Retail is defined in Webster's Unabridged Dictionary as "to sell directly to the consumer."[1]

Retailer is a merchant middleman who sells goods mainly to the ultimate consumer.

Retailing is the business activity of selling goods or services to the final consumer.

A *retail store* is a place of business in which merchandise is sold primarily to the ultimate consumers by a retailer. Sometimes that retail store is owned and operated by a manufacturer or by someone other than a retailer.

A *sale* is a retail sale when the ultimate consumer purchases the product.

The overall goals of retailing involve enticing the customer into the store and making sales. The interior design of the store plays only one part in achieving these primary goals. However, this is a very important part.

The goal of retail design is to enhance the space so as to encourage the increased and continuous sale of merchandise. This goal is a paramount consideration because each retailer has specific concerns in his or her area. These concerns focus on providing sufficient space allowances for the display of merchandise, prevention of shoplifting and internal theft, liability, image of the facility, merchandise mix, space allocation and growth of the business. Now let us look more carefully at the business of retail.

Although the design of the retail facility plays a significant part in the achievement of the overall goals of a retailer, marketing and merchandising arguably play important roles as well. To fully appreciate the concerns of the retail design client, it is important to provide an overview of these key issues. *Marketing*, in the most general sense, is carried on whenever goods change hands before being used. It includes, among other functions, buying, selling, storing, transporting, standardizing, financing, and supplying market information. Retailers participate in what is called a marketing channel. A *marketing channel* is a team of marketing institutions that direct a flow of goods or services from the producer to the final consumer. The marketing channel includes the producers, the wholesalers, the retailer, and the consumer. The *marketing concept* states that the comprehensive goal of every business organization is to satisfy consumer needs while creating a profit. *Merchandising* is defined as sales promotion and is a comprehensive function including market research, development of new products, coordination of manufacturing and marketing, and effective advertising and selling. An effective *merchandising blend* combines the contents of the retailer's merchandise with the decision the consumer uses in making selections. In this selection process, the *merchant,* defined as a buyer and seller of commodities for profit, considers the benefits the consumer seeks in the product, whether the product represents a functional or psychological need, whether or not the physical properties of the product satisfy consumer needs, and the advantages of supplementary benefits to the customer such as deliveries, installation, and alterations.

The *retailing plan* is a group of activities that includes five stages: (1) defining retail environments, (2) controlling financial, organizational, human, and physical resources, (3) identifying and selecting retail marketing and sites, (4) developing and managing product, and (5) creating and implementing promotion strategies. An effective retail plan answers the questions of why, what, when, where, and how specific retail business activities are to be accomplished. The right message, the right appeal, and the right services are all considerations in retail planning.[2] It is important for the interior designer to understand this underlying philosophy of retail planning for each project in order to provide an effective solution to the interior design of the facility.

The store owner or management team's tasks and responsibilities begin with developing the merchandise blend, finding the best location, operating the store, and, of course, purchasing, pricing, controlling, and promoting the merchandise. In addition, they will provide the interior designer with ideas for the design of the interior of the store.

---

[1] *Webster's New International Unabridged Dictionary,* 3rd ed., 1971, s.v. "retail."

[2] Lewison, 1994, pp. 31–32.

In selecting a retail store's environment, the management must consider the physical and psychological emphasis the environment will have on customers and employees. One of the initial concerns is creating a store image. This image includes store location, interior design, the actual products and their presentation, price of items, and public relations. As the interior design is paramount to the space planning and visual impact of the store, the aforementioned areas affecting image must be considered in the design solution. In addition to the obvious contributions of graphics and color, the interior designer's space planning of fixed and flexible merchandising space will affect sales and the store's image. Management must also consider the consumer's interest in locating shopping areas that provide safety, comfort, and attention to aesthetics.

Consumer needs and wants motivate their buying activities. *Needs* are essential physiological and psychological requirements necessary to the physical and mental welfare of the consumer. *Wants* are conscious impulses toward objects that promise rewards. Simply, needs are things we must have, wants are the things we would like to have. There are *physiological needs* that are required for survival and basic comfort such as food, clothing, and housing. *Safety needs* refer to security and stability. In today's world, an alarm for the car, a personal defense device like Mace, and even a cellular phone are examples of goods that satisfy these needs. *Esteem needs* are those regarding self respect, admiration, and achievement. An enormous amount of goods can be involved in satisfying esteem needs, depending on the consumer's background. Antique furniture, a new car, and jewelry can be examples of esteem needs. All of these items or services are sold in stores and the image and design of the store must relate to the goods being sold.

Retailers focus on the unsatisfied needs and wants of consumers by offering goods and services that satisfy these needs and wants. One thing that retailers have discovered to assist in this process is that when the shopping experience focuses on the senses, these stimuli can operate as a motivation to purchase. One of the terms associated with the focus on the senses is *atmospherics,* which is a conscious effort by the retailer to create a buying environment that will produce specific emotional effects in buyers. An example of atmospherics in action is the aroma from a bakery, specific types of music in a high-fashion boutique, or carefully controlled temperatures in many kinds of stores. Retailers focus on a variety of these appeal techniques to entice the consumer into the selling space. The first one is *sight appea*l. The retailer uses size, shape, and color to attract the customers as well as harmony, contrast, and clash. Harmony is "visual agreement" and a harmonious environment is usually associated with a more formal environment, whereas contrast and clash, which are considered "visual conflict," are used often to create an informal shopping atmosphere. The use of paneling in a formal design in Ralph Lauren shops is an example of sight appeal using harmony. *Scent appeal* is also used by retailers. For example, in a bakery, the scent of baked goods is important. A sports equipment facility with an emphasis on fishing would focus on the scent of the outdoors. A sports equipment store could combine scent appeal with sound appeal by the use of an audiovisual system playing the sound of a rushing stream or replaying sporting events. Stores are also designed using *theme appeal,* which is establishing an environment related directly to the product, to holidays, or to special events.[3] Examples would include Christmas decorations and displays used seasonally by most stores, and special displays tied into a local event like a city hosting a major sporting event such as the Super Bowl or the Olympics.

In reviewing the basic concepts of retailing, the following points need to be considered: the definition of retailing, the difference between marketing and merchandising, and the importance of factors that affect the store's environment such as techniques that appeal to the customers' needs and wants. The next section focuses specifically on the basic considerations in the planning of the retail interior.

---

[3] Lewison, 1994, p. 269.

Types of Retail Facilities

There are a huge variety of retail stores (see Figure 6-1). Some are independently owned and operated by entrepreneurs. Others are chains or franchises that can either be independently owned or owned by the chain and managed on the local level. Chain stores require local merchants to follow policies established by corporate structures while entrepreneurs are free to explore alternative methods. The design of a chain-owned specialty store will also be mandated by the corporate owners while the design of an independently owned entrepreneurial store is controlled by that entrepreneur.

Another developing retail concept in the United States is the hypermarket. These are stores that are usually about 200,000 square feet and sell general merchandise and/or food. Hypermarkets were introduced in post World War II France and developed out of a need to distribute food to a country devastated by war.

The majority of retail facilities are located in either a central business district or a shopping center. During the 19th century, centers of commerce developed in the central city. As cities developed, as trade increased, and as the crafts developed to produce goods, a center of commerce became necessary. The switch from open markets to actual stores had began during the Middle Ages and accelerated after approximately 1840.

Shopping centers are a 20th century adaptation of the historical marketplace with accommodation made for parking cars. Stores in a shopping center are distinct from stores in a central business district because the shopping center is created and managed as a unit and provides adequate parking for the volume of shoppers. Retail stores in central business districts are both independently owned or chain stores and are under no obligation to provide parking for their customers' vehicles.

There are generally three types of shopping centers. The smallest is the neighborhood shopping center. These consist of a mix of retail stores and service business offices like accountants or travel agents. Larger neighborhood shopping centers have a supermarket as a focus or magnet,[4] often in conjunction with a drug store and a variety of retail stores and possibly small service offices. Most frequently, the retail stores in the smallest neighborhood shopping centers are independently owned and operated, not chain stores or franchises. In the larger neighborhood shopping centers that contain supermarkets, many more of the specialty stores might be chain stores.

CENSUS OF RETAIL ESTABLISHMENTS IN THE UNITED STATES:	
Category:	#'s by thousands:
Eating & drinking establishments	433,608
Food stores	180,568
Apparel & accessories	145,490
Furniture & home furnishings	110,073
Gasoline service stations	105,334
Automobile dealers	96,373
Building materials & garden supplies	69,483
Drug & proprietary stores	48,142
General merchandise	34,606
Miscellaneous:	302,538
TOTAL RETAIL ESTABLISHMENTS:	1,526,215

Source: 1992 Economic Census/Census of Retail Trade, U.S. Bureau of the Census

Figure 6–1 US Department of Commerce report depicting the percentage of types of retail stores in the United States.

---

[4]A *magnet store* is a large, well-known chain that attracts a large number of customers to the shopping area.

The community shopping center has a mix of stores similar to that of the neighborhood center except that it adds a medium-sized department store as its magnet. The community shopping center is also more likely to have some chain or franchise stores in its mix as well as theaters and individually owned shops.

The third type of shopping center is the regional shopping center, more commonly called a *mall* today. Regional malls offer a full range of shopping services comparable to small central business districts. Regional malls have two or more department stores as magnets (also called anchor stores), along with a large variety of specialty stores. Today, most specialty stores in malls are chain stores rather than independently owned stores. Regional malls have steadily increased the scope of their services and amenities and they often include food courts, recreation areas such as movie theaters, areas for small concerts, and of course, an area for holiday or other theme events. In addition to a mall complex itself, it is also common for additional stores, restaurants, hotels, and recreation facilities to be built around the fringe of the regional mall. The Mall of the Americas in Bloomington, MN, is one of the world's largest regional malls. It contains over 420 stores including 4 major department stores, 24 restaurants, 24 food courts, 9 night clubs, 2 arcades, an 18-hole miniature golf course, a 14-screen movie theater, and a 7-acre amusement park in the center of the mall. The entire mall is on 78 acres with 4.2 million square feet and 13,000 parking spaces.

Before moving on to the discussion of planning and design considerations in retail stores, it is important to briefly comment on how department stores came into being. The development of department stores was linked to the growth in the 19th century of large population centers. During the 19th century, general merchandise stores developed into department stores by broadening their inventory (Figure 6-2). During the 1920s some department stores in the United States began opening branches. The first department stores to have branches were J.C. Penney and Sears, Roebuck Company. Both of these department stores began essentially as catalog suppliers targeted to the rural areas of the United States and grew into full-line department stores in the central cities. From 1929 to the 1950s, department stores spread into the suburbs. It was in the 1950s that the discount store was created. Early discount stores were designed very simply, making customer self-service rather than service by store personnel a key ingredient in their design. In regards to interior design, store image for discount stores varies from the higher end department stores such as Nordstrom's, Bloomingdale's, and Nieman-Marcus; the discount store uses very simple finishes and has a minimal use of walls to subdivide the departments. In order to compete with the discount stores, department stores improved personnel training, and modernized their facilities, including the updating of their interior design.

As the 21st century approaches, the malls continue to dominate as the preferred shopping facility of consumers. However, the Internet, catalogs, and cable television are changing the shopping landscape. These nontraditional shopping venues provide consumers an opportunity to shop from their homes, thus avoiding traffic and saving time. The popularity of shopping at home is beginning to have an effect on traditional shopping centers. Nevertheless, interior designers need to be informed and prepared in the designing of retail facilities.

Planning and Design Concepts

The material in this section provides the student and the design professional with a background in the basic planning and design concepts that must be considered in the design of small retail stores. Although we discuss these issues in terms of the small retail store, these design concepts can be applied to the design of larger stores. Keep in mind that the exact specialty of the store will affect how these concepts are applied.

Exterior Design Concepts

The exterior design of the storefront is the first major impression that consumers have of the store. Thus the focus of exterior architectural design of the store is to attract attention,

Figure 6–2 Retail department store circa 1900 with stationary features such as display cabinetry. (Photograph used by permission, Utah State Historical Society. All rights reserved.)

create the highest level of product exposure, and maximize selling areas visible from outside. In looking at the design concepts that affect the exterior of the store, the elements that must be considered are: the exterior architectural design, signage, store windows, and the entrance.

The chief function of *exterior design* is to attract the customer into the store. A primary way this is done is through the storefront configuration. Figure 6-3 provides examples of the three basic storefront configurations: straight, angled, and arcade fronts.[5] The advantage of the straight front is that it does not reduce the interior selling space. Unfortunately, it often lacks consumer appeal from the exterior. The angled-front gives the consumer a better viewing angle of the merchandise. Angling the front also reduces the window glare. This makes it easier for customers to see merchandise displayed in the windows as well as merchandise farther into the store. The arcade front has several recessed windows, which increases area of the store's window display as well as reducing glare. Although stores generally employ their own visual merchandisers for window display, an interior designer must initially specify materials for that area. Material specification must be made for the purpose of creating an appropriate backdrop for the merchandise as well as attracting the customer into the store.

In order to enhance the goal of representing the merchandise or the character of the merchandise which is offered, well designed *signage* is required. *Signage* or *shop signs* are defined as outdoor advertisement on the premises of a store or business describing the product or services provided by the advertiser. The originators of shop signs were the ancient Babylonians. The Roman Empire developed the use of logos in order to communicate more effectively with the illiterate. This method of communication was continued throughout the Middle Ages in Europe with the logos operating as a visual symbol or sign for the merchant. As the literacy level of the general population increased, the emphasis in signage switched to written communication. Incandescent lighting was used with signs by the end of the 19th century and neon signs became popular in the 20th century. Store signs should explain who, what, and where in regards to the retail establishment. Retail franchises and chains have established logos and/or signage, which is immediately recognizable by the public due to

---

[5]Lewison, 1994, pp. 276–277.

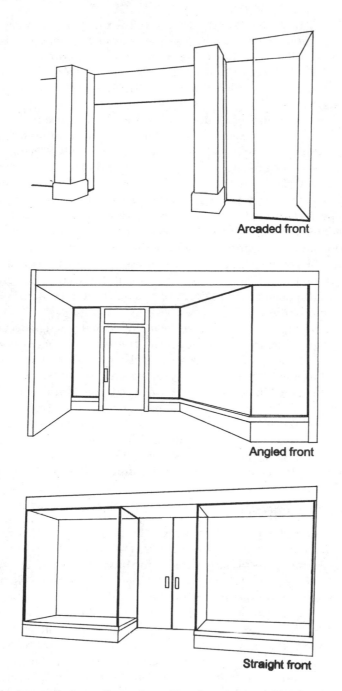

Arcaded front

Angled front

Straight front

Figure 6–3 Three basic storefront configurations. (Drawing courtesy of S.O.I. Interior Design, Houston, TX.)

the considerable advertising investments made by these organizations. Smaller retail stores may hire graphic designers who specialize in retail signage to develop their logo and written images. Occasionally, an interior designer will be asked to develop the concept.

In addition to signage, *windows* are also used to advertise merchandise. The number, size, depth, and types of windows a store uses change its exterior appearance and the general impression conveyed to customers. The most common types of display windows are: ramped, shadow box, elevated, and island. Ramped display windows have a display floor higher in back than in front. These windows can be either a wedge or a tiered display shape, either of which gives a better view of the merchandise displayed in the back. They are often used in shoe and accessory stores. The shadow box display window is small and set at eye-level. They are completely enclosed and are often used by jewelry stores such as Tiffany's. Elevated windows are display windows with floor elevations from 12 to 36 inches above the floor. Island display windows are four-sided and used with the arcade storefront. This style of display window is commonly used in clothing stores. The advantage of the island window is that it can be viewed from a variety of angles.[6]

The decision about what kinds of windows will be used for the storefront is often dependent upon the products to be sold. For example, a dress shop must have windows that display the full mannequins, thus keeping the display related to human scale. This often allows the merchant to increase display of shoes, handbags, accessories, hats, and so on, as well as general clothing items. A jewelry store display window needs to be at eye level. The customer's eye needs to focus on the much smaller objects in the jewelry display window. For this reason, the shadow box window is the perfect setting for this product. In addition, lighting can be enhanced and directed within the box, creating a miniature theater effect that helps to attract the customer.

Display windows and their lighting should be flexible to promote a variety of displays. The windows should be complementary to the exterior architecture as well. The retailer will stress the display windows since the volume of sales is influenced by the effective design of windows and displays. Remember, the majority of retailers prefer a view into the interior store as opposed to the window display blocking the view.

The actual design of the store entrance will be included in the design decisions concerning the total exterior design of the store. Many store owners view the entrance door as an important part of the visual appeal and market recognition of the store. Merchants will emphasize the style of the door and its importance in creating an inviting, welcome, and enticing entry. For example, the red door of the Elizabeth Arden Salons and the gold and maroon door of Cartier act as important symbols for those stores. The door itself is only one part of the entrance. The designer must also consider lighting and numerous code requirements. A few of these include: no steps, the use of nonskid flooring materials, sufficiently wide doors for all traffic, and no entrance clutter.[7] Ideally, the entrance doors should allow customers to see at least a portion of the interior. However, this can be governed by location, codes, weather, and other factors.

Interior Design Concepts

Once inside the store, the physical layout and design decisions concerning the architectural surfaces and elements are critical to the success of the store. These elements must be used effectively by the interior designer as the success of the business is often dependent upon these factors. Considerable research in the area of marketing and merchandising has been pursued to find out what attracts the customer, what direction and what traffic patterns within a store are effective, what height for display merchandise and which materials should be specified to attract the customer through visual, tactile, and audio appeal. The elements that must be considered in the interior design of the store are: space allocation, traffic patterns and aisles, merchandise display equipment, architectural finishes, and lighting design.

Before we begin to look at each of these elements in the total planning and design of a retail store, remember that all the decisions about the items to be discussed below are heavily influenced by the merchandise to be sold and the type of customer the store owner desires to attract. What will be sold can have an impact on how it will be displayed in the selling space.

Merchandise is grouped into product-line subdivisions. Within each of these subdivisions are three categories or types of merchandise: demand, convenience, and impulse merchandise. Demand merchandise is usually a necessary item that encourages the public to shop. A bed would be an example of demand merchandise for a furniture store. Coats and suits are examples in clothing stores. The retailers of small shops stock mainly demand merchandise

---

[6]Lewison, 1994, p. 278.

[7]Lewison, 1994, p. 278.

since these items turn over faster and produce constant revenue. Convenience items are much used items. Sheets would be an example of convenience merchandise in a furniture store, while hosiery would be an example of a convenience item in a clothing store. Impulse items are unplanned purchases by the customer. Impulse items are dependent upon good display. We have all impulsively purchased candy bars at the checkout counter of a grocery store or accessory items like scarves and ties in a clothing store.

In allocating space for merchandise, the interior designer also needs to be aware of two merchandising approaches to making space decisions: the *model stock method* and the *sales/productivity ratio method*. In the model stock method, the retailer determines the amount of floor space needed to stock a desired amount of merchandise. In the sales/productivity ratio method, the retailer allocates selling space on the basis of sales per square foot for each merchandise group. The retailer/merchant will make the decision as to which method will be used. The importance of this information to the interior designer is that it directly relates to the placement and space planning of the fixed and flexible fixtures and to the proximity relationships of other merchandise.

Once the merchandise blend for the particular store has been identified, the focus is shifted to the disbursement of the product within the selling space. In the *space allocation* of retail stores, the space is generally categorized as *selling space* and *nonselling space*. The area designated for the display of merchandise and interaction between customers and personnel is referred to as selling space. Nonselling space would be areas such as the stockroom, office, and any other areas not allocated for the direct display or selling of merchandise. The selling space is of major concern to the retailer.

The merchant usually discusses with the interior designer the approximate placement in this selling space of the merchandise in the selling space. Decisions about where the merchandise is located try to meet an important goal of the retailer: exposing the customer to all the merchandise and enticing the customer to purchase additional items. For example, demand merchandise is often placed far from the entrance. This placement forces the customer to pass convenience and impulse items prior to reaching the intended item. Convenience items are traditionally placed somewhere in the midsection of the store. Impulse items are usually located near the sales counter/cashier or close to the entry. Other important considerations in the placement of the different types of items are the cost of the items and the concerns for theft and security. Of course, merchandise placement is highly flexible and dependent upon the merchant and the product mix. The final decision about where to place goods is based on two factors: the need for exposure of the merchandise, such as impulse and convenience items, which must be readily seen, and the retailer's expected customer type in regards to their profile, their age group and their shopping frequency.

Retailers have basic guidelines when considering how the selling and nonselling spaces in stores are determined. These guidelines include:

- The space near the front of the store is considered more valuable than the space to the rear.

- Space on the first floor is more valuable than basement or upper floor space.

- The space along the aisles is more valuable than the peripheral corner space.

- Main or central aisles are more valuable than peripheral or side aisles.

- Eye level space is more valuable than space above or below eye level, especially for new items.[8]

All these guidelines must be taken into account when assisting the store owner in decisions about space allowances for types of merchandise, fixture types, fixture locations, architectural finishes, and internal signage.

---

[8] Lewison, 1989, pp. 226–229.

Traffic patterns establish the layout of *aisles* and positioning of fixtures within the store. Merchandising research has shown that the public usually turns right when entering a store. Thus the designer needs to attract the customer to the left as well in order to reduce one-way traffic. Many retailers agree that the best placement for a product is often associated with the customer in-store traffic patterns.

Easy access from the store entrance to all sales sections is very important. Small retail stores usually use one single aisle extending the length of the store. If the store is large, minor aisles would branch off from the main aisle whether the main aisle is placed directly through the center of the store or as a radial main aisle creating a circular traffic pattern. The three pattern systems used for placing aisles are the grid, the free-flow, and the boutique system. The grid system plans aisles and fixture locations to fit within the columns of the structural system. Due to the necessity of working with the columns, this aisle pattern provides very little flexibility to the overall floor plan. The free-flow system allows displays and fixtures to be moved easily. The free-flow system is recommended for most effective use of space, especially with small stores, because the displays can be changed very easily and targeted for the volume of merchandise in stock. The boutique system arranges the sales floor into individual, semiseparate areas, each possibly built around a shopping theme that focuses on the individuality of the product. Personal service, uniqueness, and ambience are all considered important elements in planning and creating a boutique atmosphere. Figures 6-4, 6-5, and 6-6 provide examples of these pattern systems.

In larger stores and department stores, stairs, escalators, and elevators play an important part in attracting customers to other parts of the store as well as functioning to move traffic. They must be easily accessible and of course, meet code requirements. Escalators are usually installed in pairs and generally located in the center of the sales area. They are used to keep shoppers in a "captive audience" situation for the viewing of merchandise. Open stairs are often placed toward the rear of the selling space, exposing the customer to more products as they proceed through the main floor to access the stairs to the upper and lower levels. Elevators are often placed on the periphery of the floor plan close to the stairways. Escalators, stairs, and elevators are placed strategically to enhance customer traffic flow as they view the merchandise. Stairs are also placed in accordance to building code requirements for safe egress.

When planning the *nonselling space*, consider the following points:

- Decide initially how much reserve stock needs to be stored.

- Plan for reserve stock areas located around the perimeter of the sales floor for easy access.

- Coordinate the moving of new merchandise onto the floor with the customer traffic pattern to avoid interference.

- Make certain that outgoing merchandise is not handled in a manner that would interfere with the sales area.

- Include facilities for docking, loading, and unloading, keeping docking areas under a roof or canopy.

- If the store is sufficiently large, use a conveyer belt to transport items from the receiving dock to the service area where they are marked and put into storage or stock.

- Provide space for store delivery trucks to load and keep it separate from the receiving area.

In addition to the above mentioned points in space planning for the nonselling areas, be alert to the in-store merchandise-handling process. After the merchandise is unloaded at the receiving dock, it should follow a traffic pattern as it is checked and marked and then sent to storage or the sales floor.

Additional storage may be needed to handle off-season stock that was not sold during the season as well as to provide space for the layaway procedure popular in small clothing stores.

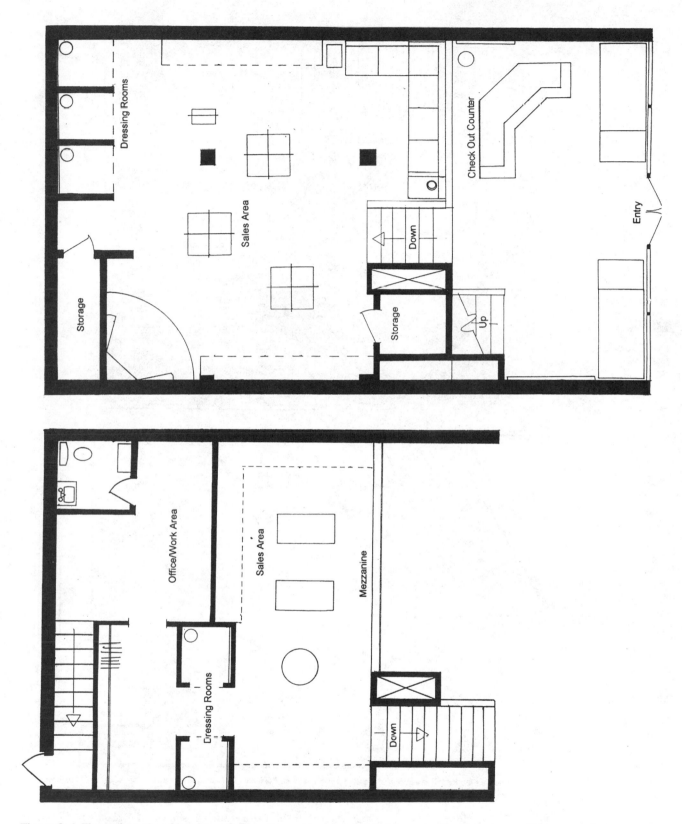

Figure 6–4 Floor plan of a tri-level free form pattern showing potential for versatile placements. (Plan courtesy of S.O.I. Interior Design, Houston, TX.)

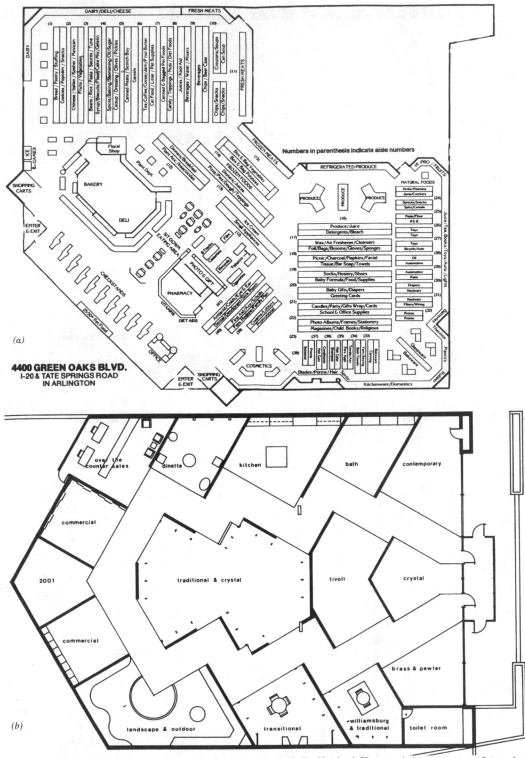

(a)

4400 GREEN OAKS BLVD.
I-20 & TATE SPRINGS ROAD
IN ARLINGTON

(b)

In the geometric plan for the showroom of **Lighting Designers, Inc., Rockville, Maryland, fifteen angled spaces present fixtures by functional and style groupings.**

Figure 6–5 (*a*) Floor plan of a grid pattern with fixed features such as shelving for products. (From Barr and Broudy, *Designing to Sell.* Copyright © 1986. Reproduced with permission of the McGraw-Hill Companies.) (*b*) In this geometric plan for the showroom of Lighting Designers, Inc., Rockville, MD, 15 angled spaces present fixtures by functional and style groupings. (From Barr and Broudy, *Designing to Sell.* © 1986. Reproduced with permission of the McGraw-Hill Companies.

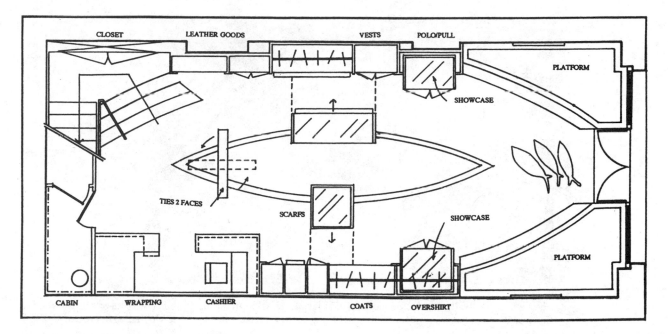

Figure 6–6 Floor plan of a boutique pattern showing creative use of space. (Plan courtesy of Jean-Pierre Heim & Associates, Paris, New York. Jean-Pierre Heim and Galal Mahmoud Architectes, DPLG, Paris.)

Work space is necessary for service personnel to perform their duties. Space should be allowed for alterations, accounting, purchasing, custodial functions, and rest rooms.

Merchandise display equipment includes counters, racks, and platforms as well as freestanding flexible fixtures. All these different types of merchandise display equipment items are commonly called *display fixtures*. Display fixtures are used to store, protect, and display merchandise. Often the interior designer is required to provide creative design solutions to the selection and specification of merchandise display equipment. Fixtures should allow for the maximum amount of merchandise to be available on the selling floor and yet these fixtures should not appear overcrowded. Display fixtures should also be flexible in use and easily moved.

Several types of fixtures are commonly used. They are the island, wall, and freestanding fixtures. The island fixture is a three-dimensional counter. These are used for the display of jewelry, scarves, handbags, cosmetics, and the majority of accessories. An often specified wall fixture on the market is the slatwall/shutterwall (see Figure 6-7). This fixture is useful in the display of apparel merchandise. For example, at the beginning of a season, the volume of the stocked items is up and the merchandise can be grouped close together. However, as the stock reduces in volume, the brackets can be moved on the slatwalls to create a feeling of space and not emphasize the reduction in stock, which often is interpreted by the customers as "leftovers." Freestanding fixtures provide customer access from all sides. The most common freestanding fixtures are the two-way, the four-way, and rounders (see Figures 6-8, 6-9, and 6-10). Often new merchandise is displayed on the two-ways and the four-ways, especially in a clothing store. For example, a new collection of skirts, pants, and jackets could be displayed on the two-way. Rounders are usually preferred for items that are sold at a reduced price. As a special sale can bring customers into a store, these rounders are often positioned at the back of the store, which forces the customer to pass by the newer merchandise. Additional freestanding fixtures are available as well as custom designed fixtures, which may be required for an individual store's needs. See Figures 6-11 and 6-12 for examples of display arrangements.

In the initial interview with the client, the interior designer will discuss the preferences for *colors* and materials. Many times, the retailer has a logo and color choices that are already

Figure 6–7 Slatwall can also be used for display alone as depicted in this photo. Four-way and waterfall fixtures in foreground and lower level. (Photograph courtesy of S.O.I. Interior Design, Houston, TX.)

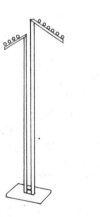

Figure 6–8 Two-way fixture with waterfalls for easy viewing. (Courtesy of S.O.I., Interior Design, Houston, TX.)

Figure 6–9 Four-way fixture to display coordinates. (Courtesy of S.O.I., Interior Design, Houston, TX.)

Figure 6–10 Rounder, often used for sales items due to potential density for hanging. (Courtesy of S.O.I., Interior Design, Houston, TX.)

established and identified with the product. The colors chosen are usually noncolors or neutralized colors for the large planes that serve as a backdrop for the merchandise. If a specific, dominant color is requested by the retailer, the interior designer must make certain that it does not interact or conflict with the changing colors of the merchandise. This is especially true in clothing stores. Remember that the colors of the current merchandise change more rapidly in the apparel market. The majority of retailers recognize the value of color and color schemes as denoting a certain period or year. Most merchants will want their store to look at least up-to-date with color schemes. However, the majority of colors used in the interiors will reflect a tint onto the merchandise. For this reason, noncolors and light neutrals are often used for walls and floors.

Materials specification is dependent upon the type of atmosphere requested by the retailer as well as fire and building codes. For example, if the retailer desired a quiet atmosphere

Figure 6–11 Mannequins in a life-like poses are often used to display merchandise, as seen in this Tommy Hilfiger showroom, New York, NY. (Design by and photograph courtesy of Peter Gisolfi Associates, Hastings on Hudson, NY.)

Figure 6–12 Unusual display arrangements can include creative solutions such as this sock display in this Tommy Hilfiger showroom, New York, NY. (Design by and photograph courtesy of Peter Gisolfi Associates, Hastings on Hudson, NY.)

for shopping, then such materials as a high-density, low-pile carpeting would be specified as well as use of commercial grade fabrics on the wall. If the retailer requested a high energy environment, then more hard surfaces, such as tile or wood floors, mirrored walls, and minimal upholstery, would be specified. In selecting materials for architectural finishes remember that soft, porous materials absorb sound, and hard, rigid materials reflect sound. The size of the store and its building type will govern the code requirements concerning architectural finishes. The reader is urged to verify code requirements for the particular project.

The type of *lighting* used in the sales area varies with the type of merchandise displayed. The primary purpose of lighting is to improve the display of merchandise. There are three basic categories of lighting: overall/general lighting, accent lighting, and peripheral lighting. General lighting is necessary to allow for overall visibility. Accent lighting is necessary to add visual impact to displays. Peripheral lighting is used to attract attention to the wall displays and merchandise. Lighting fixtures should attract attention to the items displayed. The recommended foot-candles needed for selling vary with the type of merchandise and the colors used, but according to the Illuminating Engineering Society (IES), between 100 and 500 foot-candles is recommended in merchandising areas.[9]

Another major concern of retailers is the subject of *security*, as they seek to deter customer theft or shoplifting, employee theft, burglary, and robbery. Shoplifting is the act of pilfering merchandise from a store. Shoplifters may be amateurs or professionals. Customer theft represents between 30 to 40 percent of retail theft; however, employee theft represents at least 42 to 44 percent. Retailers attempt to prevent theft by the use of mirrors, limited-access areas,

---

[9]McGuiness et al., 1980, p. 734.

security guards, computerized cash registers, observation booths, electronic tags, television monitors, and fitting room attendants. Although 79 percent of retailers use mirrors for security, research has determined that mirrors have proven effective only 2 percent of the time.[10] The most effective security measure is the electronic tag. Electronic tag measures are categorized under the term radio frequency identification. A tag containing a circuit capable of emitting a radio signal is attached to a valuable piece of merchandise. If the tag is not removed or deactivated at the time of sale, an alarm goes off at the exit, which alerts the sales staff to theft. Another kind of electronic tag or marking device can code prices onto tickets and tags that are processed by optical character recognition (OCR) systems. The designer or retailer must make certain that very expensive items are not too close to the exit unless they have a cable wire attached or are in locked display cabinets. Aside from their duties of wrapping merchandise and taking money, personnel at the cashier/sales desk must also monitor the store from this position in regards to security.

In addition to the security factor, the retailer will also discuss with the interior designer an emphasis on liability. For example, a slippery floor material used at an entry might cause a customer to fall; a sharp edge on a cabinet or fixture at eye level could cause an eye injury; stair steps that do not meet the codes could cause a fall.

The display of merchandise in store windows and in other locations in the selling space is called *visual merchandising*. Visual merchandisers or display designers are hired specifically to deal with the visual merchandising for the store. The objective of visual merchandising is to encourage the completion of the sale once the customer is in the store. A talented, creative display designer can bring customers to and into the store based on the reputation of the designer's show window and vignette work. Retail displays expose the product, enhance the look of the product, create interest, give information, aid sales transactions, ensure security, provide storage, and increase sales. Visual merchandising is considered a form of nonmedia advertising. It aids in creating a store image to customers. Many stores have visual merchandisers on staff. Formerly referred to as display staff or window dressers, their ability can draw consumers to the windows as well as to the interior design display throughout the store. An interior designer working as a visual merchandiser has an excellent opportunity to develop and increase portfolio work rapidly. Thus it is a good position for an entry-level designer who needs to increase his or her work experience as well as accumulate portfolio items.

Design Applications

It would be impossible to discuss specific design applications for each type of retail store. However, it is important to look at how the planning and design concepts discussed in the preceding section apply to a particular facility. For the purpose of brevity, this section on design application focuses on small clothing stores and residential furniture stores. These types of facilities were selected because students' and professionals' exposure to clothing stores and furniture stores is greatest at this point. Figure 6-13 shows some typical retail presentation drawings.

Clothing Stores

One of the initial responsibilities of the designer when contracted to design a clothing store is to organize the merchandise areas into logical selling groups and allocate space and design layouts that are conducive to selling. The interior designer will be given information from the retailer as to a logical grouping of merchandise that will aid the customer in locating and selecting merchandise. The interior designer is responsible for making the shopping experience logical and comprehensive.

---

[10]Lewison, 1989, p. 237.

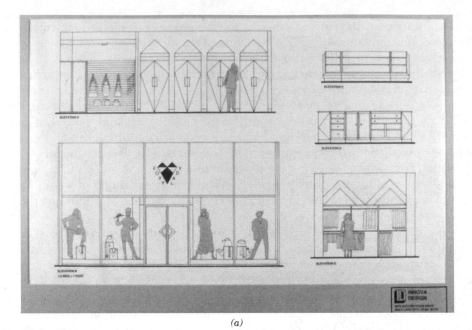

(a)

(b)

Figure 6–13 (*a*) Exterior elevation drawing of the tri-level free form pattern store. Designers are involved in the total design of the retail facility. (Drawing courtesy of HENV/USU. Drawing by Lee Brinegar.) (*b*) Designer's sketch of a store interior. (Drawing courtesy of S.O.I., Houston, TX.)

Space is at a premium in a small clothing store. The retailer will request that the maximum square footage be used for merchandise display while a small amount of space be allocated to nonselling functions. It is the designer's responsibility in the space planning process to present the client with the most flexible and functional plan. It is important to remember in apparel merchandising that the volume of stock varies greatly, depending upon what is actually being sold. For this reason, the designer needs to plan space using those fixtures that will give the store owner or manager the greatest flexibility in merchandise display.

Men's and women's clothing stores contain a wide variety of items that can be logically organized using the space planning principle of *in close proximity,* which means items used together are displayed next to or near each other.[11] For example, blouses/tops are placed near skirts, pants, jackets, and accessories such as belts and scarves. The close proximity of one product to another allows the salesclerk easy access and potential for selling more products to coordinate with the outfit. Using another example, three-way mirrors are placed strategically to entice the customer to leave the dressing room and view the outfit from one of the larger mirrors. At this point, the salesperson has an opportunity to sell more items to complete the outfit if some of the accessory items are close to the mirror and the customer.

Impulse, demand, and convenience items all occur in volume in this type of store. An example of demand merchandise would be coats, dresses, and suits; convenience items would be gloves, sweaters, and socks; and impulse items would be costume jewelry and other accessories.

In most cases, the free-flow traffic pattern system is the one used in clothing stores. This is due to its flexibility, potential for creative placement, and its economical use of space. Displays can be changed very rapidly. The majority of small retail outlets use one single, straight center aisle extending the length of the store. This aisle can vary depending upon the placement of the fixtures. The width of the main aisle is usually 6 feet with minor aisles from 3 to 4 feet. Stairs, escalators, and elevators must be easily accessible and are an important factor in determining the traffic pattern.

Once the zoning and the traffic patterns have been identified, the interior designer can then commence the specification of fixtures, both flexible and fixed. The most commonly used fixtures in clothing stores are two-ways, four-ways, spirals, and rounders—the flexible fixtures—along with slat wall and modular perimeter frames, which are the fixed fixtures. Since merchandise volume changes from season to season, it is important that the clothing store fixtures be flexible in order to display the varying products to their full advantage. One way this is done is to plan retail stores on a 4 foot module to accommodate standard retail fixed fixtures.

Clothing stores always have a few furniture items other than merchandise fixtures that need to be specified. The most common item specified in a small clothing store will be chairs or other seating units. Chairs are most commonly placed close to the three-way mirrors and are generally used by individuals accompanying the shopper. The scale of the chairs should be small but versatile enough to seat persons of varying sizes with a standard seat height. Avoid chairs and seating pieces with sharp edges and make certain that the chair does not tip or roll. Banquettes are sometimes specified for boutiques to provide seating for trunk showings (Figure 6-14).[12]

Each dressing room needs to be provided with a stool, chair, or bench, a shelf for handbags or accessories, several hanging hooks, and a full length mirror. In the majority of small clothing stores, the retailer prefers the three-way mirror to be in the selling space to allow the salesclerk to suggest additional items for purchase to enhance the outfit. Remember that a three-way mirror must be specified at a 120 degree angle or it is ineffective for viewing three dimensionally. In most locations, at least one dressing room will have to be accessible.

---

[11] Note that "in close proximity" is also used in many other types of retail stores.

[12] A *trunk showing* is a merchandise demonstration by the designer or manufacturer within the retailer's store.

Figure 6–14 Custom designed banquettes provide seating for trunk showings. (Photograph courtesy of S.O.I., Houston, TX.)

Interior designers will also be required to design and specify the counter(s) space that houses the cash register, the merchandise wrapping systems, and storage required at the cash register area. It is important that the designer have as much information from the retailer as possible about how this space will be used in order that the designer can best meet the needs. A two level counter is usually preferred, with the higher, narrower portion used for the check writing and the inside section used for the salesclerks' accounting procedures. In addition, a lower, outer shelf, placed appropriately for holding customer handbags and packages, is often provided. The higher counter area allows for better security of the cash register. In designing this space, make certain that the cash register is not visible from the exterior. The Americans with Disabilities Act (ADA) now requires that a portion of the main counter on the customer's side be no higher than 36 inches or that an auxiliary counter with a maximum height of 36 inches be provided. Remember to include the toe kick space for the entire counter area to allow the customer and sales staff to stand flush to the space.

In many stores, the cash wrap desk will be supplied with a computerized cash register. These specialized computers will help the store owner or manager perform many management control functions. Besides printing out the receipt for the sale, the computer will also keep an accurate inventory and make ordering new merchandise faster. A computer will also help the small store owner with bookkeeping and accounting functions. Of the design concepts for a computer workstation described in Chapter 1, the most important in the retail store will be lighting to prevent glare and veiling reflections.

The selection of colors and materials are a little different for clothing stores than for stores in general. As stated earlier, it is very important that the color of the walls, floor, and ceiling not reflect a tint of a specific color onto the merchandise. It is always best to specify noncolors and neutrals for large volume planes in the interior. Color distortion of merchandise is to be avoided. Lighting also affects color and must be specified to allow color to read accurately.

Nonselling areas in clothing stores provide facilities for storage of merchandise, receiving incoming stock, shipping outgoing items, moving stock around in the store, and also store administration. These support spaces include the administration and service areas, which involve receiving and signing, unpacking and inspection, prep work, ironing and/or steaming, sewing, repair work, hanging new goods, and layaway. Storage includes cleaning supplies, boxes, bags, bookkeeping papers, and sales receipts. Space must also be provided for the mechanical equipment that furnishes heating, cooling, light, and other utilities.

The design of a small clothing store uses the same principles in space planning as many large clothing stores. These principles include space planning for zoning, traffic pattern design, fixture placement, sales area planning, location of dressing rooms, and nonselling spaces, colors and material specification, lighting, and acoustics.

Furniture Stores

It is obvious that not all retail stores offer only clothing, accessories, and small gifts. Many retail stores sell furniture, appliances, hardware, and other nonapparel items, what the retailing industry calls hard goods or hard-line merchandise. Clothing, linens, shoes, and many accessories are called soft-line merchandise or soft goods. The hard goods or hard-line store should be designed to induce the shoppers to recognize quickly the kind and quality of the merchandise. The layout of the store must allow for easy viewing of the merchandise, which is commonly large in scale. It is also important in specifying of a hard goods specialty store to reflect the quality and nature of the product and services offered. A discussion of the application of design and planning concepts to a furniture store is included so that students and professionals can understand how these general planning concepts affect a store that carries hard goods.

Due to the nature of hard-line merchandise, specifically in our example furniture, there are some additional considerations in regard to the overall layout and design of this type of retail store. Although this section primarily discusses the residential retail furniture store, the principal ideas would also apply to the commercial office furnishings dealer as well as to a manufacturer's showroom. A brief discussion of the differences of these three furniture stores appears at the end of the section.

Some furniture stores offer very specialized merchandise while others offer a complete line of home furnishings. Specialized stores might sell only contemporary styles or only traditional styles. Others may sell only a particular furniture line—that is, furniture from only one manufacturer. Residential retail furniture stores in general, however, offer a broad line of merchandise and usually stock many styles of furniture, area rugs, window treatments, bedding, lamps, and a wide variety of accessories from many manufacturers. Often a furniture store will offer interior design services as an impetus to further purchasing by the customer.

The exterior architectural design of the furniture store, especially the windows or show window display, is paramount in exposing the potential customer to the available products. Show windows for a furniture store should be large enough to display completely furnished rooms. Window displays are predominanly done as vignettes[13] and are used not only to entice the customer into the store but to preview for them how a grouping of furniture can look in a home or commercial facility. The advantage exterior design can contribute to potential store business is the exposure to the public via passing traffic. A building or storefront is easily viewed from an automobile and its design can immediately attract or repel a potential customer. For example, a store displaying a Georgian storefront immediately portrays a traditional approach and the consumer can assume that more traditional furniture items are sold there.

The *entrance doors* should appear to welcome the customers by allowing them to see inside. It is also important that the entrance be sufficient to provide a wide view of the interior of the store. When entering, the customer usually encounters some display to each side of the door. The purpose of these displays is to expose customers to new products, or to create an inviting entry, and/or to introduce the customer to a specialty item carried by the store.

The *space planning* of a furniture store is done with specific goals in mind. The design of the traffic paths should lead directly into the store where the customer is usually greeted by a receptionist or a salesclerk, depending upon the size of the facility. From there, the traffic

---

[13]A vignette is a display of furniture and accessories that is created to look like an actual room.

paths lead the customer along the periphery of the store in order to see the window displays from another angle as well as to view the vignettes along other sides of the facility. As with the show windows, the internal vignettes are composed in an aesthetic, creative manner using new products or products on which the management is focusing for sales.

The *merchandising* of a furniture store is generally planned with categories of merchandise in mind, just like any other retail store. For example, the high-end furniture lines are given visual priority and often placed toward the front, taking up perhaps a quarter of the available floor space. Depending upon the configuration of the show windows, the high-end products may be placed to the right side of the store, as customers generally walk to the right upon entering a facility. Often a variation in flooring materials is used for the traffic paths and the display space.

Ideally, furniture should be arranged in natural groupings rather than lined up. Natural groupings are often used by higher-end and mid-priced furniture stores with the less creative approaches to display used in stores that sell budget furniture. Electrical outlets placed in recessed floor boxes should be abundant for mobility in furniture placement on the main sales floor. Living room, dining room, and bedroom furniture are popular items and the areas where customers will view them need to be planned for easy access. Accessories, used throughout the store to enhance the realism of vignettes, are also often allotted an area where they are grouped, should a customer be looking for only accessory items. Lamps are often grouped together using step fixture case goods display cabinetry for better display.

In residential furniture stores, *furniture placement* plays an important part in the layout of the store. If a furniture store is on more than one level, the first floor often contains living room and dining room furniture, lamps, and china. The second floor may contain bedroom furniture and mattresses. Area rugs and carpets are placed toward the rear or side of the store on either the first or second floor. Depending on the price levels of the products and the actual product mix of the store, a portion of the displace space may also be allotted to outdoor furniture as well as kitchen equipment. Of course, each individual store with its own merchandise blend will determine the focus of its particular products. The interior designer will rely upon the retailer for this specific information. In the majority of furniture stores, sale items at a reduced price are placed at the back of the store or in a basement. This encourages the customer to walk through the entire facility, which encourages additional exposure to products and potential sales.

Just as with a clothing store, a furniture store will have nonselling areas. The cashier's desk can be incorporated into the accounting/bookkeeping area at the back of the selling space with a window for receiving money and orders. Salesclerks are assigned their own individual desks, placed strategically throughout the facility. If the store has an interior design department, these individuals are often grouped together in a "design studio" space, which is commonly placed off the main sales floor. Many furniture stores have a restricted area for customer refreshments, which allows the customer and possibly the salesclerk to relax and discuss the products under consideration. It is important that this area be restricted, as food and drink should not be allowed on the sales floor for protection of the product.

Other nonselling areas will be areas like storage space, employee lounges, employee rest rooms, shipping and receiving areas, refinishing areas, and administrative offices. Most furniture stores have either an attached warehouse or a warehouse at a remote location, which is used to receive merchandise from manufacturers and store backup stock.

The interior design and *materials* used in a furniture store must predominantly be a background for the display of the products being offered for sale. The majority of large wall spaces are specified as light, noncolors, such as off-white or neutrals. Vignettes of products that may be the mainstay of the store will use stronger colors, wallpapers, or wood paneling specifically chosen to enhance the products displayed. Flooring materials need to allow for easy mobility, not only for customer access and comfort, but also for the moving of furniture. In specifying carpet, the designer should stay with a guideline of high density, low pile carpet, usually installed with the glue-down method. Many furniture stores have specified hard surface flooring for the main traffic aisles and use carpeting for the display and minor traffic aisles. Due to the volume of fabrics on a furniture store selling floor, the acoustical issue is not as much of a problem in that the fabrics and materials absorb some degree of sound.

Lighting becomes a paramount issue in the selling space as it has to focus on the individual groupings and represent the colors accurately. For this reason, the overall lighting of a furniture store requires considerable expertise from a lighting consultant. Retailers often request a combination of fluorescent, incandescent, and halogen fixtures for versatility. Lighting should be planned to accommodate the accurate depiction of any color on display and to enhance the product displayed. Lighting in furniture stores can be used effectively to establish mood in the setting as well as to affect the buyer.

Security in a furniture store or any hard-line store has a different focus than that in a clothing store. It is obviously difficult for a customer to shoplift a chair or dresser. Small accessory items on the sales floor, however, are a target for customer theft and may have an electronic tag attached, much like items in clothing/gifts stores. However, burglary is an issue during off hours. For this reason, many furniture stores have on-site security officers or a security service available. Employee theft also represents a portion of the security problem in a furniture store. For this reason, a large furniture store will have an employee checkout exit with a security guard or monitoring device in the area.

Liability in the design of a furniture store is also an issue. Materials specified as well as the configuration of the design must be carefully considered. The designer should avoid sharp edges in fixed features, slippery surfaces, uneven flooring, and exposed electrical wiring from lamps on display. The interior designer needs to be alert to the fire and safety codes as well as the building codes as required by law. The interior designer must think strategically in regards to the liability factors in the design of furniture stores, or in the design of any store, for that matter.

An office furnishings store is a type of furniture store that exclusively displays, stocks, and sells commercial quality furniture rather than residential quality furniture. Many office furnishings stores are also dealerships for one or more specific types of furniture. This specific furniture is usually office systems furniture but it could also be case goods furniture. The principles of layout and design for the selling spaces in a commercial quality furniture store are very similar to those of a residential store. It is in the nonselling spaces that the design varies. Members of the sales force and interior design department are grouped off the main selling floor, maybe even in a secluded section of the facility. Even though they may be somewhat segregated, the spaces for the salespeople, designers, even the bookkeeping departments, are still considered "selling space" as the office layouts may be the mechanism of the store or dealership to display certain kinds of furniture products.

A manufacturer's showroom is a facility mainly used by interior designers for the purpose of specifying and purchasing goods for their clients (Figure 6-15). Most furniture manufacturers have showrooms located in or near the trade market places like the Merchandise Mart in Chicago, the Pacific Design Center in Los Angles, and the Trade Mart in Dallas. Some of the largest manufacturers have multiple showrooms in a variety of cities. The manufacturer displays the furniture items in vignettes, both open and closed, throughout the space. The majority of the floor space is allotted to furniture with each area fully accessorized. Groupings are located in the space dependent upon what the manufacturer is trying to focus sales upon at any given time. For example, a new line or style of items will be located at the front of the showroom while standard items will be located toward the back. Nonselling space is provided for sales representatives, bookkeeping, and other general office functions.

The furniture store layout and display can be an excellent method of design exposure to promote reputation and to secure additional clientele. Just as the design of any design studio or office is a selling space for the designer's creative and space planning ability, the design of the furniture store gives the potential customer an impression of how the designer or sales people will assist them in their needs. A successful furniture store relies on customer traffic for sales. A creative interior designer can develop a reputation that brings customers to the store, thus promoting the store and the designer.

Figure 6–15 Knoll, Inc. showroom located in Houston, TX. (Photograph courtesy of Knoll, Inc. Designer: Kenji Ito.)

Summary

Retail interior design is an interesting and exciting specialty within commercial design. In this venue, the client has very specific needs in terms of space planning, and materials or support product specification. And yet the client who hires the interior designer is not the only client that must be satisfied. The store's customers and what they expect from the store must also be considered in the planning and design. In addition, the actual product type and mix of the store merchandise will also impact what is done in terms of planning and specification.

This chapter has focused on an explanation of the business of retailing, as well as providing basic information for the student and professional to help them understand how to approach the design of a retail facility. Depending upon the reader's background in commercial design and retail design specifically, this background information should be supplemented with further research. The references listed below provide the reader with a great deal of general and specific information on the design of retail stores.

References

Barr, Vilma and Charles E. Broudy. 1986. *Designing to Sell.* New York: McGraw-Hill.

De Chiara, Joseph, Julius Panero, and Martin Zelnik. 1991. *Time-Saver Standards for Interior Design and Space Planning.* New York: McGraw-Hill.

Fitch, Rodney and Lance Knobel. 1990. *Retail Design.* New York: Watson-Guptill.

Israel, Lawrence J. 1994. *Store Planning/Design.* New York: Wiley.

Lewison, Dale M. 1989. *Essentials of Retailing,* 4th ed. Columbus, OH: Merrill.

———. 1994. *Essentials of Retailing,* 5th ed. New York: Macmillan College.

Lopez, Michael J. 1995. *Retail Store Planning and Design Manual.* New York: Wiley.

Mason, J. B., M. L. Mayer, and H. F. Ezell. 1991. *Retailing.* Boston, MA: Irwin.

McGuiness, William J., Benjamin Stein, and John S. Reynolds. 1980. *Mechanical and Electrical Equipment for Buildings,* 6th ed. New York: Wiley.

National Retail Merchants Association. 1987. *The Best of Store Design 3.* New York: PBC International.

Ragan, Sandra L. 1995. *Interior Color by Design: Commercial.* Rockport, MA: Rockport.

Spence, William P. 1972. *Architecture.* New York: McKnight and McKnight.

Webster's New International Unabridged Dictionary, 3rd ed. 1971. Springfield, MA: G. C. Merriam.

Weishar, Joseph. 1992. *Design for Effective Selling Space.* New York: McGraw-Hill.

Additional references related to material in this chapter are listed in Appendix A.

Chapter 7

Health Care Facilities

Health care or medicine is concerned with the science and art of dealing with the maintenance of health and the prevention, alleviation, or cure of disease. Health care facilities include many types of business facilities that allow health care providers to prevent, treat, or possibly cure diseases or ailments. The interior designer may work with many of the medical professionals listed in this chapter. Although there are many similarities among the various specialties, each has its own needs, which will require individual design solutions.

The experience of visiting a doctor or receiving medical treatment is almost universal to the majority of the population of North America and many other parts of the world. We have a basic understanding of this field through our own experiences, which begin with childhood checkups and illnesses and continue through a multitude of adult complaints and diseases. Perhaps the design student or professional has had experiences with specialists such as family practitioners, gynecologists, surgeons, obstetricians, sports physicians, orthopedic surgeons, psychiatrists, cardiologists, gerontologists, or other medical specialists. Other health care providers, such as dentists, orthodontists, optometrists, ophthalmologists, and others, are also common to design students and professionals.

Despite this type of personal experience, the health care field is far more complex and diverse than any one individual's experience will encompass. To be effective in the area of designing medical facilities, the interior designer needs to have, at minimum, a solid understanding of the overall health care field, an understanding of the terminology associated with medicine, and the laws and regulations that apply to the design of health care facilities.

As with previous chapters, this chapter begins with a discussion of the subject field, health care, in order to give the reader a greater understanding of the work of his or her potential clients. It identifies and discusses the medical specialties and subspecialties as well as allied health care workers, describes the basic facilities from an interior design standpoint, and presents general solutions for design considerations in a variety of facilities. Due to the broad scope of health care, it is necessary to limit specific discussions to only a few examples of interior design solutions. These examples are included in the section on planning and design concepts.

An Overview of Health Care/Medicine

It is important for the interior designer to research and develop a basic understanding of the health care field before accepting any interior design assignment in this sector of commercial design.

Part of the responsibility of the interior designer in any aspect of commercial interior design is to become acquainted with common terminology used by the potential client. Basic terminology for health care is extensive. Fortunately, there are many medical dictionaries available in the many public libraries as well as medical libraries. A few are listed at the end of this chapter. The terms listed below are related to information in this chapter and are provided to aid the student and the interior designer more easily understand the subject matter. Additional terms are provided in other parts of the chapter.

Acute care patients are those requiring immediate or ongoing medical attention for a short period of time.

Primary care physician (PCP) is usually the first physician the patient sees for treatment or other consultation.

Skilled nursing facility (SNF) is a state licensed health care facility that provides 24-hour nursing care to patients.

Health maintenance organizations (HMO) are large groups of multispecialty health care providers offering services to member patients at either group clinics or a physician's medical office suite.

Medical office building (often referred to as *MOB*) contains one or more office suites for specialized medical practitioners.

Assisted living facilities (ALF) are semi-independent living facilities for those who require minimal nursing or other care. They are also sometimes called residential care facilities.

Continuing care retirement communities (CCRC) provide rental or purchase living facilities for retirees who may need anything from no assistance up to and including skilled nursing.

Hospice is a facility or program designed to provide a caring environment for the terminally ill.

Redundant cueing is the sending of a message to more than one sensory mode, such as a change in floor texture.

The overall goal of health care is to provide the patient with the most effective and successful treatment. Treatment may consist of preventive medicine, treatment for disease and/or illness, or health maintenance. It may occur for a short term or long term, and to improve the patient's quality of life. The goal of health care design is to understand each specialized area, the design needs of the specific assignment, and to develop appropriate design solutions and specifications. Since the health care industry is one of the fastest-growing components of the economy, it is a worthwhile focus for the interior designer.

There are approximately 24 accredited major medical specialty areas and subspecialties. The most commonly recognized and consistently encountered physicians are the primary care physicians, which include general practice (GP), pediatrics, family practice, and internal medicine. These physicians deal with the overall health of the patients. When necessary, the PCP refers the patient to the appropriate specialist.

Physicians have a variety of employment choices. They may work as a solo practitioner, in a group practice, or as a salaried physician. *A solo practitioner* provides professional services to the patient and is personally responsible for that care. Solo practitioners represent approximately 60 percent of all practicing physicians engaged in one of the specialties or subspecialties. This physician is one of the most frequent clients of the interior designer engaged in health care design (see Figure 7-1).

Group medical practices represent the second most common form of medical practice. The American Medical Association (AMA) defines the medical group practice as

The provision of health care services by three or more physicians who are formally organized as a legal entity in which business and clinical facilities, records, and personnel

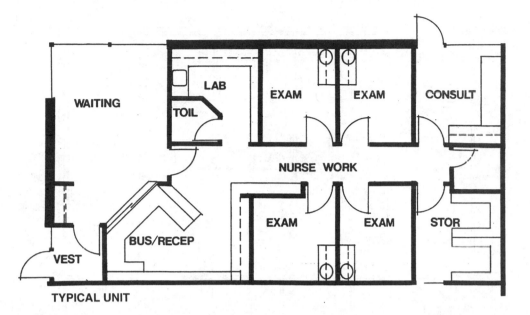

Figure 7–1 Floor plan of a medical office designed for a solo practitioner. (Plan courtesy of Architectural Design West.)

are shared. Income from medical services provided by the group are treated as receipts of the group and distributed according to some prearranged plan.[1]

A group can be an association of solo practitioners, a partnership, or a corporation. The members can combine their resources and expenses, which also provides more equipment and facilities as well as increases nursing and technical staff (see Figure 7-2).

Salaried physicians generally do not have private practices like those physicians discussed above. Rather, they have positions in hospitals or other health care facilities, government agencies, private and commercial companies, and the armed forces. The majority of the positions available are in private hospitals where physicians work in departments such as the emergency room, as consultants, as medical directors, or as department heads.

In discussing the various types of employment for the physician, it is important to include information regarding HMOs, as they seem to affect all physicians today. There are three types of HMOs: (1) HMOs where the doctors are involved as partners of the group, (2) staff arrangement HMOs where doctors involved are on staff and are salaried, and (3) HMOs where the doctors are part of a group practice affiliated with the HMO. The HMO supplies only approximately 10 percent of the patient load for these physicians.

In concert with the physician is the nursing staff, which is generally comprised of registered nurses and licensed practical nurses. A registered nurse (RN) has an undergraduate degree in nursing whereas a licensed practical nurse (LPN) has graduated generally from a two year nursing program. Nurses also often specialize in an area of medicine. The designer will also encounter nurse practitioners, who will generally have both bachelor's and master's degrees, and physician's assistants, who work with physicians but are not nurses.

There are innumerable specialists, assistants, and allied health professionals with which the patient may come into contact or who in some way may affect his or her care.

Dentistry is another facet of health care. The dental office generally includes a dental hygienist and a dental assistant who are both supervised by a professional dentist. The dental hygienist performs procedures such as removing deposits and stains from teeth, applying

---

[1] Havlicek, 1996, p. 1.

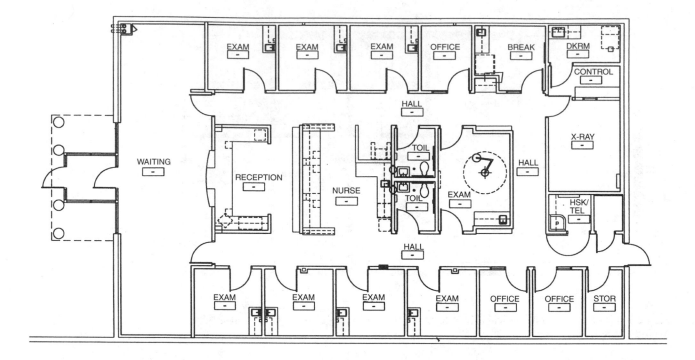

Figure 7–2 Floor plan of medical offices designed for a group medical practice. (Plan courtesy of Architectural Design West.)

medication, and taking dental X rays. The dental assistant may perform these same functions as well as other duties such as sterilizing instruments, mixing filling compounds, and assisting the dentist in the drilling and filling of teeth.

Another important area of the overall medical field is *veterinary medicine.* Interestingly, most of the techniques, equipment, and materials used in human medicine are similar to those used in veterinary medicine. Most veterinary specialists are on staff at veterinary school hospitals or at a private referral animal hospital.

Interior designers provide irreplaceable services that can enhance and insure the successful completion of a health care facility to these professionals. An endless variety of designs can be created for the client that not only meet the specific health care profile but also abide by the governing laws that are mandated in this area of commercial design. It is preferable that the interior designer be included in the initial planning process of a medical facility because all of the areas are affected by the design. Of course, that may not always be the case.

Types of Health Care Facilities

Health care facilities fall into arguably about seven types. Hospitals, MOBs, dental facilities, and senior's facilities are the ones most familiar to the student. These facilities along with emergi-centers, mental health facilities, and veterinary facilities, provide services to different user groups of patients and family members.

Although most of these facilities have been around in one form or another for countless years, the services provided have gone through many changes as technology and science have evolved. This section briefly discusses the purposes and functions of different types of health care facilities, emphasizing hospitals, MOBs, and facilities for seniors.

Hospitals

A hospital, as defined by the American Hospital Association (AHA), is a:

Health care institution with an organized medical and professional staff and with in-patient beds available round the clock, whose primary function is to provide in-patient medical, nursing, and other health related services to patients for both surgical and non-surgical conditions, and that usually provides some outpatient services particularly emergency care; for licenser purposes, each state has its own definition of hospital.[2]

A hospital can be a center for research, technology, and education. It is a place where doctors can treat their patients from a standpoint of both in-patient and out-patient needs. Several criteria used to classify hospitals include types of medical problems, general or specialized medicine, short-term or long-term patient stay, size, ownership, and whether the facility is a teaching or nonteaching hospital.

The functional relationships and the administrative structure of a hospital are quite complex. Understanding the chain of command and knowing who the decision makers are within the organization as it impacts the design job is very important to the interior designer. Depending upon the size and scope of the design project, the decision maker with whom the interior designer deals will change. When a project does not involve a major renovation or new construction, the interior designer can begin work with the purchasing or physical plant supervisor and coordinate with the department head for whom the design work is being done. These working relationships affect the design process, delivery, installation, financing, and overall client satisfaction. The following represents only a brief overview of many variables in regards to hospital organizations.

The organization and management of hospitals, particularly voluntary hospitals, commonly includes a governing board. This board selects an executive head, often referred to as the hospital administrator or the medical director. The board also establishes and is involved in the policies of the hospital. The hospital administrator, as the executive head, has associate administrators who are responsible for several departments. These departments are usually headed by a supervisor. Some of the nonmedical departments include purchasing, fiscal affairs, physical plant, security, housekeeping, dietary services, and personnel.

A percentage of the medical staff work in the hospital but are not usually employed by the hospital. Rather, they have private practices and are granted the privilege to treat patients in the hospital. There are, of course, some medical staff who are employees of the hospital. Physicians who belong to the medical staff of the hospital are in essence employed by the hospital and usually report to a chief of staff. This method of management is typical of the voluntary hospital. The most common medical departments in a hospital include obstetrics, pediatrics, surgery, acute care medical units, diagnostic imaging (also called radiology), pathology, rehabilitation therapy, emergency, and clinical services.

The attending physician, sometimes in concert with consulting physicians, is responsible for the diagnosis and treatment procedures required for his or her patients. A resident is a doctor who has finished an internship and is extending training in some specialty. An intern is a medical school graduate who is working to gain practical experience in the hospital.

Nursing departments are generally organized by patient wards or units. There is a head nurse (also called a charge nurse) for each unit. Reporting to the head nurse are RNs, LPNs, student nurses, and aides. Nursing services usually represent the largest component of hospital personnel. The department of nursing commonly has a director with several supervisors in charge of a unit. A nursing supervisor is in charge of a group of patient units and supervises the standard of care of the patients. Nursing units are also a part of operating rooms, recovery rooms, intensive care units, and emergency rooms, to name a few. There are, of course, additional hospital services.

---

[2]Kiger, 1986, p. 27.

Historically, hospitals were first associated with religious groups; then government or public funding became more common. For example, ancient Roman institutions for the care and shelter of the sick were referred to as *valetudinaria,* or infirmaries, and were used for slaves and free Romans. During the Crusades the *hospitia,* which provided food, lodging, and medical care to the ill, were located adjacent to monasteries.

The authors would like to mention several interesting points about the development of hospitals in the United States. Early hospitals in this country were used to treat the poor. The wealthy preferred to be treated in their homes or hotels, as this was viewed to be more comfortable and safer in terms of infectious diseases. Physicians could bill for care delivered in a home whereas it was considered unethical to bill hospital-based patients. In the American colonies, the first hospital opened in 1751 in Pennsylvania. During the 19th century, three developments occurred that resulted in the use of hospitals by larger segments of the population: (1) discovery of anesthesia, (2) introduction of antiseptic techniques, and (3) establishment of the nursing profession. At this point, hospitals became teaching centers for doctors. In the 1880s, hospitals added specialized facilities and staff for surgery, which encouraged the performance of advanced surgical procedures. By 1900 the use of hospitals by physicians and patients resulted in increased cost of medical treatment. Private rooms for the affluent, as well as semiprivate rooms for the middle class, added to the use and cost of hospital care. Interestingly, hotel-like comforts, which are common practice in hospitals today, were added for affluent patients at the turn of the century.

From their own experience readers are somewhat familiar with the multitude of changes in medical treatment and diagnostic procedures that have come into use during the 20th century. It is beyond the scope of this book to discuss them all. It is important, however, to briefly discuss one of the innovative changes in hospital planning developed in the past 20 years, as it affects design.

There has been a trend toward patient-centered health care to meet the emotional needs of hospitalized patients. The term usually associated with this approach is *healing environment.* The philosophy of the healing environment centers on providing visual and acoustic comfort by adding some aesthetic comforts of home with such design elements as carpets to absorb noise, soothing colors, artwork, access to nature, and soft lighting (see Figure 7-3). All of these techniques aid in creating a residential-like atmosphere, which research has shown aids patient healing.

Jain Malkin, in her book *Hospital Interior Architecture,* wrote, "the new frontier for health care design will be the creation of healing environments."[3] According to many studies, the healing environment planning approach increases patient comfort as well as improves staff satisfaction. It has been noted that patients take better care of themselves in hospitals with healing environments as opposed to traditional hospitals. This trend in hospital design and organization attempts to blend soothing, efficient surroundings and emotional support with quality medical care—a blend between high technology and humanism. Ideally, facilities designed with a focus on healing environments are designed with large windows and lounge areas, and appear inviting. Readers who are interested in detailed information on the concepts of healing environments should review some of the materials referenced at the end of the chapter or contact the Center for Health Design, Inc.

Medical Office Buildings

Medical office buildings, often referred to as MOBs, are constructed for the purpose of providing medical practice space for physicians (see Figure 7-4). MOBs can be entities separate from the hospital campus or can be adjacent to a hospital. They are generally owned by a physician, a group of physicians, or a health care corporation.

---

[3]Malkin, 1992, p. 13.

Figure 7–3 Elements used in planning healing environments are evident in this photo of an Alzheimer care facility. (Design by Taliesin Architects, Elizabeth Rosensteel, Principal. Photograph © 1997 by Robert Reck, 505-247-8949.)

Figure 7–4 Exterior view of a medical office building, generally located in close proximity to a hospital. (Photograph courtesy of Architectural Design West.)

Interest in hospital-based MOBs began during the Depression of the 1930s. Hospital space was underutilized as many patients could not afford hospital services during the Depression. Hospitals turned empty patient rooms into physician's offices. After World War II, there was a rapid remodeling and expansion of hospitals as veterans, their families, and the general population sought improved health care. New government programs increased the use of health care, thus, health care became more centralized around the hospital facility.

The number of MOBs near hospitals continued to grow, primarily because of four developments that took place after World War II. They were: (1) increased scientific knowledge and technology, (2) the complexity of care for the patients, (3) specialization of physicians, and (4) the emphasis on ambulatory care rather than in-patient care. In particular, increased specialization of physicians required them to consolidate locations for more effective consultation systems. As hospitals emphasized ambulatory care, the need for outpatient diagnostic and treatment services expanded. This created a need for outside laboratories and radiology facilities and other outpatient services.

Occupants of these MOBs can generally be grouped into three major categories: (1) physician tenants, (2) hospital departments or diagnostic services, and (3) commercial establishments such as a restaurant or pharmacy. Careful grouping of tenants in one building aids the patient because the consulting physicians, pharmacy, laboratories, and other outpatient facilities are nearby, saving the patient time.

Facilities for Seniors

The population of seniors, traditionally those age 65 or older, is growing tremendously. This makes senior housing facilities a major market for interior designers. In the 1990s, age 55 has been considered by many as the beginning of the "senior" adult designation. Seniors require different types of medical care facilities based on age, medical condition, and personal choice.

There are basically two groups of medical care facilities that are directed toward the senior adult. One is generally called a long-term care facility, such as a nursing home, where the individual requires continuing or custodial care 24 hours a day. The other group is referred to as congregate care, assisted living facilities, or retirement communities (retirement facilities), where individuals may or may not need some assistance, but do not need continual medical care (see Figure 7-5). The actual name of the type of senior facility may vary somewhat from those mentioned here. Discussion of senior facilities throughout this chapter focuses on the nursing home.

A nursing home is a "privately operated establishment providing maintenance and personal or nursing care for persons who are unable to care for themselves properly."[4] Nursing homes offer care and monitoring for those patients requiring help with eating, dressing, bathing, or using the bathroom because many of these patients are bedridden and/or "wheelchair bound." Statistically, there are two to three times more nursing homes than hospitals in the United States, in part since one-fifth of citizens over 85 years of age live in nursing homes. These numbers are expected to increase dramatically as the longevity of US citizen expands. Nursing homes also often function as temporary convalescent facilities where patients can recuperate from injuries such as a stroke or fractures until they regain their strength. Within the general categories of facilities for seniors, there is some overlapping of the type of residents for each facility. For example, a retirement facility may have one section for assisted living and another for skilled nursing or other assistance. Another example is a nursing home that has a retirement facility wing where the residents live independent of nursing care, a wing for residents who need 24 hour skilled nursing care, a wing for Alzheimer patients, another for Medicare short-term or skilled care rehabilitation, and additional wings where the patients need generalized nursing care.

Senior facilities are commonly owned by private corporations or HMOs. This is especially true of long-term care facilities. Congregate care and retirement facilities may be owned by a corporation. In some cases the individuals who live in the congregate care or retirement facility own their space since they may have the option to purchase their living space as they would purchase a condominium or single family dwelling (see Figure 7-6).

---

[4] *Merriam-Webster's Collegiate Dictionary,* 1994, p. 799.

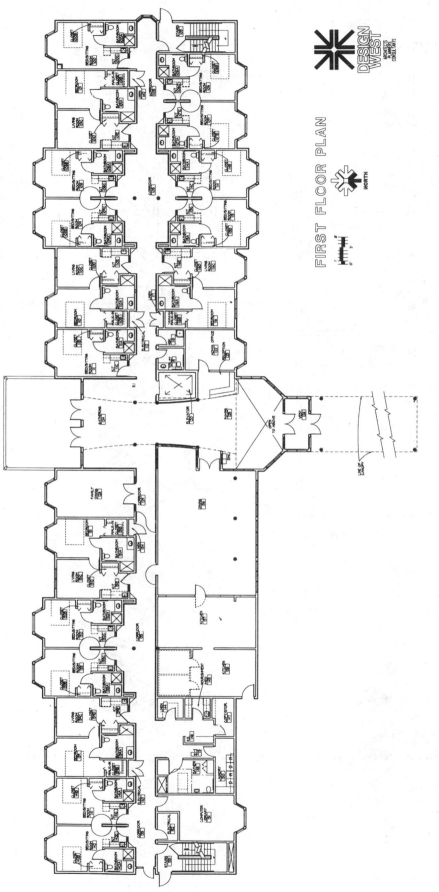

Figure 7–5 Floor plan of the main floor of an assisted living facility. Note the use of bay windows for an additional light source. (Plan courtesy of Architectural Design West.)

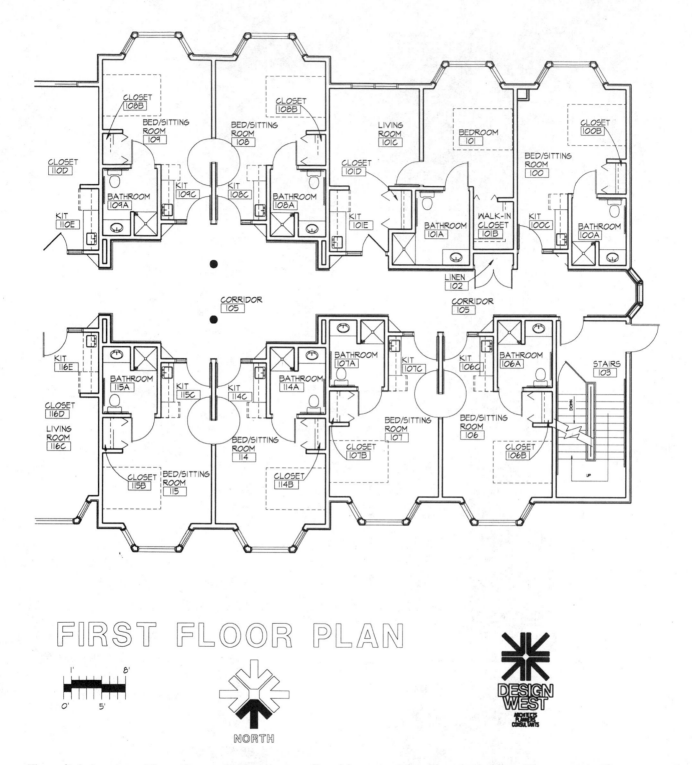

FIRST FLOOR PLAN

NORTH

DESIGN WEST

Figure 7–6 A variety of floor plan configurations are offered for potential residents' selection. (Plan courtesy of Architectural Design West.)

Other Health Care Facilities

There are other types of health care facilities about which the reader should have some understanding. The first are those that relate to hospital services. *Emergi-centers* are freestanding facilities that provide treatments comparable to a hospital emergency room for nonurgent patients. They are primarily owned by hospitals and HMOs. Emergi-centers are open 24 hours, 7 days a week, providing an alternative to hospital emergency rooms. *Surgi-centers* are freestanding facilities where ambulatory outpatient surgery can be performed. They may be owned by hospitals, HMOs, or private corporations. The procedures are often those that do not require an overnight stay in a hospital bed. These facilities have become increasingly popular because the cost of treatment in a surgi-center is less than in a hospital. Other normal hospital services can also be obtained in freestanding facilities. The most common are diagnostic imaging, cardiac and general rehabilitation, and oncology. These medical centers may also be owned by hospitals, HMOs, or private corporations.

Additional freestanding medical facilities include primary care health centers, rehabilitation centers, mental health facilities, and birthing centers. A primary care health center, also called a neighborhood health care center, provides nonemergency care similar to that of a hospital outpatient clinic. *Rehabilitation centers* provide care for patients recovering from such things as strokes, amputations, or paralysis. Some level of 24 hour nursing care is often required; however, many other hospital services may not be provided. The patient in a rehabilitation center is typically medically stable and is ready to begin rehabilitation therapy. Mental health facilities are those that specialize in the treatment of a variety of mental disorders. A birthing center is a "nonhospital facility organized to provide family-centered maternity care for women judged to be at low risk for obstetrical complications."[5] This type of facility gained acceptance in the 1980s when middle-income families insisted upon the newer methods of childbirth. Birthing centers may be freestanding facilities or within a maternity ward in a hospital.

Another type of health care facility is the hospice. A movement originating in Europe, *hospices* provide a place for the terminally ill and/or their families to receive care. The concept is that there should be a place where dying patients can spend their remaining time in as comfortable a setting as possible. The hospice staff provides nursing care and nurturing for these patients and their families. After the death of the patient, the hospice often aids the family in dealing with their grief.

Dental offices are another type of health care facility. The design of dental offices provides the interior designer somewhat different challenges than exist for physicians' suites, hospitals, and other medical care facilities. Since dental care is still considered by many to be something to fear, dentists know that making their patients comfortable in the office setting is very important. Aesthetic design choices, space planning, and acoustical control are key elements in creating environments that put patients at ease. Space planning decisions and material specifications are also very important to the successful functional design of a dental office. It is not the same as designing a physicians' suite and should only be undertaken after gaining an understanding of the dental profession.

The final type of health care facility mentioned here is the veterinary facility. Veterinarians, of course, deal with small and large animals, not humans. Although the design of veterinary clinics is not thought of by most as a part of health care, it is technically part of the overall health care industry. It is also a specialty in commercial interior design that most interior designers neglect. Key issues in the design of a veterinary clinic are presented at the end of the chapter.

---

[5]Malkin, 1992, p. 235.

Planning and Design Concepts

All medical facilities have many similar design considerations. The size of an exam room in a hospital clinic is similar to that in an MOB. Materials specifications for a nursing home are similar to those for a hospital patient room. Professional appearance is also a design consideration that crosses over all medical facilities. Of course, hospitals will have the greatest code restrictions and more limitations on materials specifications due to state health department regulations. Medical suites in MOBs will have different restrictions, based on the size of the building and whether it is attached to a hospital or freestanding.

For most projects in this commercial design specialty, the interior designer must work in concert with an architect, contractor, or other consulting professional. Of course, the designer will coordinate design decisions with the building owner, or a representative of the ownership of the facility. Design responsibility may involve space planning, materials specification, lighting design, signage design, color coordination, and mechanical interface with building and medical equipment. Space planning and specification work are also impacted by building, life safety, and accessibility codes.

This section discusses specific design and planning principles with emphasis on the medical suite in a MOB. The medical suite is emphasized since it is the most common type of facility that students would be asked to design. Brief discussions on limited areas of hospitals, nursing homes, dental offices, and veterinary offices are also provided.

One issue common to all the different types of health care facilities is materials specification. Selection of *architectural finishes* cannot be made only on aesthetic considerations. Codes, sanitation, cleanability, allergens, and bacteria growth are all very important in the selection of materials. Color and pattern selections based on psychological factors must also be taken into account. The interior designer must research carefully to insure that the materials specified in a medical office suite or other health care facility meet the aesthetic requirements of the client as well as the applicable laws and regulations.

Health care facilities are one of those particular facilities where some occupants may have limited mobility and thus may be dependent on the staff for help in an emergency. Corridor architectural treatments, therefore, are of the highest importance for fire safety and must be chosen carefully. Freestanding MOBs and dental offices are commonly classified as business offices rather than institutional facilities, giving them more versatility with materials in regards to codes than hospitals and MOBs attached to hospitals. Nursing homes are considered institutional occupancies. In most situations, materials in corridors must be Class I, while materials in rooms and other smaller spaces can be Class II or even Class III. Beyond flammability issues, architectural treatments must be easily cleanable and durable due to frequent cleaning.

Paint and wallcoverings are the most common wall treatments used. Paint is still the easiest and most versatile *wall treatment.* Unlimited colors and color combinations are possible and paint is very economical. However, painted walls can easily be marred by carts, chairs, and equipment. Fortunately, there are a large variety of wallcoverings on the market that are acceptable for the majority of codes. Textured, cleanable wallcoverings are often preferred as they not only aid in acoustical control but also function to diminish glare. The selection of a wallcovering depends upon the effect the client desires. For example, if in a medial office suite the physician would like to portray a feeling of warmth and coziness, a textile wallcovering in the waiting room could be effective. Codes must be verified to allow for the use of textile wall coverings.

Flooring is another important specification. Depending on the use of the space, the designer may be able to specify any of the hard or resilient surfaces or carpeting. In areas such as the lab or a minor surgery space in a medical suite, resilient materials are preferable. Vinyl sheet goods or vinyl tile flooring can be used very successfully in most cases. Many of these materials meet the standards regarding cleanability and durability and have the reduced opportunity for bacteria growth required in such areas. Hard surface flooring, such as hard wood or ceramic tiles, should be specified cautiously as slippage could be an issue. This is especially true in cold and wet climates and in sites where the majority of patients have difficulty walking.

The use of carpeting in medial facilities varies greatly with the type of facility, function of the space, and code requirements. Hospitals use carpeting in public spaces, offices, and some patient rooms. A medical office suite might have carpet in the waiting room and business office and perhaps some exam rooms. The wide use of carpeting is due to its versatile character, acoustical control, static control properties, antimicrobial factors, and ability to buffer against injuries. It is important to specify high-density, low-pile carpet to ease the movement of wheelchairs and wheeled carts or equipment.

Window treatments also must be carefully specified for medical interiors. In many situations, all windows are specified with neutral colored vertical or horizontal blinds, which meet the applicable codes and give a consistent exterior appearance. However, the client and designer do have the option to add window treatments in some spaces to change their interior appearance. For example, adding draperies or curtains in the exam rooms in a medical office suite or the lobby of a nursing home helps to create a more residential look. However, any fabric hanging must meet applicable codes. Textiles that are not Class A cannot be used unless treated with fire retardent chemicals, and this treatment can change the colors and hand of the fabric.

It has been shown that *color* can play an important part in the healing of patients in health care environments. According to Mahnke and Mahnke, "A correct color environment contributes to the welfare of the patient and the efficiency and competence of the staff."[6] Color choices can range from subdued, greyed, or dulled tones to full saturation color, depending upon the type of medical facility and the use of the space. Generally, the physician and staff are aware of the color range that will work for their specialty.

Medical Office Buildings and Suites

The majority of independent interior design assignments in the health care area are with physicians leasing spaces or owning property in a medical office building. An MOB can be a single story structure or a multifloor building. On the first floor of a multistory MOB, one will find a variety of services offered to the patient and the public. There might be a restaurant or coffee shop, a retail store specializing in medical supplies, a pharmacy, an optical store, or possibly other retailers.[7] Upper floors are leased to various physicians representing a variety of specialties (see Figure 7-7).

Multistory MOBs can have a service core with the elevators, stairs, mechanical equipment, and public rest rooms in the center of the building or can locate these building services at the ends of a double-loaded public corridor (see Figure 7-8). Of course, other building configurations may also exist. Single story MOBs commonly have direct access to each suite from an exterior courtyard or parking lot. Layout of the basic public corridors and specification of architectural finishes for these areas are primarily the responsibility of the architect. Within the interior of the leased office space, the physician has flexibility in regards to the placement of walls and selection of materials. These can be the responsibility of the interior designer since interior partition walls are rarely load-bearing.

Easy access to office suites is important to the patient and the physician. Good legible signage at the entry to the building, in the lobby, and on each floor is mandatory (see Figure 7-9). Way-finding in medical facilities (especially hospitals and large MOBs) is very important to avoid sensory overload and provide guidance to help patients, family members, visitors, and facility employees find their way around. In a large well-planned MOB, an information booth[8] will have a map of the building to assist patients in locating the offices. "You-are-here" maps in the main entry as well as on additional floors aid the patient and visitors in way-finding.

---

[6] Mahnke and Mahnke, 1993, p. 85.

[7] Such service spaces might also be located in a single story MOB.

[8] The information booth in an MOB may also serve as a security center for the building.

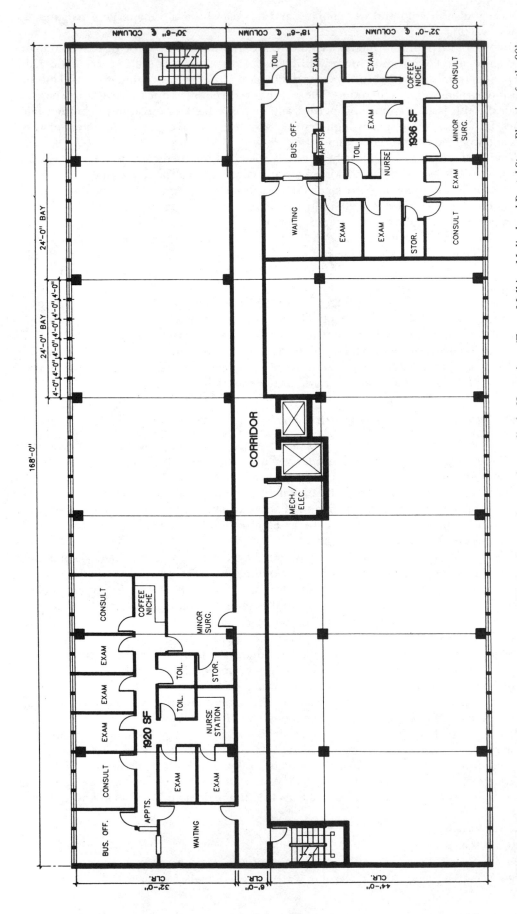

Figure 7-7 Floor plan of an upper level in a multistory MOB showing two layouts for medical office suites. (From Malkin, *Medical and Dental Space Planning for the 90's.* Copyright © 1990. Reprinted by permission of John Wiley & Sons, Inc.)

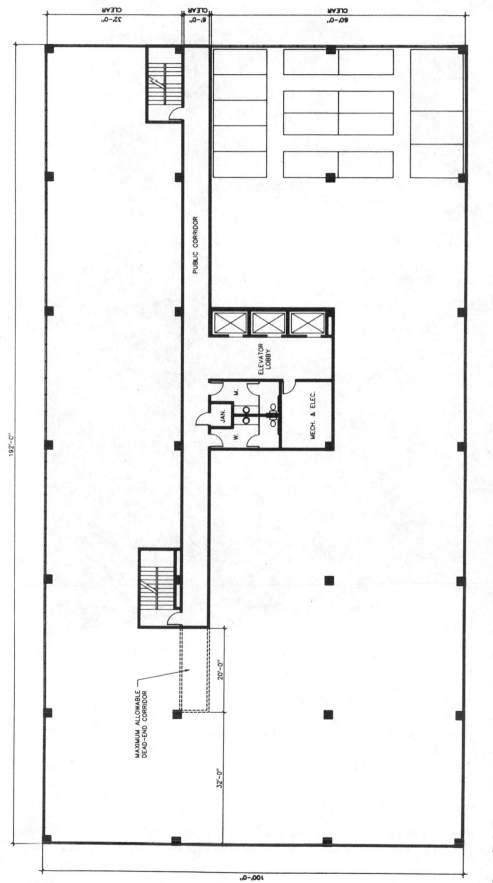

Figure 7-8 Floor plan showing the service core of a MOB. (From Malkin, *Medical and Dental Space Planning for the 90's*. Copyright © 1990. Reprinted by permission of John Wiley & Sons, Inc.)

Figure 7–9 Signage at the entrance of a MOB aids patients and visitors in the way-finding process. (Photograph courtesy of APCO Graphics, Inc., Atlanta, GA, 404-688-9000.)

The entry door to the physician's suite is specified by the architect, contractor, or corporation. Usually, the style of the door and the entry cannot be changed by the lessee due to the codes. Leasing agreements also limit all corridor design in order to achieve consistency. Door security is very important due to the cost of equipment, the security of medical records, and possibly the storage of medical drugs in the office.

Interior Design Concepts

The interior design of a medical office suite should provide a pleasing environment that puts patients and family members at ease. It also must provide an environment that supports the medical functions of the practice. This is a delicate balance, which challenges the interior designer.

Each medical specialty will require somewhat different planning and design specifications. Designers who choose to specialize in medical design do not have to become experts in each medical specialty—although that would be an ideal advantage for both the designer and the client. However, the interior designer should have an understanding of the nuances of the medical specialty for which the project is planned so that informed questions can be asked. This section looks at the planning of a generic general practitioner's office suite.

The interior designer is often responsible for *space planning* within the suite. There are space standards for office functions such as sizes of exam rooms. However, the space allocation needs of the space will be guided by the desire of the doctor or doctors and other staff. This information is obtained during programming. Of course, building, fire safety, and accessibility codes will also impact the space allocation and planning of the suite. Medical office suites are generally considered business occupancies by the building codes and must meet Americans with Disabilities Act (ADA) guidelines for a medical care facility, unless otherwise required by local conditions.

The typical medical office suite can be divided into two general functional areas: medical and support functions. Medical areas include one or more nurse's stations, examination rooms, laboratory space, and medical storage. Additional medical areas, depending on the specialty, could include small surgeries, an area for physical rehabilitation, cardiac testing, or other spaces needed by the specialty. Support function spaces include waiting room, receptionist and secretarial area, business office, medical records storage, offices for doctors, rest rooms, office supply storage, possibly a conference room and lunchroom.

Reception and Waiting Room

Upon entering the medical suite, the patient's first impression of the physician and the practice is established by the appearance of the waiting room. Today's medical suites are designed to be residential in feeling with colors and patterns selected to ease patient stress (see Figure 7-10). Very clinical looking waiting rooms are rarely installed.

Figure 7–10 This cardiologist's waiting room requires stable chairs, soft textures, and good lighting instead of a clinical appearance. Chairs, tables, and lamps are Italian design. Wallcoverings by Sunar-Hauserman. (Photograph courtesy of S.O.I. Interior Design, Houston, TX.)

The waiting room is, of course, where patients will check in for appointments and wait until it is time for their examination. In planning the layout of the waiting room and reception area, sufficient space at the entry door is needed for ambulatory patients and possibly those in a wheelchair. A good traffic path should be allowed to insure easy access to the receptionist desk or area and to the door into the main suite.

It is quite common that the waiting room be separated from the remainder of the suite by a door. This provides acoustical and visual privacy as well as security. That door is generally adjacent to the receptionist window and leads the patient into the corridor that will take him or her to an exam room. The receptionist should be able to see all areas of the waiting room as well as be visible to patients entering, waiting, and exiting the office. Many receptionists are located at a workstation that is separated from the waiting room by a window. This is done to provide privacy and security of patient records. The design of the receptionist window and area should be an inviting, creative focal point. In addition to greeting the patients, the receptionist's duties often involve doubling as a secretary, recording medical records, receiving payments, and assisting the physician in obtaining patient information.

Furniture layout in the waiting room is sometimes suggested by the physician or staff. For example, some physicians may want to encourage interaction with other patients (see Figure 7-11). In this case the designer will place the seating units in the waiting room together, facing inward to promote conversation. This is called *sociopetal spacing* according to Dr. Edward T. Hall. However, other physicians may prefer spacing that does not promote interaction, called *sociofugal spacing*. In this situation, seating units are lined up and the distance from row to row is such that it does not promote conversation. There are no code requirements on the spacing of traffic aisles around the seating units. However, 36 inches should be allowed for wheelchair clearance.

The majority of physician's waiting rooms are designed using chairs since they provide versatility in furniture placement and help create a psychological barrier between waiting patients. This is especially true if the chairs have arms. Chairs with arms also make it easier for senior patients and others, who often lean on chair arms to get in and out of the chair (see Figure 7-12). It is important to select a secure, stable chair that will not easily tip and that does not have splayed front or back legs, which might cause the patient to stumble.

Settees or love seats are used when it is important for a family or other groups to sit together for the purpose of monitoring children or providing close contact with family members. Settees or love seats can also be beneficial for patients who are oversized and require a broader width than an armchair allows.

Depending on the specialty, the materials specified for the seating unit will vary. For example, a dermatologist will often request easily cleanable fabrics, such as a top grade vinyl, and will avoid heavy woven textures that might suggest a repository for bacteria. A pediatrician's office or a veterinary clinic may request plastic or a hospital-grade vinyl to aid in the problem of accidents with children or pets. A psychiatrist may request a woven texture, which might suggest comfort and security. Small nonvibrating visual patterns comfort the patient whose illness may lead to being bothered by large patterns and bright or contrasting colors. Pediatricians are more likely to accept contrast in pattern than other physicians, due to the metabolic response of their younger patients. Whatever the specialty, consider maintenance, soiling, and spilling in the selection of textiles for seating in the waiting room.

Lighting is another element to be specified in a waiting room. Many waiting rooms will have a combination of overhead lighting, possibly wall sconces, and table fixtures. Wall sconces provide uplighting as well as warmth to the area, counterbalancing the harsher light from ceiling fixtures. Designers will often specify table lamps to give additional lighting not only for acuity but to create pockets of warm, inviting lighting.

Waiting rooms are accessorized with artwork, magazine racks, and displays of medical information the physician makes available to patients. Fish tanks and small play areas if young children are patients are other possible accessories.

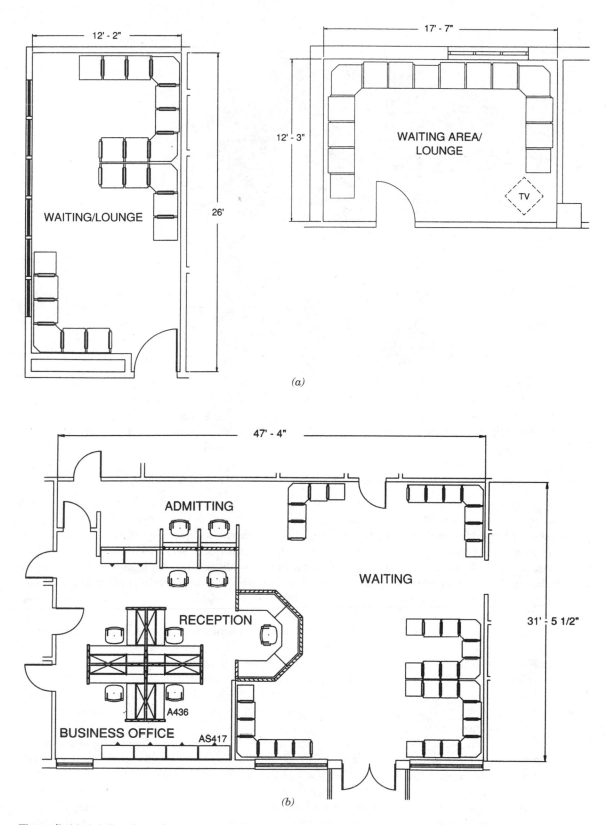

Figure 7–11 (*a*) Furniture layout in the waiting room can encourage or discourage interaction between patients. The left plan shows sociopetal spacing while the right shows sociofugal spacing. Figure (*b*) provides an example of the plan relationships of reception & business office. (Drawings courtesy of Milcare, Inc.)

Figure 7–12 Chairs designed for health care reception areas must be stable, comfortable, and devoid of sharp edges, as shown in this photo. (Photograph courtesy of Carolina Business Furniture.)

Receptionist and Business Office

As mentioned above, the receptionist greets patients, answers the phone, and performs other support duties. Individuals in the business office often include a bookkeeper and one or more other office workers to handle billings, receive payments from patients, set up additional appointments, be responsible for medical records, and other secretarial and office duties. Depending on the size and overall space plan of the medical suite, the business office may be adjacent to the receptionist area or in a separate location. Large medical practices will have separate rooms for reception and the business office while smaller ones will have a space with combined functions.

The receptionist's workstation is often custom cabinetry, although the use of systems furniture is also popular. For the custom cabinetry, the designer must specify durable, cleanable surfaces such as laminates and sealed wood. Remember, countertop surfaces throughout the suite should be smooth for staff to produce legible patient notes and records. Based on recommendations from the field of ophthalmology, the designer should specify light work surfaces, as dark surfaces can cause eyestrain as the office worker's eyes shift from white paper to a dark surface.

Furniture for the receptionist and business office usually involves specifying good quality posture chairs that will provide adaptability in regards to employee size and use. The kinds of ergonomic chairs discussed and shown in Chapter 1 would be appropriate here. Fabric for the secretarial chairs needs to be durable and comfortable. Because of the medical suite functions, care in selection of fabrics should be taken to reduce bacterial and allergy issues.

Effective lighting in the receptionist area and business office is paramount in providing an effective, productive work area. Overhead lighting provided as part of the built-out allowance and task lighting are both needed for this space. The Illuminating Engineers Society recommends 150 foot-candles for the office areas.

Desks, chairs, credenzas, or surfaces for computer terminals are common for most of the functions in the business office. Needs will be determined in programming and are similar to some of the offices described in Chapters 1 and 2.

Storage of medical records deserves some attention. Most states require the maintenance of the actual paper medical records for several years. Primary care physicians will maintain patient records in more depth than specialists who see patients as referrals. The amount of medical records that must be maintained can be quite large, overwhelming the standard vertical or lateral file cabinet.

Most medical office suites use open filing or mobile filing units that can hold a very large amount of records. Establishing the volume of files is a first priority. Once the number of filing inches currently needed plus allowances for anticipated growth is determined, the designer can determine which filing solution is appropriate for the client. Open filing units are open shelves that allow for side-tab file folders. Shelves can usually be stacked six or seven high, providing more filing that the standard lateral file. Figure 1-15 in Chapter 1 shows an example of this type of file unit. They are an inexpensive solution for the smaller practice. Mobile filing units that move on tracks can be an efficient space saver for larger practices (see Figure 1-14 in Chapter 1). Depending on the cabinet, units move from side to side or back to front in order to allow more filing in less floor space.

Examination Room

Basic examination rooms for most practices are fairly standard in size. Rectangular rooms approximately 12 feet by 8 feet are common. Equipment in a typical exam room is shown in Figure 7-13. Note that the stool for the doctor is specified without arms. Ideally there is a cubicle curtain surrounding the dressing space for privacy, a place to hang clothes, a chair or stool for the patient, and a mirror. As can be seen in Figure 7-14, the door into the exam room is often hinged on the opposite jam to insure privacy to the patient waiting on the exam table.

In planning the interior of the exam room, the designer must allow sufficient space for the physician and nurse to stand on either side of the exam table. The standard size of the exam table is 27 inches wide by 54 inches long with a pull-out extension and stirrups at one end.[9] In addition, the physician must be able to easily reach the countertop and sink without getting up from the mobile stool. Counter space or a pull-out writing tablet should be provided so that the physician or nurse can write notes on the patient's chart.

Furniture and fabrics in the exam room are very simple and easy to maintain. The small armless stool for the doctor is usually covered in vinyl and has a sit-down seat height. Guest and patient chairs are small arm or armless chairs, commonly covered in vinyl or tightly woven fabrics. Cabinets are stock or custom cabinets with smooth surfaces to allow for clear, accurate recording of medical information and prescriptions. The examination table is generally purchased by the physician through a medical supply house rather than an item specified by the interior designer.

Colors and architectural finishes, especially wall treatments, in the examinations rooms are very important, as the wrong choices can increase a patient's anxiety and affect certain aspects of diagnosis. Certain colors have been shown to work more effectively or to cause anxiety. For example, wall treatments in a pediatric practice can be colorfully patterned. Certain pastels, such as pale coral, can be appropriate for a dermatologist's office since it does not detrimentally accentuate the skin color of the patient. But full saturation of the color red should not be used in many specialist's offices since it will raise blood pressure.

A few tips on color choices in medical office suites are provided to assist the student in understanding the importance of color choices. Warm, homelike feelings can be achieved by using the colors of nature such as hardwood floors in waiting and consultation rooms. Pastel yellows, blues, and greens can help calm children in pediatric offices. Brighter colors

---

[9] Malkin, 1990, p. 44.

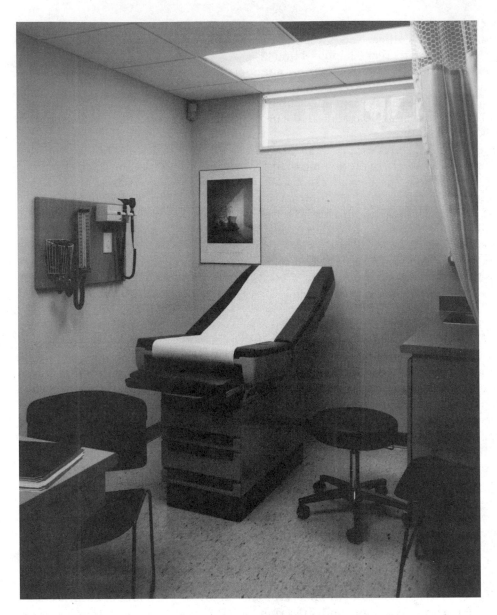

Figure 7–13 Well-designed and equipped patient examination room. (Photograph courtesy of Architecture for Health Science and Commerce, PC.)

are permissible in geriatric specialties. Avoid saturated colors in the exam rooms because the color can influence the diagnosis.

Painted walls provide versatility in color selection, allow for easy cleaning when semigloss paint is specified, and are economical. When a wallcovering is specified, make sure it is easily cleaned and meets code requirements. Consider whether or not the pattern is too large and contrasting, which may give the patient the feeling that it is closing in. Use borders wisely so that the patient does not feel "hemmed in." Wallpaper only one or two walls and paint the remaining two in a coordinated color to add interest. These techniques will provide for an interesting treatment of a small space.

Lighting specification is another element in the design of an exam room. It is, of course, important for the physician to be able to see clearly when examining a patient, when using equipment, and when writing prescriptions. Approximately 100 foot-candles should be provided as general lighting, supplemented by task lights as might be needed by the specialty.

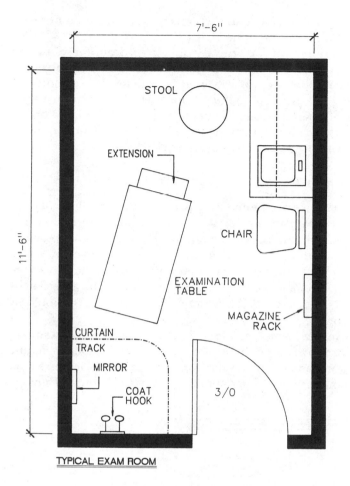

7'-6"

11'-6"

STOOL

EXTENSION

CHAIR

EXAMINATION
TABLE

MAGAZINE
RACK

CURTAIN
TRACK

MIRROR

COAT
HOOK

3/0

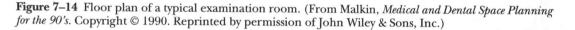

TYPICAL EXAM ROOM

Figure 7–14 Floor plan of a typical examination room. (From Malkin, *Medical and Dental Space Planning for the 90's*. Copyright © 1990. Reprinted by permission of John Wiley & Sons, Inc.)

The lighting needs to be planned so that the physician and/or the nurse can control the lighting during the examination. As most medical suites are provided with fluorescent ceiling fixtures for general lighting, the designer should suggest the specification of lamps that do not adversely affect the color of skin tones.

Accessories in an exam room are simple and often include a small bookshelf for a few magazines or patient education pamphlets. Photos, prints, drawings, and other appropriate wall hangings enliven rooms that are psychologically anxiety producing. Plants are used by some physicians to add their warmth and homelike feeling. The designer should not forget the importance of accessories in the exam room as one more method of creating a healing environment.

Physician's Office

The physician's private office, sometimes called a consultation room, is a place where he or she needs to either meet with patients for special consultations, or to retreat for study, to review business matters, and to rest. This office is planned more or less like any other mid-level executive office with the exact details depending on the preferences of the physician. Furniture for this private office generally consists of an executive desk, chair, credenza, and space to accommodate a computer. Two chairs for patients, bookshelves for the multitude of literature required in this profession, lockable filing cabinet for private information, and sometimes a safe are also standard. If the private office has ample space, a small conference table with four chairs can be added. Physicians such as surgeons or others who do not have regular hours need a sofa in their office for resting (see Figure 7-15).

Finishes and accessories in the private office often vary quite a bit from those used in the medical areas of the suite. Color is a matter of client preference and is not subject to the concerns that affect color choices for areas primarily used by patients. It is common to upgrade wall treatments and flooring specifications in the private office. Many physicians will have some of their academic and professional accomplishments framed and displayed on the walls of their office or in the corridors. This is not because they crave ego satisfaction; rather it is an attempt to establish confidence in the patient as to the physician's skill and experience.

Nurse's Station and Laboratory

One of the responsibilities of the nurses is to monitor the patient traffic anywhere beyond the waiting room and business office. Ideally, the nurse's station is close to the reception area as well as to the exam rooms and any laboratory space. Depending on the size of the practice, there can be more than one nurse's station. A nurse's station in a small practice may be a length of counter with cabinets or any larger size space or room appropriate to the size of the medical practice. The nurse's station is not just used by the nurse, but also by the physician or other medical personnel employed by the practice. If a laboratory is planned, it is commonly located adjacent to the nurse's station.

Many different tasks are done in the nurse's station and laboratory. The key examples include, instrument sterilization, preparation or dispensing of some medications, routine lab tests, weighing patients, paperwork, and other routine tasks. The primary furniture item needed in the nurse's station are countertops, ergonomically designed seating, and storage

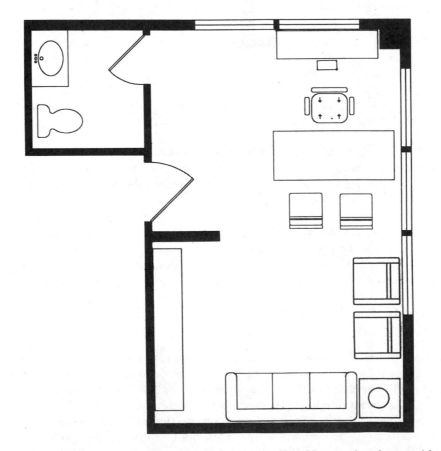

Figure 7–15 Floor plan of a physician's private office. Note zoning that provides the physician a rest area as well as a work area. (Drawing courtesy of Pei-Hsi Feng.)

cabinets. Depending on the preference of the physician, some or all of these counters will be at stand-up height since much work is done while standing. Higher stools such as drafting stools are provided, however, when the nurse needs to be seated. In some large medical offices, small fold up units are installed on the walls of the corridors to provide temporary work space for nurses and doctors (see Figure 7-16). The nurse's station in most physician's offices still maintains the barrier concept in design as opposed to the innovative open nurse's stations now used in some hospitals.

Laboratory areas in MOBs are highly regulated by the Occupational Safety and Health Administration (OSHA). Because of the stringent requirements of OSHA, laboratory areas in medical office suites are often small and only capable of performing simple blood, urine, and other minor tests. If one is provided, a laboratory area requires countertops, cabinets, one or more double-compartment sinks, a refrigerator for medical supplies, and extra electrical outlets to accommodate equipment. Counters are again a combination of stand-up and sit-down areas. Sanitation and cleanliness are very important in the lab area. Many practices now provide one rest room adjacent to the laboratory so that patient specimens can be easily passed from the rest room to the lab via a pass through opening without the patient having to go into the general corridor. In consideration of ADA requirements, this is the rest room that should be ADA accessible.

Color specifications and lighting are important in the laboratory. Generally the color preference is to use a white or off-white as the overall color for walls, floors, and cabinetry. Color can be added with vinyl upholstery on the stools. The laboratory generally needs to be pattern-free and contrast-free; ideally there should be no windows that might admit light.

Other Support Spaces

There can be a wide variety of other support spaces in a medical office suite, depending on the medical specialty and the range of services provided. These would include many specialized treatment rooms, storage spaces, a staff lounge, and rest rooms.

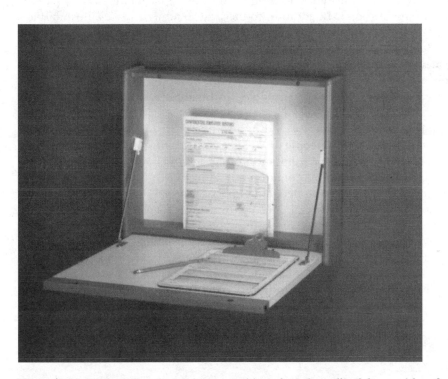

Figure 7–16 Fold up dictation units are positioned on the walls of the corridors for easy access by the medical staff. (Photographs courtesy of Peter Pepper Products, Inc.)

A few examples of specialty medical treatment rooms follows, though no discussion of interior design treatments is given. A radiology or small X-ray room for simple diagnostic exams, such as a chest X ray, may be found in many general practice medical suites. If X rays are taken, the designer must carefully research and specify special wall construction and treatments to prevent the radiation scatter through normal walls. A small darkroom is generally needed as well. For a cardiologist, a special exam room for cardiac stress tests will be needed. And many general practitioners and internists have small surgery rooms for simple outpatient surgical procedures.

Storage is another necessary support space. Medical offices must store quantities of gloves, patient gowns, sterile supplies, office supplies, certain pharmaceutical items, as well as housekeeping items like rolls of paper towels and mops. Specialized examination equipment may be stored in the exam rooms or in a storage room. Storage of medical supplies needs special consideration to prevent theft and outdating.[10]

The lunchroom or break room can challenge the designer to produce a creative, entertaining, relaxing space for the physician and staff. A lunchroom needs a small refrigerator, a sink and cabinetry, room for a microwave, a dishwasher if space allows, tables and chairs, a telephone, and magazine rack. Depending on the overall design of the suite, lockers may be provided in this room so that staff members have a place to securely leave belongings and a change of clothes if desired. Larger practices will have a separate employee locker room.

Finally, patient and staff rest rooms are necessary. The number of rest rooms depends on the number of occupants and the codes. A very small practice may need only one unisex accessible rest room. In most cases today, medical suites have separate rest rooms for males and females. A rest room in a medical suite is commonly a one-user space provided with only one water closet and lavatory and must meet ADA guidelines. Finishes are specified as for any other public rest room.

Hospitals

General hospitals are complex facilities housing numerous departments to treat patents as well as hundreds of patient rooms. In addition to medical treatment spaces, hospitals are also office complexes housing admitting, billing, medical records, and other office functions. But that is not all. Hospitals also provide food service to patients, visitors, and employees through inpatient meals and public or semipublic food services facilities. Gift shops, floral shops, and the receiving and distribution of thousands of bits of supplies are also handled in a hospital. Calling a hospital a complex design problem for the architect and interior designer is an understatement.

All of the hospital's functions are performed in a setting that is generally perceived as "hostile" by the patient and visitor. Most people do not like to visit a hospital either as a patient or a visitor. Hospital environments have a reputation of being cold, antiseptic places. Those cold institutional environments are not as common any more. Over the last few decade or so, hospital environments have changed to become more residential in feeling, with greater attention to design and better color, pattern, and textural uses. The healing environment, mentioned several times in this chapter, has made the modern hospital a more comfortable place to spend time, whether as a patient, staff member, or family member.

By their nature, some medical areas like surgery and intensive care remain somewhat sterile in their appearance. Other medical areas, such as maternity, diagnostic imaging, and physical therapy, have become more interesting and colorful. Patient floors have become more residential in appearance and nursing areas provide better environments for staff concentration and comfort. The interior design of a hospital must unify these multiple spaces into a descriptive design solution while at the same time adhering to rigorous code, regulation,

---

[10]Many kinds of medical supplies must be used by a specific date. Any supplies still at hand after that date are considered out-dated and cannot be used.

and safety considerations. Because of space limitation and complexity of the facility, our design discussion of hospitals focuses on the main lobby and a typical acute care patient room.

The Lobby

The nonemergency patient's first encounter with the facility is the *hospital main lobby.* Today's hospital lobby is designed using a residential or hotel lobby emphasis. It functions as a place for family members and other visitors to sit, relax, and talk quietly. Although the hospital lobby has to accommodate a large number of people, this is commonly achieved by grouping seating units in such a way that the waiting family members feel like they are in a comfortable environment, not a waiting room. These spaces are designed using plants, sculpture or other artwork, possibly water fountains, low wattage lighting, and comfortable seating units to help alleviate family and friends' anxiety levels. Gift and floral shops are located off the lobby and the entrance to a public restaurant may also be available directly from the lobby (see Figure 7-17).

An incoming patient's needs focus on the location of the admitting area while a visitor is seeking information on the room location of a patient. An information center or reception desk, easily visible from the main entrance, will help both of these groups. To reduce patient anxiety, the organization and communication between the lobby and admissions area needs to function effectively. The configuration of the admitting area will vary with the operational needs of the hospital. It can be a visible part of a section of the lobby or it can be in a separate area close to the lobby. A certain level of privacy should be maintained as the patient checks in and discusses personal information with admitting staff. Desks with panels or counters with half-height walls creating booths provide privacy for these discussions. Computers, forms, and filing are part of this admissions area as well. The interior designer needs to maintain the warm and inviting atmosphere that began in the lobby. Once admitted, the patient is usually taken to his or her room.

Way-finding and cue-searching techniques help the incoming patient, the visitor, and staff members easily find their way around the hospital. Good signage and graphic symbols that clearly lead the visitor to the different departments on a floor or other floors is an important step. "You-are-here" maps at elevators along with color coding techniques all help make travel easier.

The interior design of the hospital should make a transition from public lobbies to the patient rooms and medical spaces. Colors, textures, and materials used in the lobby can be simplified in corridors to ease the transition.

Patient Rooms

Space planning of patient rooms is primarily the responsibility of the architect. Interior designers provide input on architectural finishes, movable furniture specification, and perhaps some planning suggestions, depending on the designer's experience. Heating, ventilation, and air conditioning (HVAC) and other mechanical systems are designed by the architect, and the interior designer has very little control over these matters in patient units.

Standard acute care patient rooms are divided into units where a nurse's station and a variety of supporting spaces serve a group of patient rooms. A nurse's station has many functions. Not only is it a center for recording medical information, it is also an area of communication between physicians, nurses, other medical personnel, and patient family members. It also is an area for filling out forms, scheduling the staff, and for small shift meetings as well (see Figure 7-18).

The design and layout of the nurse's station plays an important part in nursing efficiency and patient and nurse interaction. The nurse's station is located to reduce the amount of time it takes for the nurse to move from the station to any patient room in the unit. Since several people may be at the nurse's station at one time, sufficient space must be provided to accommodate multiple users. A common design of a nurse's station has a 42 inch high counter creating a

Figure 7–17 Reception area in an emergency room at a children's medical center. (Design by The Hillier Group and Karlsberger Companies Photograph © Robert Benson.)

privacy barrier from the corridor and desk height or stand-up height counters on the interior for the nurses and other medical personnel. Computers, patient call equipment, and in some situations, patient monitoring equipment will be within the nurse's station. Access to storage of medical supplies and some pharmaceuticals will be through the nurse's station. An innovative approach to the nurse's stations is to design it without the barrier approach, leaving the space more open to facilitate patient-nurse communication. In larger hospitals, small satellite fold up stations can be placed along the corridor for use by the staff (see Figure 7-16).

Interior design specifications for standard acute care patient rooms are important in making the patient feel comfortable and secure. The most common type of patient room is a semiprivate room. The semiprivate patient room has two beds separated by a cubicle curtain

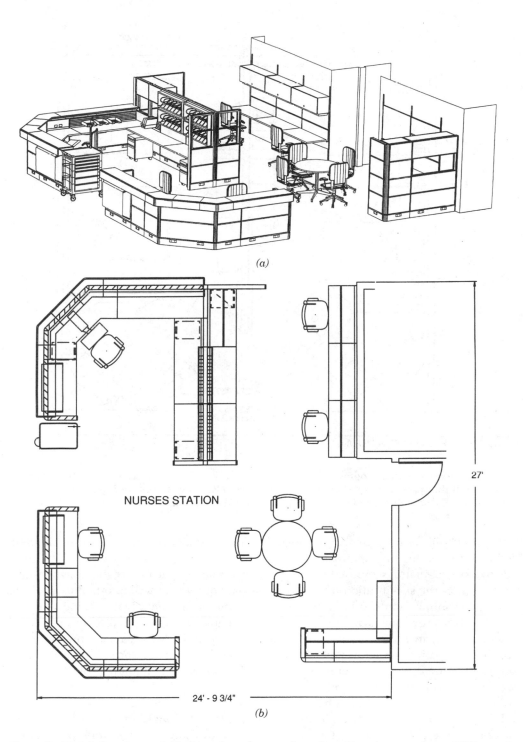

(a)

NURSES STATION

27'

24' - 9 3/4"

(b)

Figure 7–18 (*a*) Drawing and (*b*) floorplan of a nurse's station. (Drawings courtesy of Milcare, Inc., Zeeland, MI.)

(see Figure 7-19). Each bed is provided with a headwall that contains lighting fixtures and connections for medical gases such as oxygen. The headwall may have a self-contained night stand with drawer space or this item may be freestanding. Each patient will also have one or two chairs (Figure 7-20), individual television, a telephone, light controls, a closet, and a mirror. A shared bathroom is provided. Some patients request or require the option of a private room.

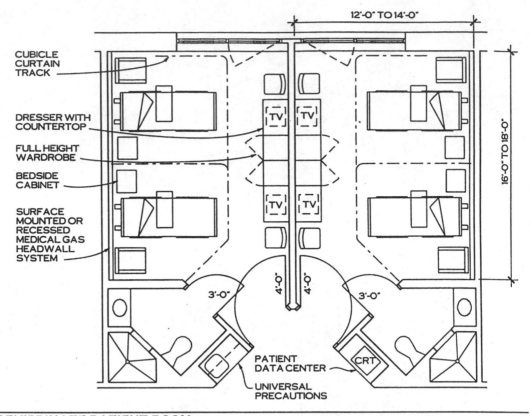

CUBICLE
CURTAIN
TRACK

DRESSER WITH
COUNTERTOP

FULL HEIGHT
WARDROBE

BEDSIDE
CABINET

SURFACE
MOUNTED OR
RECESSED
MEDICAL GAS
HEADWALL
SYSTEM

12'-0" TO 14'-0"

16'-0" TO 18'-0"

TV   TV

TV   TV

3'-0"   4'-0"   4'-0"   3'-0"

CRT

PATIENT
DATA CENTER

UNIVERSAL
PRECAUTIONS

SEMIPRIVATE PATIENT ROOM

Figure 7–19 Semiprivate patient rooms in a hospital generally have two beds, which are separated by a cubicle curtain in the space between the beds. (Drawing from Ramsey, *Architectural Graphic Standards,* 9th ed. Copyright © 1988. Reprinted by permission of John Wiley & Sons, Inc.)

A private room will be furnished in a similar fashion to a semiprivate room though some additional visitor seating may be provided.

Due to strict regulations imposed by the codes and health departments, the designer must be very careful in the specification of materials for patient areas as well as other areas of the hospital. For example, nontextured laminates for counters, antimicrobial flooring, hospital grade vinyl fabrics for some seating units, and scrubbable paints and wallcoverings are all necessary in this environment. Seating units that are stable and safe for patient and visitor use are important in patient rooms as well as in the lounges that are often located on each floor. Designing the patient room in a noninstitutional manner, while still abiding by all hospital codes, is important in healing design.

Colors in patient rooms should be selected to lift the spirits and make rooms cheerful. Once light green or a clean white was used in all areas of hospitals and other health care facilities since green was considered a soothing color and white seemed "antiseptic." Many colors are used today in patient rooms to create a pleasant residential environment that calms and comforts patients. For example, soft yellows can assist in the healing process, blues can help reduce blood pressure, and shades and tints of many colors create a soothing environment.

There are several other factors that contribute to a healing environment in patient areas. Incorporating design elements from residences or vacation hotels has become an important part of creating a healing environment in patient areas. Windows, plants, atriums, and perhaps the sound of water in small fountains are all design features used so that patients may connect with the sights and sounds of nature and aid in creating a healing environment. Privacy for

(a)

Figure 7–20 Three different specialty chairs used for patient comfort and mobility. Often these chairs are mobile and can transport the patient from room to room. (*a*) Care Chair. (Photograph courtesy of Kusch + Co., Huntington Station, NY, 516-271-6100. (*b*) "It Rocks" Chair designed for Alzheimer and dementia patients. (Photograph courtesy of Primarily Seating, New York, NY, 212-838-2588. (*c*) QC Chair. (Photograph courtesy of La-Z-Boy Inc., Monroe, MI, 313-241-4700.)

the patient and protection from unwanted interactions with the patient in an adjacent bed and attention to auditory control should also be planned.

Other areas requiring interior design expertise are the waiting rooms, especially those close to the major treatment areas such as surgery. Often family and friends spend many hours in these waiting areas. An effort to create a functional, friendly, comfortable environment is important. Television, magazines, and telephones, plus some form of food and beverage within the area aid in creating a comfortable space. Some hospitals may provide a private room for families under emotional stress.

Hospitals are designated as institutional spaces by the building *codes*. In states that have adopted California Technical Bulletin 133 (CAL 133 or TB 133) regarding seating units, fabric and seating unit specification will also be carefully monitored by the local fire marshal. Of course, a hospital and all its public areas must be accessible and designed in accordance to the ADA guidelines. In addition, 10 percent of patient bedrooms and toilets must meet the ADA guidelines. Accessible patient bedrooms must have a turning space 60 inches in diameter. A one bed room must have clear space between the wall and the bed of 36 inches, while 48 inches between beds is required in a two bed room. Of course, additional ADA guidelines also apply. The student should carefully consult the ADA guidelines for complete information.

Nursing Homes

Patients in nursing homes, also called long-term care facilities, are generally over age 65 and are in the nursing home for physical and/or mental infirmities. Many of these patients require 24 hour nursing care, while others require only some assistance. The sizes and types of nursing homes vary from a conversion of an existing residence into a nursing home to a facility built specifically for the purpose of treating and housing the infirm geriatric patient. This chapter briefly discusses a few key design criteria for the latter.

There are many design factors to consider in specifying for these facilities. This information is generally communicated via the head administrator of the nursing home and the nursing staff. It is important to remember that the ADA accessible guidelines apply to nursing homes and will play an important part in the overall design solution of the facility. For example, 50 percent of patient bedrooms and toilets must be accessible.

A general layout of a nursing home will have both patient and visitor areas as well as staff and support areas. It will vary based on the specific needs of the patients primarily housed in the nursing home (see Figure 7-21). Alzheimer patients will require different layouts and areas than patients with brain damage from strokes or accidents. For example, the Alzheimer patient is often a restless, mobile patient who has a tendency to walk, often ending in a dead corner unable to move. A continuing corridor encircling and within the wing is a solution for this situation (see Figure 7-22). Newer designs in nursing homes provide more residential design concepts and amenities. For example, small family kitchens and eating areas are placed within a unit of patient rooms. In this way, the visiting family can occasionally prepare a patient's favorite meal.

Designing for aging adults focuses on physical and mental impairments. For example, as people age, they need more light to see clearly, their motor ability may be impaired, or mental processes may have deteriorated due to diseases such as Alzheimer's. For those with cataracts, colors and color saturation become less clear so that color selections for the interior become very important. A significant concern for seniors is the fear of falling and breaking bones. Careful selection of flooring materials must be made to prevent slipping while not impeding the use of wheelchairs and walkers. A senior suffering from one of the many diseases associated with dementia is often easily confused and can become lost in the facility if improper design decisions are made.

The interior design of a nursing home requires some special considerations, especially in regards to material specification. Let us look at a few of those related to floor and wall treatments. This section also provides some tips on the specification of furniture for a nursing home.

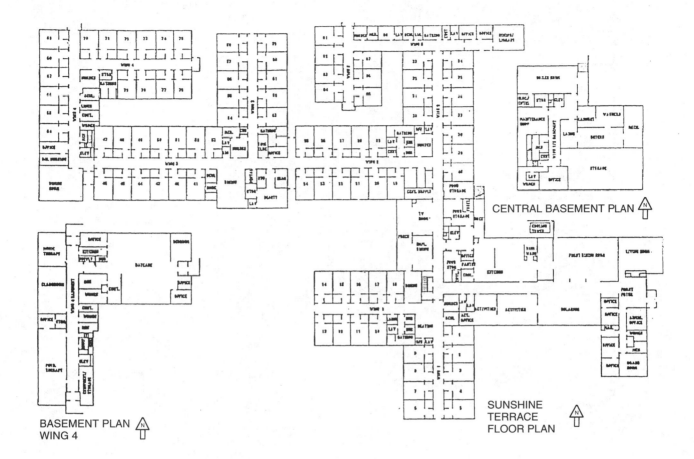

Figure 7–21 Floor plan of a 72,000 square foot nursing home. (Plan courtesy of Sunshine Terrace Foundation.)

The designer should specify a nonpatterned or a nondominant patterned floor covering. Some patients become dizzy or confused when strongly patterned flooring is used. In other cases patients may interpret the pattern as an object on the floor and attempt to step over it or pick it up, which could cause the patient to fall. Hospital grade vinyl tile for nursing homes is commonly specified as it is easily cleanable. However, this causes acoustics problems, resulting in some specification of carpeting. It is very important when specifying carpeting to use a carpet that is easily cleanable and that has been treated to reduce the growth of bacteria. It should also have a high density/low pile uncut surface to allow for easy mobility over the carpet by patients in wheelchairs or using walkers. It is also a good idea to establish a visual demarcation between the floor and the wall. For example, the baseboard should be a contrast to the flooring, thereby establishing borders.

Wallcoverings in corridors must be Class I while those used in patient rooms and many other rooms may be Class II. Specify wallcoverings that offer durability, cleanability, subtle patterns, and soft colors. Insist on excellent installation since some patients may pick at wallpaper seams and damage wall treatments. Avoid dark colors and high contrast colors on the walls as the geriatric patient needs more light to see clearly. Strong contrasting and bold prints may also cause dizziness. Painted walls need to be finished with a semi-gloss paint for cleanability. Painted walls offer a variety of colors and are easier to repair than wallcoverings.

Use handrails along the corridors. Make certain that the handrail is not awkward or uncomfortable for the patient to grasp. Handrails must be easily cleanable, durable, and be able to sustain antibacterial cleaning agents as they need to be disinfected often. The dado

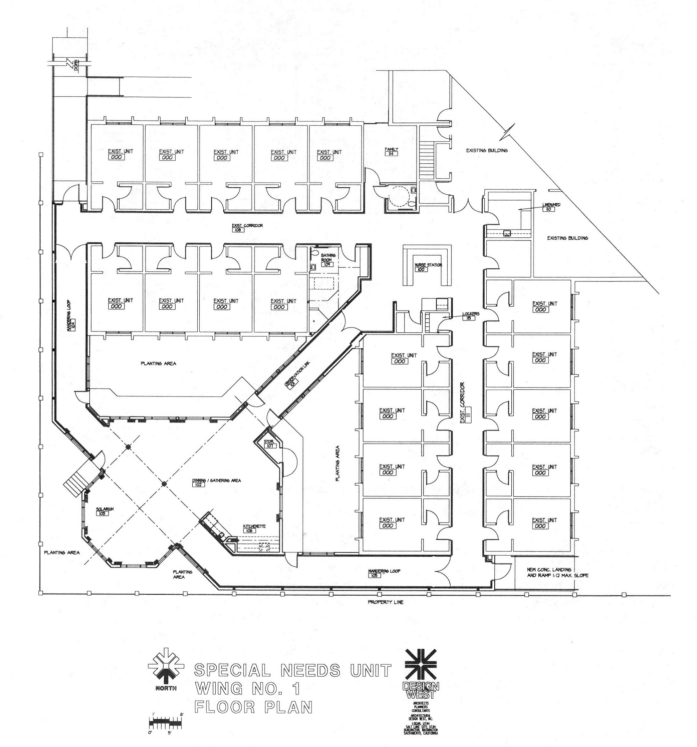

Figure 7–22 Floor plan of an Alzheimer unit showing an effective corridor that can provide continuous mobility for the restless patient. (Plan courtesy of Architectural Design West.)

area between the baseboard and the handrail is a good area to specify acoustical cloth or some wallcovering with sound absorption as well as durability. However, it must be Class I material.

There are a few special considerations in the specification of furniture for nursing homes. It is important for the patient rooms to have their own individual identity (Figure 7-23). When specifying wallcoverings for these areas, make certain that no two adjacent rooms have identical

Figure 7–23 A patient room in a nursing home uses traditional-styled furniture which promotes a residential atmosphere to the space. (Photograph courtesy of Sunrise Medical Continuing Community Care Group, Stevens Point, WI.)

wallcoverings as it aids the nursing home patient in locating his or her room. Another design method is to have individual boxes, bulletin boards, or signs posted where the patient may display family photos or other memorabilia of importance and recognition. When selecting furniture for patient use in family areas or in the patient room, be certain that you consider the type and size of furniture required for these patients. For example, due to the patients' difficulty in getting out of a chair, the designer will specify seating with a height of 20 inches rather than the average seat height of 18 inches. Remember also to include arms on the sofas, chairs, and any seating unit as these aid the patient to stand up. Fabrics specified for this furniture need to be cleanable, durable, and attractive. Vinyl fabrics are most commonly used as incontinence needs to be constantly addressed when specifying for a nursing home.

When specifying dining room furniture, test the chairs for strength, weight, and an inability to tip over. Many nursing homes prefer a style of chair that has a handle on the back so staff can assist the patient in pushing back the chair from the dining table. Round dining tables are best as they avoid sharp corners as well as allow for a varying number of patients per table. Tables that have adjustable heights, casters with stops, spill-proof edges, and tilt top for storage are in popular demand in these settings (see Figure 7-24).

Dental Facilities

Another type of health care facility that many interior designers find an interesting challenge is the dental office. Some designers, as in any other type of commercial facility design, specialize in a narrow type of dental design projects while others design dental offices as an extension of their medical design specialty. The majority of dental practitioners go into general practice or a specialty such as orthodontics or endodontics. There are usually one

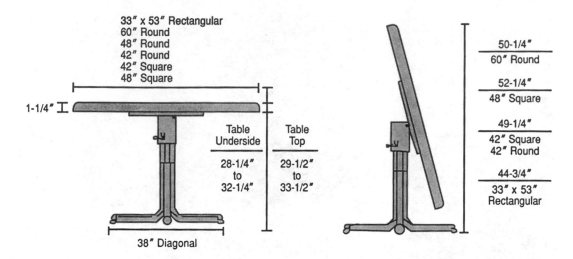

Figure 7–24 Tilt top table allows for nesting, storing, easy movement, and easy cleaning. Base has casters that can be retracted. All these features are important for a dining room in a nursing home facility. (Drawing courtesy of Sunrise Medical Continuing Community Care Group, Stevens Point, WI.)

or more dental assistants and dental hygienists, depending on the size of the practice and a number of treatment rooms. Business office personnel includes at least a receptionist and perhaps one or more office workers.

Dentists recognize the value of sales and marketing in their specialty. This is partially due to the fact that many dental treatments are elective and often performed for cosmetic purposes. This value on marketing translates into a heightened concern for the interior design and aesthetic environment of dental facilities. According to Malkin, "dentists were among the first to advertise, use color coordinated uniforms, open offices in shopping malls, and attend seminars on office design, stress reduction, and the psychology of dealing with patients."[11]

Paramount to understanding the dentist as client is the emphasis in the dental community on infection control. In 1988 OSHA commenced compliance with Centers for Disease Control (CDA) and American Dental Association (ADA) asepsis[12] control regulations. That goal is to protect the dentist, staff, and patients from contracting HIV or hepatitis B virus from cross-contamination. Material specifications are especially affected in maintaining an antiseptic environment.

The layout of the dental office varies more than that of a physician's suite. This is primarily due to the variation in size and layouts of the dental treatment area, called an *operatory*. Exactly how the dentist works concerning the delivery of instruments (from the side, rear, or over the patient) will change the layout of the operatory (see Figure 7-25). It is important to the work of the dentist that the operatory be functionally designed so that the dentist has easy access to a sink upon entering the operatory without walking around the chair or through the assistant's work area. Depending on the size of the operatory, a separate sink may be specified for the assistant. Work counters hold instruments and supplies needed for both the dentist and the assistant. Drawers are not common as antiseptic practice requires sterilized tray setups rather than removal of instruments from drawers.

Since the operatory is the place the patient spends the most time, optimal effort to create a pleasant surrounding is important (see Figure 7-26). A window is common. Some dentists design their offices with a walled garden surrounding the operatories so that patients have a beautiful natural setting to look at while dental procedures are performed. If windows cannot be accommodated, pleasant landscape prints, murals, or other artwork on the walls and/or

[11]Malkin, 1990, p. 332.

[12]*Asepsis* refers to the methods used to prevent infection.

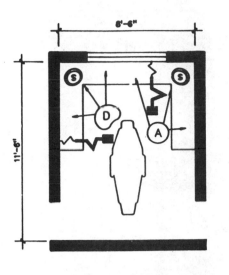

PLAN A · SIDE DELIVERY

"U" DESIGN OPERATORY DENTIST AND
ASSISTANT WORK OFF OF FIXED CABINETS.
CABINET MOUNTED INSTRUMENTATION PULLS
OUT ON A FLEXIBLE ARM.

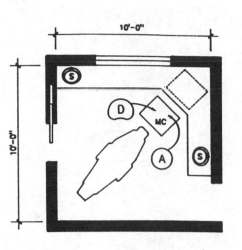

PLAN B · REAR DELIVERY

DIAGONAL CHAIR PLACEMENT WITH SINGLE
DUAL-PURPOSE MOBILE CART BEHIND PATIENT'S
HEAD. DENTIST AND ASSISTANT WORK OFF THE
SAME CART.

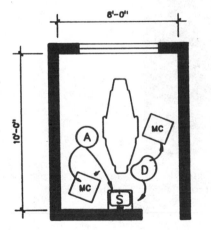

PLAN C · SIDE DELIVERY

ASSISTANT AND DENTIST WORK OFF
OF SPLIT (SEPARATE) MOBILE CARTS.
NO FIXED CABINETRY IN ROOM.

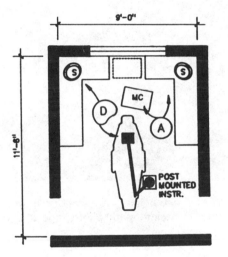

PLAN D · OVER-THE-PATIENT

MODIFIED "U" ARRANGEMENT FOR STORAGE OF
MOBILE CART. ASSISTANT WORKS OFF OF
MOBILE CART BEHIND PATIENT AND DENTIST
RECEIVES DYNAMIC INSTRUMENTS OVER THE
PATIENT'S CHEST (INSTRUMENTS ARE POST
MOUNTED).

Figure 7–25 Four plans for dental operatories. (From Malkin, *Medical and Dental Space Planning for the 90's.* Copyright © 1990. Reprinted by permission of John Wiley & Sons, Inc.)

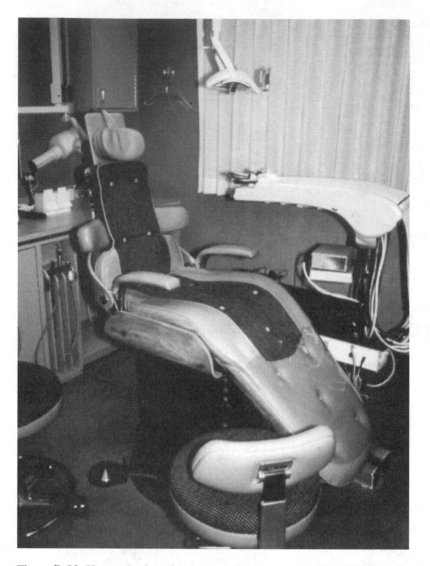

Figure 7–26 Photo of a dental operatory showing materials specified for the chair, walls, cabinetry, and floor. (Interior design by and photograph courtesy of S.O.I. Interior Design, Houston, TX.)

ceiling help to relive the anxiety of patients. Pleasant wall colors or commercial grade vinyl wallcoverings and easily cleanable hard-surface floorings are common in operatories. Level loop carpet can be used, but that is a matter of preference by the dentist.

The dental profession uses natural daylight lamps for overhead lighting due to the importance of "true" color in the identification of tooth color in capping. Task lighting for the dentist is part of the dental equipment purchased through medical supply houses. Again, in the specification of architectural finishes and graphics for the operatory, cleanability and control of asepsis are of paramount importance.

Furniture and finishes in the waiting area, business office, and dentist's office are similar to what can be used in a physician's medical office suite. The waiting room should be inviting and is usually furnished with chairs, although some dentists do provide a love seat or settee so that a mother and child can sit together. The reception window is generally not closed off as is often the case in a physician's suite. A counter of 42 inches above the floor is open and inviting for the patient to check in and pay bills after completing procedures. Waiting areas are commonly designed to be more residential in character than many physician's offices, in part because they are smaller in size, needing to seat fewer waiting patients.

Even with modern painless dentistry and the reduced noise produced by drills, acoustical control is important in the dental office. As most suites do not have a door between the waiting area and the corridor and treatment rooms rarely have a door, hearing ambient noise can be a problem for waiting patients. A good sound masking system throughout the suite, sound absorbing carpeting in the waiting room, and acoustical wallcoverings can help reduce this problem. It is also a good idea not to locate any operatory adjacent to the waiting room. Separation can be obtained by locating storage rooms, the dentist's office, and even rest rooms next to the waiting room.

One final comment concerning the design of dental offices: It is important that all architectural finishes and general lighting fixtures be in place before any of the dental chairs or other large equipment is ready for installation. This will make the final installation of large, cumbersome pieces of medical equipment much easier and create a cleaner interior installation.

There are many other design considerations important to the successful dental office project. Proper design and shielding of X-ray equipment, location and layout of the darkroom, public and staff rest rooms, location of the laboratory for sterilization of instruments and preparation of some compounds, and support spaces like storage areas and staff lounges are all important to the general dental practice. Should the student or design professional undertake the design of a dental office of any kind, he or she should investigate some of the resources listed at the end of the chapter or other references.

In reference to code considerations, dental offices are considered business occupancies as relates to the building and fire safety codes. Exact requirements will vary based on the number of occupants, though most dental practices will have an occupant load under 50. Architectural finishes in corridors and exit ways must be Class I while those in operatories and most other areas can utilize Class II or III materials. Corridor and doorway sizes must meet ADA and building code requirements for a business occupancy.[13] At least one public rest room must be accessible and at least one operatory must be ADA accessible. All other ADA requirements for commercial public spaces will also need be met, especially for new construction and major remodeling projects. The designer should consult with the local building official with jurisdiction to insure proper code compliance.

Veterinary Facilities

Veterinary practices include small and/or large animal private practices, clinics and hospitals, group practices, research, teaching, as well as positions working for the federal government. Due to the popularity of pets in US homes, small animal veterinary clinics are abundant. The area is an excellent source of clientele for the interior designer. Many large animal veterinary clinics are found in rural areas. For the rural large animal owner, the focus is on the care of the animal as an investment concern.

There are approximately 48,000 veterinarians practicing within some parameter of veterinary care in the United States. One of the most common types of facilities is a clinic that focuses on small and/or large animals. In some respects, the layout is similar to that of a human outpatient clinic. A small animal clinic generally includes the waiting area, ideally sectioned off separately for cats and dogs, a receptionist, and an office area that includes the billing area and possibly the veterinarian's office. There are also examination rooms similar in size to exam rooms in physician's suites, as well as laboratories, surgery, boarding areas, kennel runs, and grooming areas (Figure 7-27). Specialized exam rooms will be provided if the veterinarian also treats large animals.

---

[13]Some of these code requirements have been detailed in Chapter 1.

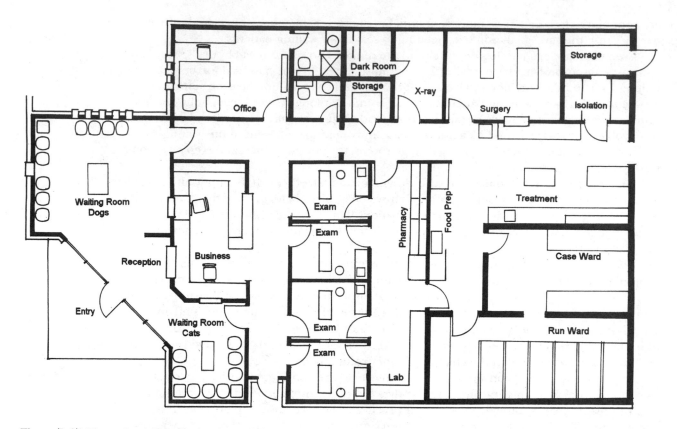

Figure 7–27 Floor plan of a solo practice veterinary hospital. Note the division of spaces planned for cats and dogs. (Plan courtesy of Spencer Animal Hospital, Inc., Dennis Mangum, D.V.M.)

There are obvious major concerns regarding the interior design of veterinary facilities. The veterinarians are concerned with durability, cleanability, antibacterial properties, as well as the overall professional appearance of the clinic (Figure 7-28). In specifying materials for a waiting area and all examination rooms, it is important to use cleanable surfaces as accidents can occur while the pet is waiting to see the veterinarian. Vinyl tiled flooring or a commercial grade sheet vinyl are commonly used. A continuous cove base molding is specified to avoid as many seams as possible, as they can collect bacteria and dust. Needless to say, avoid woven textiles for seating in the waiting area. Chairs should be open-legged, tandem, or wall hung; a built-in bench might be used instead. Many veterinarians prefer wood furniture for the waiting area to relate the space to nature.

The veterinarian often has preferences for colors and materials specific to his or her facility, sometimes based on the geographic location. Color preferences generally include white, off-whites, and pale tones for the wall and floor areas. Colors associated with nature, such as forest green, brown, and rust, are some of the preferred colors for accents within the clinic. Treatment areas, such as the surgery and the acute care areas, are generally treated with an off-white for the walls. The kennels are generally kept in a light tone. Studies regarding cats and dogs and their response to color are still in progress. However, there has been some interesting data in regards to pet response to color.

Client preferences also include vinyl flooring, nonporous furniture surfaces, incandescent lighting in the waiting room and fluorescent lighting in the exam rooms. Of course, veterinarians commonly use photographs of animals and birds as accessories. Needless to say, an odorless clinic is also a preference. The interior designer should avoid live plants in a veterinary facility as some plants are poisonous to animals. The interior designer must consider the interior environment's effect on the pet owner as well as on the pet itself.

Figure 7–28 Creatively designed reception area in a veterinary clinic. Note the lack of sharp edges. (Photograph courtesy of Hugh A. Boyd Architects, Montclair, NJ.)

Supposedly, a pet reacts to the mood of its owner, which can therefore affect the pet's reaction to the visit.

Summary

Health care design is an exciting and exacting specialty within commercial interior design. Designers who engage in any area of health care design must become familiar with medical terminology and have an understanding of the business of health care. As several designers who have specialized in health care design have told the authors, it is not the same as doing an office, a hotel, or other types of commercial interior design. Specialized knowledge of medical practice is important for the interior designer to produce a successful project.

To help the reader, this chapter has attempted to provide the design student and professional with an overview of health care. However, it is difficult to provide a complete reference on this matter within the space limitations of the chapter. Considering the complexities of health care design, it is imperative that the designer use this chapter as a guideline only and add considerable research from additional texts concentrating on the specific area of health care design assignment. The references listed at the end of this chapter are a good starting point for further reading.

This chapter has also provided some specific guidelines regarding the design of the most common health care facilities that a student may encounter in assignments. Design guidelines have been given for the general practice medical office suite, specific areas of a hospital, the nursing home, and a dental office. In addition, brief design comments have been provided for the design and specification of a small animal veterinary facility. This was provided since it is a specialty design area often ignored by interior designers.

References

Anderson, Kenneth N. (Editor). 1994. *Mosby's Medical, Nursing and Allied Health Dictionary*, 4th ed. St. Louis, MO: Mosby.

Berger, William N. and William Pomeranz. 1985. *Nursing Home Development.* New York: Van Nostrand Reinhold.

Burt, Brian A. and Stephen A. Eklund, DDS. 1992. *Dentistry, Dental Practice and the Community*, 4th ed. Philadelphia, PA: W. B. Saunders.

Bush-Brown, Albert and Dianne Davis. 1992. *Hospitable Design for Healthcare and Senior Communities.* New York: Van Nostrand Reinhold.

Christenson, Margaret A. and Ellen D. Taira (Editors). 1990. *Aged in the Designed Environment.* New York: Haworth.

Cox, Anthony and Philip Grover. 1990. *Hospitals and Health-Care Facilities.* London, England: Butterworth.

Doble, Henry P. 1982. *Medical Office Design.* St. Louis, MO: Warren H. Green, Inc.

Dorlands Illustrated Medical Dictionary, 28th ed. 1994. Philadelphia, PA: W. B. Saunders.

Farr, Cheryl. 1996. *High-Tech Practice: Thriving in Dentistry's Computer Age.* Tulsa, OK: PennWell.

Field, Marilyn J. (Editor). 1995. *Dental Education at the Crossroads.* Washington, DC: National Academy.

Foner, Nancy. 1994. *The Caregiving Dilemma.* Berkeley, CA: University of California Press.

Friedman, JoAnn. 1987. *Home Health Care.* New York: Fawcett Columbine.

Goodman, Raymond J., Jr. and Douglas G. Smith. 1992. *Retirement Facilities.* New York: Watson-Guptill.

Hall, Edward T. 1966. *The Hidden Dimension.* Garden City, NJ: Doubleday.

Havlicek, Penny L. 1996. *Medical Groups in the US: A Survey of Practice Characteristic*s. Chicago, IL: American Medical Association.

James, Paul and Tony Noakes. 1994. *Hospital Architecture.* Singapore: Longman Group.

Johnston, Ivan and Andrew Hunter. 1984. *The Design and Utilization of Operating Theaters.* London, England: Edward Arnold.

Kiger, Anne Fox (Compiler). 1986. *Hospital Administration Terminology.* Chicago, IL: AHA Resource Center.

Klein, Burton and Albert Platt. 1989. *Health Care Facility Planning and Construction.* New York: Van Nostrand Reinhold.

Kovner, Anthony (Editor). 1995. *Jonas's Health Care Delivery in the United States*, 5th ed. New York: Springer.

Laughman, Harold (Editor). 1981. *Hospital Special-Care Facilities.* New York: Academic.

Lebovich, William L. 1993. *Design for Dignity.* New York: Wiley.

Liebrock, Cynthia. 1993. *Beautiful and Barrier-Free.* New York: Van Nostrand Reinhold.

Mahnke, Frank H. and Rudolf H. Mahnke. 1993. *Color and Light in Man-Made Environments.* New York: Van Nostrand Reinhold.

Malkin, Jain. 1990. *Medical and Dental Space Planning.* New York: Van Nostrand Reinhold.

————. 1992. *Hospital Interior Architecture.* New York: Van Nostrand Reinhold.

Marberry, Sara. 1995. *Innovations in Healthcare Design.* New York: Van Nostrand Reinhold.

————. (Editor). 1997. *Healthcare Design.* New York: Wiley.

Marberry, Sara and Laurie Zagon. 1995. *The Power of Color: Creating Healthy Interior Spaces.* New York: Wiley.

Martensen, Robert R. 1996. "Hospital, Hotels and the Care of the 'Worthy Rich.' " *Journal of the American Medical Association.* January 24.

Merriam-Webster's Collegiate Dictionary, 10th ed. 1994. Springfield, MA: Merriam-Webster.

Merriam-Webster's Medical Desk Dictionary. 1993. Springfield, MA: Merriam-Webster.

Miller, Richard L. and Earl S. Swensson. 1995. *New Directions in Hospital and Healthcare Facility Design.* New York: McGraw-Hill.

Ragan, Sandra L. 1995. *Interior Color by Design: Commercial.* Rockport, MA: Rockport.

Rakich, Jonathon S., Beaufort B. Longest, Jr., and Kurt Darr. 1992. *Managing Health Services Organizations,* 3rd ed. Baltimore, MD: Health Professions Press.

Sacks, Terence J. 1993. *Careers in Medicine.* IL: NTC Publishing Group.

Schmidt, Duanne Arthur, DDS. 1996. *Schmidt's Anatomy of a Successful Dental Practice.* Tulsa, OK: PennWell.

Snook, I. Donald, Jr. 1981. *Hospitals: What They Are and How They Work.* Rockville, MD: Aspen Systems Corp.

Spivak, Mayer, and Joanna Tamer (Editors). 1984. *Institutional Settings.* New York: Human Sciences Press.

Stedman's Medical Dictionary, 26th ed. 1995. Baltimore, MD: Williams and Willkins.

Toland, Drexel and Susan Strong. 1981. *Hospital-Based Medical Office Buildings.* Chicago, IL: American Hospital Association.

Weinhold, Virginia. 1988. *Interior Finish Materials for Healthcare Facilities.* Springfield, IL: Thomas.

Wilde, John A., DDS. 1994. *Bringing Your Practice into Focus.* Tulsa, OK: PennWell.

Additional references related to material in this chapter are listed in Appendix A.

Chapter 8

Institutional Facilities

The area of commercial interior design identified with institutional facilities represents a wide variety of businesses and types of buildings. The groupings within this category vary greatly based, to some degree, on personal opinion or experience in designing any type of institutional interior. The authors' review of a large number of design related dictionaries, encyclopedias, and textbooks finds no conclusive definition of what types of projects are considered "institutional." In fact, these books do not even offer a definition of institutional design. A brief yet broad definition of the term "institutional" would be to identify an institution as an "established organization or corporation, especially of a public character."[1]

The strongest consensus for a definition of institutional design indicates that it is primarily the design of publicly funded facilities. Generally that includes museums, theaters, religious facilities, libraries, educational facilities, government and public buildings such as post offices and courthouses, as well as prisons and reformatories. In some cases, designers interpret financial organizations and health care facilities as institutional since that is their designation in the building codes.

The authors acknowledge the reader's right to argue whether one or more of the facilities described in this chapter are institutional or not, for we have argued that issue ourselves! It is hoped that the reader will take the interpretation that the facilities discussed in this chapter are public spaces used by large numbers of people, even if some are privately owned and receive little if any public funding. The building or interiors types addressed in this chapter are: banks, museums, theaters, religious facilities, libraries, and educational facilities. Unfortunately, not all types of institutional spaces can be covered. These particular types were chosen since they are the types of institutional assignments given as studio assignments in many interior design programs around the country.

Overview of Institutional Design

In assessing the design needs of institutional facilities, the designer must be able to work with a diverse group of "clients" who commonly have different agendas for the project. There is, of

---

[1] *Merriam-Webster's Collegiate Dictionary*, 1994, p. 606.

course, the client who has initiated the project and is likely the primary authority or user of the space. Then there will be the person or group that funds the project. There may be a facilities department that oversees all physical plant elements of the organization. Staff members who currently work at the existing facility will want or need to have some input into the project or portions of the project. Benefactors or others who are in the habit of donating large sums to the facility may want or expect input. Finally, the public that will come to use the facility in one way or another will definitely express approval or disapproval by the extent they patronize the facility. The designer must use what some refer to as "group psychology" in dealing with all these interested parties. In this context, "group psychology" means that the designer must understand and apply, as much as possible, all the needs, interests, and preferences of the group to the project. This is not an easy task.

In many cases, institutional facilities are financed with public funds and are therefore open to scrutiny and criticism from the public. The designer must be sensitive to the public as a client even though the actual client is the director, manager, or owner of the facility. In many people's minds, spending taxpayer, benefactor, or contributor money on unnecessarily expensive design treatments or furniture, fixtures, and equipment (FF & E) in museums, religious facilities, or libraries is a terrible waste. Complaints are constantly heard after construction of any government building is complete, as many taxpayers will believe the agency has misspent public funds. The designer must walk a fine line when designing and specifying institutional facilities, satisfying those who actually work in the space and those who fund the space.

Institutional design is an opportunity for the commercial interior designer to showcase his or her abilities to a larger volume of the public than normally encountered with the majority of interior design projects. For example, the interior design of a residence is experienced basically by the owners of the house, their family, and friends. The interior design of a medical office is experienced by a somewhat small group of patients, professionals, and staff. However, a public facility such as a museum, a library, or a theater is used and experienced by a large cross section of the public. Therefore, an institutional design project can expose the interior designer's talents to numerous potential clients.

The interior designer must recognize the emotional content and response by the public to institutional facilities as it can affect their acceptance or rejection of a facility. Some of these emotions can be excitement, happiness, joy, fun, or the expectation of pleasant memories being created; however, anxiety, frustration, tension, and distrust are also possible. For example, a bank is a repository for the individual finances of the general public. With this in mind, the interior designer needs to create an interior representing security, stability, and longevity. Another example of an assignment guaranteed to evoke emotional responses from the public is the interior design of a religious facility. These facilities represent the user's personal spiritual life, heritage, and his or her approach toward life. Each user will feel and respond personally to the interior design of these structures. Thus the interior design of most institutional projects must represent the group client as well as the "personal" client.

Interior designers who choose to specialize in one or more types of institutional interiors need to be prepared to uncover these diverse interests and facilitate and coordinate them into a completed project that accomplishes diverse goals and satisfies varying interests. They also must take it upon themselves to gain a deeper understanding of the business of the specialty area and the many specific requirements that are common to any of these types of interior spaces. Institutional designers also need to be superior project managers, have excellent organizational and communication skills, and have a deep regard for the functional concerns of the client over and above personal aesthetic expression. Knowledge of codes and local regulations is a must and the ability to work successfully within a team that will often consist of consultants outside the designer's own firm is also important. The challenges are great, but the rewards are exceptional.

This chapter presents information about selected types of institutional facilities in a format similar to the previous chapters. Due to space limitations, however, the discussions on each type of space are limited, and some elements have been presented in a very limited manner. All discussion about design concepts or applications is incorporated into the sections on Planning and Design Concepts. Separate Design Applications sections provided in some of the other chapters are not included in this chapter. The chapter concludes with a discussion concerning the planning and design of multifixture rest room facilities as are found in any of the large installations discussed in this book.

Banks

Banks are a type of institutional facility that provides for the depositing, lending, and protection of moneys and other financial assets. It is important for a bank's customers to feel that the work of the bank is done in trust and that the deposits and other transactions made there are secure. A customer wants to feel that the banking operation is stable and that the bank management acts in the best interests of the depositors and other investors. In some measure this is achieved through the interior and exterior design of the facility though, of course, it ultimately has more to do with the management of the bank.

A commercial bank, the type of banking facility with which the reader probably has the most experience, provides a place for many customer services. Savings and other forms of deposit, checking accounts, safe deposit boxes, loans, credit and guarantee cards, and trust management are the most common services of the basic commercial bank. More specialized commercial banks may emphasize business loans and services, large real estate development loans, commercial paper transactions, investment counseling, or other services. Though some other banking facilities will be briefly mentioned, this section focuses on the basic commercial bank providing standard consumer services.

Overview

The design of banking facilities has always had a strong connection to what goes on in that facility. In early banks, classical motifs and cashier cages were used to give the impression of security and stability. Today, security cameras, modern designs, and even powerful advertising inform the public of the safety and security of a bank.

Let us begin with a few common terms associated with the functions of banking facilities.

Commercial banks provide the kinds of services described above. They may be chartered by the states or the federal government.

Unit bank is another name for the main bank (or individual bank) when a banking facility has more than one location.

Branch bank is a satellite of a main bank such as a branch of a commercial bank. Branch banking is allowed in most states.

The *Federal Deposit Insurance Corporation (FDIC)* is a federally operated institution that guarantees the deposits held within FDIC banks.

The *Federal Reserve System* is the central banking system of the United States. A primary responsibility is to control the nation's money supply. The Federal Reserve System is made up of 12 Federal Reserve Banks and other centers.

Banks are chartered either by the states or by the federal government. Those chartered by the federal government have more prestige and those charters are more difficult to obtain. Federally chartered banks are required to join the FDIC, to have funds on deposit at the federal reserve district bank, to purchase stock in the district reserve bank, and to meet other conditions. State chartered banks must join FDIC if the bank wishes to be a member of the Federal Reserve System.

As with all commercial interior design projects, the more the designer knows about the client's business, the better the design project can be created and executed. A commercial bank is structured much like any major corporation. It will have a board of directors with a chairman of the board who oversees the operations of the bank. A CEO or president and vice presidents will work at the main unit bank and supervise all branch managers. Corporate officers at the main branch may include loan committees, trust committees, public relations, personnel, and other corporate services as described in Chapter 1. Branch managers will be in charge of the daily operations of a branch and will supervise a group of loan officers, tellers, secretarial staff, accounting staff, and others with specific job functions at the branch.

A design project may be started through the bank's facility office at its corporate headquarters, or directly by a branch manager. In most situations, the decision-maker for the bank will be someone from the corporate office or the branch manager. This is an important distinction as the designer must satisfy the demands of the corporate decision-maker as well as the local branch manager.

Like many corporations and types of commercial interiors facilities, the bank may have design standards that influence decisions of the interior designer and architect on the layout and specifications of the facility. This information is obtained from the branch manager or corporate facilities planner during programming and must be taken into consideration.

Types of Banking Facilities

Banks have been in existence since the earliest times of commerce. Sometimes temples and other strongholds were used to store items of wealth. Banking began to emerge as an entity in the Renaissance when commercial families like the Medici took on functions of deposit and credit. The introduction of merchant bankers who dealt in goods and coins developed out of the economic strength of the guilds. By the 1600s, England was a leader in the banking institution where the practice of deposit banking accelerated.

Banking in the United States grew rapidly, mirroring the rapid changes and expansion of the country's economy. The first bank structure in the United States was opened in 1792 in Philadelphia.[2] It established the design concept of banks using classical motifs, a concept that was imitated for many years. As banking gained sophistication and government regulation added stability, new services were added to attract customers. The first savings bank was established in the early 1800s and the first trust company was formed in 1822. The Federal Reserve System was created in 1913 to regulate bank credit and the money supply. The first drive-in bank was built in Chicago in 1946.[3] As the US economy increased after World War II, banking institutions continued to change.

New types of financial institutions were added such as credit unions and savings and loan associations. *Credit unions* are member cooperatives that receive funds from depositors. *Savings and loan associations* are financial institutions in which deposits are obtained from customers and loaned to members or other customers. Credit unions and savings and loan associations generally offer fewer services than commercial banks. Credit unions are limited by law as to the services they can offer. New services have been added to many commercial banks, in particular, credit, debit, and check guarantee cards have become very popular with customers and a source of new revenues for the banks. Automatic tellers, banking services on the Internet, and other electronic banking services are changing the design of banking facilities and the way a customer interacts with his or her banker.

The design of banking facilities in the United States has been inexorably tied to the changes in banking itself. The first banks relied heavily on the classical styles of ancient Greece and Rome (see Figure 8-1). Classical motifs represent longevity and stability, an emotional device believed important to attract customers. The monolithic appearance of these buildings created a sense of security for depositors. Interiors with high ceilings, tall ornate columns, and cage-like teller areas projected a sense of security, continuity, and importance. At the turn of the 20th century, architects like Louis Sullivan ignored the conventions of the classical eras and designed modern banks that exposed the customer to the new methods of materials and design elements.

---

[2] Wilkes and Packard, 1998, Vol. 1, p. 388.

[3] Packard and Korab, 1995, p. 36.

(a)

Figure 8–1 (*a*) Exterior view of a traditional bank facade with classical motifs. (From Whiffen, *American Architecture Since 1780*. Copyright © 1969. Reprinted with permission of The MIT Press.) (*b*) Interior of a bank building circa 1900. Note the high teller cages and barred windows. (Photograph used by permission, Utah State Historical Society. All rights reserved.)

New construction methods allowed for the ever growing use of high-rise buildings with glass-curtained exterior walls. Banks are often located on the street level of a high-rise building, housed in very open spaces. This allowed the pedestrian to see into the banking facility. Designers were then faced with finding ways to keep the open feeling while still providing the security desired by the customer. Branch banking allowed for smaller facilities and new designs that could relate better to the customer in a specific location.

These 20th century design concepts remain in effect as we approach the 21st century. New challenges for the designer and bank management in the 21st century are numerous:

- The expanding utilization of technology in the bank and for banking services

- Implementation of Americans with Disabilities Act (ADA) guidelines in the design of public spaces in a bank

- Reductions in the number of tellers and bank employees as services are conducted by electronic means

- A growing concern with security for employees and customers as bank robberies occur too often

- Movement of banking facilities to different branch sites such as automatic teller machines in shopping malls and branches with limited services at grocery stores.

There are a variety of banking facilities and it is important for the student and designer to have a basic understanding of these different categories. The most commonly recognized bank is the *commercial bank*, defined above. It is the type of banking facility with which the interior designer will most commonly become involved for a design project. There are unit banks, which are the main bank facility, and branch banks, which are satellite locations. The savings and loan association and the credit union, defined above, is also familiar to most readers. The interior design of these types of facilities is quite similar to that of any commercial bank.

Trust companies are banking facilities that specialize in the administration and control of large amounts of funds held in trust. Funds held in trust are funds that one person or entity has put aside for the benefit of another person or entity, but that are not under the direct control of the person or entity to be benefited. The person holding the money is the trustee. Many commercial banks act as trustees; however, they commonly administer smaller trusts such as a parent's trust account for a child. Trust banks also make loans. The interiors of a trust company are more like a professional corporate office than a commercial bank facility.

Clearinghouses are establishments maintained by banks for settling mutual claims and accounts.[4] Several banks will voluntarily create a clearinghouse at a location separate from the member banks to expedite the exchange of checks and other claims. The interiors are similar to the operations areas of commercial banks.

Investment banks serve as middlemen in the buying and selling of securities such as stocks and bonds. Their principal activity involves the buying and selling of securities and they will have few other banking functions. This type of bank most commonly advises corporations but can also work with the wealthier individual investor. This facility would also be designed more like a professional office than like a commercial bank.

Savings banks emphasize savings and thrift to customers. Services focus on customer savings accounts. The term is used by some interchangeably to mean a *mutual savings bank*. Design problems will be similar to those of a commercial bank.

Central banks are operated by the federal government such as the Federal Reserve System banks. They function as a depository bank, making loans and providing other services to banks, not to the individual consumer or business.

---

[4] *Merriam-Webster]s Collegiate Dictionary*, 1994, p. 213.

Understanding the differences in the types of banking facilities is important to the interior designer seeking a contract to design such spaces. Although the space planning and design needs of a state chartered versus federally chartered commercial bank may not vary greatly, these needs for a central bank branch remodeling or a trust bank will be significantly different. These differences must be honored in order to have a successful design project.

Planning and Design Concepts

In the planning and design of a banking facility, the interior designer generally is part of a team that includes the architect, facilities people from the bank, and bank staff. The design concept is strongly influenced by the image the bank wishes to see expressed as well as by the need to convey psychological impressions of security and stability. Specific design challenges will be space planning, furniture and materials specifications, color schemes, codes compliance, and security issues. The last is the responsibility of the architect.

The location of the bank can have a significant influence on the design of the interior and exterior. Banks located in the central business district, whether the unit bank or a branch, seek a different image and design appearance than a unit or branch bank located in the suburbs or a rural area. A bank branch in an affluent part of a suburban area can also be quite different from a branch of the same bank in some middle class neighborhoods. These location and customer differences are important for the interior designer to understand. The bank management may feel that architectural finishes, for example, that are appropriate in an affluent neighborhood are not to be used in a middle class neighborhood.

Banks are quite aware of how important image is in the design of their architecture and interiors. The need to project a feeling of power, stability, and security is critical to banks seeking customers in all neighborhoods. The exterior design must project an image that the customer can identify. Some customers may prefer traditional, classical designs that give the impression of longevity. Brick, stone, and classical columns all help create that image of conservative policies and safe, reliable management. Other customers prefer modern designs that use large windows and open planning. New contemporary designs give an impression of the bank being on the cutting edge of technology and thinking, which appeals to many customers.

Today's bank designs must maintain a balance between a stable, secure look and an open, honest appearance. Layouts must provide the privacy that customers want when discussing financial issues and the bank's need to insure security and safety. Space planning must make it easy for customers to make their way around the public spaces easily and quickly. Employees must be given the functional work spaces to accurately and securely conduct banking activity.

The basic commercial bank or bank branch can be divided into two basic spatial areas. The first is the public spaces in which the customer will enter to make deposits, withdrawals, and conduct other banking business. The second group of spaces is the operations area, which includes the vault where safety deposit boxes are located, counting rooms, storage, lunchrooms, employee rest rooms, conference or meeting rooms, and records rooms (see Figure 8-2). For a main unit bank, other spaces will be needed for the corporate officers, specialty functions like securities work, and other spaces common to a corporate office. We discuss only the public areas of the commercial banking facility.

When the customer enters the bank, an atmosphere of welcome and friendliness should be combined with an equal atmosphere of safety and security. This is often accomplished with finishes and furniture pieces similar to those that can be found in many hotels, homes, and other offices. A receptionist or security guard may be present to help the customer find the appropriate employee to assist the customer in completing his or her business. In larger banks, the lobby or entry area may also serve as the location of the automatic teller machines. Space for forms, adequate lighting for after-hours banking, and security cameras are necessary to allow the customer to use this equipment in safety.

It is common that banks provide a small amount of seating near the entry for those customers who must wait to see a bank employee or for family members accompanying a

Floor plan

A. Covered parking
B. Foyer
C. Lobby
D. Waiting room
E. Check counter
F. Conference room
G. Private office
H. Break room
I. Tech center
J. Commercial lane
K. Drive-thru

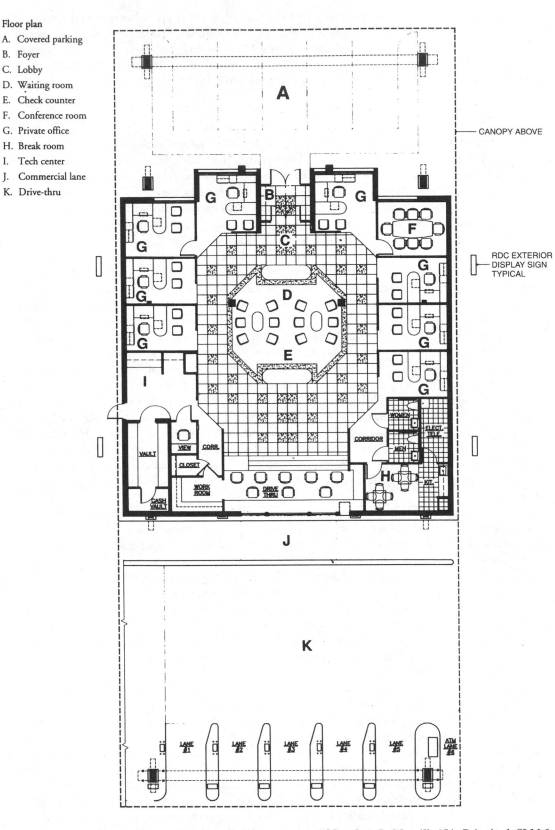

Figure 8–2 Floor plan of a commercial bank. (Plan courtesy of Stephen L. Morrill, AIA, Principal, SLM & Associates, Architects.)

customer. Depending on the size of the bank and the array of services provided, this waiting area may consist of a few small armchairs or be a comfortable group of soft seating units such as a sofa, love seat, or settee and individual club chairs. However, it is most common to provide some sort of individual chair rather than multiple seating units. In most cases, these seating pieces are covered in a commercial grade woven textile. Patterns in the upholstered goods help to break up the monotony of large quantities of simple finishes commonly used in the public areas.

The purpose of the majority of customers entering a bank is to deposit or withdraw funds. The customer usually proceeds to a standing height counter, called a *check-stand*, to fill out the required transaction forms. Check-stands are usually custom millwork. They require a smooth surface for the top and numerous pigeon holes or slots for the storage of transaction forms. The exact design of the check-stand will be guided by the bank's requirements. Today's banks provide a sit-down height check-stand or other accommodation to meet ADA guidelines.

From the check-stand the customer moves to a teller window (or cage) or, more often, to the line for the tellers. Space must be allowed to accommodate a line of customers waiting to approach one of the teller windows. The teller area is created by the use of custom millwork (see Figure 8-3). Each teller window should have an opening of a minimum of 24 inches. Generally the teller counter is designed so that a stand-up countertop at least 42 inches above the floor is provided. Modern banks seldom use grilles at the teller windows, but banks in a traditional design scheme may ask for a grille as part of the cabinet design. Small openings provide privacy for the customer as money is deposited and especially when it is counted out for withdrawals. The inside working area of the teller cabinet is a highly specialized design that is guided by the bank. It must contain room for adding machines, computer terminals, storage for forms of various kinds, and locking drawers for cash and coin. Designers often have the opportunity to design exciting cabinet faces on the customer's side of the teller cabinet while still operating within the strict parameters of sizes and needs expressed by the bank for the inside of the stations. A separate teller window or desk may be required for customers who seek to gain entry to the vault where customer safety deposit boxes are located. Tellers may be provided with a high stool with a back. Employee access to the drive-in window is from the teller area so that at least one section of the teller line is placed along an exterior wall.

Banks also provide sit-down versions of the teller cabinet to meet accessibility guidelines. These accessible stations generally have a larger window opening or a more open desk to provide more convenience to those in wheelchairs or with other disabilities. They should be placed alongside or adjacent to the teller windows. Guest seating that can easily be moved is provided only at sit-down teller stations.

Most customers will exit the bank after visiting a teller. However, some will have come to the bank for other specific needs (Figure 8-4). Banks will also have workstations consisting of freestanding desks, systems stations, or millwork with partial-height walls dividing the stations to meet these other needs. The area where these other services are conducted is often called the *platform*. A new customer must visit with a new accounts representative. Or the customer may be applying for a credit or debit card and must meet with a representative for this service. Other customers are seeking personal or small business loans or other services that require discussing personal finances and filling out forms. These activities are not generally the responsibility of tellers.

Privacy for customers who visit the platform is very important. Customers are discussing personal financial information and do not want that information to be overheard by waiting customers or customers at other desks. Privacy is commonly achieved by the use of upholstered panels, credenzas with overhead storage units, or plants placed between desks.

Appropriate furniture items must be selected for all the activities conducted on the platform. Standard desks can be used for all these tasks, though some banks prefer case goods style systems furniture. It is interesting to note that some banks use different sizes of desks to indicate the status of these other bank employees. For example, a loan officer has a higher status in the bank than a new accounts representative or the receptionist. Therefore, the receptionist might be given a 30 by 60 inch desk while the loan officer might be given a

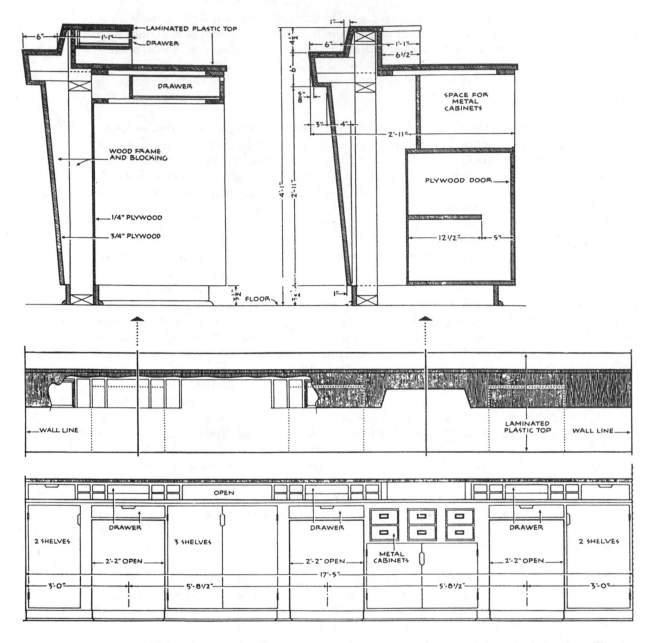

Figure 8–3 Detailed drawing of custom millwork for a tellers' area in a bank. Note the changes in design from Figure 8-1*b*. (Reprinted with permission from *Design Solutions Magazine,* published by the Architectural Woodwork Institute, Reston, VA.)

36 by 72 inch desk. Chair size and type is another way of showing subtle status. Desk chairs with higher backs and upholstered arms are commonly specified for the loan officer while smaller secretarial or transaction style chairs are commonly specified for the receptionist and new accounts station. Guest chairs can be different but most banks do not vary guest chairs in order to maintain a coordinated appearance in this section of the public spaces.

Larger bank branches and main banking facilities occasionally provide meeting places where customers can gather to hear a presentation by a bank employee. These spaces may be a simple room with small chairs, a conference room similar to those discussed in Chapter 1, or spaces that are almost lounges, with soft seating and even a small coffee bar.

Architectural finishes for floors, walls, windows, and ceilings in the main public banking

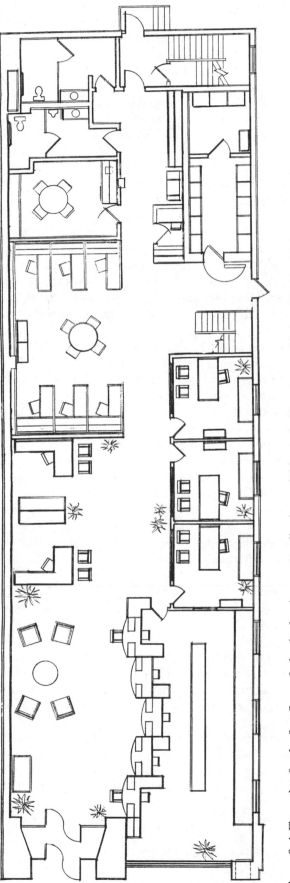

Figure 8–4 Floor plan for the first floor of a bank, showing entry, tellers' area, lobby, and officers' area. (National Bank of Arizona, Flagstaff, AZ. Design by and plan courtesy of Carl E. Clark, FASID, Design Source, Flagstaff, AZ.)

spaces are limited to some degree by building and fire codes. Banks are generally considered business occupancies by the building and fire codes and Class II and III materials will be required in most public areas. Flooring materials should be specified with consideration for safety, noise, and cleanability. Many locations use slip resistant hard surface materials at the entry. If other materials are used at the entry, the designer must also provide floor mats. It is possible to use a glue-down high-density low-pile tufted carpet in the public areas and behind the teller line. This type of carpet will be easier to clean, allow for moving chairs, and provide safety for all ages of customers. Small patterns are often used for carpeting in banking, though larger patterns help to hide traffic paths. Ease of maintenance and elimination of static charges that could damage sensitive equipment are key issues in the selection of carpeting.

Walls, windows, and ceilings also require careful specification. Walls can be treated with many kinds of materials. Paneling is always a favorite when a more traditional or homey look is desired. Textured vinyl wallcoverings can provide many different looks. Commercial grade textile wallcoverings treated for fire retardency can also be used. Large windows walls are commonly left without any window treatments unless the windows face the west or south. Vertical or horizontal blinds are the preferred window treatment for large areas of glass. In private offices such as the bank branch manager's office, vertical or horizontal blinds may also be used, to keep a consistent exterior appearance. In a more traditional interior, overdrapes or swags can be added over the blinds. The designer must determine whether drapes must be fire retardent fabrics.

Color schemes for a bank interior could be based on a corporate color scheme or freely determined by the bank manager and the designer. Traditional banks rely heavily on wood tones and the traditional hues of the colonial period. Contemporary banks use a variety of color schemes to establish a modern feeling. Contemporary styled banks do not want to look dated within a few years, so the designer needs to be wary of developing color schemes around trends rather than good color concepts. It is quite common for the architectural surfaces to play the part of the background of the large open spaces of a bank. Subdued patterns or essential solid colors or finishes are normal on these surfaces, with patterns and louder colors inserted in seating, accessories, and perhaps area rugs.

Lighting is important since many employees are not working on source documents.[5] Good lightning is needed to insure that errors are not made by employees or even the customers as banking business is transacted. Most banks are designed providing general lighting levels at the same levels as those in offices—approximately 70 to 150 foot-candles—and task lighting at workstations requiring additional illumination.

The impact of the computer on banking is of increasing importance. The computer has supplanted paper work in many cases as the public uses the computer for a variety of bank transactions, bank records, loan applications, and Internet uses of banking services. Employees use computers for all kinds of banking functions. Tellers, loan officers, secretarial employees, managers, and operations personnel all use the computer. Furniture specification and millwork design must be done with an eye to housing the computer. Employees such as loan officers, who may be seated at a computer all day, should be provided ergonomic seating and furniture properly designed to accommodate the computer hardware. The reader is urged to refer to the section on computers in Chapter 1 to help in the design and specification of computer workstations.

Needless to say, the interior design of a bank should produce a feeling of stability, safety, and quality. Accessories are a final touch in regards to creating this atmosphere. Functional accessories such as trash receptacles at check-stands, as well as plants, artwork, and sculpture, should all be of excellent quality and in keeping with the theme of the bank.

---

[5]A *source document* is the original of a document.

Museums

A *museum* is an institution that collects, stores, and exhibits art objects and/or antiquities for the purposes of preservation, display, study, and education. Museums offer the general public and special interest groups an opportunity to be involved in the museum by attending exhibits, funding, and sharing collections. Sometimes museums are referred to as galleries, as the National Gallery of Art in Washington, DC. The distinction is important to clarify. A museum contains a permanent collection while a gallery generally does not, but depends upon changing displays obtained from other museums for its exhibits.

Museums provide educational opportunities for the general public through the display and study of the objects in their collections. A wide variety of subject matter is collected and includes objects and information concerning: the fine arts, the decorative arts, historic documents, science and technology, the natural sciences, anthropology, and furniture, to name a few. Museums that may be familiar to the reader include: the Metropolitan Museum of Art in New York City, the Smithsonian Institution in Washington, DC, and the new Getty Center in Los Angeles, CA. Of course, this brief list of museums does not remotely represent the breadth of museums across the United States.

The majority of museums in the United States are private institutions with the remainder operated by federal, state, or local governments. Funding is a constant problem for any museum. Much museum funding is obtained from private donations and endowments. Donations may be monetary or may be donations of items to add to a museum's collection. Many museums, even those privately owned, seek funding from the government through such agencies as the National Endowment for the Arts and the Institute of Museum and Library Services.

Education is the major focus of museums. Exhibits allow visitors, students, and scholars to view and study pieces "up close and personal." For example, the impression made on a patron studying a painting or piece of furniture in a museum will last much longer than the impression of seeing that same item as a photograph in a book. Programs are developed to assist teachers in exposing elementary and secondary students to the arts and sciences. Trained volunteers often give guided tours to school groups and other visitors.

It is most likely that a student or nonspecialized interior design professional will be retained to design a small art gallery or perhaps a small community museum. Only designers who have specialized in museum design or have worked in a museum would likely be retained to design a major museum or gallery space. Although some discussion of larger museums has been included, the focus of this chapter's discussion of this type of institutional space is on a small museum, not the major national museums.

Overview

In many ways, a museum can be considered to be similar to a retail store with extensive office and other specialized functions. Museums are like stores in that they must display art or artifacts for public viewing as merchandise for sale is displayed. Museums also receive, store, and restore objects in back areas of the facility, much like the back areas of a retail store. Museums have more extensive office areas for curators and office staff. Of course, a museum, being a large public structure, often provides food service for employees and the public, a gift shop, and other public facilities.

Let us begin the overview of the organization of a museum with a few typical terms.

A *curator* is the individual in charge of a portion of a museum such as the curator of decorative arts.

A *gallery*, in addition to the distinction made at the beginning of this section, is a room or series of rooms for the display of works of art, objects, and antiquities. A gallery can also be a freestanding commercial facility for the display and sale of art, objects, and antiquities.

Museology is a program of advanced study that prepares an individual to work in the administration of museums.

Conservation is specialized work performed on items in a museum's collection or that come into the collection in order to stabilize and save the piece of artwork or antiquity.

Docents are volunteers that provide tours and educational presentations, as well as assist in fund-raising and other support services.

Guild members are also volunteers; they may perform tasks similar to those undertaken by docents and they sometimes focus on fund-raising.

The administration of museums varies depending upon the ownership and focus of the facility. The majority of museums have a *museum director,* one or more curators, an advisory board, salaried staff, volunteers called docents, and other volunteers called guild members. The museum director oversees the administration of the facility, its organizational structure, staff, meetings, and exhibits. The director will also be responsible for fund raising and working for continued donation of items for the collection, if there is a permanent collection. Staff include secretarial, admissions, sales, display, custodial, and possibly food service workers. Conservation staff might be included if the facility engages in any conservation work on premises.

Client concerns and needs when planning, renovating, or remodeling a museum are many. Funding is a key issue since most museums do not have an endowment the size of the Getty Center in Los Angeles. Museums are nonprofit organizations and must obtain sufficient donations, revenues from admissions fees, food service, or gift shops to cover the expenses of operation. Of course, facility changes and additions to the collection are paid for from these same sources. Gallery designs that help set the appropriate backdrop for exhibits are very important. Sufficient and appropriate storage of the collection and items being received for exhibits is another major concern. Large double doors, even overhead garage doors, are needed at the receiving dock of the museum. All these issues must be addressed through the design program to insure a quality project solution.

Additionally, security, mechanical systems, and other public services spaces are part of the concerns of the museum. Security is very important and is discussed in depth with the architect or security consultant for the best systems design. Mechanical systems are very critical to a museum. The heating, ventilation and air conditioning (HVAC) system for air quality and temperature control is very important as it relates to the preservation of the collection.

Many museums have auditoriums for public lectures and media presentations. Conference rooms for benefactor use as well as advisory board meetings are important spaces in many museums. Additional spaces for the public such as rest rooms, food service facilities, and even a gift shop are all part of the museum facility. Last, but certainly not least, the client wants assurances that designers meet building, fire safety, and ADA codes and regulations; these are paramount in the design of the facility.

The museum staff and administration are not the only client that must be satisfied. Patrons of the museum expect exhibits to be displayed in appropriate fashions so as to provide education and access. The public has come to expect places to sit and study significant pieces and comfort areas such as the rest rooms and gathering places. Patrons of even the smallest community museum are looking for gift items to purchase, and larger museums like the Metropolitan Museum of Art have gift shops that are special treats for visitors. Food service is also expected in the larger facilities.

All these concerns and requirements are part of the programming and design considerations that will challenge the interior designer and the design team. To what extent each item is an issue will depend upon the size and complexity of the project, the funding available for the project, and the experience of the project team members.

Types of Museum Facilities

Museums originated in Renaissance Italy when objects of antiquity were collected by the monarchs, the Vatican, and wealthy families. Galleries to display art works were incorporated into palaces, many of them, like the Louvre in Paris, later becoming public museums. There was a great expansion in the development of museums and galleries to house antiquities and art objects in the 17th century. One of the first official museums was opened by Oxford University in 1683.[6] As more and more ancient artifacts were discovered in the 18th century, collections at pubic museums grew.

By the 1800s, the growth and popularity of museums was fueled by the Industrial Revolution. Increased education of the masses created public interest in the arts and artifacts of the masters and the ancient worlds. Explorations of relatively unknown worlds and discoveries of ancient civilizations made thousands of objects of all kinds available for display and study. From the 1850s to the 1950s, new categories of museums evolved. Early museums followed the popular architectural styles, especially those of the Renaissance and Classical Greek and Roman motifs. High ceilings were used to give the feeling of grandeur by imitating palaces from history.

One of the first museums in the United States was founded in Philadelphia in 1786 where the painter Charles Willson Peale displayed a collection of paintings and other items.[7] The Smithsonian Institution in Washington, DC, was begun in the mid 19th century, and most other early museums in the United States were not opened until the later half of the 19th century. Many other museums opened throughout the United States and the world, to the delight of the public, in the 20th century.

Retail galleries for the display and sale of the work of artists may have started in the late 18th century as craftsmen and artists sought a venue for their work beyond waiting for a commission from a wealthy patron. Retail galleries can be found in all but the most rural communities. They seek out artists and craftsmen whose work shows quality, originality, and sales potential. These retail sales galleries are a type of institutional space that many interior designers find challenging.

The 20th century saw an explosion of museum construction, slowed only by the Depression and both World Wars. Museums became larger, displaying greater numbers of items and requiring more space for preservation and conservation. Museums also became more specialized in the 20th century, zeroing in on a specific type of display such as a museum of fire that might only display old fire equipment. Many of these museums and sites of the early part of the century maintained designs of the classics. But those built after World War II were often more contemporary in architecture. The Museum of Modern Art, the Guggenheim Museum, I. M. Pei's addition to the Louvre, and even smaller museums such as the Des Moines Fine Arts Museum in Iowa, with three adjoining sections designed separately by Eero Saarinen, I. M. Pei, and Richard Meier, are only a few examples.

Types of museums relate to items in the collection or that are regularly displayed at the facility, rather than a "type" as might be recognizable with types of lodging facilities. Museums and galleries collect and display:

- Fine arts such as painting, sculpture, drawings, and photographs

- Decorative art objects such as furniture, lamps, china, silver, and glass works

- Items related to the sciences and technology such as those displayed at the Museum of Science and Industry in Chicago, IL

- Historical information and historical artifacts or documents such the Constitution displayed at the National Archives in Washington, DC

Museums are also created to preserve:

- Historical sites, where land, architecture, and artifacts within buildings are preserved, such as Mount Vernon and Monticello

---

[6] Wilkes and Packard, 1988, Vol. 3, p. 502.
[7] Wilkes and Packard, 1988, Vol. 3, p. 507.

- Historic villages, which preserve a whole or part of a community or recreate a community. Examples would be New Salem State Park, IL, which preserves the log cabin of Abraham Lincoln's early adulthood, and Williamsburg, VA.

- Large or important private homes or mansions that have been donated to a the state or federal government for preservation such as the home of General Ulysses S. Grant in Galena, IL, and the Hearst Castle, CA. Mansions might provide a place for exhibit of the architecture and interiors of the house itself as a residence, or might serve as a backdrop for a collection presented in a historic setting.

Museums in the 21st century will continue to be challenged by such issues as the necessity of changes in the interior structure and the mechanical systems of the building to insure the preservation of delicate art objects and antiquities. Museum design and construction has changed to address such concerns as interior climate, security, lighting, display methods, and storage. Specialists in conservation must be consulted in planning a new or for the renovation of an existing museum. Even fine retail sales galleries will have a conservation consultant work with the design team to insure that the interior and systems preserve the works displayed. Interactive education and integration of the computer to help students and scholars learn more about the museum's collection without even being in the museum is a challenge already being met by many museums. The challenges in museum design are exciting and never-ending.

Planning and Design Concepts

The interior designer will be directed by an architect, an advisory board, a museum director or curator, and possibly a benefactor as to the focus and interpretation of the design. This will include the museum's approach in regards to color schemes, materials selections, and display methods.

Many factors come into play when the designer becomes involved in any kind of museum or gallery project. Careful programming is vital to understanding the needs of the museum, the focus and mission of the museum, and the makeup of the collection. Of course, the degree of public use, the physical plant, the staff, and general needs are also important in dealing with the design of museum or gallery spaces.

Museum collections and exhibits affect public exposure to the arts as well as public opinions (Figure 8-5). The general public varies in its preferences for the fine arts and reacts to both the items exhibited and the environment of the exhibit. The designer must create an environment that can be a suitable background for a variety of exhibits and promote comfort for the majority of the public.

The design and layout of a museum is dependent on the focus of the collection. Generally, the areas or zones for the fine arts and the decorative arts museums include the entry and reception area, all the exhibit rooms open to the public, the gift shop, cafeteria, and public rest rooms. In addition, office space, conference rooms, a library, storage spaces for the collections, and other support spaces are needed.

The entrance lobby is the key point for a visitor to orient himself or herself to the museum. It is quite common that an information desk is convenient to the entrance. Ticketing or a monitored entrance to the galleries, coatrooms, and auditoriums should be easy to find off the lobby. Museum information desks and cabinetry with public relations brochures and announcements are designed to attract the visitor. Cabinets in light tones allow the visitor's eyes to focus on the brochures and educational materials displayed in this area. Gift shops, rest rooms, visitor orientation spaces, and possibly food service spaces can also be found off the lobby. Because of the amount of activities that occur in and around the entrance lobby, the designer and architect must carefully consider traffic flow, materials specification, and any millwork or furniture items that will be placed in the space. Signage is very important to help visitors find an appropriate auxiliary space or their way to the galleries. Benches are commonly used to provide patrons a place to sit.

Figure 8–5 Entrance hall inside the entrance pavilion of the J. Paul Getty Museum at the Getty Center Los Angeles, CA. (Architect: Richard Meier. Photographer: Scott Frances/Esto. Copyright © J. Paul Getty Trust.)

The majority of museums have flexibility in the layouts and design of the exhibit and gallery spaces. This is needed to accommodate varying options for the display of visiting exhibits as well as to accommodate the different items that may be part of the museum's permanent collection. Large, open galleries may be subdivided by movable partition walls for some exhibits. Space planning of the various galleries should be done to help move the visitor from one gallery to another without the visitor feeling lost and/or bringing the visitor back to the lobby. The design of exhibit galleries is often guided by a specialist in exhibition design. The interior designer and architect must make decisions for design treatments in the galleries according to the advice of these specialists.

Appropriate display methods are an important issue that must be carefully correlated to the items in the collection or to items that might be obtained for special exhibits. See Figure

8-6. Display fixtures in a museum are commonly custom-made in the museum shop or by another cabinet maker. Some display fixtures used in retail stores can also be used. Lighting design, color schemes, architectural finishes, and space planning for proper traffic patterns for viewing of exhibits are all critical decisions, and all related to design for the gallery spaces.

As with banks, the security factor is very important in the design of art museums. Surveillance is accomplished not only with sophisticated cameras monitoring each area of the entire museum, but also by security guards or docents who monitor each room. Curtailing theft and preventing the damage of art collections is a constant and major concern of the museum director and staff.

For the most part, architectural materials and color schemes for exhibit spaces and galleries are chosen to create a background for the items to be displayed. Although this traditional approach is used by many museums, some are using bolder colors and more interesting materials for the backdrops for many exhibits—whether or not they are contemporary in nature. A key issue for the wall treatments is to select those than can be easily changed or will readily hide holes from picture hangers. Textured wall coverings and paints are common wall treatments.

The designer is also responsible for the specification of flooring for exhibit spaces. The lobby and major traffic corridors are commonly specified with a hard surface flooring. These materials will be easier to maintain along the main traffic paths. Galleries are often specified with a commercial grade, high-density, low-pile carpet. This will allow wheelchairs, walkers, or baby strollers to be operated effectively on carpeted areas. Carpeting helps to warm large gallery rooms and helps with acoustical issues. Carpeting is more comfortable on the feet for both visitors and staff. Obvious patterns are generally avoided as the eye is focused at eye level for the majority of the displays. Generally, a neutral color or medium values of carpets with color can be specified. Borders are usually avoided as they restricts the versatility of the placement of some exhibits.

Lighting in the exhibit spaces is, of course, a major concern for the museum. It is necessary for the proper viewing of the art work but can also contribute to the damage of the pieces. Filtered natural light is preferred in some situations while other galleries depend upon a

Figure 8–6 Pedestals are generally used to display three-dimensional art pieces. (Photograph courtesy of the Nora Eccles Harrison Museum of Art.)

variety of artificial light sources. Lighting designers and engineers are generally consulted in regards to a museum's specialized lighting needs.

Another design specification made by the designer is the selection of seating in the exhibit areas. Sturdy upholstered and unupholstered benches are usually specified in the galleries. Benches allow the visitor to view any area of the exhibit room from any seating position. Since benches are not as comfortable as chairs, they do not encourage long-term lounging. The absence of a chair back increases safety as it is easier to tip over a chair than a bench, and benches aid security monitoring since there is "no place to hide" on a bench. It is rare that other kinds of furniture items for use by the visitor are specified in any exhibit spaces. Fabrics such as vinyls and tightly woven nylons are preferred when upholstered benches are used.

Of course, interior designers may be involved in the space planning, specification of materials, lighting design, and furniture items for areas other than the exhibit galleries. As mentioned in the beginning of this section, food service facilities, a gift shop, libraries, auditorium spaces, public rest rooms, and offices may require design specification. Many museums provide eating facilities for the public. This feature is common in larger museums as it invites the public into the interior, thereby promoting increased traffic, exposing potential visitors to the exhibits, and can be a means of funding for the museum. Planning the food facility is an important issue for the architect and interior designer in that it must not impact the exhibit space. Designers need to select tables, chairs, and banquettes that are easily cleanable, comfortable, and space efficient. The gift shop or bookstore has become commonplace in large and even small museums and galleries. These retail shops can help the public learn more about the artworks on display and take home a cherished momento of the visit. Gift shops have also become an important source of revenue for museums (see Figure 8-7). Libraries are common in museums. Documents, texts, original manuscripts, and other items common in university libraries are just some of the items stored and made available for scholars and students. Design considerations for libraries will be presented later in this chapter. Auditoriums are provided in many museums for lectures and large group meetings. Many of the design considerations for auditoriums in museums are covered in the next section on theaters. Public rest rooms are often located off the main lobby and in wings of larger galleries. Finally, offices for staff will be located in the back of the house areas. Planning and design concepts for these areas are very similar to those of generic spaces discussed in previous chapters of this text.

Due to the number of people that are commonly in a museum, it is classified as a Group A or assembly occupancy by the building and fire safety codes. This means that strict guidelines for exit ways, door sizes, corridor sizes, and materials specification will be enforced. As a museum is also a mixed occupancy, other building code requirements may be applied to food service, retail, auditoriums, libraries, and office spaces. ADA requirements must be met for new construction and existing structures must meet guidelines to allow for physically challenged visitors to have access to the museum. This will include accessible height counter areas at the information desk, ticket counters, food service facilities, and gift shop. Appropriate sized corridors, passageways, doorways, floor surface specifications, ramp designs, and signage must also be provided as part of the design team's responsibilities.

The design of museums, galleries, and other types of exhibit spaces offers incredible challenges to the interior designer and the rest of the design team. Appropriate space plans that provide adequate exhibit space, materials that aid in creating a multiuse backdrop, and specialized problems in lighting design are only a few of the interesting challenges in this area of commercial design. Students interested in this type of work should seek additional course work in such areas as arts management, museum studies, history, and lighting design.

Theaters

Theaters are buildings, parts of buildings, or outdoor venues in which performances of one kind or another are presented to an audience (Figure 8-8). They are facilities that attract and

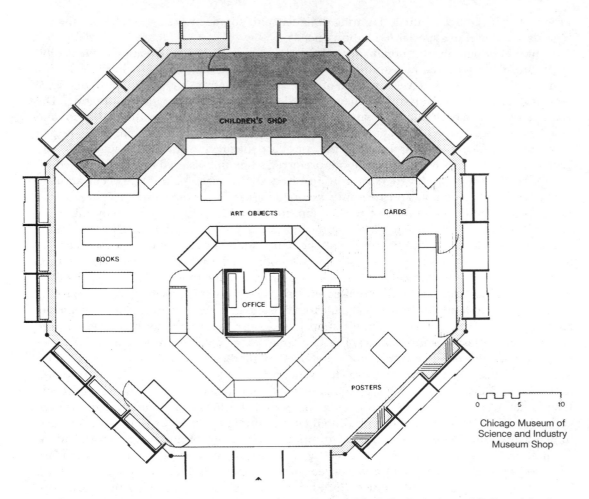

CHILDREN'S SHOP

ART OBJECTS   CARDS

BOOKS

OFFICE

POSTERS

Chicago Museum of
Science and Industry
Museum Shop

Figure 8–7 Floor plan of a gift shop in a museum. (From Barr and Broudy, *Designing to Sell.* Copyright ©
1986. Reproduced with the permission of the McGraw-Hill Companies.)

entertain the public. The most common types of performances are musical, acting, dance,
opera, oratory, movies, and other visuals. The term *theater* comes from "the Greek verb *theatai,*
meaning to see, watch, look at, or behold." [8] The design of a theater space is related to the
type of performance or performances that will be presented, though today many aspects of
the design of different types of theaters are similar.

Theaters present many technical challenges to designers. Audiences must be comfortably
seated for performances that may last for two or three hours. It is important that the design
treatments of the architectural elements set the proper mood for the type of performances
that will be presented. Since a theater is considered an assembly occupancy by the building
codes and since large numbers of patrons are in the space, codes compliance is of utmost
importance. Acoustics must be carefully designed so that even the person in the farthest
reaches of the facility can hear. And lighting must help set the mood for the performances to
be offered.

Some theaters are used for only one purpose and all the planning and design decisions
focus closely on that one performance type. Others are more multifunctional, presenting a play
one week, a musical performance the next, and even movies at other times. This challenges
the designer even further as these multiple uses require specific design specifications.

---

[8] Wilkes and Packard, 1988, Vol. 3, p. 52.

Figure 8–8 Interior of the American Conservatory Theatre auditorium, San Francisco, CA. (Architect: Gensler. Photographer: Marco Lorenzetti/Hedrich-Blessing.)

The challenges of a theater space are rarely undertaken by an interior designer acting alone. The brief discussion on theater spaces is presented in this chapter since interior designers will be part of a team of architects, specialty consultants, and the owners.

Overview

As with a museum and many other commercial facilities discussed in this book, the client may actually consist of two or more different groups. One client is the organization or person who initiates the project, for example, a theater department in a university. A second client will be the person or organization that authorizes spending for the project. In this example, the university administration and even the university's governing body would only be able to authorize expenditures. Another client for this type of facility is the public and other users of the facility. Be assured that the maestro of a major symphony will have input into the design or remodeling of the theater for a resident symphony. The patrons' comfort and enjoyment of the space is also important, as evidenced by recent remodeling of movie theaters to make them more comfortable.

Terminology that might aid the student and the designer in understanding the client and the subject matter could be extensive. A few terms are included to assist in the following discussion.

Auditorium is that part of a theater where patrons sit to watch the performance. It can also mean a room in a building such as a school, used for performances, meetings, or educational programs.

The *house* is a term used to refer to the part of the theater the audience occupies.

Proscenium is the part of a stage in front of the curtain.

Orchestra in Greek theater meant a circular space used by the chorus in front of the proscenium.

Greenroom is the room where benefactors are met and performers relax.

Balcony refers to a projecting area of seating in the upper areas of the theater.

Backstage is the production and storage spaces in a theater. The stage is the major component of the backstage area.

Legitimate theater indicates a professional performance by members of Actors Equity or other professional performance unions.

Mezzanine is the lowest balcony in a theater.

Repertory theater is a theater that presents several different productions each year.

Summer theater is a repertory theater organized for the summer season.

Staging or *staged* is a term that means putting on the performance. Of course, *stage* also means the part of the theater where the performance actually takes place.

Ownership of a performing arts facility can be very broad. Some theaters are governed by local governments. These can be large enough to house a resident company such as a symphony or they may be small community theaters. Many theaters are commercially owned, built for the profit of a company. Movie theaters are just one example of a commercially owned theater. It is common for educational institutions to own one or more theater or auditorium spaces. These theaters exist so that performances can staged by students, classes, or rented to outside promoters. Private theaters may be owned by such other organizations as religious groups, amateur dramatic companies, community organizations, and art galleries.

Each ownership group will have different uses, concerns, goals, funding situations, and needs for the facility. And each group will have a different administrative structure to oversee the facility and the performances that are staged. It is very important for each member of the design team to research and gain an understanding of the goals of their specific project rather than deciding what worked for a previous theater client will work for a current one.

Management structure will, in one way or another, involve these types of individuals:

- Owner of the facility or primary user of the spaces
- The funding authority
- Administration staff, who will be responsible for such activities as public relations and financial issues
- The house manager and others who work with the public
- Artistic and event management staff
- Performance staff such as directors and stage hands
- Building maintenance staff.

The needs and concerns of these client groups are extensive. Providing the best quality building and system to present performances is at the top of that list. An adequate sized stage, storage spaces, dressing rooms, and costume areas only begin to explore the client needs in terms of performance. Lobbies that attract the audience into the theater, possibly refreshment areas or gift areas where additional revenues can be generated, and comfortable seating of a capacity to meet revenue needs list some of the issues for the patron. Safety is also an issue and the client assumes the designer will plan and specify a building and interior that satisfies building and fire codes, meets ADA guidelines, and takes into account other practical and legal factors.

Types of Theaters

The origin of theater is not known, though early records indicate that it existed in ancient Sumeria, Egypt, and Athens and was associated with religious festivals. Theater was also used as an educational tool to teach morals and to tell of historic events. Theaters of the ancient Greeks housed 10,000 to 20,000 people, who were seated in amphitheaters constructed on hillsides. Performances were usually staged with a large floor or orchestra for the chorus and an elevated platform behind for the speaking actors. Backdrops were used and rearranged depending upon the drama presented, and cranes were used to aid in the representation of gods in flight. All actors wore masks and were referred to as thespians.

Ancient Rome adapted the Greek theater though dramatic presentations were overshadowed by spectacular productions such as gladiator sports. But it was the Romans who first built theaters on flat land with raised seating, rather than building into hillsides. During the Middle Ages, there were religious dramas as well as entertainers such as singers, dancers, and jugglers whose purpose was to entertain the public and royalty. During the 1400s, morality plays became popular in England as well as on the Continent and identified problems man was encountering with the emergence of the individual. The Baroque theater produced the horseshoe proscenium stage. From this point on, the *orchestra* diminished in size and the seating area increased.

Probably the most recognizable dramatist of the English Renaissance period is William Shakespeare, whose plays flourished under the reign of Elizabeth I. Shakespeare's Globe Theater is one of the most famous early theaters. It was in the shape of an octagon with much of the space allotted for public seating as the charge of admission supported the existence of the theater company. It is being rebuilt in England using the same construction methods used in Shakespeare's day. Opera and ballet were some of the preferred productions during the 1600s. Productions focused on middle class interests by the 1700s as these people attended performances in greater numbers. During the 1800s, many theaters were built including music halls and vaudeville theaters. With the introduction of gas lamps in 1803, theater production became more versatile.

In America, the first theater was built in the mid 18th century in Philadelphia. Plays and other performances were popular throughout the development of the United States and most major cities had at least one repertory theater company. Everyone enjoyed performances of every kind as large and small theaters were built in most cities where resident or traveling performers would come to entertain. By the 20th century, US theater was moving toward the preference for realism in the productions. Major developments in stage machinery, lighting with the use of electricity, and other technological advances helped to enhance this realism. The horseshoe floor plan continued to be used until about the end of the 19th century when Adler and Sullivan, architects, produced a fan shaped auditorium that gave better sight lines for the audience. Operettas and musical comedies became popular in the 19th century and the introduction of movie theaters in the early 20th century opened up new avenues for entertainment. In the 1930s, attendance at stage productions was affected not only by the Depression but also by competition from the increased use of the radio and from movie theaters. Television had an especially hard impact on theater patronage. However, as the old saying goes, "the show must go on," and theatrical performances of many kinds are increasingly popular and are likely to remain so in the 21st century.

Different types of theater buildings are developed to house different kinds of productions. Of course, some are multiuse facilities capable of staging many kinds of performance. Theaters are also categorized by the kind of floor plan used to develop the auditorium, stage, and backstage areas.

Let us define a few of the most common types of theaters based on the production. An *amphitheater* is generally an outdoor theater. A theater with the stage in the middle of the auditorium with seating surrounding it is technically called an *arena theater,* though it is often referred to as *theater in the round.* An *opera house* primarily presents operas and other musical performances, and a *concert hall* primarily presents musical performances, especially for orchestra and singers. Familiar to the reader is a *movie theater,* which is a place where motion pictures are shown. There are thousands of theaters around the United States and the world. A few well-known theaters for the performing arts in the United States are: Lincoln Center for the Performing Arts, New York City; the Wortham Theater, Houston, TX; and the John F. Kennedy Center for the Performing Arts, Washington, DC. Of course, this does not begin to list the fine theaters around the world.

Types of theaters vary in floor plan as well. The major schools of stage design include proscenium style and the open stage style. The *proscenium style* of floor plan has a heavy curtain or wall that frames the stage (see Figure 8-9). A curtain is also hung in the proscenium opening so that sets can be changed out of view of the audience. The *open stage floor* plan projects a portion of the stage into the audience so that the audience sits partially on three sides of the stage. In this case, there is only a curtain between the stage and the audience. The sides of the stage behind the proscenium and open stage out of sight of the audience are called the *wings.* Actors gather in the wings for entrances and exits. A small amount of necessary scenery material can be stored in the wings as well. Most scenery and accessories are stored in the very back of the backstage area or in property[9] and scenery rooms.

Theater types also vary by the floor plan of the audience seating. Main floor seating may be designed with aisles along the walls as well as intermediary aisles providing easier access to central seats. This type of plan is called the *American* or *conventional seating plan.* When the main floor seating is planned so that aisles are designed only on the perimeter sides, the plan is called a *Continental seating plan.* The house will also often have balcony seating, perhaps both a mezzanine and a balcony.

One other consideration in determining theater types is production style. Some facilities produce a variety of performances throughout the year. For example, a concert theater such as Carnegie Hall in New York City might offer a solo performance by a popular singer or group one month and a symphony the next. Some are home to resident companies such as symphonies. Others host temporary productions such as a summer stock or road shows. Community theaters might offer a variety of dramatic and musical performances and resort areas often offer summer theater with short runs. All of these differences are important in the design programming, planning, and specification of a theater project.

Planning and Design Concepts

As can be seen from the above, there are many kinds of theaters and performance types. Although each has different issues and concerns specific to the type of theater and the planned productions to be staged, many planning and design concepts are common. To simplify the discussion regarding the planning and design concepts in theater interiors, this section concentrates on the proscenium layout for dramatic presentations.

The theater may be a freestanding building or nestled between other buildings in a downtown location. Generally, an entrance will set the mood for the facility. Often the entrance is prefaced with large windows such as in the Jesse Jones Hall in Houston, TX. These large

---

[9] *Property* or *props* are the small accessory pieces used to finish the design of a set or supplement scenery. Props are also used by actors.

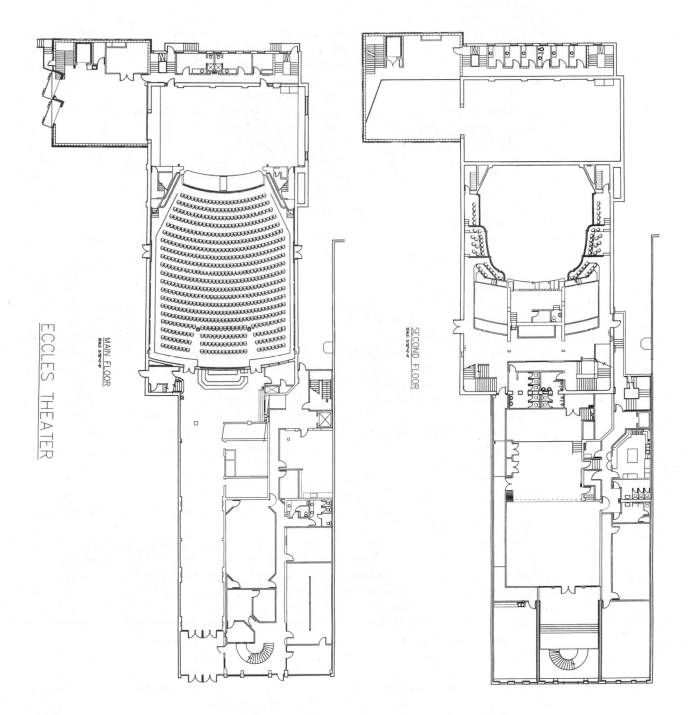

Figure 8–9 Proscenium style of floor plan, Eccles Theatre, UT. (Plan courtesy of Jensen Haslem Architects PC. Project Architect and Designer: Lanny Herron.)

windows promote the feeling of space. A strong feature of the exterior that might involve an interior designer are the entrance doors. Due to the numbers of patrons of the space and code requirements, numerous exit doors must be specified. Older theaters often have beautiful polished brass doors or otherwise ornate exterior doors inviting the patron into the theater. Modern theaters seldom use these expensive ornate doors, opting for simple contemporary ones.

Once inside the entrance doors, the patron moves to the entrance lobby. In most theaters there is a box office lobby where tickets can be purchased and some patrons can wait until the doors to the main lobby are opened. Patrons are then welcomed through a second set of doors, where their tickets are checked, and they are directed to the proper entrance to the auditorium. The role of the interior designer at this point is to make design decisions that will enhance the experience for those in attendance, guided by the limitations and needs expressed by the client. Architectural finishes are selected to be long wearing and to be able to stand up to the abuse of crowds. Hard surface flooring is common though floor mats are necessary in wet climates. Heavy duty commercial wall treatments, such as stone, wood paneling, and some textured vinyl wallcoverings, can be used effectively.

After entering the main lobby, traffic patterns lead patrons to monitored coat checks, possibly refreshment areas, rest rooms, water fountains, and beyond this area, entrance to the main auditorium. Exciting design specifications can be suggested in the entrance lobby. Its role is to set the mood, promote good will, and possibly be a memorable space in regards to design (see Figure 8-10).

The theater design must provide service spaces for the audience. Public rest rooms, water fountains, and telephones are usually grouped in a convenient area off the lobby. Today, these public rest rooms must meet ADA guidelines. The total number of fixtures required will be determined by the total number of occupants of the auditorium and office areas. A coat check off the main traffic paths but convenient to the front entrance is necessary, especially in cold or wet climates. Food service is often provided in one form or another since it brings needed revenue to the theater. In legitimate theaters, it is most common that refreshment stands are provided that serve simple types of beverages and perhaps some packaged foods. If liquor is served, the location of refreshment areas needs to be planned in consideration of delivery of liquor cases and lockable storage after hours.

Traffic is heavy in these areas and when carpet is specified, it must be a very high quality commercial grade carpet designed specifically for high use areas. Designers often specify patterned carpet in the lobby since it will show less soilage and hide traffic patterns. Smaller patterns or tweed styles should be used on stairways to the balcony since larger patterns can be visually confusing to some patrons. Acoustical wallcoverings or acoustical panels help to control the noise problems generated by the large crowds in the lobby. Any wall treatment in this area needs to be a Class I material or otherwise treated for fire protection. Lighting is usually provided by wall sconces, strip lighting along soffits, or other subdued indirect lighting to help set a mood for the space.

Furniture items in the lobby are generally sparse as this area is specified for traffic. However, some seating must be provided for those who cannot stand for a long period of time or those who leave the auditorium but are waiting for companions. As in museums, this seating is commonly specified as benches placed along one wall, if the corridor is of a size to allow for benches. In some situations, the building code will not allow benches due to a smaller size corridor. In this case, benches can be recessed into alcoves along the corridor.

Designers have a variety of challenges with the auditorium portion of the theater in much the same way as with museums. The stage and the main auditorium become the "display" area, which requires that the design be the background and not in competition with the production. Especially in theaters producing plays, it is important to place the attention on the stage and the production without peripheral interference. One effective method is to specify colors that do not contain yellow tints as they reflect too much light. Theater designers usually opt for pale tones of grey, dusk purples, or any tone that absorbs light during the performance. When a play is in progress, the walls of the main theater should not reflect light once the house lights have been dimmed. Reflective surfaces such as foil wallcoverings are generally avoided in the peripheral viewing areas. However, the reader may get to experience the beauty of gold foil on peripheral walls in historic theaters.

The layout of seating is one of the first considerations in the design of the auditorium. Seating for the main floor is usually arranged at a pitch calculated to provide for proper sight lines to the stage. The size of the theater and the exact configuration of the stage will determine whether a continuous pitch from the back of the auditorium to the stage is allowed or if stairs will be required. Usually the main floor will have a continuous pitch while mezzanines and

Figure 8–10 Lobby of the American Conservatory Theatre, San Francisco, CA. (Architect: Gensler. Photographer: Marco Lorenzetti/Hedrich-Blessing.)

balconies will be stepped. Rows of seats on the main floor are usually arranged in a slight curve so that patrons sitting on the far aisles will have good sight lines to the stage. Another preferred area of seating is box seats, which, depending upon the design of the theater, are above the main floor facing and flanking the stage on either side. To the rear of the house will be the mezzanine or balcony seating.

The designer will find that the seating specifications for the main auditorium, the box seating, and the balcony vary depending on the space allotted. Comfort, leg space, plus passage of others are factors in determining chair sizes and row widths. Spacing between rows is dictated by the building and fire safety codes. Seating laid out based on the American seating plan allows row spacing to be closer together since intervening aisles are provided for quick exit. When seating is laid out using the Continental seating plan, spacing between rows must be larger since a patron sitting in the middle of the house will have to travel farther to get to an aisle. Of course, spaces must be left for wheelchairs and a percentage of seats are required to have accommodation for assisted listening devices. The architect and the designer can consult the ADA guidelines for appropriate dimensions and numbers.

Theater and auditorium seating manufacturers are plentiful. The designer and the client need to sit in the variety of theater seating offered on the market prior to purchasing. Seats on the main floor are usually bolted to the floor while box seats are often freestanding. All seating must be selected on the basis of comfort, stability, versatility as to size and height of patrons, durability, and aesthetics. Fabrics selected for the seats first must be very durable and easy to clean. Wools and tightly woven nylons are commonly specified. Fabrics for the box seats may be more customized as long as they are acceptable to the fire codes. Box seats are generally the more expensive seats and are often targeted for benefactors.

The designer will also specify flooring for the auditorium. Dense, tufted carpet is commonly specified to aid in acoustical control. If hard flooring is preferred, carpeting in the aisles can be specified to reduce noise and aid in walking up and down pitched aisles. It is best to avoid high contrast patterns in the auditorium as they can be visually too active.

Lighting design for the auditorium and lobby and mechanical systems are all items that are strictly the responsibility of the architect. Of course, the interior designer may be involved in the selection of wall sconces or chandeliers, which might be used in the auditorium, boxes, and balcony. Signage is very important. Signs directing patrons from the lobby to sections of the auditorium are necessary. Additional signage is needed to direct patrons to the rest rooms and refreshment areas. Easily viewed egress signage is mandatory for safety in the auditorium.

Backstage spaces include the dressing rooms, set storage and preparation, costume storage and maintenance, rest rooms for staff, artist's lounge, a greenroom, as well as loading docks. Walls are painted black or charcoal in the stage area and near the stage openings. Designers usually assign neutral tones of all values for other backstage spaces other than dressing rooms and the greenroom (which is rarely green anymore). Kitchen facilities are commonly included in the greenroom.

Dressing rooms can be a large space used by several cast members and separate small rooms for stars and featured actors. It is generally recommended that a minimum of 16 square feet per person be allowed for dressing rooms. They must be very functional and light with emphasis on good lighting to help in preparation for makeup application. Furniture in private dressing rooms not only includes the makeup areas with lavatories but also chairs, perhaps a sofa or day bed, tables, lamps, full-length mirrors, space to hang costumes, and a dressing area.

Finally, theater offices will be planned for the staff. The amount of space given to office areas will depend on whether the facility has a resident company or rents space to touring productions. Resident companies will require a larger amount of office space. If at all possible, offices should have exterior views, good lighting, and as generous an amount of space per office as is practicable. Case goods office furniture, or even some systems furniture, is appropriate in the offices.

Theater design requires teamwork and input from a variety of professionals associated with the theater, construction, and the design team. The interior designer represents a segment of this team and can directly affect the ambience, safety, comfort, and appeal of the facility.

Religious Facilities

Religious facilities are "a building, or group of buildings, such as a church, a synagogue, sometimes called a temple, or a mosque, in which people worship, or other buildings used for religious or secular purposes by the worshipers."[10] Varying religions plus the variety of

---

[10] Packard and Korab, 1995, p. 531.

interpretations within each denomination make this area a specialty field where research and preparation are critical to the success of the project. Generally an interior designer retained to plan a religious facility is not designing for his or her own denomination, or even to express his or her own spiritual contribution. More often the designer is dealing with a congregation where each individual can feel passionately and intensely personal about the interior space, the use of the structure, and the exterior design as well. In this sense, religious structures are an institutional facility where the group considerations are mainly based on the overall philosophy of the denomination.

Places of worship have been built by all religions throughout most of history. They have always been places where the membership could go to satisfy and intensify spiritual feelings, study the precepts of the denomination, and feel safe in their emotions. Religious facilities are also places where members can feel a part of a community of individuals who share common beliefs. Thus these facilities have always been designed and built with great care. The fact that cathedrals, churches, temples, synagogues, and mosques date from our earliest architectural history attests to this fact. For centuries, buildings associated with religious orders have had an enormous influence on architectural and design styles. And while changes in building technology, presentation, and even a congregation's interests may have changed, the design of a religious structure remains a focal point for communities.

Religious structures vary greatly based on the actual denomination. Although certain requirements will be similar, the specific design elements and concepts for structures in each religion are different. The Crystal Cathedral (Figure 8-11b) is an example of a modern design for the Dutch Reformed Church of America. An in-depth discussion of the many and various religious structures existing in the world today is beyond the scope of one chapter. Therefore, the discussion here focuses on those facilities and floor plans typical of the Christian church and the synagogue. In no way does this intend to deny the importance of the religious facilities of other religions not covered in this section.

Overview

For religious facilities, the most important element is the sanctuary, which is incorporated into the building commonly know as the church in Christian religions and the synagogue in the Jewish faith. When a congregation undertakes to build new facilities, this is the space usually built first. It is the focal point of the activities of the congregation and its planning and design will seek to express the most profound characteristics and emotions of the congregation. A particular religious facility will also include supporting spaces or structures. Assembly rooms, possibly with a small kitchen, classrooms, perhaps a small library, offices for the ministers, priests, or rabbi, other administrative offices if the congregation is large enough, and even nurseries can be part of the campus of the church or synagogue. Our discussion, however, focuses on the sanctuary.

Terminology to assist the student and the designer in understanding the subject matter could be quite extensive in order to clarify issues of the various denominations. The following list of terms is provided since they are the terms used throughout the discussion on the functions and design of religious facilities. The authors acknowledge that some of these terms may have slightly different meanings, based on a specific denomination's interpretation

Sanctuary is the most sacred part of a religious facility. It is where the altar, if one is used, is placed.

Nave is the long narrow part of a cruciform/Latin cross floor plan. It is where the congregation stands or sits during the service.

Transept is the transverse segment of a cruciform floor plan, which crosses over the nave at the chancel end. Additional seating can be placed here and small chapels may be located at the ends.

Vestibule is a passage or small room between the entrance and the interior of a building.

Sacristy is a room attached to the church where the vestments and sacred utensils are stored.

Chancel is the name most often given to the sanctuary in most Protestant churches.

Baldochino is an ornamental canopy over an altar or seat of honor.

Rood screen is a screen separating the chancel from the nave.

A *priest* is an ordained clergyman in an Anglican, Eastern Orthodox, or Catholic church.

A *pastor* is the head of a Catholic church parish.

A *rector* is the head of some denominations of Protestant and Anglican churches.

Diocese is the district of churches governed by a bishop.

Synagogue is a house of worship for a Jewish congregation.

Rabbi is the ordained teacher of Jewish law and the head of a local synagogue.

Cantor a synagogue official who sings or chants religious music.

In designing religious facilities, the client represents a broad profile of administrators as well as members. The administrative structure varies with the denomination. For example, in the Anglican church, a bishop governs a diocese, which is comprised of districts containing established congregations as well as mission churches. A rector is the head priest of a parish. A vicar is in charge of a mission or a chapel. Deacons are laypersons trained to assist the priest. Catholic parishes have a parish priest with additional priests if the congregation is large enough. At higher levels will be monsignors and a bishop, archbishop, or cardinal, depending on the size of the diocese. On the local level, approvals for all but the smallest projects will have to come from one or more of these higher levels. In the Jewish faith, the rabbi is the leader of the local synagogue. The remainder of the organizational structure in a specific synagogue or district will depend substantially on what sect of Judaism is practiced at the location. The designer needs to remember that ultimate decision-making concerning major renovation or a new facility generally stems from those above the minister, priest, or rabbi at the local level.

Generally client needs and concerns are similar in all sects and include safety, security, application of building and fire codes, ADA applications, comfort needs via the HVAC systems, funding, time involved in the new construction or renovation, and transitional spaces to use during construction. Public concerns, needs and responses regarding religious facilities vary. As these structures are related to the individual's personal spiritual life and yet represent the history and combined consensus of the group, the designer may find that the members express strong opinions in regards to design decisions. Interpreted, this means that although the design project is for an institutional group, in this particular case the individual member may respond emotionally to the use, change, or application of the design elements.

Types of Religious Facilities

The traditional Christian church floor plan, which includes the transept and the nave, is identified as the Latin cross or *cruciform floor plan* . This floor plan has origins in ancient Egypt as the hypostyle hall. Jewish worship in ancient times took place in temples where an outer court, open to women, led to an inner court, which in turn led to the ark in its sanctuary, which was open only to men. Ancient Romans adapted the floor plan and the structure of the hypostyle hall to conform to their government structures or halls of justice, known as basilicas. When the Roman Empire fell, the existing Christian population took over the basilicas and used them as churches. With the advantage of the cross barrel vault in the Middle Ages, the transept was extended to create the cruciform floor plan. Variations of the cruciform floor plan were seen in Constantinople and parts of eastern Italy and Greece. This floor plan is referred to as the Greek cross floor plan and is identified as being in the shape of a square.

With the Reformation in the 1500s and the rebellion against the Roman Catholic church, structures began to change in an attempt to create a floor plan based on the new philosophy. The design of church architecture after the Reformation was quite varied as it was influenced by the different forms of worship. For example, many denominations built meeting houses rather than churches so that both religious services and community meetings could be held in the same building. Church buildings became simpler in size and detailing, in contrast to the scale and grandeur of the cathedrals.

The first church in America was probably built in Jamestown, VA, in the early 1700s, while the first synagogue in America was built in Newport, RI, in the mid-1700s. Spanish churches, which were based on the Roman Catholic religion, existed in the Southwestern part of America in the 16th century.

Church architecture not only has been influenced by the denomination, but also by the geographic area where the church was located. Protestant congregations of New England used wood as a common building material for their churches as it was readily available. If the church building was small, the interior was mainly a central aisle leading to the pulpit with pews flanking each side. Church structures in the southern colonies were brick and often constructed in a Georgian style (see Figure 8-11a). In the middle and southern colonies, the Anglican church predominated and maintained the cruciform floor plan for the majority of the religious structures. Spanish missions in the southwest used adobe bricks, a material made of clay, straw, and water. Floor plans of these missions were styled after traditional Roman Catholic churches with a central aisle leading to the altar in the sanctuary. As the US population increased and moved west, so did the variety of religious facilities.

Today's religious architecture reflects the continual changes in religious philosophy, and new congregations want facilities that meet their particular needs. Denominations abound, religious governing bodies vary, congregational profiles are infinite, thus making design preferences dependent upon the philosophy and historic practices of a particular religion. This means that should an interior designer decide to specialize in religious facilities, an understanding of the various religious groups and their philosophies is necessary. Careful consideration of each congregation's needs is always important, as the designs that worked for one church may not work for another, even if both churches are of the same denomination.

The primary types of religious facilities are the churches, synagogues, cathedrals, mosques, and temples that are built to house the primary religious services of a denomination. Religious facilities can also be typed by the support spaces of the main church (for simplification). Community or social spaces, classrooms, offices, and possibly residences for the clergy are some examples. Several denominations provide extensive classroom and other educational spaces as part of their church campus, creating parochial schools for the congregation's children. Of course, there are also private universities sponsored by religious denominations. There are monasteries, seminaries, and convents, places to become educated in religious principles in order to become part of the clergy of a denomination. Residences for higher ranking clergy in many orders are provided on or near the campus of primary religious facilities in many dioceses or districts. And some other types of facilities associated with a particular denomination exist as well.

All of these different types of facility provide project opportunities to designers who have specialized in this area of commercial interior design. As in other cases, it is impossible within the scope of this book to cover all these facilities. As noted previously, this section focuses on the sanctuary.

Planning and Design Concepts

The floor plan for a religious facility can affect the interaction of the worshippers with the ministers, priests, or the rabbi. Floor plans of religious structures vary and have gone through evolutionary changes over time. The traditional cruciform plan was used by most denominations for hundreds of years. Churches are now experimenting with new floor plans; one example would be a church in the round, which creates the potential for greater participation by the congregation. Many churches are duplicating some principles of theater design to produce an auditorium imitating the fan seating plan. Contemporary religious structures, whether churches or temples, generally want to present an open, welcome atmosphere to all. Part of the designer's job is to fulfill this request.

The following brief section will provide a background for the reader on the different approaches to the floor plans of Christian and Jewish religious facilities. In the Roman Catholic

(a)

(b)

Figure 8–11 (*a*) Exterior view of a church building constructed in a traditional style. (Photograph courtesy of S.O.I. Interior Design, Houston, TX.) (*b*) Exterior of Crystal Cathedral, Garden Grove, CA. Architects: Philip Johnson, Richard Neutra, and Richard Meier. (Photo courtesy of the Crystal Cathedral, Dutch Reformed Church of America, Garden Grove, CA.)

church, the focus of the plan will be rows of pews facing the altar in the sanctuary. A cross will be hung behind or above the altar and a tabernacle, which is, in a way, a decorative strong box, will be on the wall behind the altar. The tabernacle holds the Holy Sacrament. The sanctuary is where the priest will conduct the service, called a mass. The sanctuary is usually raised and may be divided from the seating portion of the nave by a railing called a communion rail. The congregation kneels or stands at the rail to receive communion. The sermon, called a homily, may be given as the priest stands in front of the altar or from a pulpit to the side of the altar. A sacristy, where religious garments and some other articles are stored, is to the side of the sanctuary, usually in a separate room. To the back of the church will be a baptistery, which is a fountain used to baptize infants, along with confessionals, which are small cubicles where the priest can hear the confessions of parishioners in private. The vestibule or lobby serves as a transition from the outdoors to the church nave. A Roman Catholic church campus often has other spaces or buildings for offices, community rooms, classrooms, and living quarters for the priests.

Protestant churches vary considerably based on their exact denomination and philosophies. Church architecture may be very elaborate, as in many Episcopal churches, to very simple in many Reformed denominations. However, Protestant church facilities are generally divided into two main elements: the nave, where the congregation sits, and the chancel or sanctuary, where the minister or other officiate performs the religious service. It is common that the sanctuary have an altar with a cross near or above it. The pulpit is also a common feature in the chancel. In those denominations in which the priests or ministers use liturgical garments, a sacristy will be located in the back of the church in a private room. A vestibule or lobby is also provided as a transition from outside to inside the nave. Baptism rites differ among the various denominations, so that the location of the baptism area can vary greatly. Protestant church campuses also require spaces for offices, meeting rooms, community rooms, and classrooms. Some congregations provide housing for the minister or priest on the campus.

The sanctuary in a Jewish synagogue can be different depending on which sect of Judaism is the focus of the congregation. However, the focal point will always be the spot where the Torah is kept. The Torah is the sacred scrolls that contain the first five books of the Bible. The Torah is kept in an ark or niche generally located on the eastern wall of the sanctuary, covered by a curtain called a *paroche*. In front of the ark is a table or platform called a *bimah*, much like a pulpit in other churches. The rabbi will remove the Torah from the ark and place it on the platform as readings are made to the congregation. Seating is provided in rows, generally with a central aisle and side aisles. A vestibule or lobby is at the back of the synagogue, similar to Christian churches. Synagogues also provide community meeting places, offices for the rabbi and staff, and classrooms. The community rooms are used for special services and rituals such as the Passover meal. Because community rooms can be used for certain rituals, extra care is needed in the design of these spaces.

If the design assignment involves restoration of a religious facility listed on the National Register of Historic Places, the interior designer will need to increase research measures to make certain that all guidelines are followed for these structures. A good reference is the national organization, Partners for Sacred Places. The purpose of this organization is to educate, aid and assist religious facilities and members as to resources, funding methods, and provide a multitude of information. It also gives an annual award to recognize outstanding restoration of a religious facility (see Figure 8-12).

In the selection of products and materials for this type of institutional facility, it is important to understand the philosophy of the denomination and its response to product needs, materials, and colors as they relate to the specific church. It is impossible to fully cover the unique diversities of design concepts for the various religious denominations. However, some design considerations can be applied to most denomination's churches.

Let us begin with color schemes. Some churches request an overall color scheme that will be compatible with the colors used in conjunction with the church calendar. For example, purple may be used for the Lenten season. Some churches will request that no black or dark

Figure 8–12 Interior of a Spanish Gothic cathedral recently renovated. (Cathedral of the Madeleine, UT.)

colors be used as it is inconsistent with the concept of "light as opposed to darkness." This means that most churches will have a rather neutral color scheme for major surfaces with accents in wall hangings that can be changed with the season.

Many traditional church walls are treated with paint or wood paneling. However, as experiments in contemporary floor plans are being used, the use of textured wallcoverings and acoustical cloth is being specified. The Anglican and Methodist churches have retained some features of the hammer beam truss ceilings from the late Gothic period in England. Consistent with this design is the use of white or off-white plaster walls. Synagogues may use dramatic wall treatments to help focus attention on the ark. However, this will vary greatly with the sect of the synagogue and the philosophies of the congregation. Many churches hang banners related to the seasons along some of the walls to add color accents.

Floor coverings are another specification item for the church. Many smaller churches use carpeting to help with acoustics. But some argue that carpeting dampens the acoustics for singing. If carpeting is selected, it should be a dense, tufted pile installed with the glue-down method. This will give better wear, show traffic paths less, and be an aid to older members who may use a walker. Hard surface floorings such as wood, stone, and even resilient materials are also commonly specified. The actual material will be specified with aesthetic, acoustical, and maintenance issues important to the congregation kept in mind.

Of course, the major furniture element will be the pews or other seating. Seating for the congregation was not provided until around the Middle Ages. Before that time, the congregation stood or sat on the floor. Catholic churches in particular use pews with kneelers. The kneeler is usually padded and covered with a vinyl fabric. Pews are, of course, fixed to the floor for safety. Many churches request pew cushions, which require durable, easily cleanable fabrics. Churches that are more traditional in design or even many new churches just getting started use small chairs. It was very common for chairs to be used in cathedrals in the earlier centuries and some cathedrals still use chairs rather than pews. While the spacing between pews and sizes of the aisles are regulated by codes, the central aisles in many churches are larger than required in order to better accommodate processions like a wedding party.

Pews are rarely custom made but come from vendors that specialize in liturgical and religious products. Some of these suppliers can be found in the annual resource guides published by the trade magazines. Furnishings needed in the sanctuary or chancel are either available from these suppliers, or may be custom made.

Window treatments in the nave and sanctuary are rarely provided. In many churches, stained glass windows are used to enhance the spiritual ambience of the interior. Stained glass windows were used in early churches to help educate the masses who were unable to read. The pictures in the windows taught certain biblical lessons important to the denomination. Contemporary windows more often use religious symbols such as the cross or a lamb rather than detailing a biblical passage as in older cathedrals. These windows make an important statement and are used in many religious facilities.

Lighting in churches and synagogues varies based on need and atmosphere. Spot and track lighting are often specified for the nave and sanctuary. These fixtures can be controlled by a rheostat to create focus and mood where desired. Of course, sufficient lighting must be provided for the congregation to read.

Building codes and accessibility requirements need to be strictly adhered to in new construction and major remodeling of church structures. Churches and synagogues are considered assembly occupancies. This restricts not only which materials can be specified for architectural finishes, the width of the aisles, and the number of entry doors, but also the spacing between rows of pews. Accessibility guidelines will also require that a percentage of pew space be reserved for wheelchairs and that assisted listening devices be installed in some pews.

Historic churches and synagogues that are listed in the National Register of Historic Places are exempt from many of the ADA guidelines as long as some accommodations are provided. For example, a historic church or synagogue would not need to include a ramp at the main entry if it would be inconsistent with the historic character of the building as long as a secondary entrance has a ramp and signage is supplied.

The interior design of religious facilities can be a very rewarding endeavor. Whether one becomes part of his or her own church or synagogue building committee or specializes in the design of this type of institutional space, gaining an understanding of the philosophies and religious practices of the potential client is very important. To be successful in this area of commercial interior design it is crucial to put aside one's own thoughts about how a church or synagogue should be designed, and instead to express those feelings that the congregation wishes to express, in accordance with their denomination's teachings.

Libraries

A *library* is a term referring to a collection of books as well as to the building that houses the collection. In addition, a library is also a repository for collections other than books. The reader most likely became familiar with libraries as a child. Visiting and borrowing books from a community library for the first time is a thrilling experience to children. Library visits become more frequent as children move through the elementary grades. Preparing book review cards and book reports not only helps teach children to read, but introduces them to the wonders of the enormous amount of information that a library contains. Secondary school students find library resources useful to help them make career choices and decide what college or postsecondary training they might want. Of course, that seemingly never-ending need to write a book report or research project continues in secondary school. Whether the high school graduate pursues further education in college or seeks enrichment and information from libraries for other reasons, the need to use the resources of a library never seems to end.

Libraries collect, preserve, and make available for use and study the thoughts of the civilized world. Whether the library is the smallest of community libraries in a rural area, the Library of Congress, or something in between, it helps people shape their lives through information (see Figure 8-13). Library design an interesting and rewarding specialty area of educational and institutional interior design.

Overview

Libraries are administered by local, state, and federal authorities, and by private interests. No doubt, interior design students have visited their college or university library numerous times. The federal government also maintains libraries in many of the agency office buildings, and one of the greatest federal libraries is the Library of Congress in Washington, DC. Here copies of all published books and copyright registered materials are stored and cataloged. First established as a library for the Congress in 1800, it was rebuilt after the War of 1812 with the resources of the private library of Thomas Jefferson. It is the largest library collection in the United States.

Figure 8–13 Small Carnegie library typical of structures built in small towns throughout the United States. (Photograph courtesy of S.O.I. Interior Design, Houston, TX.)

Public libraries are not the only ones that exist, however. Many museums, religious organizations, association headquarters, nonprofit groups, corporations, and businesses large and small have library collections. Law libraries are indispensable to legal offices. Museums make their library collections available to students and scholars. The Vatican Library is indispensable to religious scholars. And interior design students find their resource libraries necessary to complete projects.

Libraries not only collect books, magazines, and audiovisual materials, they also archive historical documents donated by individuals or groups. A visit to a state historical society library allows students to explore original documents, manuscripts, and rare photographs of their community, learning what life might have been like in earlier decades. Many libraries have audio books on tape and Braille books to assist the blind. Libraries also sponsor exhibits of historical artifacts or the works of local artists and craftsmen. Educational opportunities such as lectures, seminars, and community programs are available, generally free of charge to community members. Libraries do indeed provide a valuable service to all who seek out their resources and comfort.

Terminology referring to library science is extensive. A small number of terms the interior designer might encounter during a library project are provided.

Carnegie libraries are facilities funded by the Carnegie Foundation, founded in 1911, to aid community libraries and schools.

The *stacks* refer to the open shelves containing the library materials.

Open stacks means the shelves of materials are open to the public to freely access and use.

Closed stacks means the materials are available only by checking them out from library staff. Many community libraries will keep the historical materials about the community in closed stacks.

Special collections are usually historical or special archival materials that require special care to protect them from damage. Most materials in special collections are in closed stacks.

Catalog systems are the methodologies used to catalog all the materials in a library into categories to make it easier for a patron to find needed materials. The two systems used are the Dewey Decimal system and the Library of Congress system.

Carrel tables are small enclosures, usually freestanding, for individual study.

It is important for the designer to research and recognize the chains of command and identify the decision-makers for a library facility design assignment. Administration is dependent upon the type of library. A public library in most US cities and towns is administered by a library board and a head librarian. Several librarians, secretarial staff, and volunteers are responsible to the head librarian and the board. A public school library in an elementary or secondary school operates with a head librarian, assistants, and perhaps adult volunteers as well as the student volunteers. The head librarian reports to the school principal, and indirectly to the superintendent of schools and the local board of education. The board of education is an elected body; therefore, the profile of the board changes on a regular basis, creating an interesting challenge concerning decision making authority during many school library projects. A special collections or archival library has a head curator, much like a museum, who administers, researches, makes presentations, and monitors the collection as well as determines the direction of the collection. Assistants, secretarial staff, and volunteers report to the curator. The assistant is usually the primary contact for the public using the special collections.

College and university libraries have a complex administrative structure. Starting at the level the patron might encounter, students and secretarial staff are commonly the first point of contact with a student patron. Librarians and assistant librarians report to the university librarian or head librarian and work in such areas as: multimedia, reference, cataloging, periodicals, documents, information systems, materials acquisition, serials and binding, computer services, and instructional laboratories. The university librarian is commonly on the same administrative level as a college dean. Deans report to a provost or academic vice president, who reports to the president of the university. Universities and colleges also have outside governing boards. These may be called boards of regents or boards of trustees. There are also specialized libraries on many campuses as well as in some college buildings within the university.

The chain of decision-making and planning in the design of an addition, major remodeling, or renovation is similar in each case. The process will usually begin with the head librarian making a request to the city manager (for a public library in a smaller city), to the principal (for an elementary or secondary school library) or to the provost (for a university or college library). If planning approval is given, the plans and budgeting for the project will work their way up through the chain of command. Smaller projects are less likely to go through this extensive approval and reporting structure and may be handled directly by the head librarian. Daily project decision-making during the course of a project is primarily handled on a local level, such as by an assistant librarian. In larger facilities, a representative from the facilities department will also commonly be involved.

Types of Library Facilities

Libraries have been in existence since ancient times with records showing that as early as the 3rd millennium BC a Babylonian temple had an area or room set aside for storing clay tablets. Other ancient civilizations, such as the Assyrians, also maintained records via these tablets, and ancient Greece had libraries housed in some temples. By the 4th century BC, the first institutional libraries are recorded. In ancient Rome, Julius Ceasar planned the first Roman library.

During the Middle Ages, books were created and preserved within the monasteries and made available. A *scriptorium* was a place for the copying of books, mainly of religious content, within a monastic community. Due to the value and rarity of books, many of the collections were chained to shelves for security purposes. With the Renaissance came a broader emphasis on reading, writing, and learning. Johann Gutenburg's invention of movable type in 1450 helped create the need for libraries, since it was suddenly easier to produced printed works rather than handwritten manuscripts. The increase in the number of books helped to eliminate the securing of books to shelves with chains. This allowed books to be taken to early "reading rooms."

Not only were books collected by the monasteries, the universities, and the monarchs, but the merchant class also had private libraries. In 1571, the collection of Lorenzo de Medici was opened as a public library while the Vatican also developed its extensive library at the same time. Libraries continued to grow in size and stature over the following centuries as education increased and the masses were able to take advantage of the information contained in great university, national, and religious libraries.

Early libraries in the United States were private, housed in the residences of scholars and wealthy merchants. The first public library in the United States was founded in Boston in 1653, and Harvard University has had a library since 1638.[11] By the end of the 1700s in the United States the public need for the circulation of books was being met via book lending clubs. By 1850, libraries were being organized in the United States. Later in the 19th century and into the early 20th, Andrew Carnegie, an industrialist, donated millions of dollars for the construction of community libraries.

Until World War II, libraries in the United States were designed with a traditional or classic theme, as was the case for most institutional building up to that point. The GI Bill of Rights, established after World War II, gave thousands of veterans the opportunity to attend colleges and universities, and was just one reason why the use and construction of libraries expanded tremendously in the 1950s. New construction methods allowed for larger interior open spaces, providing enhanced comfort and flexibility to the library environment. Library architecture and interior design, as well as library services, continue to change as technology provides new methods of storing and making materials available. The 20th century library has expanded to

---

[11]Packard and Korab, 1995, p. 382.

include not only books in print but also microfilm, videos, computer facilities, Internet, and periodicals of all sorts. One of the early uses of the Internet was for scientists and scholars to exchange information and make library resources available to remote locations.

Much of the difference between the types of libraries is in the ownership and/or focus of the users. *National* libraries are owned by the federal government. The example most familiar to the reader will be the Library of Congress, previously mentioned. There is also a National Library of Medicine and the National Agricultural Library. Their use is limited to scholars, though the Library of Congress is open to public use on a limited basis.

Another type of library is the *public library* owned by communities. These libraries exist for the residents of the community and serve to augment school libraries. Public libraries often emphasize children's books since some elementary schools do not have very large libraries, if any. They also provide multimedia services, educational programs, or community use of assembly spaces. This type of library may be a small public facility with a few thousand books or a large city library with millions of items in the collection. The New York Public Library is one example of a public library on a grand scale.

A third type of library is the *school library*. The majority of elementary and secondary schools have libraries for the use of students. Their collections are generally not very large, often smaller than many city libraries. However, they provide a convenient place for students to research material for class assignments, use computers to research on the Internet, and have a quiet place to study.

Academic or university libraries make up a fourth type of library (Figure 8-14). With the increase in the number of students attending colleges and universities after World War II, university library collections expanded and new services were instituted. Undergraduate, graduate, and specialized libraries grew to meet needs of some of the specific colleges on a campus. Library users are primarily students and faculty but community members are also granted certain library privileges. Academic libraries provide many technical and convenience services to users, such as media centers where videos, films, audio tapes, and other recordings can be checked out. Copy centers provide on-site copying, as long as it does not violate copyright laws. Extensive collections of periodicals are maintained so students and faculty may have access to current information. Government documents are deposited at academic libraries so users can read the latest information provided by the federal, state, and local governments. And most university libraries also have a special collections section where items of historical significance to the university and surrounding community can be preserved and studied safely.

Special libraries are facilities that focus on a certain subject matter; they can be privately owned or supported by a government or a university. An example of a special library would be the National Academy of Sciences. Additional libraries under this category would include the Huntington Library in California, the DAR genealogical facility in Washington, DC, as well as the Mormon genealogical library in Salt Lake City, UT.

Archival libraries are facilities that have focused their collections on documents that have some historical value. State archive facilities, which may be housed at state capital buildings, collect documents and books that relate to the history of the state and its cities. The National Archives in Washington, DC, is the most famous archival library.

Private libraries are owned by individuals and businesses. From the small collection of books the student has already accumulated to large private research libraries housed at corporation facilities, private libraries bring collections of an assortment of materials to very focused and specialized subject matter.

Interlibrary loan and the Internet have brought the libraries of the world to most users. With an interlibrary loan program, a user can request a book not available at a local library. The Internet allows users to log into the catalogs of major libraries throughout the world. Information about the books can be obtained so that an interlibrary loan can be achieved or, in some situations, the book can actually be read and downloaded to the user's computer.

Library patrons, regardless of their age or focus, seek information that they cannot get at home. The first goal of any library is to assemble a collection that meets the needs of the

(a)

Figure 8–14 (*a*) Interior of a university library in a contemporary style. (*b*) Exterior of the same library. (Architect: Edward Larabee Barnes. Photograph copyright © Utah State University Photography Services.)

(b)

patrons. However, some people go to libraries simply to get away from home for a few hours, to quietly socialize, or even to people watch. Thus libraries also must have as a goal the creation of a pleasant, comfortable atmosphere that allows all these patron needs to be met. The interior designer, architect, and the rest of the design team help the library accomplish that goal.

Planning and Design Concepts

Whether the library is a public library, an academic library associated with a school system or university, a museum library, or a genealogy library, the planning and design concepts are similar. As with all the other sections and chapters, space prevents a detailed discussion of each type of library facility. The remainder of this section focuses on the main floor of a generic pubic library. Offices, back work areas, public rest rooms, and meeting rooms are not discussed.

The design job may be a renovation, an expansion, adaptive use, or new construction. The designer will work with the head librarian and primary library staff for a public library. Generally, a representative from the city government will also be involved, probably from the city planning or engineer's office. The interior designer will be part of a design team led by an architect, and will likely include one or more specialty consultants, depending upon the actual scope of the project.

The client will first be concerned with space planning to insure that the layout of the functional areas is efficient and easy for the patron to use. The head librarian will also seek expert advice in the selection of appropriate furniture items, materials specifications such as flooring, wallcoverings, window treatments, and any upholstery fabrics. Lighting design and proper specification of mechanical systems to insure interior climatic environments to protect the collection are critical in the architect's specifications. The secondary client to the project, that is the public using the library, will judge the library on the ease of use of the facility, comfortable chairs and tables, computer accessibility, rest rooms, ADA accessibility, and, of course, all texts, references, and periodicals that the library staff has made available.

Generally libraries are divided into distinctive areas based on function. Let us first look at the areas concerning the most common function of the library, the book stacks. Patrons enter a small lobby before entering the actual library and approach the checkout, book returns, and information desk. Beyond this point is the main library space where the user will find book stacks, current periodicals, special reference materials, media materials, the children's library, special collections if available, browsing areas, and adult reading rooms. In addition, spaces for the library staff include offices, cataloging space, workrooms, possibly a board room or staff lunchroom, as well as storage and custodial space.

The use of the computer has made card catalog units extinct in most libraries today as librarians have discovered the space saving value of technology. Computers are commonly placed near the front of the library, near the checkout or information desk. This area of the library may also be the location of other devices used to conserve valuable space, that is, the viewers used for microforms particularly microfilm and microfiche. These devices use special films on which newspapers, magazines, catalogs, and dozens of other types of documents are retained.

Materials checkout is done at the entry desk. With the exception of the smallest community libraries in rural areas, users will exit through some sort of security device to insure that books and other materials are not leaving the library without having been properly checked out.

Tables and seating are traditional furniture specifications for libraries. Let us first look at tables. Library tables can be arranged for six or eight patrons at a table with the overall depth of 42 inches to 48 inches to supply study space at each position. Standard table height of 29 inches needs to be used. Carrel tables are especially prevalent in university libraries and may also be found in some public libraries. As most readers know, a study carrel is double-faced to allow for privacy (see Figure 8-15). The standard floor footprint of a double faced carrel is 35 inches wide by 48 inches deep plus space for the chairs. It is especially important that the designer specify light colored surfaces for carrels as the light can be easily blocked by the high side panels and the overhead shelf. Light colored surfaces for tabletops also help prevent eyestrain. Small tables or carrels with reduced height backs and sides are often specified for media equipment such as microfiche viewers and sometimes the computer terminals.

Seating at study tables and carrels usually consists of small chairs with a seat height between 16 and 18 inches, a seat depth of no more than 20 to 22 inches, and a back that gives some shoulder support. If at all possible, these chairs should be ergonomically designed to avoid back fatigue and discomfort. However, as the reader probably knows, most public libraries use a small wooden chair that is not particularly ergonomically designed. This type of chair is selected because of its ease of maintenance, resistance to abuse, and low cost.

Browsing or reading rooms are often designed with comfortable, upholstered chairs. These chairs can be fully upholstered with thick cushioning and a comfortable fabric or leather. The chairs can be placed in a sociofugal or a sociopetal arrangement. An example of the sociopetal placement would be to arrange four big upholstered chairs in a full circle facing a central low table for magazines or periodicals. Though the chair arrangement encourages talking the table creates a psychological barrier. An example of the sociofugal placement would be to arrange the large reading chairs in a back to back configuration with possibly a sofa table in between the two units. Fabrics can be specified as solid colors, patterns, or textures as long as they are commercial grade materials that can take the heavy use and abuse expected in libraries.

The designer can create unique and appropriate custom cabinetry for the checkout and information desk, and perhaps other cabinets on the main floor. The design criteria for these cabinets are specified by the head librarian and library staff since each library will handle these functions differently. The specification of smooth countertop materials for ease of writing, light surfaces to reduce eye fatigue, and sufficient work space for the librarians are all important issues. The checkout desk in particular should have a lowered counter section to meet ADA guidelines and to invite children to use the desk. Reference and information desks are also required to have a lowered counter section or other appropriate accommodation for accessibility if these are separate from the main desk.

Figure 8–15 Seating and carrels in a university library. The carrels allow for privacy whereas the sociopetal placement of chairs allows for some interaction. (Photography copyright © Utah State University Photography Services)

Bookshelves for the stacks, many cabinets to hold documents, and storage for specialized collections like video tapes or records are selected from manufacturers that specialize in library equipment (Figure 8-16). The names of many of these vendors are listed in source guides published by the interior design trade magazines such as *Interior Design, Contract, Interiors and Sources*, and *Interiors*.

The predominant requirements for materials specifications for a library are for the architectural finishes and furniture or cabinet items. Any type of color scheme for these materials can be selected; however, lighter values are commonly used to reduce eyestrain and eye fatigue, and to help with light reflectance. Walls can be painted or covered with a textured commercial grade wallcovering. Textured wallcoverings are used as an aid in reducing noise within the facility and to add interest. Patterned wallcoverings and paneling are sometimes used in the reading areas since these areas are designed to seem more like a living room than a study space. Floors are usually carpeted with a high-density, tightly tufted carpet that has been installed using a glue-down method. This aids those in wheelchairs as well as making it easier for staff to move book carts around the library. Carpets are usually tweeds or small patterns to hide traffic paths and soilage.

Whether the children's section of the library is off in a corner of the main floor or in a separate room, different considerations must be incorporated to make this space a pleasant and user friendly space. In the children's section of the library, child-sized tables and chairs are necessary (see Figure 8-17). Some adult size tables and seating should also be provided in the reading area so parents and preteen children will have furniture that is comfortable for their body size. Book stacks will be lower since it would be unsafe for a child to try to reach books on shelves over four feet high without assistance. If the library is in a large city, a separate information desk is often placed in the children's library. Designers can really use their creativity in their design of wall finishes in the children's section of the library. Murals and bright colors help achieve an atmosphere that is fun for children, which helps encourage them to come back to the library.

Figure 8–16 Book stacks in a library require continuous and sufficient lighting. (Photographs copyright © Utah State University Photography Services.)

Figure 8–17 Children's library requires a smaller scale of furnishings than the average library. (Architect: Dekker/Perich, Albuquerque, NM. Photograph copyright © Kirk Gittings.)

Lighting is a particularly tricky design challenge as all the book stacks cut any daylight that might be available from windows and block direct ceiling light solutions. The Illuminating Engineering Society recommends 30 foot-candles in the stacks and 70 foot-candles in most other areas. Task lights are often provided on the study tables and carrels in older libraries or those with very high ceilings since these areas are difficult to light with ceiling fixtures. As previously mentioned, light values of colors are ideal since they aid in light reflection and reduce the chances of eye fatigue. High contrast in colors and finishes should also be avoided as it causes eyestrain with the movement of the eye from light to dark surfaces. For example, white paper placed on a medium to dark wood laminate top causes eyestrain due to the increased visual activity caused by the contrast.

Ergonomically designed computer workstations are the ideal in a library, however, most public libraries will not provide these to the public. They should carefully designed for staff as comfort and healthy work areas are important for library employees, whether they are at the checkout desk or behind the scenes in offices. The design elements of computer workstations detailed in Chapter 1 will also apply to libraries.

The designer may be asked to select artwork to enhance the facility. In some communities, artwork is on loan to the library from local artists. In this case, the head librarian may ask the interior designer to consult on how to hang or best display the work. Artwork accessories are most likely to be needed in the reading rooms. Pieces that represent the city or geographic area are commonly used.

A few quick comments are in order concerning the codes as they relate to libraries. Since the occupancy load of this type of facility will likely exceed 50 in most situations, it is classified as an assembly occupancy in the building and fire codes. All exiting, aisles, corridors, finishes, and other like decisions should be made in accordance with this classification. In addition to the standard ADA guidelines for accessibility for an assembly occupancy, libraries must meet a few additional conditions. These apply to all the areas that the public may use. At least 5 percent of any fixed seating must be accessible and clearances between any fixed accessible tables must adhere to the dimension guidelines in Section 4.3 of the ADA. Checkout desks must have a lowered counter or other acceptable provision for an individual in a wheelchair. Security gates must also allow clear passage for a wheelchair. Space between stacks and any cabinets must be a minimum of 36 inches clear with 42 inches being preferable. The designer should research the appropriate guidelines and codes to insure the library design meets all applicable local regulations.

A library is an interesting design challenge for commercial interior designers. Satisfying the primary client and others who have an interest in the project, including the general public, is not an easy task. The emphasis will always be on the collection of materials available to the public with the building and interiors a background, creating a pleasant place to spend a few minutes or several hours. Whether the project is a small public library or a new academic library facility, the designer must research the administrative structure, the type of facility, and all of its needs to insure that a professional solution is provided.

Educational Facilities

The last segment of this chapter focuses on educational facilities. Education, that is teaching and learning, can be conducted in many different settings. Educational programs take place in corporate training rooms, in hotel conference centers, at meetings held at restaurants, during consultation with patients in medical suites, in presentations at museums, in classes held in religious settings, and in countless other settings. This section, however, focuses on facilities that offer structured publicly funded educational programs, such as elementary and secondary schools and college or university facilities.

Success in the different levels of education rests squarely on the student and the teacher. The student must be interested and participate in the learning experience. The teacher must provide methods and guidance to help each level of student understand information that can be puzzling and mysterious until recognition—and learning—take place. The school district, however, must provide an environment that encourages and assists in the learning process within a budget acceptable to the tax payers or others who fund the facility. Creating that environment is the role of the interior designer and other designers who specialize in educational facilities.

A discussion of the concepts behind different philosophies of education for the different levels as relates to the design of educational facilities is beyond the scope of this book. The discussions in this section focus on the elementary school, although some comments concerning design elements particular to the secondary school are made. University, college, and specialized postsecondary school facilities are not discussed in any depth.

Overview

For many centuries, children were educated at home in the ways of the world and to the extent that their parents had any of what was called formal education. Lessons in reading and writing were withheld from all but the ruling classes for many centuries. Lessons in simple mathematics and writing were given to apprentices as they learned their trades from master craftsmen. Gradually, parents wanted their children to have more formal education and formal school opportunities began to increase, at first for boys only, and later for girls as well.

Today, educational opportunity is a privilege and a right of all students under the age of 16. Most states require that students under 16 be provided educational opportunity that meets certain minimal requirements. Although some parents provide that education at home, most children receive their basic education in public and privately funded formal school environments.

Here are few terms regarding educational facilities for clarification.

K-6-3-3 is an educational plan calling for one year of kindergarten, six years of elementary school, three years of junior high school, and three years of high school. It is the standard school plan in many districts in the United States.

Parochial school is a school owned by a religious denomination.

Multipurpose rooms are classrooms or activity spaces that can accommodate more than one kind of educational or social experience.

Chancellor is a title given to the head of a university. The chancellor (or president) may be responsible for one school or, in some states, several schools.

Provost is a title given to the faculty member who has overall responsibility for academic programs at a university or college. The provost reports directly to the president or chancellor and the deans of the college report to the provost.

It is important for the student and the designer to understand the administrative network regarding responsibility and decision-making as it can impact the success of the design project. The ultimate audience for a school project is not just the principal (or other head) and faculty at a particular educational facility. The audience for the project is also the whole administration of the facility, the students and other users, as well as the public. The public's interest is based to some degree or another on tax dollars as well as on the concern for the quality of the educational experience, and safety and comfort of the student in the educational setting.

The administrative structure of a school depends a great deal on the type of school. For example, with primary and secondary public schools, the district schools are usually governed by a superintendent of schools and a board of education. Each school in the district will have a principal, vice-principals, teachers, specialists, support staff, and professional staff such as librarians, school nurse, and school psychologist. Members of the board of education are elected to their positions, which means that the membership profile can change with the elections. The superintendent of schools is hired by the board of education. A superintendent of schools oversees all the educational programs and employees of a school district.

The administrative structure will be somewhat similar for privately funded schools. A governing board or board of directors serves the same basic function as the board of education and superintendent of schools. There will then be a principal or headmaster or headmistress along with assistants, teachers, support staff, and professional staff. Should the school be funded or supported by a specific outside group, such as a religious denomination, the school administration and policies will also be under the scrutiny and judgment of advisors or representatives from the supporting group.

If the design assignment is for a university or four year college, then the administrative structure changes. Depending on the way the state supported universities have been chartered, one or more forms of a state board of regents or governing boards using other names will have overall control of a group of universities. However, the board of regents (for simplification) must answer to the state legislature, which appropriates and determines the apportioning of funding for the various universities. Generally, there is either a division within the state government or a branch of the board of regents that handles facilities management and represents a very influential element in the administrative and construction processes. A university in the system may have its own board of trustees or an executive council consisting of the university president (sometimes called chancellor), provost, several vice presidents, and the deans of the colleges. Each college has a dean, several department chairs or heads, a group of faculty, and support staff. There are also staff departments for campus planning and facilities management, physical plant managers and staff, and staff for maintenance, dormitories and student services, food services, and purchasing, to mention a few.

The president is the head of the university and deans are the heads of academic programs needing instructional space. However, the campus or facilities planning offices generally oversee all construction projects for the university. Smaller remodeling projects might be funded on the "local level" through a dean's office, but would still need to be approved by the campus planning office. Because of the complex administrative structure on university and college campuses, it is important that the architect and designer, whether hired directly by the university or by the architectural firm contracted by the university, be aware of the chain of command and the identity of the ultimate decision-maker.

Projects for four-year private colleges, universities, community colleges, and privately owned trade or professional schools will be similar to those described above. Almost all schools, regardless of type of student or school, have facilities managers who oversee construction and renovation projects.

What are some of the priorities, needs, and concerns of the administration in the design of a publicly funded elementary or secondary school? With a new school building, the board of education, the superintendent, and usually the principal of the building are involved directly in the planning process. Needs involve providing sufficient space for all the educational activities encountered by students and staff as well as that of projected plans for the future. A major concern involves the cost of the structure. The board of education and the superintendent confer regarding methods to finance the project. Most likely, this will be accomplished through a bond issue on which the citizens will vote in an election. The concerns of the users will focus on function, capability of the structure as it relates to the potential quality education it will offer the student, plus the ease of use. Concerns of the public encompass those of the board of education and include the cost and the potential for a quality education facility. Once these basic concerns and needs are identified and a funding strategy is developed, a request for proposal (RFP) is issued, presentations by several architects are made to a selection committee, and a contract for the work will then be awarded. These last issues are discussed in detail in the next chapter on project management.

The educational philosophy utilized in a particular school will impact the space plan and perhaps the design elements of the facility. For example, a school that has embraced a philosophy of team teaching may use more multipurpose spaces for classrooms than a school that has one teacher per classroom. Computers have had a dramatic impact on the classroom in all grades and the use of computers for learning and the design of computer classrooms needs to be carefully considered by the designer. The interior designer also needs to be alert as to how the environment, through lighting and color, can affect the learning situation. Education journals have published reports on lighting, color, surface materials, acoustics, climate control, and seating as they impact student learning and behavior.

Types of Educational Facilities

The formal structured education of most children, of course, begins with the elementary school experience. Elementary schools provide children from age 5 to 12 an introduction to formal education and the learning process (see Figure 8-18). The earliest forms of education focus on reading and writing and also serve to introduce cultural mores to the children. Children progress into secondary or high school, gaining better mastery of basic subjects and obtaining introductions to more specific and specialized areas of learning. The high school years, serving as a bridge to adulthood, are structured with greater freedom in the student's choice of subject matter to be learned. After graduation from high school, teens may elect to attend an academic college or university, a community college, or some other form of formal education such as a technical or trade school.

As previously mentioned, education and learning take place in a variety of locations. The elementary (or primary) school, secondary school, and undergraduate and graduate advanced education in colleges and universities are the most familiar. Professional education in advanced university settings in such areas as law, medicine, dentistry, and veterinary science are another familiar setting. In addition, there are preschools and nursery schools for young children, as well as specialized schools, which might focus on special education for those with learning disabilities, for the highly intelligent, or for the disabled. Furthermore industrial, technical, and trade schools also exist, providing specialized training in a variety of career options.

Of course, a secondary factor in the definition of these types of educational facility is whether they are publicly or privately funded. Publicly funded elementary and secondary schools are those that receive all or most of their operating and building funds from local school districts through taxes. Public universities and colleges may receive their funds from local taxes, in the case of most community colleges, and or from state legislatures for most universities and four year colleges. Private schools at any level have been funded by endowments, donations, funding through a supervising body such as a religious denomination, and receive additional

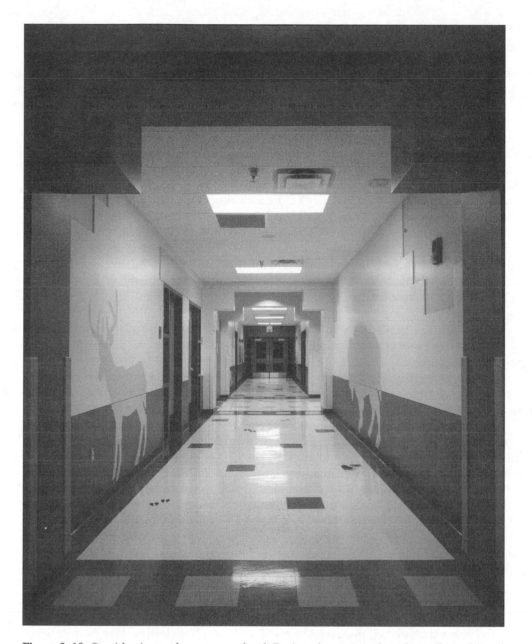

Figure 8–18 Corridor in an elementary school. Design elements such as the wall graphics, the step arch, and the floor tiles aid in reducing the appearance of length to the corridor. (Architect: Dekker/Perich, Albuquerque, NM. Photograph copyright © Kirk Gittings.)

annual funding through tuition and fees. Some private trade or professional schools are "for profit" and may have obtained initial funding like any other business and continued funding through tuition and fees.

The reader is well aware that public and many private schools not only provide classroom and laboratory spaces for formal education, but space for social, cultural, and athletic activities as well. A school campus will have classroom buildings, offices for the administration and the faculty, a cafeteria, gymnasium, auditorium, library, vocational education classrooms, and perhaps other spaces for auxiliary activities. Depending on the type of school and the educational focus, other spaces may be provided to meet specific needs.

Throughout history, education has been important. In ancient Egypt, the priests controlled the educational process and promoted homogeneity within the culture. The students studied reading and writing from age 5 until their teen years, when they were guided into a more targeted form of training. In ancient Israel, the mother taught the young child and the father directed the sons in religious, social, and moral laws. In ancient Athens, education became centered around democracy, civil life, and cultural activities. In ancient Rome, the mother and father were the educators of the child until the age of 16. The Romans adopted Hellenistic methods of education such as oratory, the Greek language, and the musical arts. When the Roman Empire became Christian, classical education in the liberal arts expanded.

Education continued to change during the Middle Ages. At this time the church took over much of the responsibility for education and studies had a definite religious emphasis. Generally, only the clergy and the nobility were formally educated. Renaissance and Reformation education emphasized the importance of the individual man and became centered on the classics and new ideas. Universities were founded in the 17th century, which helped lead the way to the formal training of teachers and the further expansion of secular knowledge.

The first schools in the New England colonies were founded in Boston in 1635. The first secondary school in America was Boston Latin, and the first university in America was Harvard, which was founded in 1636. Most formal education was for the wealthy in the early years of America and did not become available for the different social classes until the 18th century. Strict discipline in many one room schoolhouses was the educational philosophy in the 18th and early 19th centuries. In a one-room schoolhouse, one teacher would be responsible for teaching all the elementary grades. Secondary school was uncommon except for the wealthy until the late 19th century.

Schools in the United States went through many changes in the 20th century, not the least of these being the construction of separate facilities for elementary and secondary classes as well as individual classrooms for each grade and even each subject matter. Of course, one room schoolhouses existed in many rural communities until about the time of World War II. As the country gradually changed from an agricultural to an industrial society, education became increasingly important for all classes and at all levels. Universities developed in part due to an increased population and affluence, advanced technology, and the desire to get better employment. The Land Grant Act of 1862 provided for the development of state universities in many states. The intensive expansion of technology to meet the needs of World War II production and leadership heightened the need for better education and facilities. University student populations exploded after World War II as the GI Bill of Rights gave veterans the opportunity to attend colleges of their choice at very favorable costs. This gave all classes of Americans an opportunity to obtain a college education.

The philosophy of how to educate students more successfully at all levels continues to evolve. Open classrooms, closed classrooms, programmed instruction, individualized instruction, distance learning by use of television and the Internet are just some of the ways educational opportunities are directed toward all levels of students. The classroom and educational campus must also change to meet these challenges and the challenges of the 21st century.

Colleges and universities have become more market-minded with some of the recruiting emphasis placed on the appearance of the campus (see Figure 8-19). Technology has provided long-distance education through advanced telecommunications. And budget crunches at the universities have forced many schools to look for new funding sources. For example, business schools at major universities have offered residential conference centers on campuses for executive seminars. The Wharton School of Business at the University of Pennsylvania is one of the best known for this activity.

The computer has been one of the major elements in changing traditional education in that it offers a variety of information quickly. Students in all age groups are discovering how the computer can be a learning tool, an information source, and a tool to work better and faster. The computer has been critical in aiding teachers and professors in their academic activities as well as providing an effective tool for teaching in the classroom. This technology and the technologies to follow will not only change how education is delivered and learned, but change the facilities in which education takes place.

Figure 8–19 Reception room at a University. The traditional elements are used to enhance the inference of longevity and stability, features that have aided in recruiting students. (Photograph © USU Photo Services.)

Planning and Design Concepts

As the reader can see from the above, the design of educational facilities is so broad, it is difficult to provide specific planning and design concepts for each category of school facility. In addition, each category of facility has many different requirements, needs, and design issues, which compounds the issue. Thus it is necessary to make this section focus on the public elementary school classroom.

Floor plans for basic elementary classrooms over the past century include the one room schoolhouse where all grades are taught in the same room, traditional one classroom per grade spaces, or settings that require students to move from classroom to classroom depending upon the subject. As the reader will recall, the classroom is furnished with student desks in rows facing the front of the classroom where the teacher's desk may be on a raised platform. This type of classroom design was used extensively at all grades until the 1960s. At that time, the open classroom concept emerged. In this setting, classrooms were built without interior walls and students were grouped in "pods" of interest and subject matter (see Figure 8-20). Later, large open classrooms were subdivided with movable partitions and by other means. Today, many school districts have at least partially abandoned the open classroom and have returned to more secluded classroom settings.

There have been a few other planning attempts used in schools to aid in the learning process. One is classrooms without windows. It was thought that no windows would help students learn more rapidly without those distractions. Another is the design of classrooms that can be flexible and adaptable. In this case, a classroom might serve as a math classroom in the morning, individual study pods for history in the afternoon, and after-hours community instruction in the evening.

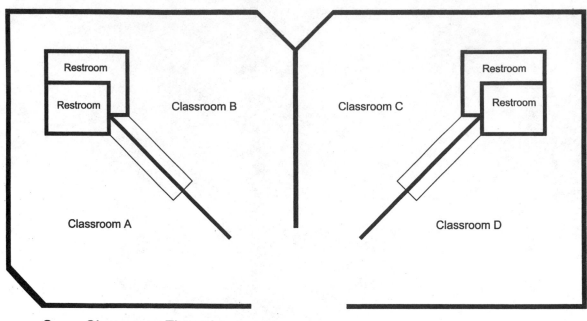

Open Classroom Floorplan

Figure 8–20 Open classroom. (Drawing courtesy of Cody D. Beal.)

Classroom furniture at all levels can be either very specialized furniture products available from educational product vendors or, at the high school and university levels, incorporate some items of standard commercial furniture products. Trade magazine resource books can again be referenced for suppliers of classroom and laboratory furniture. Furniture in the elementary school will be specified at different scales of furniture for the different age groups. Safety from sharp edges on tables, desks, and cabinets is very important. So to is the selection of chairs when individual chairs are used. They should be designed to resist tipping. To resolve the safety issue, many school districts use student chairs and desks that are one unit and can be bolted to the floor. Of course, this does impact how the educational process can be conducted in the classroom and must be discussed with the principal.

Educational facilities have moved away from the drab institutional colors schemes of the early 20th century. Research studies have shown that children are not adversely affected when bright colors are used as accessory items in classrooms. However, walls and floors should be specified in light values and neutrals. "Classrooms for young children profit from the use of brighter colors, usually in warm tones; the use of primary colors, however is an undesirable cliché."[12]

Materials in secondary schools must be selected with consideration for ease of maintenance, resistance to abuse, and safety. Wall finishes need to be easy to clean or refinish inexpensively. Textured wallcoverings can be useful for acoustical control, though they may be harder to clean. Window treatments are primarily vertical or horizontal blinds in a neutral color. Window treatments are, of course, needed when the teacher wishes to show a movie, slides, or other projected visual materials. Floor treatments must be specified with safety in mind. Hard surface and resilient materials are commonly selected because of their lower cost and ease of maintenance. However, it is easier for children to slip and fall on these types of flooring materials. Commercial carpets with dense, tufted piles can be used in classrooms where spillage of ink or other liquids is expected to be minimal.

---

[12]Pile, 1995, p. 284.

Impacting the change in classroom design is the computer. Classrooms with computers require specialized furniture, lighting, and climate control. The elementary classroom will require computer desks that are suitable for the various age groups of students who will be using that equipment. The reader is directed to Chapter 1 for specific design considerations for computer stations.

Of course, floor plans, corridors, aisles, furniture layouts, and architectural finishes must meet the building, fire codes, and ADA regulations. Elementary and secondary schools are considered education occupancies by the building and fire codes. Special code considerations are necessary for exit and egress design in educational occupancies. Most rooms or areas other than exit passageways may be finished in Class III materials. Exit ways must be finished using at least Class II materials. University classrooms are classified as business or assembly occupancies, depending on the occupant load. Classrooms such as laboratories, shops, and other areas that may involved hazardous materials will have additional code requirements, regardless of the type of school. A school must meet all applicable ADA guidelines in effect in the location. Remember that special accessibility considerations will be enforced in a school library and cafeteria. It is the designer's responsibility to research and apply all applicable local codes and guidelines to the project.

Finally, classroom needs will vary based on the actual use of the classroom space. The designer must know the purpose of the space and the teaching methods used in each space in order to solve the planning and specification challenge successfully. Specialized classrooms such as for music, art classes, science laboratories, sports, and vocational education will have other needs that must be addressed.

Educational facilities are one more interesting and challenging specialized institutional facility. Whether the design project involves an elementary, secondary, university, or specialized school facility, the designer must research the needs of the client very carefully. Designing educational facilities is considered by some to be part of a sacred trust in assisting students at any age in the pursuit of learning and cultural development. The designer must not take this sacred trust lightly.

Planning Public Rest Room Facilities

Of course, many of the projects discussed in the preceding chapters and sections require public rest room facilities. In some cases, the location, planning, and design of those facilities will be the responsibility of the interior designer or architect as part of the overall project. In situations where a tenant is moving into an existing building, rest room facilities will be in place in a building core or some other location in the building. The space planning of rest room facilities in commercial businesses creates problems for many design students. This last part of the chapter briefly discusses a few primary concepts in the planning and design of public rest room facilities.

The interior designer's responsibility in the planning and design of rest room facilities generally concerns the location of the restroom in the space plan and the interior specifications of materials. Plumbing diagrams for commercial interiors are rarely if ever completed by the interior designer. Plumbing locations are generally checked with the architect, who may also have to have the locations approved by a plumbing engineer. The locations of the rest rooms must be coordinated with a building core, access to water and waste water lines, and any wet columns planned into high-rise buildings.

The number of water closets and lavatories required for any one type of commercial interior space is regulated by the building and plumbing codes. Local building authorities may have supplemental requirements that supersede the model codes. The ADA and regulations in other countries concerning accessibility will influence the design of the facility as well.

Each model code has a supplemental plumbing code. They are:

- Uniform Plumbing Code (UPC) for the Uniform Building Code

- Standard Plumbing Code (SPC) for the Standard Building Code

- BOCA National Plumbing Code for the National Building Code

It is important to clarify a few terms for the fixtures that are discussed in this section.
A *water closet* is a plumbing fixture in rest rooms also called a toilet.
A *urinal* is a specialty water closet typically found in a men's rest room.
A *lavatory* is the term used for a sink for washing hands.
Sink is the term used for all other sinks, such as service, janitor's, and kitchen sinks.
Single-user rest room is one in which only one person occupies the space at a time.

The number of any of the plumbing fixtures required in any space is based on the occupancy type and the number of occupants of a space. For a business occupancy, which is the focus of this discussion, at least one water closet must be provided for the building or portions of the building. It is generally necessary to supply separate facilities for men and women when the occupancy contains both sexes and has more than four employees. However, some jurisdictions will allow a unisex restroom for businesses that have a small number of employees. The ratio of lavatories to water closets for a business occupancy is one lavatory for every two water closets. Other specific requirements for the numbers of fixtures can be found in an appropriate table in the building code or the plumbing code adopted by a jurisdiction.

Each floor of a building must also have provision of rest room facilities. If one or more office suites are on a floor of a high-rise building, the building core will provide the necessary rest room facilities for that floor. When the office is a leased space as part of a series of office suites on a one story building, each suite will likely require its own rest room facilities.

If a single-user rest room or unisex facility is allowed, a layout similar to that shown in Figure 8-21 is generally appropriate, since it also meets accessibility guidelines. Some other sizes and arrangement are possible. The reader may find other examples in an ADA guidelines reference. No partitions to separate the water closet from the lavatory are necessary in this situation. If separate rest rooms for men and women are required, each can be of this design. In a single-user restroom for men, it is not required that a urinal be provided in addition to a water closet unless local codes require both fixtures.

Location and planning of the rest room in the whole of the floor plan must also provide privacy. Care should be taken in where the door into the rest room is placed. With a single-user rest room, it is best if the door into the rest room is not in a direct line with any corridor or aisle so that someone walking in the corridor can see directly into the rest room. With multifixture rest rooms, it is common to have a set of double doors to enter the rest room or at least a full-height wall as a screen at the entry. Either of these planning techniques provides privacy for those in the rest room when someone walks past the entry to the rest room facility (see Figure 8-22).

Partitions between fixtures are most often obtained from specialty vendors. These specialty vendors also supply paper towel dispensers, built-in trash receptacles, soap dispensers, and other items of a similar nature. However, designers may be able to use three-quarter height or full-height stud walls to create the partitions between water closets. The limiting factors will be local code restrictions and the added expense of building and finishing stud partitions.

Location of mirrors and specification of lighting are other concerns. Of course, mirrors are generally located over the lavatories. If additional mirrors are used, they should not be placed so that someone walking past an open door to the rest room can see a reflection of those inside the rest room. General lighting is provided with ceiling florescent fixtures or a combination of spotlights, accent lights on the walls by the mirrors, and ceiling fixtures.

Architectural materials in the rest room should be selected with consideration for moisture, ease of maintenance, even purposeful user damage. Although ceramic tiles for the walls are the easiest to maintain and the hardest to damage, the added expense prevent their use in

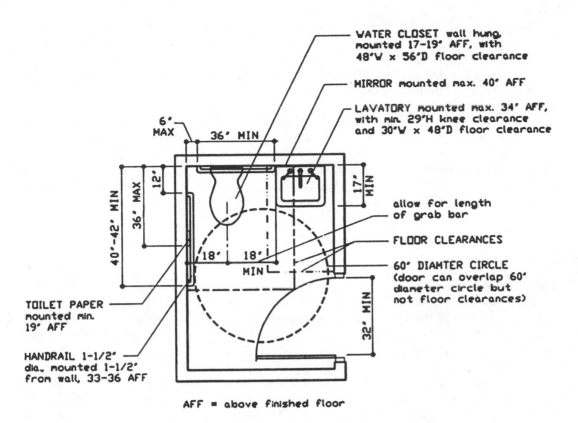

Figure 8–21 Single-user rest room. (From Harmon, *The Codes Guidebook for Interiors*. Copyright © 1994. Reprinted by permission of John Wiley & Sons, Inc.)

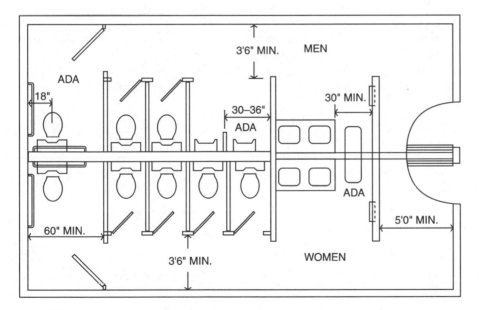

Figure 8–22 Multifixture rest room. (Illustration by Author.)

many facilities. Vinyl wallcoverings and high-gloss paints are more economical and easier to repair. Floors are generally finished in a nonslip ceramic tile since it is easy to clean and lasts a long time. Some small single user rest rooms may be able to be specified with a vinyl tile or sheet goods if allowed by local codes. Carpeting is rarely used in the rest room facilities themselves in commercial spaces due to difficulty of maintenance and potential bacteria growth.

Some locations, such as hotels, large restaurants, department stores, and large corporate office facilities, may provide a ladies lounge along with the rest room. This is planned so that the patron walks through the lounge before entering the rest room proper. A few chairs or a sofa may be placed in the lounge. Some facilities provide a separate makeup counter with low stools or chairs in the lounge. In this case, a mirror and lighting appropriate for putting on makeup is necessary.

The design of rest room facilities can be made an interesting part of the whole facility or actually be a disappointment in the total design. Beautiful lounges and rest rooms were the norm in high-rise and specialty business spaces in the early and mid-20th centuries. Unfortunately, many businesses do not allow designers to make the rest rooms as interesting in design as the rest of the space. Although function is very important, design of the rest room can be an interesting design challenge to any interior designer.

Summary

Institutional facilities involve a great number of very specialized commercial interiors. This chapter has discussed some of the key issues in the design of a few of the types of interiors often classified as institutional spaces. Designers who become involved in the interior design of one or more of these types of facilities will be challenged in many ways in order to create interesting spaces that meet the varied needs of the client and the users of the interiors.

It is very important for the interior designer to research the business and characteristics of the business prior to the initial interview with the potential client. Understanding the client and the client's needs is of paramount importance to any client, not least of which would be any of the specialized client spaces reviewed in this section. Recognizing the needs and goals of the ownership or management of institutional interiors projects brings together the designer's skills in preparing program statements, space planning decisions, specialized furniture specifications, materials specification, lighting design, and codes compliance.

This chapter has briefly discussed the key elements in the planning and design of banks, museums, theaters, religious facilities, libraries, and educational facilities. It has also included a discussion in the planning and design of public restroom facilities. The references listed below can provide more detailed information on the planning of these interiors and help the reader gain a fuller understanding of the functional concerns of institutional facility design.

References

American Association of Museums. 1998. *The Official Museum Directory*, 28th ed. National Register Publishing.

Appleton, Ian. 1996. *Buildings for the Performing Arts: A Design and Development Guide.* Oxford, England: Butterworth Architecture.

Architectural Record. 1977. "The Getty Center." November. Pp. 72–105.

Barrie, Thomas. 1996. *Spiritual Path, Sacred Place: Myth, Ritual and Meaning in Architecture.* Boston, MA: Shambhala.

Bennett, Corwin. 1977. *Spaces for People.* Englewood Cliffs, NY: Prentice-Hall.

Brawne, Michael. 1982. *The Museum Interior.* New York: Architecture Books.

Brown, Catherine R., William B. Fleissig, and William R. Morrish. 1984. *Building for the Arts: A Guidebook for the Planning and Design of Cultural Facilities.* Santa Fe, NM: Western States Arts Foundation.

Clawney, Paul. 1982. *Exploring Churches.* Grand Rapids, MI: W. B. Eerdmans.

Copplestone, Trewin, Editor. 1963. *World Architecture*. London, England: Hamlyn.

Deiss, William A. 1984. *Museum Archives*. Chicago, IL: The Society of American Archivists.

Dillon, Joan and David Naylor. 1997. *American Theaters: Performance Halls of the Nineteenth Century*. New York: Preservation Press.

Dober, Richard P. 1992. *Campus Design*. New York: Wiley.

Fisher, Bobbi. 1995. *Thinking and Learning Together*. Portsmouth, NH: Heinemann.

Forsyth, M. 1987. *Auditoria: Designing for the Performing Arts*. London, England: Bartsford.

Fraser, Barry J. and Herbert J. Walberg. 1991. *Educational Environments*. New York: Oxford.

Graves, Ben E. 1993. *School Ways—The Planning and Design of America's Schools*. New York: McGraw-Hill.

Green, Edward E. 1996. "Fitting New Technologies into Traditional Classrooms: Two Case Studies in the Design of Improved Learning Facilities." *Educational-Technology*. July-August.

Harrigan, J. E. 1987. *Human Factors Research*. New York: Elsevier Dutton.

Harvey, Tom. 1996. *The Banking Revolution*. Chicago, IL: Irwin Professional.

Holly, Henry Hudson. 1971. *Church Architecture*. Hartford, CT: Mallory.

Izenour, George C. 1988. *Theatre Design*. New York: McGraw-Hill.

Jackson, Philip W. 1991. *Life in Classrooms*. New York: Teachers College Press.

Jankowski, Wanda. 1987. *The Best of Lighting Design*. New York: PBC International.

Klein, Judy Graf. 1982. *The Office Book*. New York: Facts on File.

Lake, Sheri. 1997. "Government/Institutional Design Specialty." *ASID Professional Designer*. May/June. Pp. 24 ff.

Lord, Peter and Duncan Templeton. 1986. *The Architecture of Sound*. London, England: Architectural Press.

Maguire, Robert Alfred. 1965. *Modern Churches of the World*. New York: Dutton.

Mahnke, Frank H. and Rudolph H. Mahnke. 1987. *Color and Light in Man-Made Environments*. New York: Van Nostrand Reinhold.

McGahey, Richard, Mary Malloy, Katherine Kazanas, and Michael P. Jacobs. 1990. *Financial Services, Financial Centers*. Boulder, CO: Westview Press.

Merriam-Webster's Collegiate Dictionary, 10th ed. 1994. Springfield, MA: Merriam-Webster.

Moore, Kevin. 1997. *Museums and Popular Culture*. London, England: Cassel.

Munn, Glenn G., F. L. Garcia, and Charles J. Woelfel. 1991. *The St. James Encyclopedia of Banking and Finance*, 9th ed. Chicago, IL: St. James Press.

Museum of Fine Arts, Houston, TX, and Parnassus Foundation. 1990. *Money Matters: A Critical Look at Bank Architecture*. New York: McGraw-Hill.

New Encyclopedia Britannica, 15th ed. 1981. Chicago, IL: Benton.

Packard, Robert and Balthazar Korab. 1995. *Encyclopedia of American Architecture*, 2nd ed. New York: McGraw-Hill.

Patterson, W. M. 1975. *A Manual of Architecture for Churches*. Nashville, TN: Methodist Publishing House.

Pevsner, Nicholas. 1976. *A History of Building Types*. Princeton, NJ: Princeton University Press.

Pile, John. 1990. *Dictionary of 20th Century Design.* New York: Facts on File.

———. 1995. *Interior Design,* 2nd ed. Englewood Cliffs, NJ: Prentice-Hall.

Propst, Robert. Date unknown. *High School: The Process and the Place.* Report from Educational Facilities Laboratories, Inc., New York.

Raschko, B. B. 1982. *Housing Interiors for the Disabled and Elderly.* New York: Van Nostrand Reinhold.

Reznikoff, S. C. 1979. *Specifications for Commercial Interiors.* New York: Watson-Guptill.

———. 1986. *Interior Graphic and Design Standards.* New York: Watson-Guptill.

Solinger, Janet W. 1990. *Museums and Universities.* New York: Macmillan.

Steele, James. 1996. *Theatre Buildings.* London, England: Academy Editors.

Tillman, Peggy and Barry Tillman. 1991. *Human Factors Essentials: An Ergonomics Guide for Designers, Engineers, Scientists, and Managers.* New York: McGraw-Hill.

Violan, Michael and Shimon-Craig Van Collie. 1992. *Retail Banking Technology.* New York: Wiley.

Wheeler, J. L. 1941. *The American Public Library Building: Planning and Design with Special Reference to its Administration and Service.* New York: Scribner.

Wilkes, Joseph A. (Editor in Chief) and Robert T. Packard (Associate Editor). 1988. *Encyclopedia of Architecture, Design, Engineering, and Construction.* Volumes 1 through 5. New York: Wiley.

Williams, Peter W. 1997. *Houses of God: Architecture in the US.* Urbana, IL: University of Illinois Press.

Additional references related to material in this chapter are listed in Appendix A.

Chapter 9

Project Management

Many clients assume all interior designers can more or less do the same thing, that is, can create an appropriate interior. Often there is little difference in the client's mind between the creative skills of interior designer "A" and interior designer "B" when considering award of a design contract. What does differentiate between firms and what matters to clients in today's market is the firm's ability to manage a project from beginning to end. Commercial projects such as those discussed in the previous chapters require more than excellent creative skills; these complex projects also require management skills to coordinate massive amounts of detail and numerous activities executed by teams of designers. In other words, these large projects require project management as well as creative design solutions.

Project management should be important to interior designers regardless of the size of the firm. For so many interior designers, fees from project work are the major source of revenue, and mismanaging the project can consume profit margins. Effective project management provides the opportunity for greater profits and helps to minimize problems. Unfortunately, too many firms do not use effective project management techniques, leaving themselves vulnerable to irate clients and inadequate profitability.

To successfully execute a design project, interior designers depend on a process of work that takes them from initial information gathering through final installation and client move-in. This design process is mirrored by a project management process that assists the designer in successfully completing all the required work. Students must gain an appreciation of project management in order to better navigate their way along the process and understand that completing an interior design project is more than aesthetic problem solving.

This chapter begins by defining project management and discuses the responsibilities of the project manager. The main body of the chapter covers the project management process with emphasis on working relationships, proposals, scheduling, and budgeting. It will also briefly review postoccupancy evaluations and the role of computer applications in project management.

What Is Project Management?

In design practice, *project management* is a systematic process used to coordinate and control a design project from inception to completion. Project management requires leadership, planning, coordination, and control of a diverse set of activities, people, money, and time in order to accomplish the goals of the design project. Good project management permits the design firm to take the project from inception to conclusion as successfully, painlessly, and profitably as possible. A successful project is one that is completed on time, within or under budget, and that meets the design goals of the project and client. Poor project management leads to dissatisfied clients, frustrated team members, and possible litigation.

The overriding goal of project management is to bring the project to a successful conclusion. What "successful conclusion" means varies with the party. To the client, a successful conclusion may mean moving into rearranged office space or into a remodeled and updated restaurant on time and within the budget. To the design firm, a successful conclusion could mean making a profit on the design fees. Knowing those different meanings is part of the project manager's job.

Project management is not solely focused on the creative solution to the project, but involves all aspects of the project. Documenting all meetings, maintaining project control books for the specification of merchandise, and insuring that construction drawings are prepared correctly are a few project management activities. In addition, accurate determination of the scope of work, control of the budget, quality assurance of the work performed by the design team, and control of the schedule are also important.

The person responsible for the project is the project manager, referred to as the PM by many firms. An excellent project manager is one who plans the project process and determines who will be responsible for all the project design requirements, determines how to meet client expectations and goals, leads the decision-making, and successfully anticipates problems and manages resources. He or she will also be responsible for documentation, scheduling, and communication between the parties involved. The next section looks in detail at the project manager's responsibilities.

The Project Manager

In essence, the responsibilities of the project manager do not vary by much in a small firm versus a large firm. Of course, large firms will be engaged in projects of larger scale and complexity than most small firms. Who serves as a project manager does vary, however. In small firms, the project manager is commonly the principal or the designer assigned the project. He or she will not only design the project, but will also make all the decisions, keep all the records, attend all the meetings, and be fully responsible for the execution of the project. In large firms, the project manager is usually an experienced designer, with over 5 to 10 years experience, who has shown capabilities of handling the scheduling, planning, leadership, and control qualities necessary to manage a large design project.

As can be seen in Figure 9-1, the project manager must wear many hats. He or she must be comfortable and experienced in all aspects of interior design project work and know how to get things done. Many of the qualifications of a good project manager are shown in Figure 9-2. Of course, individual project managers may want to add other responsibilities and qualifications to these lists. To some degree or another, all these qualifications are necessary when executing any size project regardless of the title the designer holds. The importance of these skills only intensifies when the project is large and complex. Let us look at how these qualifications apply to the work of the project manager.

Planning involves determining the scope of work to be done, by whom, and how, as well as scheduling the project. Ideally, the PM is involved in the development of the project definition and scope. Unfortunately, some firms are set up so that a different individual makes the contact with the client and develops the project scoping statement[1] rather than any designers who will be responsible for executing the project. This can lead to confusion and omissions in what

---

[1]A *scoping statement* details what will be done and possibly the estimated fee for the project.

Determine scope of services
Determine project team members
Determine how the project will be done
Prepare, review, and control schedule
Prepare, review and control budgets
Manage and motivate the project team
Manage the project
Interact with client
Interact with technical consultants and other stakeholders
Technical supervision, especially codes compliance and mechanical interface
Act as agent between design firm and the client
Must be ready to make a decision when needed to keep the project moving
Serve the client
Control project budget
Billing reports and possibly preparation of invoices
Marketing to obtain new jobs
Proposal preparation and presentation/negotiation
Control project quality standards
Resolving conflicts
Lead the project team to insure work is done according to specified standards on time and on budget.

Figure 9–1 Project manager's typical responsibilities.

Effective communicator both speaking and writing
People manager
Good negotiator
Very organized
Strong technical knowledge of interior design
Self-motivated
Good decision maker
Good personal professionalism
Sense of humor

Figure 9–2 Qualifications of a good project manager.

must be done as well as conflicts between what must be done and the amount of fee available to do the work.

Planning also involves selecting the design team members. The project manager will oversee the design team as designers are commonly assigned to actually do the design and specification work. The manager must control the work of the project team to insure a satisfactory level of quality in the production of design drawings, constructions documents, and specifications. Designers have different skills and abilities and the project manager, in conjunction with the design director or principal, should select team members who are best suited for the project, not those who are available. The project manager must be familiar with the working methods of each team member so that he or she will have an easier time in motivating and controlling the work output of the team members. Design directors and principals should refrain from being all-involved with the selection of the team and scheduling of the work, thereby negating the importance of the project manager.

Scheduling is another important responsibility and relates to the project manager's need to be fully aware of how long it takes for phases of the design and construction/installation work to be executed. The project manager will be responsible for determining when each phase of the design project is to be done starting from the expected move-in date and working backwards. Then he or she will coordinate with the owner's representative and general contractor concerning the schedule for actual build-out of the interior. Project managers must control the schedule to insure work is done on time and in proper sequence. In addition, the project manager may work with the vendors supplying products and services to insure that goods arrive on time and only when needed during the construction project.

Project management also requires management of finances. In order to obtain the contract to do the design project, the PM and the principal in charge must determine the budget for salaries and project costs to design and supervise the project. This estimate must be prepared carefully to cover direct and overhead costs as well as earn an expected profit. In addition, budgeting may also be necessary for certain construction and installation costs, depending, of course, on the role and responsibility of the interior design firm. The project manager and the principal must control the budget to insure that the project design, specification, and actual work invested in the project remain within the budget constraints of the client and those projected for the actual project work.

It is also important for project managers to be good communicators and negotiators. A project manager must be talented at working with other designers, design professionals, and clients. He or she will have meetings not only with the client, but also with the project architect and the general and subcontractors. He or she will enter into discussions with vendors and installers, perhaps even with employees of the client not directly involved in the project. The project manager needs to know how to motivate and encourage his or her design team, and negotiate and collaborate with subcontractors and vendors not directly under his or her authority. Good communication and negotiation techniques are necessary to alleviate problems and concerns between parties.

It is easy for the reader to see that executing a project is much more than the creative problem-solving of designing a restaurant, church, office, store, medical facility, or whatever the space. In the opinion of many experienced designers, the creative side is the easy part. Project management is the harder part and the part that truly determines whether or not the firm makes any money on the project. The remainder of this chapter deals more directly with the responsibilities of the project manager as the project management process is discussed in detail.

The Process

By now the reader has gained an appreciation for the complexities of project management and the activities for which the project manager is responsible. Project management is a process of planning, organizing, and controlling design activities and responsibilities, and its goal is the same as that of most other aspects of interior design: a project that ends successfully for the client and the design firm. This section discusses the process and covers the key topics of working relationships, proposals and contracts, the work plan, scheduling methods, budgeting, and documentation.

Working Relationships

A major project such as those discussed in the previous chapters requires the coordination and teamwork of many individuals. The project manager must be able to supervise those team members in the design firm assisting on the project and be able to negotiate and communicate with many others. Stakeholders is a term associated with the many individuals and groups involved in any design project. In fact, *stakeholders* are individuals who have a vested interest in the project such as the design firm principals, design team, client, architect, general contractor, vendors, and so on. Here we discuss the roles of many of the stakeholders in relationship to the project manager, starting with the design firm.

The principals of the firm are, of course, the owners of the design practice. In many commercial design projects, the principal is directly involved in the project and may, in fact, act as the project manager. Principals are involved for two primary reasons. First, they like to remain actively involved in design. Second, clients like to have the owners involved, even be the key designer and manager of the client's project. In the largest firms, however, the principals play a smaller role, turning over most of the responsibility and activity to the project manager and design team. In these larger firms principals are more likely to attend the final marketing presentations to the client, review proposal documents, participate in the planning and negotiating of the contracts, and be kept informed of the progress of all work in the firm. Of course, in smaller firms, the principal will be more directly involved in the whole of the project.

Determining the design team might be one of the hardest parts of project management. Personal interests should be put aside as the project manager must select team members based on their abilities and experience. Too often someone who has the time to do the project may not be the best person because of a lack of experience, while those with the experience become overcommitted and have a more difficult time performing at a high level on each project. Thus the project manager is constantly playing a balancing act in determining who should gain experience by working on the project in a minor role, while not overcommitting more experienced designers.

An important part of the project manager's working relationship with the design team is knowing how to delegate responsibility and trust members of the design team. Project managers and principals accept overall responsibility for the project. However, if they require team members to show them every small detail for approval, the project will be slowed down and, frankly, team members will be frustrated. In order for delegation to work effectively, the project manager must select the right tasks to be delegated. This begins by understanding what can be done by team members and what the manager must do himself or herself. If the client expects the PM to be highly involved in the design of the facility, then that manager should not delegate all design responsibility to others. Delegation also involves control. Providing important scheduling and setting time limits on delegated tasks are part of the project manager's job and are helpful for team members. In addition, progress reports and meetings should be regularly required so that the project manager is comfortable in knowing the work is getting done on schedule. Meetings give each team member and the project manager a chance to discuss any issue about the progress of the project openly, as well as the opportunity to consider options for resolving problems. Progress reports have become common as firms increasingly use computer scheduling and other project management software to take care of record-keeping.

Clients come in two basic types—those who have worked with an interior designer or other design professional before and those who have not. The first group can be further subdivided into those who have worked successfully with a design professional before and those who have had a bad experience. It should be easy to see that the clients who have not worked with a designer before or who have had a bad encounter will require careful communication and strategies to keep them comfortable with the design process and the way the firm works. Whatever the previous experience a client has had with designers, there are also those clients who like to "micromanage" a project and those who just want to be kept informed. A client who likes to micromanage all aspects of his or her business will require far more of the project manager's time as he or she must make more frequent phone calls and site visits, and send more memos to that type of client.

Regardless of the client's prior experience with design professionals, it is important that the project manager and the design team understand who the client is. Of course, it is the individual or company that has hired the design firm. But many commercial projects also have other "clients," such as the employees and users of the interiors. For institutional projects, the clients also include the governmental agency responsible for the space. Not all of these "clients" will be part of the decision-making process, but they must all be understood and satisfied none the less. Clients are looking for designers who understand the client's business first, understand the wishes of the client second, and take care of the designer's interests last. What is it that clients want?

A key issue is who at the design firm is in charge. Clients want to know to whom they should go for answers to their questions—a *single source of contact*. Clients want that single source of contact to get answers to all their questions. For example, a client wants to know who can tell him or her why the wallpaper hanger isn't on the job site when, according to the schedule and design firm's responsibilities, he is supposed to be there. The project manager is naturally that single source of contact.

Clients want to be kept informed about the progress of the project. In many cases this is because they must report to a boss about the project and no one ever wants to look foolish to his or her boss when asked a questions about a project. When the work plan and schedule have been completed, it is therefore important for the project manager to review these items with the client—and furthermore to keep him or her informed throughout the project. The client has a business to get organized or keep running while he or she is trying to prepare for move-in. Thus the client will worry about the construction and installation schedule as much as the design firm.

Clients want to know how things will be done. This is an important point for clients right from the beginning of negotiations. It is not just a matter of what will be done, but how. Companies that have worked with different designers in the past will understand that firms work differently and the client will want to understand how this firm goes about completing a project. Clients who have rarely worked with designers will need to be educated on the whole process of design as conducted by the design firm.

Clients also expect technical competence. Knowledge of the client's business, how to design for that type of business, and the many codes and regulations that affect the design of the project are among the technical competencies expected by clients. Many projects include technical issues that may go beyond the expertise of the average interior designer. When this is the case, the design firm may want to enter into a joint venture with another firm in order to provide the necessary competencies required for the project. Plunging into a project that is beyond the experience scope or the technical competence of a design firm is serious business and should not be undertaken.

Finally, clients want designers who understand budgeting and cost control. The deep pockets that many clients had years ago, and that interior designers enjoyed, have vanished. Projecting a workable budget for the project, and sticking to that budget are very important in today's economy. Unfortunately, it is also true that many clients still want that "silk purse from a sow's ear." Achieving that requires budgeting and good design sense. The concept of value engineering has become very important in large commercial design projects. As it applies to interior design, *value engineering* means considering both the initial capital costs of the design or product specified and the life cycle costs of maintenance and replacement concerning that concept or item. The idea is to come up with a design or an item that is not judged on initial cost alone, but on its value over the useful life of the project or product as well. "Value engineering gets closer to cost control because it looks at ways to reduce costs on specific items or activities. It focuses only on specific items in the design, procurement, or construction area."[2]

The architectural firm involved in the project is another stakeholder with whom the interiors project manager must work. In some cases, an interior design firm may have a strong working relationship with one or two architectural firms that will prepare and seal drawings[3] for the interior designer. In commercial projects such as those described in the preceding chapters, the design firm often will be hired as a subconsultant or as a party to a joint venture with the architect for the completion of the design of a project. In other cases, the client will hire the architectural firm and the interior designer on separate contracts, yet still expect them to coordinate and work together to complete the project.

Contractors and subcontractors are another group of stakeholders. For most large construction projects today the client will hire a construction manager (CM) to oversee the entire process. In many cases, the CM has taken over some of the responsibilities formerly held by the

---

[2]Ritz, 1994, p. 243.

[3]A *sealed drawing* is a reference to the architect affixing his or her seal, which signifies that the architect is licensed by the state. A seal cannot generally be affixed to drawings produced by someone outside the architectural office or without the supervision of the architect.

architectural firm. The construction management job grew out of the former architectural field superintendent who was on the job site most of the day observing the construction work. A CM is a lot like a project manager in that he or she must plan, control, and organize the construction process and will work with the interiors project manager throughout the course of the project.

A general contractor (GC) is a firm that has overall responsibility to actually build the project. The GC is usually represented by a lead individual, also called a project manager, who is supported by a field superintendent. The GC will obtain bids from various trade subcontractors (often called subs) for the pieces of the building puzzle. After evaluating these bids, the general contractor determines which companies he or she will use for bidding on a particular project. Should the bid go to the GC, the subs will be hired to do the actual work. The GC meets with various stakeholders to review the progress of the job and whenever questions about the work occur.

The trade subcontractors are the companies or individuals who are doing the actual work on the job site, the framers, masons, electricians, plumbers, painters, and so on. The subs work for the general contractor who reports to a CM or to the project owner. On small projects, such as a small remodeling project, subs might be hired directly by the client since a GC might not be needed. Due to the complex interrelationships of construction documents, clients should be directed by the project manager not to communicate directly to the trade workers on the job site. Project managers and construction managers must make it clear to the client that if the client has a question about some work being done on the job site, then that question should be directed to the project manager and/or the construction manager, who will then check on the inquiry and take care of the issue.

Proposals and Contracts

To many designers, a proposal and a contract are the same thing, and that may indeed can be the case for many projects that are not extremely complicated. However, for larger firms both a proposal and a contract is prepared. A *proposal* is a marketing document that outlines what will be done and how it will be done, who will do it, and other information the client has requested or the design firm wishes to provide. It does not generally hold the same kind of legal weight as a contract since it generally does not include the fees for the work. Today, most large projects begin with a request for proposal, or RFP. A *request for proposal* is a document prepared by the client that provides an overview of the scope and the client's goals for the project. Its purpose is to avoid the client's having to interview a large number of design firms, while still obtaining the kinds of information about firms that would have been obtained at personal interviews. It is, in a sense, a form of bidding for the job, though fees are not necessarily part of the RFPs requirements.

Depending on the size of the job, the proposal can be quite lengthy. It is very important for the design firm to focus its response in terms of the stated or interpreted needs expressed by the RFP. Not answering specific questions could mean the firm does not get an interview, let alone the project. Many firms utilize a certain amount of "boilerplate" information in preparing proposals. Those items might include descriptions of how the project will be done, the resumés of team members, and certain kinds of information about the firm.

Should the client require a specific outline, the firm must use that, of course. Otherwise a common outline for a formal proposal or the design firm's response to the RFP includes a cover letter, an executive summary providing the highlights of the total proposal, and a table of contents. These parts would be followed by the problem analysis, which is the firm's opportunity to explain its interpretation of the client's needs; scope of services; project approach, which will explain how the firm would go about the project; staffing; project schedule; budget; qualifications, which defines the firm's credentials and ability to do the project; and references or client list.

Proposals are looked at very carefully by clients and review committees. Reviewers will look for different things, but the important criteria always come down to certain issues. Does the firm understand the project needs? Does the firm have the experience to do the project? Can they do the work on time and within budget? Is the fee competitive and in range with the client's budget for the fee? Of course, other issues could also be relevant to the client or the project.

Before a contract is awarded, the client will determine a short list[4] of firms for personal interviews. Clients will review all the proposals and through their own decision-making process determine perhaps three or more firms who seem most qualified to execute the project. It is these firms that make up the short list. Design firms then have time to prepare a presentation in which they provide additional information about how they work. At the interview the design firm will provide a contract, which adds the all important fee structure to the information the client needs to make a decision. Presentations also provide the client with the opportunity to meet the project manager, principal, and some of the design team who will work on the project. After all the presentations are completed, the client will determine which firm seems most appropriate to meet their design and fee needs and will enter into any final negotiation on the contract.

Interior designers can use standardized contracts such as those available from ASID or AIA or can draft contracts of their own authorship. The reader may wish to review materials in Berger, Jenks, Piotrowski, Thompson, or others referenced at the end of this chapter for guidelines and examples of design contracts used in interior design projects.

The Work Plan

After the award of the contract, the project manager will develop a work plan. The *work plan* defines all the tasks that are needed to take the project from inception to completion. It will define what must be done, resources needed, how tasks will be accomplished, budgeting, and when tasks must be completed. Once written, it is not set in stone, as it must live and breathe along with the project itself. Situations will occur requiring modifications in the work plan due to such things as a missed completion date, unexpected delays in receiving goods, a change in the design team due to illness or someone leaving the company, or unanticipated price increases that create the need to respecify products.

The foundation for the work plan is the recognized project process made up of six steps. Those steps are: programming, schematic design, design development, construction document, contract administration and postinstallation. Figure 9-3 shows the typical activities of each phase.

What must be executed is defined in the scope of services. The scope of services in the design contract spells out in reasonably definite terms all the parts of the project determined to be necessary. The scope of services should be detailed enough to limit the work of the design firm to what is needed without leaving the firm open to doing additional work without proper compensation. However, the firm does not want to give the impression that they are unwilling to do additional work. It is suggested that a clause in the design contract deal with extra services as a separate item.

The scope of services will also dictate other tasks. The kind of documentation to be provided, such as construction drawings, specifications, and sample boards, must be finalized. These tangible design products are called *deliverables*. In addition, it is necessary to estimate and finalize the expected number of meetings required with clients, consultants, subconsultants, vendors, and others.

When each task must be started and accomplished is laid out in the schedule. This is particularly important for large projects, but administering a project schedule is important for any size project. The project manager along with team members will estimate the work schedule. Of course, the schedule will also need to be coordinated with the client, and possibly the architect, general contractors, and perhaps some vendors. Scheduling techniques are discussed in greater detail later in this chapter.

---

[4] *Short lists* refer to when design projects are bid out by the client to obtain the actual design firm. Since numerous firms often respond to the request from the client, a short list of the top firms are determined for actual interviews.

Programming
   Client interviewing and project information gathering
   Determine client project goals
   Furniture, equipment inventories
   Determine new furniture and equipment preferences
   Aesthetic preferences
   Obtain base building plan or measure site
   Lease review
   Develop scoping statement
Schematic Design
   Finalize scoping statement or design concept statement
   Preliminary sketches and drawings of space plan
   Preliminary drawings of elevations, details, etc.
   Preliminary selections of FF & E
   Budget
   ADA Compliance survey
Design Development
   Finalize space plan
   Finalize furniture layouts
   Finalize FF & E selections
   Finalize budgets
   Prepare bid specifications (furniture and equipment)
Construction Documentation
   Prepare and finalize construction drawings and documents
   Prepare construction specifications
   Prepare construction schedules
   Prepare other construction drawings such as:
      Demolition plan
      Millwork plans and elevations
      Reflected ceiling plan/lighting plan
      Systems furniture installation plans
Construction Administration
   Bid analysis
   Observation of construction/installation work
   Preparation of change orders
   Ordering of FF & E if this is the designer's responsibility
Project completion
   Inspecting job site for complete installation of FF & E
   Create punch list of omissions and damages
   Post-occupancy evaluations

Note: this list is not all-inclusive, but details the most often executed activities. Of course, these phases also include meetings with the various stakeholders and can involve out-of-town travel to the job site.

Figure 9–3 Typical activities for each step in the work plan.

Who will be involved in the project is another aspect of the work plan. As discussed above, the project manager must determine which design staff members will be involved in the project and each of their responsibilities. Clearly defined roles and responsibilities are necessary and discussed up front to insure that the project keeps moving along toward on-time completion. In addition to the design team, the project manager must know who is the single source of contact at the client's place of business. It is very difficult for the project designer to have to answer to multiple individuals "in authority" during the process of the project.

An additional consideration that overlays most aspects of the process is quality control. Project managers must be sure that the quality of the work produced by team members meets the standards established by the firm. Quality control goes beyond insuring that the "look" of the drawings and documents meet standards. Design documents must also indicate that the project has been designed to meet code requirements, standards of construction quality necessary for the project, the budget, and generally accepted practice. In a time when litigation seems commonplace, it behooves the project manager to insist on and check for quality standards.

It is important that the design team be involved in the development of the work plan. Those that must execute the work plan should have input into it in order for them to "buy into" what must be done. Having the team members take part in developing the work plan also means that work efforts will not be duplicated during the life of the project.

Scheduling Methods

Project schedules are important for any size design project, and are, of course, critical to large or complex projects. Few if any of the project types discussed in the preceding chapters could be successfully accomplished without a detailed schedule. Project schedules are important for another reason. Few designers are working on only one project at a time, day in and day out. In some firms, it is not unusual for a designer to have some portion of the responsibility for six, ten, maybe more projects in any one month. Individual time management techniques are necessary for the team members to handle the amount of work on these varying projects. Time management will not be included in this chapter. The reader is directed to the references at the end of the chapter or other references on time management techniques.

Initial schedules are determined at the time the fee for the project is developed. This preliminary schedule must be broad, but must be based on sound planning principles. Detailed schedules generally would be completed when the contract has been awarded for the project. This section discusses methods of detailed scheduling of the project.

The key issue in scheduling complex projects is to break the project down into manageable parts. The scope of services begins that process by dividing the project into the steps in the project process and determining which tasks will be performed within each step. Unfortunately, a copy of the scope of services alone does not break down those tasks into those smaller tasks. Good project management requires that the work plan break down tasks into small steps. That task is necessary to successfully create a useful project schedule.

Project schedules can be done in different ways. The simplest scheduling method is the use of a *milestone chart* (Figure 9-4). In this approach tasks are listed on the left with three additional columns of information. As the figure shows, another column indicates who is responsible for each task and a third column gives a target date for the task. This target date is usually the completion date. Additional columns can be provided for start dates and actual completion dates. Although this technique can be used for commercial projects, today most design firms do not use it as their main scheduling technique for such projects.

Another simple method is a Gantt or *bar chart* (Figure 9-5), developed by Henry Gantt.[5]

Activity Description	*Start Date*	*Target Completion Date*	*Actual Completion Date*
Programming	8/4	8/8	8/7
Schematic Drawings	8/8	8/22	8/22
Finalize Floor Plans	8/25	9/5	9/8
Finalize Specifications	8/25	9/5	9/5
Complete Construction Documents	9/4	9/24	
Construction	9/8	10/3	
Finishes Installation	9/22	10/1	
Furniture Installation	10/1	10/10	
Client Move-in	10/13	10/15	

Figure 9–4 Sample milestone chart.

---

[5] Lewis, 1995a, p. 50.

It consists of a list of activities on the left and bars representing the amount of time (in days, weeks, or months) from start to finish for each task. Bar charts can be further differentiated by who is responsible for each task or parts of the tasks through symbols or color coding. Two important disadvantages of this scheduling method are that it does not easily show the interrelationships of tasks and that it is not easy to see the status of the project. To a degree these disadvantages can be overcome by the actual design of the bar chart—additional information can be shown through symbols and color coding. But at some point on a complex project, these additional bits of information go beyond the bar chart's simplicity, creating confusion.

For complex projects, it is more common for design firms to use the *Critical Path Method* (CPM) of scheduling. The critical path method was developed in the 1950s to help better control construction projects. It is similar to another method called Program Evaluation and Review Technique (PERT) developed by the Navy, also in the 1950s.[6] The difference is that PERT uses three time estimates while CPM uses only one. CPM schedules are not concerned with the day-to-day details unless someone has specifically set up a daily schedule. It is more common for the CPM schedule to be set on a weekly or monthly schedule, depending on the size and overall duration of the project. CPM is the method we discuss here, since it is more commonly used in interior design, architecture, and construction.

"The key to CPM is the determination of the task or tasks which are perceived to take longest to perform within a given overall time frame. Accomplishing these tasks then comprises the 'critical path' to timely completion of that portion of the project schedule."[7] The critical task(s) controls the project. If the task is not completed on time, other tasks cannot be completed, or maybe even started, on time so that the project falls behind schedule. In other words, each task must be completed in order. For example, assuming one task cannot start until the preceding one is complete, the electrical plan cannot be started until the wall locations are finalized.

For a schedule based on CPM to be most useful, it must be detailed and be easy to understand. For example, if during the construction administration phase the project manager used the phrase "construct walls" with no other defined task indicated, it would neither be detailed or nor fully understandable as much information would be missing that is needed to make this term meaningful. Walls can be constructed of wood studs or metal studs or with some other method that meets code requirements. The "construct walls" note also does not specify the complete finishing of the wall. For example, will drywall be used, lath and plaster, or paneling?

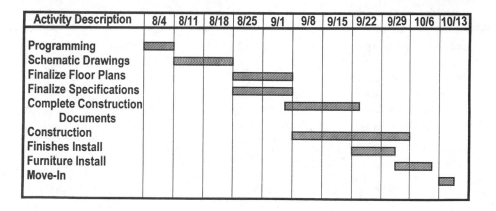

Figure 9–5 Sample Gantt or bar chart.

---

[6]Lewis, 1995a, p. 51.

[7]Birnberg, 1992b, p. 258.

The CPM diagram itself is based on blocks that identify the tasks along with lines or arrows that show the paths (Figure 9-6). As can be seen from the figure, the lines show the direction of the work and which sequence of tasks must be performed before the next task or set of tasks can be performed.

There are basically four steps in developing a CPM schedule. First, of course, would be to determine what must be done. Second, the project manager must determine the interrelationships between tasks. For example, Task A (programming) must be completed before Task B (schematic design) can be begun. In some cases, one task need only be partially completed before the next task starts. For example, in a multistory building, assuming all construction work is completed, carpeting can be installed on the first and second floors while construction work continues in its final stages on upper floors.

The third step in the scheduling process is to determine how long it will take for each task to be accomplished. Experienced project managers will have knowledge and standard guidelines that will tell them how long it will take to plan and design a project. They will also work from experience and with the help of general contractors to understand the length of time of the construction process. In that way, the PM can determine the amount of time needed to design, specify, and complete the construction and installation of the interior for which he or she is responsible. Of course, it is most wise to plan for an optimum and contingent time. The shortest reasonable time is the optimum time. Contingent time is a small allowance for minor problems that might occur.

With these three steps accomplished, the project manager is ready for the fourth step, preparing the actual schedule or entering information into the project management scheduling software. The CPM schedule will identify the tasks as either rectangles (or some other shaped symbol) or bars, depending on the methodology chosen by the project manager. These graphics will show clearly the tasks that cannot be started before the next task and those that can be started before the previous task needs to be finished. As this information is graphed, the critical path becomes obvious. Although all tasks need to be managed and controlled by the project manager, the critical path requires particular attention as it can hold up other parts of the project if left undone somewhere along the line.

Computerized scheduling methods using any of the scheduling approaches furnish the project manager an extra advantage. Modifications or updates to the schedule will automatically update the rest of the schedule. If a problem occurs so that the working drawings cannot be completed on time, the project manager can insert the new date and update the schedule, providing these changes to the general contractor and client. A change like this is very important since it may well result in a delay in the whole of the project. Most of today's commercial design firms use some type of computerized project scheduling software. Computer applications are discussed at the end of this chapter.

A note of caution concerning schedules is in order, however. Breaking a schedule down into "microelements" can create a staggering job for the project manager trying to keep up with changes. Even with the use of computer applications for scheduling, it is better to keep the schedule as simple as possible, focusing on proper sequencing rather than minutiae. Schedules are communication tools developed to keep the design team on course and the other stakeholders informed of the project's progress.

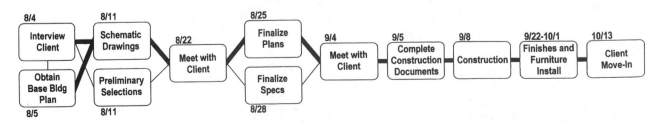

Figure 9–6 Sample CPM diagram. (Illustration by: Alisha Newman.)

Students should begin to use scheduling methods on their studio projects. Students who keep accurate time records on how long it takes them to complete various phases of a design project, begin to learn an important professional skill—time estimating of their work. Added to time records is the actual estimation of time to complete a project at the inception of receiving a studio assignment. This skill will help students better manage time while working on class assignments and prepare them for their professional activities to come.

Budgeting

The project manager should be involved in the determination of the budget for design services. The project manager will also have input into the interiors construction and specification budget for the furniture, fixtures, and equipment (FF & E). He or she has very little if any control over the budget for structural architectural work.

The project manager and principal of the firm will very likely work together to develop the fee the firm will require to complete the work. Like any kind of interiors project, the fee must cover the salary costs of all staff involved in the project, the overhead and expenses related to that project, and a measure of profit.

Two other factors that will also be considered in determining the fee are the competitive nature of the project and the duration of the project. The project manager must make some effort to determine who else might be bidding on the job in order to make the best decision on the final fee methods and amount. For large projects, such as a hotel or hospital, which will take years to complete, the PM should consider the future cost of doing the project. Salaries will likely increase, as will expenses. If the fee does not take into consideration the potential increases in costs, the project could end up losing money rather than being profitable.

Budgeting begins with an analysis of the costs involved to complete the project. First on that list are salary and benefits calculations for each team member including the project manager and any secretarial support personnel. Many firms use the direct personnel expense (DPE) calculation to determine this cost (Figure 9-7). Depending on how a firm has organized the charging of operational costs, certain expenses like copying, blueprinting, telephone calls, faxs, and even some supplies that are used directly in the execution of the contracted project are considered direct expenses and are chargeable to the client. All these estimates can be matched against historic data on similar projects. This will help the project manager estimate how long each phase of the current project will likely take and make for a better fee budget.

An FF & E budget is necessary so that the client understands how much it will cost to furnish and equip the project. The budget for furniture and the rest of the FF & E is commonly set by the client. It is rare that clients provide an unlimited budget to the interior designer for any size commercial project. Commercial clients who have developed properties before are familiar with the costs of furnishing their particular kinds of spaces and will insist the designer work with their budget. New entrepreneurs, such as a small retail store or a bed and breakfast facility, are likely to be less informed on the amount of money required to design, construct, and finish the interiors of their space. In this case, the interior designer will be very helpful in determining the budget.

The most straightforward method of project budgeting is to utilize experience and historical data the design firm has developed to produce budget ranges on the space design and specification of FF & E. For example, with knowledge of the scope of services and an understanding of the goals of the client, the design firm could offer a range of prices for items such as a dining room chair in a restaurant project. Combining the estimated costs of all items required for the interior, the designer establishes the furnishings budget. Cost estimates for construction and finishing materials can be obtained in a similar manner.

Some designers estimate FF & E budgets by a square footage method. In this case, the firm has determined that a type of commercial project generally will cost so many dollars a square foot to furnish. The estimate is arrived at by simply multiplying the square footage of the project by the dollar factor.

DIRECT PERSONAL EXPENSE

Expense Type	(Average Monthly Amount)		
	Design Staff	Support Staff	TOTAL
1. Annual Salary			
2. Projected Salary Increases			
3. TOTAL ANNUAL SALARY EXPENSES			
4. Paid Vacations			
5. Paid Holidays			
6. Sick Leave			
7. FICA			
8. Unemployment Compensation			
9. Workman's Compensation			
10. Group Health Insurance			
11. Group Supplemental Insurance			
12. Life Insurance			
13. Retirement Plan			
14. Profit Sharing Plan			
15. Professional Association Dues			
16. Educational Fees			
17. Other:			
18. Other:			
19. Other:			
20. TOTAL ANNUAL BENEFITS (line 4-19)			

$$\frac{\text{Total Annual Benefits (line 20)}}{\text{Total Annual Salary Expense (line 3)}} = \text{\% of Benefits as Part of Salary Expense}$$

Yearly Billable Salary = Annual Salary Expense of Design — Unbillable Salary
(Subtract % value in dollars)

Figure 9–7 Sample DPE worksheet. (From Piotrowski, *Interior Design Management*. Copyright © 1990. Reprinted by permission of John Wiley & Sons, Inc.)

For FF & E budgets, designers also need to calculate such things as applicable sales tax and freight, delivery, and installation charges. Depending on responsibility, the project manager may also need to estimate moving costs.

For those times the interior designer is involved in some way with construction budgeting, the designer may use one of the following methods for budgets. Construction costs estimates can be obtained by discussing the project with a consulting general contractor who can estimate ranges of construction costs for all phases of the building project. Designers who do not wish to work with a consulting general contractor in this way can utilize cost estimating references published annually. However, these references may not be accurate for the location of the job and should be used with a certain amount of caution if no other reference of construction costs is obtained.

For the student and professional inexperienced in budgeting commercial projects, references like *Means Interior Cost Data* and *Means Interior Estimating* can be helpful. When these references are not available, the inexperienced budgeter must resort to reviewing catalogs and obtaining information from manufacturer's representatives or suppliers.

Documentation

The execution of design projects generates a great deal of documentation or paperwork. Part of the project manager's responsibility, and a very important part of the process, is maintaining that documentation. Firms use job books or file folders to hold all the paperwork associated with a project. Even if many pieces of paper are generated on computer disks, no one has yet figured out how to really have a paperless office, resulting in numerous hard copies.

What has to be documented? Figure 9-8 provides an answer to that question. As the reader can see by these examples, quite a bit of material must be recorded and maintained as a record of the progress and work for a design project. Many of these items will be updated and the full series of items maintained until the project is completed. Should any disputes arise, these copies will be very important to validate the design firm's position in the dispute.

Some of the most important pieces of documentation that should be kept on hand and recorded are all correspondence to and from the client as well as to and from the designer to other stakeholders in the project. Meeting notes, telephone call notes, copies of faxes and E-mails, and transmittals, are the primary examples of correspondence that can be vital for record-keeping. Of course, copies of the RFP, the proposal, and the contract are all additional necessary items of record.

Correspondence
   RFP from client
   Proposal from design firm
   Contract
   Letters, memos, transmittals from design firm to client and other stakeholders
   Letters, memos, transmittals from client to design firm
   Other general correspondence
   Meeting notes
Project Correspondence
   Project schedules
   Meeting notes
   Memos to vendors
   Furniture specification forms
   Client interview forms
   Job-site analysis forms
   Existing furniture inventories
   Budgeting forms
   Other project correspondence
   Post-occupancy evaluations
Design Documents
   Preliminary floor plans and other design drawings
   Preliminary specifications sheets
   Samples
   Client approved drawings and specifications
   Final furniture and construction drawings
   Final specifications
Internal Documents
   Time records
   Billing records
   Expense records
   Invoices
   Post-project evaluations (internal)

Figure 9–8 Documents commonly maintained in a project job book.

Another important piece of documentation that larger firms in particular generate are project status reports. Time records, updated schedules, budget reports, and billing information are the kinds of information that can be used to produce status reports. The simplest of these to produce would be a type of variance analysis that can be used to look at the projected schedule and actual schedule. Whatever scheduling method was used will show what the estimated due dates were as well as perhaps estimates as to how long each significant task would require. Actual dates of completion and time records can be easily obtained and compared against estimates in order to view current status as well as successful estimation.

Time records and billing statements can be used to develop budget status reports on the service fees. Although the project manager wants the design work to be done creatively and accurately, it is also important to produce work profitably. The project manager must keep on top of the time invested in the design project by the team members to be sure both that they are keeping accurate time records and that they are working productively. For many firms, "time is money," and productive work by team members is a key way the firm remains profitable when completing any design project.

Of course, any kind of information that the firm needs to record progress on a project can be converted to status reports. Reimbursable expenses, direct project expenses, overhead contribution, consultants' expenses, additional services, time spent in meetings, and other factors can be recorded and studied. All these different status reports help the project manager and the team members to control the project and control budgets as well as project progress. And while status reports are useful during the course of the project, they also can be used after the project is completed to help the principal, project manager, and design team make better estimates for similar projects in the future.

Record-keeping of the project documents is not a job only for the project manager. He or she will be the central holder of all this paper, but each member of the design team should also be keeping his or her own records. Time sheets, meeting notes, schedules, and correspondence to and from suppliers are some of the records that team members will need to maintain on each project. As it might be easy for the reader to imagine, volumes of documentation could be generated for large projects. However, all of it is necessary, either as hard copies or on disks (and backup disks), to protect the team and firm from problems, even possible litigation.

One project management task that design students can easily apply to their school project work is dating all documents. It is important to have a dated record of each item in the job book so that a reasonable sequence of events can be determined. Students should begin dating each sketch, drawing, set of notes—whatever—for their design projects so as to learn the important habit of dating materials.

Postoccupancy Evaluation

Postoccupancy evaluations (POE) are reviews of the completed project obtained some time after move-in. The purposes of the POE are to obtain feedback on the successes and problems encountered in the project, to fine-tune the project to resolve problems, and to assess needs for any additional products. The POE may be a very formal program of intense evaluation of each space in the project or an informal walk-through and discussion with the owners to determine satisfaction and to insure resolution of problems.

Unfortunately, POEs are not commonly contracted for by clients or even offered by design firms. This is because they take time and can cost hundreds, even thousands, of dollars. Clients are often unwilling to pay for this extra service since they are too busy with their business to care about this important feedback. Designers also loose interest in a project after it is completed and the glaring problems or issues that came up at move-in have been resolved. However, the feedback obtained for the design firm and the client from a POE is very useful and important.

The focus of the POE is on the building, interior, and users. From the clients' point of view, the POE provides for professional handling of any problems they may have encountered with the building and its design since move-in. This might be as simple as reordering a missing chair or repairing paint that was chipped when furniture was delivered; it might be as major as redesigning cabinets that do not meet their intended function. For the design firm, the POE provides information that will help the firm perform this type of project more effectively and efficiently next time. In fact, a good post-occupancy evaluation will help the design firm create all future work better to some degree or another.

The key activity in a POE is data collection. Some firms use formal printed forms or surveys that are completed by the users and managers. Others may walk around the facility observing and recording building or product problems such as damaged walls or broken furniture. The designer can informally interview employees or other users of the interior to obtain feedback on satisfaction with the appearance and functionality of the design.

Another data collection method would involve use of a camera. The designer can walk through the space and photograph conditions and activities. Photography might be especially useful to see how ADA designs are being utilized. Designers using photographic data collection should be aware that both employees and, especially, the customers of commercial spaces might object to being photographed. Careful explanations may be necessary to insure the privacy of customers.

For the design firm, a postproject review is just as important as the post-occupancy evaluation for the client. A postproject review allows the project manager and design team to analyze the performance of the design team in the project. Perhaps shortcuts in the execution of drawings, for example, developed during a particular project, should be incorporated into the firm's standard procedures. Maybe a certain product did not perform as expected in a certain application and should be more carefully considered in the future. A review of this kind helps everyone involved be more productive and perhaps even more creative on the next project.

Post-occupancy evaluations are done to investigate the success and problems encountered by the design firm in the design of the project. Client satisfaction in the work is paramount to the firm so that a satisfactory ongoing relationship with the client can be maintained.

Project Management Software

Design firms today have access to many kinds of computer software to help make the management process a little easier. To start, it is obvious that few firms handling the larger scale projects of commercial interior design could get by without word processing, database, spreadsheet, CAD, and networking software. As most students and professionals are familiar with how each of these types of software are used by designers, they are not discussed here.

Project management software is a little different. Project management software is a type of specific application program that helps designers and all members of the interiors, architecture, and construction industry support and keep track of projects. This type of software attempts to provide easier planning, scheduling, tracking, and analysis of projects. Depending on the actual program, the software will also provide the manager with reports that help track time, money, and employee productivity. Some of the reports that can be generated by project management specific software can also be done using word processing or spreadsheet software. For example, integrated word processing and spreadsheet programs can create productivity and budget reports quite easily. If a firm is utilizing project management specific software, it is in order to take advantage of the scheduling and schedule tracking features of the program.

One feature of project management software that many firms like is the ability of the program to produce "what if" analysis reports. A "what if" analysis looks at the basic schedule, for example, and creates an analysis of what happens to the schedule "if" a certain new element, like a three week delay in the electrical work, occurs. This type of analysis can be applied to each task so that the firm is better prepared with contingencies for any known or typical problem areas.

The reader should not get the impression that project management software takes the place of the manager. It does not. It only provides one more aid with text and graphic reporting capabilities to help make the project manager's job just a little easier and more accurate. Although the authors do not recommend any specific software product, some of the most commonly used as of this date are: Project™ by Microsoft, Primavera Project Planner™ from Primavera Systems, both IBM/compatible, and Mac Project™ by Claris for the Macintosh.

Summary

Project management is a complex and time-consuming set of responsibilities that should be undertaken by all design firms, regardless of size of the firm and the project. Being in control of the project can mean the difference between a successful project with a happy client or disaster. Successful projects, of course, bring on other potential projects. Disasters turns clients away from the design firm, leaving the firm vulnerable to poor public relations and even litigation.

Project management requires knowledge of the design process as well as the technical knowledge that goes with the different specialized spaces. Project management also requires excellent organizational skills and excellent communication skills. And project management also requires confidence in one's knowledge and abilities along with the willingness to seek help when necessary. Even the most experienced project manager can't know everything about everything. Project management is an ongoing learning process that begins in school and continues throughout the career of the professional interior designer, regardless of specialty.

This chapter has reviewed the basic characteristics of the responsibilities and goals of project management in commercial design projects. Of course, these same responsibilities and goals apply to any kind of design project. The chapter has reviewed the project management process, especially working relationships, the work plan, scheduling methods, and budgeting. Numerous references are noted below to provide the reader additional insights and details into the project management process in interior design.

References

Allinson, Kenneth. 1993. *The Wild Card of Design: A Perspective on Architecture in a Project Management Environment.* Oxford, England: Butterworth Architecture (Butterworth-Heinemann).

American Society of Interior Designers. 1997. "Clients Are Impressed by Project Management." *ASID Professional Designer.* March/April. P. 17.

Berger, C. Jaye. 1994. *Interior Design Law and Business Practices.* New York: Wiley.

Birnberg, Howard G. 1992a. *Project Management for Small Design Firms.* New York: McGraw-Hill.

———(Editor). 1992b. *New Directions in Architectural and Engineering Practice.* New York: McGraw-Hill.

Burstein, David and Frank Stasiowski. 1982. *Project Management and the Design Professional.* New York: Watson-Guptill.

Covey, Stephen R., A. Roger Merrill, and Rebecca R. Merrill. 1994. *First Things First.* New York: Simon & Schuster.

Farren, Carol E. 1988. *Planning and Managing Interior Projects.* Kingston, MA: R. S. Means Co.

Friday, Stormy and David G. Cotts. 1995. *Quality Facility Management.* New York: Wiley.

Huffadine, Margaret. 1993. *Project Management in Hotel and Resort Development.* New York: McGraw-Hill.

Jenks, Larry. 1995. *Architectural Office Standards and Practice*s. New York: McGraw-Hill.

LeBoeuf, Michael. 1979. *Working Smart.* New York: Warner Books.

Levy, Sidney M. 1994. *Project Management in Construction,* 2nd ed. New York: McGraw-Hill.

Lew, Alan E. 1993. *Means Interior Estimating.* Kingston, MA: R. S. Means Co.

Lewis, James P. 1995a. *Fundamentals of Project Management.* New York: American Management Association.

———1995b. *Project Planning, Scheduling and Control,* revised ed. Chicago, IL: Irwin Professional.

Lientz, Bennet P. and Kathryn P. Rea. 1995. *Project Management for the 21st Century.* San Diego, CA: Academic Press.

Lundy, James L. 1994. *Teams.* Chicago, IL: The Dartnell Corp.

Means, R. S. Company. 1998. *Means Interiors Cost Data 1998,* 15th ed. Kingston, MA: R. S. Means Co.

Means, R. S. Company. 1996. Means Interior Estimating. Kingston, MA: R. S. Means Co.

Parshall, Steven A. and Marc R. Hart. 1993. "Does It Work?" *Contract Design Magazine.* November. Pp. 78–79.

Pinto, Jeffrey K. and O. P. Kharbanda. 1995. *Successful Project Managers.* New York: Van Nostrand Reinhold.

Piotrowski, Christine M. 1992. *Professional Practice for Interior Designers,* 2nd ed. New York: Wiley.

———. 1990. *Interior Design Management.* New York: Wiley.

Preiser, Wolfgang F. E., Harvey Z. Rabinowitz, and Edward T. White. 1988. *Post-Occupancy Evaluation.* New York: Van Nostrand Reinhold.

Ritz, George J. 1994. *Total Construction Project Management.* New York: McGraw-Hill.

Snead, G. Lynne and Joyce Wycoff. 1997. *To Do, Doing, Done!* New York: A Fireside Book (Simon & Schuster).

Stasiowski, Frank A. and David Burstein. 1994. *Total Quality Project Management for the Design Firm.* New York: Wiley.

Thompson, Jo Ann Asher (Editor). 1992. *ASID Professional Practice Manual.* New York: Watson-Guptill.

Trauner, Theodore J., Jr. 1993. *Managing the Construction Project: A Practical Guide for the Project Manager.* New York: Wiley.

Glossary

Acute care patient: A patient requiring immediate or ongoing medical attention.

Alternative officing: A term meaning any of several strategies to provide office space other than permanently assigned traditional offices.

American (or conventional) seating plan: An arrangement of rows of seats in an assembly space, such as a theater, with a central aisle and perimeter aisles.

Amperage: The amount of electrical current required to operate any kind of electrical device.

Amphitheater: Generally considered to be an outdoor theater.

Anchor stores: A large well-known chain store that attracts a large number of customers to a shopping center. It is a focal feature of the shopping center. Sometimes called a **magnet store**.

Ancillary space: A support space in an office facility. Common ancillary or support spaces include conference rooms, storage, file, and mail rooms, employee cafeterias, and copy centers.

Archival library: A facility that has focused its collection on documents that have some historical value.

Arena theater: A theater in which the stage is in the middle of the auditorium with seating surrounding the stage.

Assisted living facility (ALF): Semi-independent living facility for those who require minimal nursing or other care.

Atmospherics: A conscious effort by the retailer to create a buying environment to produce specific emotional effects in buyers.

Auditorium: The part of a theater where the patrons sit to watch a performance. It can also be a part of a building, such as a school, used for performances, meetings, or educational programs.

Back bar: The display area for the different liquors, glasses, and storage space for beer, extra liquor, and other items needed at the bar.

Back of the house: Those areas in a commercial facility such as a hotel or restaurant where employees have minimal contact with the customer or public.

Backstage: The production and storage spaces in a theater.

Balcony: A projecting area of seating in the upper areas of the theater.

Baldochino: An ornamental canopy over an altar or seat of honor.

Bank: A type of institutional facility that provides for deposits, lending, and protection of moneys and other financial assets.

Banquette: An upholstered bench along the wall commonly fronted by a table.

Bar: A small beverage facility providing a small amount of seating and little food service.

Bar chart: A type of schedule that shows a list of activities in one column and uses horizontal bars to indicate the expected length of time it will take to complete each activity. Sometimes called a **Gantt chart**.

Bay: The amount of space required to house a single standard guest room in a lodging facility.

Bed-and-breakfast lodging: A lodging facility that provides sleeping and breakfast service.

Belt-line electrical service: System furniture setup with the outlets and electrical channels at either 24 or 30 inches above the base of the panel

Beverage facility: A business, either as a section of a restaurant or as a freestanding facility, that primarily serves alcoholic beverages for on-site consumption.

Board of directors: Individuals elected by shareholders to run a company. The board is legally responsible for such things as selecting the president and other chief officers, delegating operational power, and setting policy on matters concerning stocks, financing, and executive pay levels.

Branch bank: A satellite of a main bank such as a commercial bank. Branch banking is allowed in most states.

Built-out allowance: An amount per square foot provided by the landlord to the tenant to furnish the cost of building partitions, providing basic mechanical features, and architectural finishes for leased commercial space.

Cantor: A synagogue official who sings or chants religious music.

Capital assets: An accounting term generally meaning property, buildings, and equipment that a business requires in order for that business to conduct the mission of the enterprise.

Carnegie library: A facility funded by the Carnegie Foundation, which was founded in 1911 to aid community libraries and schools.

Carpel tunnel syndrome: A type of musculoskeletal disorder that usually affects the arms, wrists, and fingers. It is associated with repetitive tasks like computer keyboarding.

Carrel table: A small enclosure, usually freestanding, for individual study.

Case goods: Furniture items made of "cases" like desks, credenzas, bookcases, file cabinets, and so on.

Catalog system: Any of the methodologies used to catalog library materials to make it easier for a patron to find needed materials.

Cathode Ray Tube (CRT): Another term for the computer screen or monitor.

Central bank: A bank operated by the federal government and functioning as a depository for other banks.

Central processing unit (CPU): The hardware "brain" of a computer where the actual computations and data manipulation take place.

Chain: Multiple locations of one restaurant or lodging facility type. Also applied to stores and other kinds of commercial facilities.

Chancel: The name most often given to the sanctuary in most Protestant churches.

Chancellor: A title given to the head of a university. The chancellor may be responsible for one school or, in some states, several schools.

Check-stand: A stand-up height cabinet in a bank where depositors fill out forms to add or withdraw funds from their accounts.

Chief Executive Officer (CEO): The highest ranking individual in a business. Sometimes called president or principal rather than CEO.

Clearinghouse: An establishment maintained by banks for settling mutual claims and accounts.

Closed stacks: Library materials available only by checking them out from library staff.

Coaxial: A data cable with a central core conductor surrounded by insulation material that is then covered by a metal sheath that acts as a second insulator. This cable is finished with an outer coating.

Commercial bank: A facility offering common banking services such as savings and checking accounts, safe deposit boxes, loans, and possibly trust administration.

Component: One of the individual items, such as a shelf, a drawer unit, or a work surface, that is used with a divider panel for an open office systems station.

Concept: An overall idea that unifies all parts of the design of a facility and provides a specific direction for all aspects of the design.

Concert hall: A type of theater that primarily presents musical performances for orchestras and singers.

Concierge: A hotel staff member who provides informational guest assistance. The term is also associated with alternative office arrangements where one office or workstation may be used by several people. The reservation to use the office space is made through the concierge at the office.

Connector: The hardware used to connect panels together in open office systems projects.

Conservation: Specialized work performed on items in a museum's collection in order to stabilize and save pieces of artwork or antiquities.

Continental seating plan: Main floor seating of an assembly occupancy such as a theater in which aisles are only located on the perimeter sides of the space.

Continuing care retirement community (CCRC): A planned community providing rental or purchase living facilities for retirees whose needs may range from no assistance up to and including skilled nursing care.

Conventional furniture: Desks, credenzas, file cabinets, and bookcases.

Corridor: Any circulation space set off by partitions, rails, or dividers of over 69 inches in height.

Credenza: A storage unit, usually 30 inches in height, to hold additional files and supplies. It is usually placed behind a desk in offices.

Credit union: A member cooperative type of bank.

Critical path method (CPM): A scheduling method that shows the variety of tasks using symbols and lines or other means to connect the items that must be accomplished in a certain order before the next set of tasks can be started.

Cruciform floor plan: The traditional Christian church floor plan, which includes the transept and the nave.

Curator: The individual in charge of a portion of a museum, such as the curator of decorative arts.

Dead load: Permanent structural elements part of the building such as partition walls.

Dealership: A retail sales and design office that is primarily associated with one or more specific manufacturers of commercial furniture.

Decibel (dB): The scale of measurement of sound.

Dedicated circuit: A separate circuit with its own hot, neutral, and ground wires having none of these wires shared with any other circuit.

Delayering: A change in business structure that eliminates layers of management.

Deliverable: A tangible design product such as a construction drawing, a furniture plan, a specification, or a sample board.

Demising wall: Any partition used to separate one tenant space from another. Each tenant is responsible for one-half the thickness of all demising walls.

Demountable wall: A type of floor to ceiling partition that is held in place by tension and can generally be easily relocated with little demolition and new construction. Also called **movable wall**.

Dentist: A health care professional who treats a patient's teeth, gums, and related tissues.

Department manager: Commonly a third level of management responsible for very specific work activities.

Deuce: A table for two in a restaurant.

Diocese: The district of churches governed by a bishop.

Direct glare: Glare coming from a light source.

Display fixture: Equipment used to display products for sale in a variety of retail stores.

Display kitchen: A cooking area in the dining room of a restaurant positioned so that the guest can watch the chef prepare food.

Divider panel: A vertical support unit that, combined with others, forms the stations in open office systems projects.

Docent: A volunteer who provides tours and educational presentations, assists in fund-raising, and performs other support services at a museum.

Downsizing: When a business reduces the number of employees with the goal of being more responsive to customers and becoming more cost-effective.

Emergi-center: A freestanding facility that provides treatment comparable to a hospital emergency room for nonurgent patients.

Empowerment: Allowing the employee to make certain decisions rather than requiring him or her to go through layers of managers.

Ergonomics: The scientific study of the physical functioning of humans in the environment.

Esteem need: Any of those human needs regarding self-respect, admiration, and achievement, such as a luxury automobile.

Facility management: The total nonfinancial asset management of a business.

Facility planning: The programming and space planning of offices and other areas of a commercial business.

Fast-food restaurant: A quick service restaurant that rarely provides wait staff service.

Federal Deposit Insurance Corporation (FDIC): A federally operated institution that guarantees the deposits held within FDIC banks.

Federal Reserve System: The central banking system of the United States. A primary responsibility is to control the US money supply.

FF & E: Acronym that stands for furniture, furnishings, and equipment.

Fiber optics: A data cable utilizing a thin glass filament wire for the transmission of signals.

Food service facility: Any retail space devoted to providing cooked or prepared foods to consumers whether that food is consumed on the premises or not.

Four pair: Four sets of two copper wires twisted together and covered by an insulating material. The most common type of voice and data cabling used today.

Franchise restaurant: One in which the owners purchase a license to operate the restaurant under the guidance and requirements of the company that holds the rights to the original concept. A franchise might also be associated with other types of commercial facilities such as retail stores and lodging facilities.

Free-address: A system of unassigned work spaces that are available to any employee of the firm on a first-come, first-served basis.

Front of the house: Those areas in a commercial facility such as a hotel or restaurant where employees have the most contact with the customer or public.

Full-service restaurant: A restaurant offering a large selection of menu items, and a wait staff member to take orders and serve the food.

Function space: One of the areas used in a lodging facility for conferences, meetings, trade shows, banquets, seminars, and other activities requiring space for large numbers of guests.

Gallery: A room or series of rooms for the display of works of art, objects, and antiquities. A gallery can also be a museum facility without a permanent collection of objects. In addition, a gallery can be a commercial facility for the display and sale of art, objects, and antiquities.

Gantt chart: See **bar chart**.

General use furniture: Conventional case goods wood or steel desks, credenzas, and file cabinets.

Glare: Uncomfortably bright or reflected light that makes it difficult for an individual to see properly.

Greenroom: The room backstage in a theater where benefactors are met and performers relax.

Group medical practice: A group of physicians who provide medical care to patients in a group office facility such as a medical office building.

Guesting: An assigned or unassigned work space provided to a visiting worker from another company.

Guest service: Any of the various services provided to enhance a guest's stay at a lodging facility, such as room service, or valet and bell service.

Guild member: A volunteer at a museum who provides a variety of services such as educational presentations and tours.

Haute cuisine: Means high food. Generally connotes very expensive food.

Healing environment: An environment providing patient-centered health care through environmental and design elements that are more comforting and soothing.

Health care: Concerned with the science and art of dealing with the maintenance of health and the prevention, alleviation, or cure of disease.

Health Maintenance Organization (HMO): A large group of multispecialty health care providers offering services to member patients at either group clinics or a physician's office suite.

Hospice: A facility or program designed to provide a caring environment for the terminally ill.

Hospital: A health care facility for the treatment, care, and housing of patients with illnesses, injuries, diseases, or other medical situations.

Hostel: A lodging facility that often caters to students and budget minded travelers who are looking for a clean room and few other services.

Hot-desk: An unassigned work space. It gets its name from the concept that the chair may be "hot" from the previous user.

Hotel: A large lodging facility that offers a variety of rooms from standard guest rooms to luxurious suites along with a variety of food and beverage services and other amenities.

Hoteling: A system of unassigned work spaces that are available to workers by reservation.

Hotel management company: A group of individuals or a company which has made an agreement with the hotel owners to operate the hotel facility.

House: A term used to refer to the part of the theater the audience occupies.

In close proximity: A space planning principle that means items used together (as in a retail store) are displayed next to or near each other.

Independent restaurant: A restaurant owned and managed by an individual or partnership, created from the individual's or partners' own imagination and creativity.

Inn: A small to medium sized lodging facility that wishes to convey a feeling of a small comfortable home.

Interlibrary loan: A system whereby a library user can request a book not available at a local library.

Investment bank: A banking facility that serves as a middleman in the buying and selling of securities such as stocks and bonds.

Just-in-time work station: An unassigned work space where a worker or group of workers can congregate.

K-6-3-3: An educational plan calling for one year of kindergarten, six years of elementary school, three years of junior high school, and three years of high school.

Key: A renewable unit in a lodging facility.

Landing site: An unassigned work space that the employee "lands" at rather than selects through a reservation.

Lavatory: The term used for a sink used for washing hands.

Lease-hold improvement: When a tenant installs architectural finishes and other construction items other than those provided by the landlord.

Legitimate theater: Indicates a professional performance by members of Actors Equity or other professional performance unions.

Library: The collection of books as well as the building that houses the collection.

Line manager: An individual responsible for the activities directly related to a company's production of goods or services.

Live load: Such things as the weight of people, furniture, and equipment added to a building.

Local Area Network (LAN): A telecommunications network that has been designed to eliminate the possibility of crossing signals that would interrupt the network.

Lodge: A lodging facility that is commonly associated with some kind of recreational activity such as skiing or fishing.

Lodging facilities: Those facilities that provide sleeping accommodations for individuals away from their permanent home. Sometimes called a lodging property or transient living facility,

Lounge: A beverage facility providing more seating than a bar, with more emphasis placed on some type of entertainment. A lounge may serve food.

Magnet store: A large, well-known chain store that attracts a large number of customers to a shopping center. Also called **anchor store**.

Maitre d': The head waiter in a restaurant.

Mall: A regional shopping center that has a large number of stores. Usually the largest shopping center in a community, offering retail stores, food and beverage facilities, and even entertainment facilities such as movie theaters.

Manager: Any individual at any level whose responsibilities are to plan, control, organize, provide leadership, and decision-making for his or her employees.

Market channel: A team of marketing institutions that direct a flow of goods or services from the producer to the final consumer.

Marketing: Activities such as selling, transporting, and supplying goods and services to consumers.

Marketing concept: The comprehensive goal of every business organization—to satisfy consumer needs while creating a profit.

Medical office building (MOB): An office building containing one or more office suites for specialized medical practitioners.

Merchandising: Sales promotion in a comprehensive group of activities that include market research, development of new products, coordination of manufacturing, and effective advertising and selling.

Merchandising blend: Combines the contents of the retail merchandise with the decision the consumer uses in making selections.

Merchant: A buyer or seller of commodities for profit.

Mezzanine: The lowest balcony in a theater.

Milestone chart: A scheduling method that lists tasks in a column on the left and columns of other information such as target finishing dates on the right.

Model stock method: A system whereby the retailer determines the amount of floor space needed to stock a desired amount of merchandise.

Motel: A lodging facility that caters to the traveler using an automobile.

Movable wall: See **demountable wall**.

Movie theater: A place where motion pictures are shown.

Multipurpose room: A classroom or activity space that can accommodate more than one kind of educational or social experience.

Museology: A program of advanced study that prepares an individual in the administration of museums.

Museum: An institution that collects, stores, and exhibits art objects and/or antiquities for the purposes of preservation, display, study, and education.

National library: A library owned by the federal government.

Nave: The long narrow part of a cruciform or Latin cross floor plan. It is where the congregation stands or sits during the service.

Need: An essential physiological or psychological requirement necessary to the physical and mental welfare of the client or consumer.

Net area required: The amount of square footage comprised of office spaces and support areas, but not including circulation and architectural features such as columns and wall thicknesses.

Nonselling space: The amount of a store's square footage allocated to storage, offices, rest rooms, stock rooms, and other spaces not directly related to the sale of merchandise.

Nursing home: A health care facility where nursing and assisted care is given to patients unable to care for themselves.

Office landscape: A design methodology developed in the 1950s using conventional furniture and plants, but few if any wall partitions.

Open stacks: The shelves of library materials open to the public to freely access and use.

Open stage floor plan: A theater space plan where the stage projects into a portion of the audience so that the audience sits partially on three sides of the stage.

Opera house: A theater that primarily presents operas and other musical performances.

Operatory: A dental office treatment room.

Orchestra: In Greek theater, a circular space used by the chorus in front of the proscenium. Today, it is the section of seats in front of the stage and/or a group of musicians.

Out-dating: Medical products have a shelf life when they can be safely used. After that date, they are no longer safely usable.

Parochial school: A school owned by a religious denomination.

Pastor: The head of a Catholic church parish.

Physical plant: A term usually associated with a building and equipment within for any kind of commercial facility.

Physiological need: Any of those needs required for survival and basic human comfort such as food, clothing, and shelter.

Platform: The area in many banks where loan officers and other account representatives have desks.

Plenum: An air space between the ceiling tiles and the structural ceiling in commercial buildings.

Porte cochere: A canopy located over the driveway by the main entrance of a building, used to protect individuals from the weather as well as call attention to the main entrance.

Postoccupancy evaluation (POE): A review of the completed project obtained some time after client move-in to obtain feedback on the successes and problems encountered in the project.

Power entry: A generic term for the point at which the building electrical service is wired to a special vertical panel in open office planning projects.

Priest: An ordained clergyman in an Anglican, Eastern Orthodox, or Catholic church.

Primary care physician (PCP): Usually the first physician the patient sees for treatment or other consultation.

Private library: A library owned by individuals and businesses.

Programming: The first phase of any project where information about the project is obtained by the interior designer.

Project management: A systematic process used to coordinate and control a design project from inception to completion.

Property or prop: Any of the accessory pieces used to finish the design of a set or supplementary scenery. Props are also used by actors.

Proposal: A marketing tool that outlines what will be done and how it will be done, who will do the work, and other information requested or provided.

Proscenium: The part of a stage in front of the curtain.

Proscenium style floor plan: A theater design where a heavy curtain or wall frames the stage.

Provost: A title given to the faculty member who has overall responsibility for academic programs at a university.

Rabbi: The ordained teacher of Jewish law and the head of a local synagogue.

Rector: The head of some denominations of Protestant churches.

Redundant cueing: The sending of a message to more than one sensory mode.

Reengineering: A method of reorganizing a business and its way of doing everything in order to achieve improved overall performance.

Reflected glare: Glare coming from surrounding equipment.

Rehabilitation centers: Medical centers that provide care for patients recovering from such things as strokes, amputations, or paralysis.

Rentable area: The total amount of square footage required for office and support spaces and including allowances for demising walls, and interior architectural features such as columns, mechanical chases, or closets, and even a portion of the exterior walls.

Repertory theater: A theater that presents several different productions each year.

Request for proposal (RFP): A document prepared by the client to request information from the designer regarding a potential design project.

Retail: Selling merchandise or services directly to the end-user (consumer).

Retailer: A merchant who sells goods to the ultimate consumer.

Retailing: The business activity of selling goods or services to the final consumer.

Retail store: A place of business in which merchandise is sold to the consumer.

Rood screen: A screen separating the chancel from the nave in a church.

Room: A separate unit, whether rentable or not, in a lodging facility.

Room mix: The configuration of different types of rooms required, based primarily on the size and number of beds in the room.

Sacristy: A room attached to the church where the vestments and sacred utensils are stored.

Safety need: Any of those human needs that relate to security and stability, such as a personal defense device like Mace™.

Salaried physician: A physician who works as an employee of a hospital, a government agency, or another organization rather than in private practice.

Sale: When merchandise and money change hands from the retailer to the consumer.

Sales/productivity ratio method: The retailer allocates selling space on the basis of sales per square foot for each merchandise group.

Sanctuary: The most sacred part of a religious facility. It is where the altar, if one is used, is placed.

Satellite office: A work center established away from the main office but convenient to the territory of outside workers. It is not generally a branch office.

Savings and loan association: A financial institution in which deposits are obtained from member customers and loaned out to members or other customers.

Savings bank: A type of bank that emphasizes savings and thrift to customers. Services focus on customer savings accounts. It can also be called a mutual savings bank.

Scent appeal: A retail merchandising technique that attempts to entice the consumer to buy through the introduction of aromas that are associated with products.

Scoping statement: A document detailing what will be done and possibly the estimated fee for the project.

Sealed drawing: A drawing to which an architect has affixed his of her seal, which signifies that the architect is licensed by the state.

Seat turn-over rate: The estimated number of times a table in a restaurant will be used in any one day.

Selling space: The amount of store square footage allocated to the display and sale of merchandise.

Service bar: The area where wait staff orders and picks up beverages for restaurant service.

Service station: A work area located in the dining room of a restaurant to provide space for storing clean and dirty dishes, glasses, and coffee service.

Shared assigned work area: An office or station shared by more than one person, perhaps by two part-time workers.

Short list: A list of three to five design firms who have been selected by the client to provide more detailed presentations on a pending project.

Sight appeal: A retailing technique to entice the customer to buy by the use of elements such as size, shape, contrast, or harmony.

Signage: Outdoor advertisement signs on the premises of a store or other business describing the product or services provided by the business. Signage also refers to any kind of sign used in the interior of a business to direct or inform customers.

Single phase electrical service: The former standard for electrical service in most commercial buildings. It provides 240/120 volt service.

Single source of contact: The one person at the design firm or client's place of business who has the authority to make decisions or provide information concerning the project.

Single-user rest room: A rest room that is used by only one person at a time.

Sink: The term used for all sinks other than lavatories, such as service, janitor's, and kitchen sinks.

Skilled nursing facility (SNF): A state licensed health care facility providing 24-hour nursing care to patients.

Sociofugal: Furniture spacing that does not promote social interaction.

Sociopetal: Furniture spacing that promotes social interaction.

Solo practitioner: A medical practitioner who is personally responsible for medical care provided to patients.

Sommelier: A wine waiter.

Source document: The original of a document.

Sparkle lighting: A type of lighting produced from a variety of light sources, that creates special effects and gives atmosphere to a space. Commonly used in restaurants and lodging facilities.

Special collection: A library or museum collection, usually of historical or special archival materials, that requires special care to be protected from damage.

Special library: A facility that focuses on a certain subject matter. It may be privately owned or supported by a government agency or a university.

Specialty restaurant: One that serves a certain type of food, features a particular theme, or offers a certain style of service.

Speed rail: A place that holds bottles of the house beverages along the inside edge of the main bar cabinet so that bartenders can get to them quickly.

Stacks: The open shelves containing library materials.

Staff manager: An individual who provides support, advice, and expertise to line managers.

Stage: The part of the theater where the performance actually takes place.

Staging: Putting on a performance.

Stakeholder: An individual who has a vested interest in the project such as a member of the design team, the client, the architect, or a vendor.

Station: An individual work area set up using open office systems furniture.

Stick furniture: A term designers use to refer to wood office furniture and seating.

Summer theater: Repertory theater organized for the summer season.

Supervisor: Commonly the lowest level of management in a business. Generally responsible for the employees who actually perform most of the work in a business.

Surgi-center: A freestanding health care facility where ambulatory outpatient surgery can be performed.

Synagogue: A house of worship for a Jewish congregation.

Systems creep: A miscalculation in drawing the amount of space that is required to install panels and components so that the stations do not actually fit the space.

Systems furniture: Divider panels and components used to provide work areas for open office projects.

Telecommuting: A work arrangement where workers spend most of their workday away from the main office and accomplish tasks by computers and modems or possibly telephones.

Theater: A building, part of a building, or an outdoor venue in which performances of one kind or another are presented to an audience.

Theme appeal: In retail design, a technique establishing an environment directly related to the product, holidays, or special events.

Three phase electrical service: The present standard in electrical service to commercial buildings. It provides 208 Y / 120 volt service.

Transept: The transverse segment of a cruciform floor plan that crosses over the nave at the chancel end.

Trunk showing: A merchandise demonstration by a designer or manufacturer within a retailer's store.

Trust company: A bank facility that specializes in the administration and control of large amounts of funds held in trust.

Twenty-five pair cable: A telecommunications cable that has 25 pairs of copper strands. Used in older commercial buildings and rarely installed in new buildings today.

Twisted pair: Two copper wires twisted together, shielded by an insulator. The simplest type of data and voice communication cable.

Unassigned office: An office station or private office not assigned to any one individual. It can be used by a variety of individuals.

Under bar: The main working area of the bartender as he or she faces the guest.

Urinal: A specialty water closet found typically in a men's rest room.

Value engineering: A system for budgetary decision-making that considers both the initial capital costs of the design or product specified and the life cycle costs of maintenance and replacement concerning that concept or item.

Veiling reflection: Reflection that occurs when a light source is reflected onto a worksurface or computer monitor, making it difficult to see paperwork or the monitor images.

Vestibule: A passage or small room between the entrance and the interior of a building.

Veterinarian: A professional who treats and cares for animals.

Vice president: A member of the second highest layer of management in large businesses. A vice president is generally responsible for a specific department or division in a corporation or other type of business.

Vignette: A display of furniture and accessories that is created to look like a real room.

Virtual office: A setup where the worker has everything needed to do the job in a briefcase so that he or she does not report to a permanent office at a commercial facility.

Visual display terminal (VDT): Device that displays the data generated in the CPU. Note that some people use the acronym VDU or visual display unit rather than VDT. Referred to as a monitor by many.

Visual merchandising: The art of displaying merchandise in store windows and other locations in the selling space.

Want: A conscious impulse toward an object that promises a reward. In this book, it is discussed in context of retail store design.

Water closet: A plumbing fixture in rest rooms, also called a toilet.

Way-finding: A methodology of signs, graphics, and directional arrows used to help individuals find their way around complex properties and building interiors.

Wing: One of the sides of the stage behind the proscenium and open stage, out of sight of the audience.

Work plan: A document defining all the tasks that are needed to take a project from inception to completion.

Worksurface: The term for the product that serves as the desktop in an open office systems project.

General References

The references listed in this appendix are those items that might be used in the design of a variety of commercial facilities.

Arthur, Paul and Romedi Passini. 1992. *Wayfinding*. New York: McGraw-Hill.

Birren, Faber. 1988. *Light, Color & Environment*, 2nd revised ed. West Chester, PA: Schiffer.

Building Officials and Code Administrators International (BOCA). 1993. *National Building Code*. Country Club Hills, IL: BOCA.

Callender, John Hancock (Editor). 1986. *Time-Saver Standards for Architectural Design Data*, 6th ed. New York: McGraw-Hill.

Deasy, C. M. 1990. *Designing Places for People*. New York: Watson-Guptill.

De Chiara, Joseph, Julius Panero, and Martin Zelnik. 1991. *Time-Saver Standards for Interior Design and Space Planning*. NY: McGraw-Hill.

Egan, M. David. 1988. *Architectural Acoustics*. New York: McGraw-Hill.

Gordon, Gary and James L. Nicholls. 1995. *Interior Lighting for Designers*. 3rd ed. New York: Wiley.

Haines, Roger W. and C. Lewis Wilson. 1994. *HVAC Systems Design Handbook*. 2nd ed. New York: McGraw-Hill.

Hall, Edward T. 1969. *The Hidden Dimension*. New York: Doubleday-Anchor Books.

Hall, William R. 1993. *Contract Interior Finishes*. New York: Watson-Guptill.

Harmon, Sharon Koomen. 1994. *The Codes Guidebook for Interiors*. New York: Wiley.

International Conference of Building Officials (ICBO). 1991. *The Uniform Plumbing Code*. Whittier, CA: ICBO.

———. 1994. *Uniform Building Code*. Wittier, CA: ICBO.

Jackman, Dianne R. and Mary K. Dixon. 1983. *The Guide to Textiles for Interior Designer*. Winnipeg, MB, Canada: Peguis.

Kearney, Deborah. 1993. *The New ADA: Compliance and Costs*. Kingston, MA: R. S. Means.

Leibrock, Cynthia. 1992. *Beautiful Barrier Free: A Visual Guide to Accessibility*. New York: Van Nostrand Reinhold.

Mahnke, Frank H. and Rudolph H. Mahnke. 1987. *Color and Light in Man-Made Environments*. New York: Van Nostrand Reinhold.

McGowan, Maryrose. 1996. *Specifying Interiors. A Guide to Construction and FF&E for Commercial Interiors Projects.* New York: Wiley.

McGuinness, William J., Benjamin Stein, and John S. Reynolds. 1980. *Mechanical and Electrical Equipment for Buildings,* 6th ed. New York: McGraw-Hill.

McPartland, J. F. and Brian J. McPartland. 1996. *National Electrical Code Handbook.* 22nd ed. New York: McGraw-Hill.

Miller, Mary C. 1997. *Color for Interior Architecture.* New York: Wiley.

National Fire Protection Association (NFPA). 1991. *NFPA 101: Life Safety Code.* Quincy, MA: NFPA.

Panero, Julius and Martin Zelnick. 1979. *Human Dimension and Interior Space.* New York: Watson-Guptill.

Pile, John. 1997. *Color in Interior Design.* New York: McGraw-Hill.

Ramsey, Charles G. and Harold R. Sleeper. 1988. *Architectural Graphic Standards,* 8th ed. New York: Wiley.

Reznikoff, S. C. 1986. *Interior Graphic and Design Standards.* New York: Watson-Guptill.

———. 1989. *Specifications for Commercial Interiors,* revised ed. New York: Watson-Guptill.

Riggs, J. Rosemary. 1989. *Materials and Components for Interior Design,* 2nd ed. Reston, VA: Reston Publishing (Prentice-Hall).

Simmons, H. Leslie. 1989. *The Architect's Remodeling, Renovation, and Restoration Handbook.* New York: Van Nostrand Reinhold.

Sommer, Robert. 1983. *Social Design.* San Francisco, CA: Rinehart Press.

Sorcar, Pratulla C. 1987. *Architectural Lighting for Commercial Interiors.* New York: Wiley.

Southern Building Code Congress International (SBCCI). 1994. *Standard Building Code,* Birmingham, AL.: SBCCI.

Templeton, Duncan and David Saunders. 1987. *Acoustic Design.* New York: Van Nostrand Reinhold.

Terry, Evan, Associates. 1993. *Americans with Disabilities Act Facilities Compliance: A Practical Guide.* New York: Wiley.

Watson, Lee. 1990. *Lighting Design Handbook.* New York: McGraw-Hill.

Wilkes, Joseph A. (Senior Editor) and Robert Packard (Associate Editor). 1988. *Encyclopedia of Architecture, Design, Engineering and Construction.* New York: Wiley.

Magazine Resources

Readers may also want to search in *Ulrich's International Periodicals Directory* for other magazine titles of interest. This directory is published annually and can generally be found at the reference desk of public and university libraries.

American Libraries
50 E. Huron St.
Chicago, IL 60611

American School and University Magazine
491 N. Broad St.
Philadelphia, PA 19108

Architectural Record
1221 Avenue of the Americas
New York, NY 10020

Architecture
1130 Connecticut Ave. N.W.,
Suite #625
Washington, DC 20036

Arts Management
408 W. 57th St.
New York, NY 10019

Canadian Interiors
360 Dupont St.
Toronto, Ontario
M5R 1VR

Contract Magazine
Miller Freeman, Inc.
One Penn Plaza
New York, NY 10119

Design-Build Business
333 E. Glenoaks Blvd., 3204
Glendale, CA 91207-2074

Design Firm Management and Administration Report
29 W. 35th St.
New York, NY 10001-2299

Design Management Journal
29 Temple Place
Boston, MA 02111-1350

Display and Design Ideas
Shore-Varrone, Inc.
6255 Barfield Rd. N.E., #100
Atlanta, GA 30328-4300

Educational Leadership
1250 N. Pitt St.
Alexandria, VA 22314

Facilities Design and Management
Miller Freeman, Inc.
One Penn Plaza
New York, NY 10119

Home Office Computing
Scholastic, Inc.
556 Broadway
New York, NY 10012

Hospitality Design
Bill Communications
355 Park Ave. S.
New York, NY 10010-1706

Hotel and Motel Management
7500 Old Oak Blvd.
Cleveland, OH 44130

Hotel and Resort Industry
488 Madison Ave.
New York, NY 10022

Hotel Management International
King's Court
2-16 Goodge Street
London W1P 1FF, England

Interior Design
249 W. 17th St.
New York, NY 10011

Interiors
1515 Broadway
New York, NY 10036

Interiors and Sources
840 US Highway One, Suite 330
North Palm Beach, FL 33408-3834

Interiors, Design, Environment, Art, Structures
    (IDEAS)
Dodi Publishing
PO Box 343392
Miami, FL 33114-3392

International Design
440 Park Ave. S.
New York, NY 10016

Journal of Interior Design
Interior Design Educators Council, Inc.
9202 N. Meridian St., Suite 200
Indianapolis, IN 46260-1810

Lodging
1201 New York Ave., N.W.
Washington, DC 20005

Lodging Hospitality
1100 Superior Ave.
Cleveland, OH 44114

Metropolis
177 E. 87th St.
New York, NY 10128

Modern Office Technology
1100 Superior Ave.
Cleveland, OH 44114

Progressive Architecture
600 Summer St.
PO Box 1361
Stamford, CT 06904

Project Management Journal
40 Colonial Square
Sylva, NC 28779

Retail Store Image
Intertec Publishing Corp.
6151 Powers Ferry Rd. NW
Atlanta, GA 30339-2941

The School Administrator
1801 N. Moore St.
Arlington, VA 22209

Store Planning and Design Review
302 5th Ave.
New York, NY 10001

Stores of the Year
302 5th Ave.
New York, NY 10001

Theatreforum
9500 Gilman Dr.
La Jolla, CA 92093

VM + SD (Visual Merchandising and Store
    Design)
407 Gilbert Ave.
Cincinnati, OH 45202

Trade Associations

The reader may also wish to reference the *Encyclopedia of Associations*, published annually and available at the reference desk of most libraries.

American Animal Hospital Association
PO Box 15089
Denver, CO 80215

American Association of Museums
1225 I St., N.W.
Washington, DC 20005

American Association of School
    Administrators
1801 N. Moore St.
Arlington, VA 22209

American Dental Association
211 E. Chicago Ave.
Chicago, IL 60611

American Furniture Manufacturers
    Association
PO Box HP7
High Point, NC 27261

American Hospital Association
840 Lake Shore Dr.
Chicago, IL 60611

American Hotel and Motel Association
1201 New York Avenue, N.W.
Washington, DC 20005-3931

American Institute of Architects (AIA)
1735 New York Avenue, N.W.
Washington, DC 20006

American Library Association
50 E. Huron St.
Chicago, IL 60611

American National Standards Institute
    (ANSI)
11 W. 42nd St.
New York, NY 10036

American Society of Furniture Designers
PO Box 2688
2101 W. Green Dr.
High Point, NC 27261

American Society of Interior Designers
    (ASID)
608 Massachusetts Ave., N.E.
Washington, DC 20002-2302

American Society for Testing and Materials
    (ASTM)
1916 Race St.
Philadelphia, PA 19103

Association for Project Managers
1227 W. Wrightwood Ave.
Chicago, IL 60614

Association of Registered Interior
    Designers of Ontario (ARIDO)
717 Church St.
Toronto, ON M4W 2M5 Canada

Association of State Colleges and
    Universities
1 Dupont Circle
Washington, DC 20036

Association for Women in Architecture
2550 Beverly Blvd.
Los Angeles, CA 90057

British Contract Furnishing Association
52 Upper St., Suite 214
Business Design Center
London, UK N1 OQH, England

Building Officials and Code
    Administrators International, Inc.
4051 W. Flossmoor Rd.
Country Club Hills, IL 60478

Building Owners and Managers
    Association
1201 New York Avenue, N.W.
Washington, DC 20005

The Business and Institutional Furniture
    Manufacturers Association
2680 Horizon, S.E.
Grand Rapids, MI 49546

Center for Health Design, Inc.
4550 Alhambra Way
Martinez, CA 94553

Center for Universal Design, The Center
    for Accessible Housing
North Carolina State University
PO Box 8613
Raleigh, NC 27695-8613

The Color Association of the United States
409 W. 44th St.
New York, NY 10036

Concert Hall Research Group
327 F Boston Post Rd.
Sudbury, MA 01776

Construction Specification Institute
601 Madison St.
Alexandria, VA 22314

Council of Educational Facility Planners,
    International
8687 E. Via de Ventura
Scottsdale, AZ 85258

Environmental Protection Agency, Indoor
    Environments Div.
401 M St., S.W.
Washington, DC 20460

Foundation for Interior Design Education
    Research (FIDER)
60 Monroe Center, N.W., #300
Grand Rapids, MI 49503

Governing Board for Contract Interior
    Design Standards
341 Merchandise Mart
Chicago, IL 60654

Guild of Religious Architecture
1777 Church St., N.W.
Washington, DC 20036

Illuminating Engineering Society of North
    America
1142-E Walker Rd.
Great Falls, VA 22066

Institute of Store Planners (ISP)
25 N. Broadway
Tarrytown, NY 10591

Interior Design Educators Council (IDEC)
9202 N. Meridian, Suite 200
Indianapolis, IN 46260

International Association of Lighting
    Designers
1133 Broadway
New York, NY 10010

International Conference of Building
    Officials (ICBO)
5360 South Sorman Mill Rd.
Whittier, CA 90611

International Facility Management
 Association (IFMA)
1 E. Greenway Plaza
Houston, TX 77046

International Furnishings and Design
 Association (IFDA)
1200 19th St., N.W.
Washington, DC 20036

International Interior Design Association
 (IIDA)
341 Merchandise Mart
Chicago, IL 60654

National Association of Display Industries
355 Lexington Ave.
New York, NY 10017

National Association of Store Fixture
 Manufacturers
1776 N. Pine Island Rd.
Plantation, FL 33322

National Council for Interior Design
 Qualification (NCIDQ)
50 Main St.
White Plains, NY 10606

National Electrical Contractors Association
3 Bethesda Metro Center, Suite 1100
Bethesda, MD 20814

National Endowment for the Arts
1100 Pennsylvania Ave., N.W.
Washington, DC 20506

National Fire Protection Agency (NFPA)
1 Batterymarch Park
PO Box 9101
Quincy, MA 02269

National Kitchen and Bath Association
687 Willow Grove St.
Hackettstown, NJ 07840

National Restaurant Association
1200 17th St., N.W.
Washington, DC 20036

National Trust for Historic Preservation
1785 Massachusetts Ave., N.W.
Washington, DC 20036

Ontario Furniture Manufacturers
 Association
6900 Airport Rd.
Mississauga, ON L4V 1E8 Canada

Organization of Black Designers (OBD)
300 M St., S.W.
Washington, DC 20024

Partners for Sacred Places
1616 Walnut St.
Philadelphia, PA 19103

Quebec Furniture Manufacturers
 Association
1111 Saint-Urbain St.
Montreal, PQ H2Z 1Y6 Canada

Southern Building Code Congress
 International
900 Montclair Rd.
Birmingham, AL 35213

Underwriters' Laboratories, Inc.
333 Pfingsten Rd.
Northbrook, IL 60062

US Institute for Theater Technology
6443 Ridings Rd.
Syracuse, NY 13206

Index